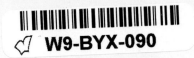

third edition

exploring the elements of design

Poppy Evans and Mark Thomas

DELMAR CENGAGE Learning

Australia • Brazil • Japan • Korea • Mexico • Singapore • Spain • United Kingdom • United States

Exploring the Elements of Design, Third Edition
Poppy Evans and Mark A. Thomas

Vice President, Editorial: Dave Garza
Director of Learning Solutions: Sandy Clark
Senior Acquisitions Editor: Jim Gish
Managing Editor: Larry Main
Product Manager: Meaghan Tomaso
Editorial Assistant: Sarah Timm
Vice President, Marketing: Jennifer Baker
Marketing Director: Deborah Yarnell
Associate Marketing Manager: Erin DeAngelo
Senior Production Director: Wendy Troeger
Production Manager: Andrew Crouth
Senior Content Project Manager: Kathryn B. Kucharek
Design Director: Bruce Bond
Technology Project Manager: Chris Catalina
Cover Design: Mark Thomas, Libby Sillis and Joe Villanova
Cover image: Design by Jason Munn for Chris Schlarb/Psychic Temple
This image appears in its entirety as part of a poster design featured on page 12.

Library of Congress Control Number: 2011935255

ISBN-13: 978-1-1116-4548-9

ISBN-10: 1-1116-4548-5

Delmar
5 Maxwell Drive
Clifton Park, NY 12065-2919
USA

Cengage Learning is a leading provider of customized learning solutions with office locations around the globe, including Singapore, the United Kingdom, Australia, Mexico, Brazil, and Japan. Locate your local office at: **international.cengage.com/region**

Cengage Learning products are represented in Canada by Nelson Education, Ltd.

To learn more about Delmar, visit **www.cengage.com/delmar**

Purchase any of our products at your local college store or at our preferred online store **www.cengagebrain.com**

Printed in the United States of America
1 2 3 4 5 6 7 16 15 14 13 12

M. T. The family upstairs—Lisa, Michael,
Max and Eli—love you
Brother Mikey
… and for every brokenhearted soul in the
whole wide universe.

To Libby and Nina

P. E. Dedicated with all my love to Mom, Dad, Evan and Rob.

contents

Poster design by McRay Magleby.

Poster design by Ames Design.

preface

INTRODUCTION

Understanding how design elements and principles work together to create effective communication is at the core of what every graphic designer needs to know. *Exploring the Elements of Design, Third Edition*, presents the fundamentals of visual organization that function as the basis and rationale for visual communication. This text is intended to empower the reader with the conceptual tools and critical skills to create confident design communications. This book explains how design fundamentals operate in all realms of the visual communication industry, supported by custom illustrations, charts, graphics and examples from student work and professionals in the field. Additional chapter content includes the use of typography, imagery in design, color in design, design research methods, digital media and design, professional preparation, as well as professional interviews and profiles.

Exploring the Elements of Design is an attempt to bridge the gap between theory and practice. Design has traditionally been taught as basic theory supported with visual examples that demonstrate the fundamentals in their simplest form. Although these methods that employ basic shape, line, textures, and color are adequate for introducing rudimentary concepts, students often experience difficulty making the leap from visual basics to more complex projects in the professional realm. This text provides an in-depth discussion of the basics as a basis for more complex design issues covered in the sequel publications, *Exploring the Integration of Design* (available in 2014) and *Exploring Contemporary Practices in Design* (available in 2015).

Intended Audience

The primary target learner for *Exploring the Elements of Design, Third Edition*, is an introductory design major in a two-year or four-year college graphic design or visual communication design program. Secondary target learners include non-design professionals in related fields who need a primer of design essentials. This text is also suited for advanced design programs in secondary art education.

WHY WE WROTE THIS TEXTBOOK

Many textbooks covering the principles and elements of design present the discussion based primarily on fine arts references. There is much to be learned about the influence and relevance of fine arts to visual communication design. In contemporary art and design, the line between the two continues to blur; however, distinguishable concerns remain: the responsibility of making meaningful connections between a visual communication message and an audience is a challenge unique to the design process. We were interested in a design basics text that relied primarily on communication design references and examples as the context for this discussion. Hearing directly from accomplished design professionals in an interview format, critical analyses of works of design, and sidebar discussions seemed to us more relevant for aspiring designers than presenting the work of fine artists and asking the reader to make the leap to design applications. With a combined 45 years of teaching visual communication design and design foundation courses, we have developed a concise and comprehensible methodology for presenting this material. This book answers both the "how" questions and more importantly the "why" questions associated with the exploration of the visual elements, principles, and hierarchical relationships.

TEXTBOOK ORGANIZATION

This book is structured so that learners are introduced to design fundamentals at the beginning of the book and progressively work their way conceptually through an understanding of design processes, strategies, and professional preparation.

In **Chapter 1**, students learn about how design works as a visual language built on fundamental principles and elements. The primary principles of unity, variety, hierarchy, and proportion are explained as they affect a design composition as a whole. Scale, balance, rhythm, repetition, and proximity are presented as support principles that govern internal design relationships within a composition. The design elements of shape, space, line, size, color, texture, and typography are also introduced as compositional content.

Chapter 2 addresses the role of typography in design. A presentation of the origins of typography leads to a discussion of the artistic and cultural forces that influenced the aesthetic evolution of type. The text continues to familiarize students with basic terms and measurement systems. Students also learn how to select typefaces appropriate to a project's design and communication goals and use type effectively in a design composition.

In **Chapter 3**, students develop an understanding of imagery's role in design. This chapter explains how symbols, logos, and trademarks function as an aspect of image representation. Students also learn the unique distinction between photographic and illustrated imagery and how to combine these with type and text to make the most of it in a design composition.

Color's role in design is explored in **Chapter 4**. Students learn about how color is perceived and processed by the eye and brain, and they are introduced to basic color terminology. Color systems and color psychology are explored, as well as strategies for choosing effective color schemes and using color effectively in a composition.

Chapter 5 presents a discussion of the origin of design in nature and the constructed environment as sources for inspiration. It also addresses graphic devices and techniques that support visual relationships and organization. The psychological effect of design is also presented, as well as how design can best be used in support of a communication goal.

Chapter 6 discusses the basis of design research methods and design processes. Connections are made between design problem solving and visual thinking to the fields of psychology and semiotics. A variety of research tools are presented to help establish informed design strategies.

Digital media options for communication artists are discussed in **Chapter 7**. Students learn about how technological advancements have affected media development and how design has adapted to new media. Web design, multimedia design, interactive design, and social media are presented and explained in the context of both digital and print communications.

Chapter 8 addresses career opportunities. An overview of the industry and career options is included, as well as advice on self-promotion, portfolio preparation, and interviewing strategies using real student examples.

FEATURES

The following list provides some of the salient features of the text:

- Objectives clearly state the learning goals of each chapter.
- Contemporary examples of graphic design from accomplished and recognized designers are presented.
- Color visuals are used to explain and analyze design fundamentals in graphic and verbal terms.
- The elements of design—line, shape and texture, color, size, and value—are defined and examined.
- The principles of design—unity, variety, hierarchy, proportion, scale, balance, rhythm, repetition, and proximity—are reviewed and explained.
- How typography and imagery can be used successfully in design is explored.
- Research strategies are presented that provide an informed basis for design decisions.
- Interviews with distinguished graphic designers are included, along with their important industry advice and inspiration examples of their work.
- Articles by leading professionals in the field give valuable insight into the creative process.
- Review questions and in-depth assignments reinforce material presented in each chapter.
- Projects relevant to the material in each chapter give students an opportunity to create work supported by the discussion of concepts and design issues.

NEW TO THIS EDITION

This third edition has been updated to reflect changes in the design profession and in communication arts that have taken place since the second edition was published in 2008. These updates address:

- Recent technological advances and their effect on marketing, visual communication, and graphic design.
- Content that includes many more examples of Web design and other interactive design applications as well as animation and motion graphics.
- More information on the technical aspects of designing for the Web and multimedia.
- How to assess design and communication in a climate where evolving technologies continue to change the way information is shared and processed.
- More examples of global design applications.
- More technical advice in the form of "production tips" within each chapter.

ANCILLARY PACKAGE

The ancillaries for this new edition are designed to enhance both the instructors' and students' use of the book. The Instructor Resources have been updated to meet new and revised content in the text. There is also a new CourseMate product that correlates with the text and provides helpful features for both students and instructors.

Instructor Resources

These instructor resources were developed to assist instructors in planning and implementing their instructional programs. They include sample syllabi for using this book in either an 11- or 15-week course, answers to the review questions found in the text, tips for assessing completed exercises assigned in the book, and a list of additional resources. It also includes PowerPoint slides that highlight main topics and provide a framework for classroom discussion.

All these features have been updated accordingly to the new content in the book.

CourseMate

Exploring the Elements of Design, Third Edition, includes a Media Arts & Design CourseMate, which helps you make the grade.

This CourseMate includes:

- An interactive eBook, with highlighting, note-taking, and search capabilities.
- Interactive learning tools including:
  - Quizzes
  - Flashcards
  - PowerPoint Lecture slides
  - And more!

Go to login.cengagebrain.com to access these resources.

about the authors

Poppy Evans is an award-winning writer and graphic designer who teaches and lectures on art and design. Most recently, she served as Assistant Professor at the Art Academy of Cincinnati where she taught for 16 years. Now retired, she continues to teach art and design at local colleges and universities. Her background includes serving as managing editor for *HOW* magazine and board member for *HOW* magazine's Editorial Advisory Board. She is also a former board member and Educational Chair for AIGA Cincinnati. In addition to coauthoring *Exploring the Elements of Design*, she is the author of *Exploring Publication Design*, 12 other books for graphic designers, and hundreds of magazine articles. Prior to teaching and writing for the design industry, she worked for many years as a graphic designer and magazine art director and continues to work as a freelance designer. Ms. Evans holds a B.F.A. in Fine Arts from the University of Cincinnati.

Mark Thomas is Professor and Chair of the Communication Arts Department at the Art Academy of Cincinnati where he has been teaching for 25 years. He has developed courses in design research methods, illustration, design systems, and a thesis program for communication arts. He is also a graphic designer, illustrator, and published author. He has designed numerous exhibitions, catalogs, and posters for graphic designers, fine artists and illustrators including Anita Kunz, Marshall Arisman, Loren Long, Malcolm Grear, Edward Potthast, and Kevin T. Kelly. Mr. Thomas holds a National Parent Center Seal of Approval for educational board game design. He also holds a U.S. patent for an educational color demonstration device and method used for teaching color theory. He has an M.F.A. and an A.B.D. in Design Education from the University of Cincinnati and is currently president of the board of AIGA Cincinnati.

acknowledgments

A debt of gratitude to Jim Gish, acquisitions editor at Delmar Cengage Learning, for his continued support and trust. Our appreciation to the following professionals for their support and expertise: Paige Williams, Libby Sillis, Michael McCuskey, and LeAnne Wagner.

The work and insightful voices of these professionals will forever resonate in our practice of designing and teaching: Lawrence Goodridge, Malcolm Greer, Hermine Feinstein (*in memoriam*), Gregory Wolfe, Roy R. Behrens, Dennis Puhalla, Noel Martin *(in memoriam*), Rebecca Seeman, Matt Hart, and Howard McIlvain. We also want to acknowledge the significant impact of Steven Jobs, who's untimely death at the time of this writing reminds us of how great design is often the ability to creatively blend art and science.

Thanks to our Delmar Cengage Learning team of professionals who offered support, ideas, guidance and trusted us to write the book we believed in: Jim Gish, Senior Acquisitions Editor; Sarah Timm, Editorial Assistant; Kathryn B. Kucharek, Senior Content Product Manager; and Bruce Bond, Design Director. A special thanks also goes to Integra, especially Sue Langguth and her team, who handled the editing and production of this text with great care and expertise.

A special thanks to Meaghan Tomaso, our Product Manager, for her support, patience, trust and gentle prodding.

Finally, to the many talented and accomplished designers, illustrators, and artists whose works appear throughout this book, our sincere thanks.

Delmar Cengage Learning and the authors would also like to thank the following reviewers for their valuable suggestions and technical expertise:

Tom Davie, MFA
Art Academy of Cincinnati
Cincinnati, Ohio

Joyce M. Dick, MS
Northeast Iowa Community College
Peosta, Iowa

Jennifer C. Dowling, MFA
Framingham State College
Framingham, Massachusetts

Julie Mader-Meersman, MFA
Northern Kentucky University
Highland Heights, Kentucky

Jill Mash, BFA, MAMS
Albany Technical College
Albany, Georgia

Patrick Schreiber, MFA
University of Cincinnati
Cincinnati, Ohio

Matthew Tullis, MFA
Western Kentucky University
Bowling Green, Kentucky

QUESTIONS AND FEEDBACK

Delmar Cengage Learning and the authors welcome your questions and feedback. If you have suggestions that you think others would benefit from, please let us know, and we will try to include them in the next edition.

To send us your questions and/or feedback, you can contact the publisher at:

Delmar Cengage Learning Executive Woods
5 Maxwell Drive, Clifton Park, NY 12065
Attn: Graphic Arts Team
800-998-7498

Or the authors at:
Art Academy of Cincinnati
1212 Jackson St., Cincinnati, OH 45202
513-562-8777

Poppy Evans: poppye@fuse.net

Mark Thomas: merj@fuse.net

one

Defining the Language of Design

Poster Design by Wolfgang Weingart.

1

introduction

Design is a visual language that is built on fundamental principles and elements. The principles are the organizational rules used in conjunction with the elements to create order and visual interest. The principles are presented as two related sets: primary and secondary (or support). The primary principles affect the design as a whole. Secondary, or support, principles affect the internal relationships of the elements. Principles can be thought of as the transparent forces that create interaction between the elements. The elements of design constitute the content of a graphic design composition. The elements are seen and exist on the surface or picture plane of a composition.

Each of these principles and the elements are defined and discussed in this chapter. Accompanying analysis using professional examples is provided, as well as illustrated diagrams.

objectives

- Understand design as a visual language that is built on fundamental principles and elements.
- Explain how the primary principles of unity, variety, hierarchy, dominance, proportion, and balance affect the design composition as a whole.
- Explain how the supporting principles of scale, emphasis, rhythm, movement, proximity, and repetition affect internal relationships of the elements within a design composition.
- Describe the uses of the design elements shape, space, line, size, color, texture, and typography as compositional content.

PRINCIPLES AND ELEMENTS OF DESIGN

The human psyche seeks harmony and resolution in everyday life. You use your senses of touch, smell, hearing, taste, and sight to perceive and navigate in the world. When you perceive that your living or work environments have become too disorderly, you are motivated to organize them so you can again function productively. You see disorder and act to reorganize or rearrange it. On a basic level, the activity of designing is a form of visual organization. The more familiar you are with the environment you want to change, the more manageable is the task of changing it.

Graphic design is the art of arranging pictographic and typographic elements to create effective communication. It is a complex discipline that requires skillful and sensitive use of the eyes for navigating, the hands for crafting, the left brain for analytic reasoning and logic, and the right brain for creative, intuitive thinking. Directing those functions of the mind and body is a demanding human activity. In fact, research in higher education ranks studying visual arts second behind medical school in its overall demand of the learner. Design is not a collection of formulas that, if followed and applied, ensures effective results. Design is a fluid process that is guided by the designer's sense of intuition, reason, and aesthetic judgment.

To manage the process, successful designers have learned that fundamental principles can be used to guide their creative design decisions. The principles provide a structure for combining the common elements of design by serving as the relationship between the parts or design elements involved. You may find it helpful to use familiar analogies when thinking about the elements of design, for example, the ingredients in a recipe, the parts of a machine, or the materials needed to build a house. Individually, those components have limited use. But when skillfully combined, they work together to form something useful. When a measure of creativity is added, the result can be not only useful but also pleasing to the senses. Design works in a similar way.

You can understand how design works by first defining an inventory of principles and elements of design. Then you can see why those principles and elements work by examining examples of design that emphasize a particular principle or element. Many lists of principles and elements of visual organization are widely acknowledged and have been written about in books on art and design theory. Most of those principles and elements are universal to any of the visual arts. The principles are often grouped together, suggesting that they have an equal role or are of equal importance. However, some principles have a more dominant function, whereas others serve a supporting role. The principles have been organized here as primary and supporting to help you see their function and relationship. In any given design, one principle can be emphasized over another.

Primary principles *affect the design as a whole* and include the following:

- Unity
- Variety
- Hierarchy
- Dominance
- Proportion
- Balance

Support principles *affect the internal relationships of a design* and include the following:

- Scale
- Emphasis
- Rhythm
- Movement
- Proximity
- Repetition

There are also visual relationships that function as variations or forms of the principles just mentioned. They also will be discussed in this chapter as they are widely used in education and the industry. Those visual relationships include economy, tension, direction, density, harmony, discord, focal point, theme, and motif. The **elements of design** include *shape, space, line, size, color, contrast, pattern, texture, and typography*. Typography is included as an element because in addition to having verbal meaning, it also functions in design in the same manner as shape and line.

Primary Principles

Through the study and practice of making works of design, you will become more familiar with the processes and strategies that govern it. A working knowledge of the principles and elements of design provides a foundation for managing design decisions. Keep in mind that the principles and elements are interrelated. You will see how in the discussion of each.

Unity and Variety

In the eye and mind of a viewer of any designed image, the viewer needs to be able to understand what he or she is seeing. An objective of any design plan is to create a sense of unity through the organization of the compositional parts. **Unity** is an overriding principle that is served by all others **1.1**. Unity is the control of variety. Often the content used in a design varies in kind and can include different typefaces, graphic elements, photographs, or illustrations.

Variety, a complementary principle to unity, is necessary to create visual interest. Managing variety is the art of balancing visual contrasts. It is combining elements that do not appear, on the surface, to have much in common. Unusual combinations of elements directed at the message often are used in the most inventive and successful designs. However, too much variety or random use of it can cause confusion **1.2a** and **1.2b**.

[1.1] In this range of merchandise from the San Francisco Museum of Modern Art, unity is achieved in several ways. The logo's individual letterforms are strong identifiers that are repeated on each item. The consistent use of a distinctive, saturated color palette also unifies each product. Changing the scale of the logo elements to accommodate the changing size of each souvenir item is a fresh, bold approach to variety. The horizontal bands on the bags mimic the banding effect of the logo applied to other items, and the bands create a layering effect that adds depth. The result is a variety of merchandise applications that tie in with each other and make a unified presentation.
Logo and merchandise design by Michael Osborne Design.

[1.2a] At a glance, the design seems unified. But a sustained examination reveals that this design is struggling for identity and unity. The manipulated photograph of the tree serves as a backdrop for type and graphic elements. Competing with the photo are two different typefaces as well as two different uses of icons. The colors in the main, central type and the typeface itself overpowers the design. The corner icons have a somber color and are graphically inconsistent with the rest of the design. The black band through the center of the composition functions to make the "green" type readable but insensitively interrupts the graphic continuity of the tree illustration. The placement of design elements itself is overly centralized. Too much variety has created a dysfunctional design.
© Cengage Learning 2013. Examples designed by Mark Thomas and Libby Sillis.

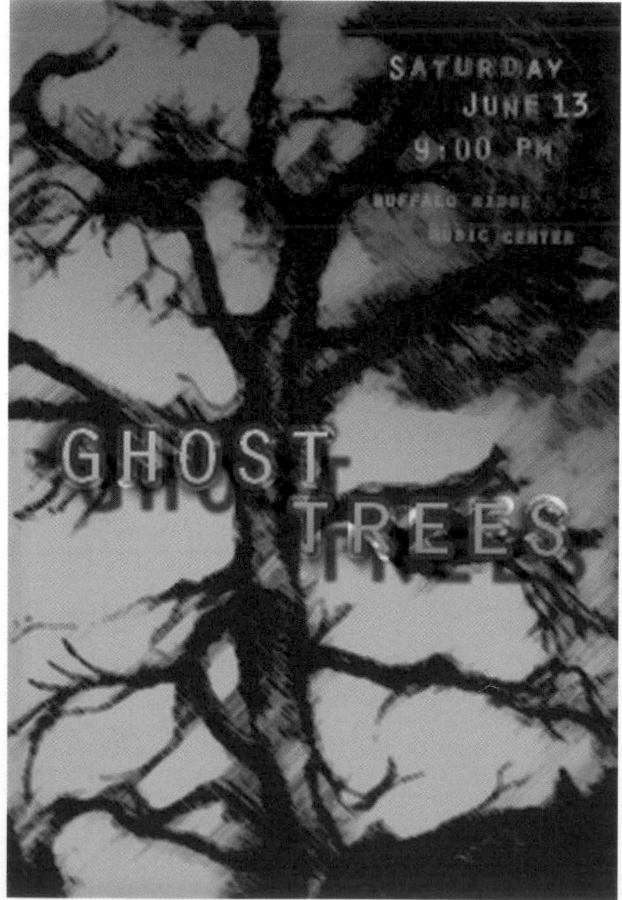

[1.2b] This solution uses one typeface, creating a subtle and more unified statement in keeping with the illustration. In this revision, unity is achieved through economy. **Economy** is the idea of distilling the design to its most essential parts while striving to be sensitive to visual relationships. The type, graphic elements, and photograph are now working in concert to enhance and support one another. The elements are reduced to the illustration and the type that is visually manipulated in response to the name of the band. The color of the type is responsive to the color in the illustration.
© Cengage Learning 2013. Examples designed by Mark Thomas and Libby Sillis.

Hierarchy and Dominance An important function of unity in design is managing visual hierarchy in composition. **Hierarchy** refers to an arranged order. **Dominance**, the prevailing influence of one element over another, and **emphasis**, the importance of one element over another, are commonly thought of as principles. But they are more simplistic, related functions of hierarchy. Hierarchy is the established order, importance, and emphasis given to visual elements, from those that are dominant to those that are subordinate. A designer must manage the size, placement, and balance of the elements used so the viewer can read the image and extract the intended meaning. Controlling hierarchy determines the path the viewer's eye takes while first scanning and then studying a design composition.

If you look at any work of design or art repeatedly, you can experience an eye-movement path. For the first few seconds of each viewing, the path is the same. Areas of high contrast, faces, or unusual shapes immediately attract the eye. Once you loop a few times around the dominant elements in a work, you become familiar with them and break away from the familiar elements to consider other features and elements that support the main ones **1.3**.

Lack of clear visual hierarchy is the reason many designs fail to attract and hold a viewer's attention. It is important to practice the art of critical analysis, or deconstruction of design compositions. A critical analysis begins through examination of the parts of a design to see how they function. That activity can help identify the visual hierarchy and the subsequent eye-movement path. Identifying the most dominant elements in a design, as well as secondary and other support elements, reveal the meaning in the message. Sharpening that skill will serve your own design.

Bias exists in the way certain cultural groups and individuals comprehend visual information, which has an impact on eye-movement tendencies. Designers must be sensitive to viewer partiality with regard to visual orientation, which is influenced primarily by the way written

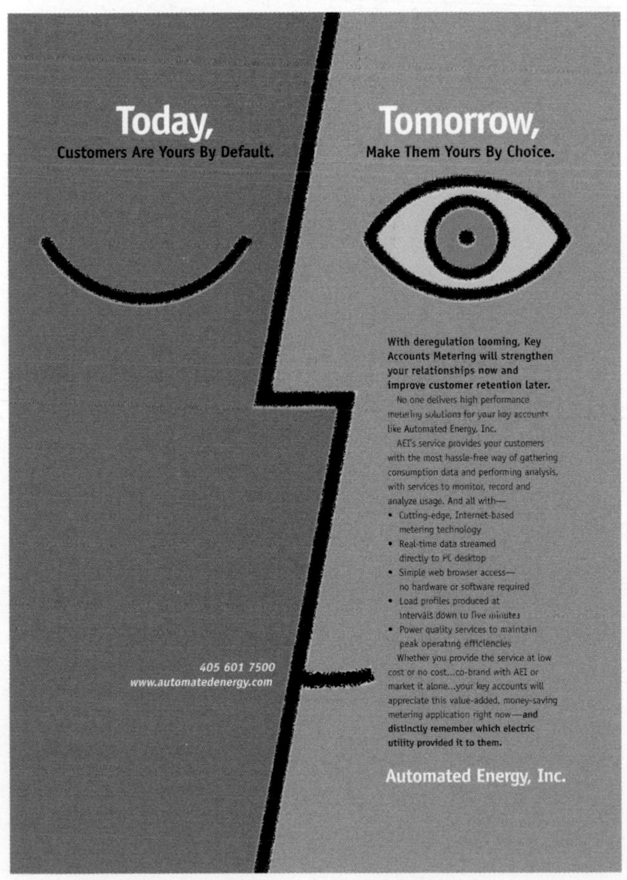

[1.3] By determining hierarchy, a designer can control the path a viewer's eye will take when scanning a design composition. In the case of this ad, the viewer is first drawn to the prominent open eye and then to the suggestion of a face. The headlines "Today" and "Tomorrow" are the first type elements that are read.

The zigzag vertical line pulls the eye down to the smaller blocks of text. Two clever graphic effects in this image are the dual read of the face from a frontal view to a profile and the completion of the mouth with typographic elements.

Ad for Automated Energy, Inc. by Steve Walker.

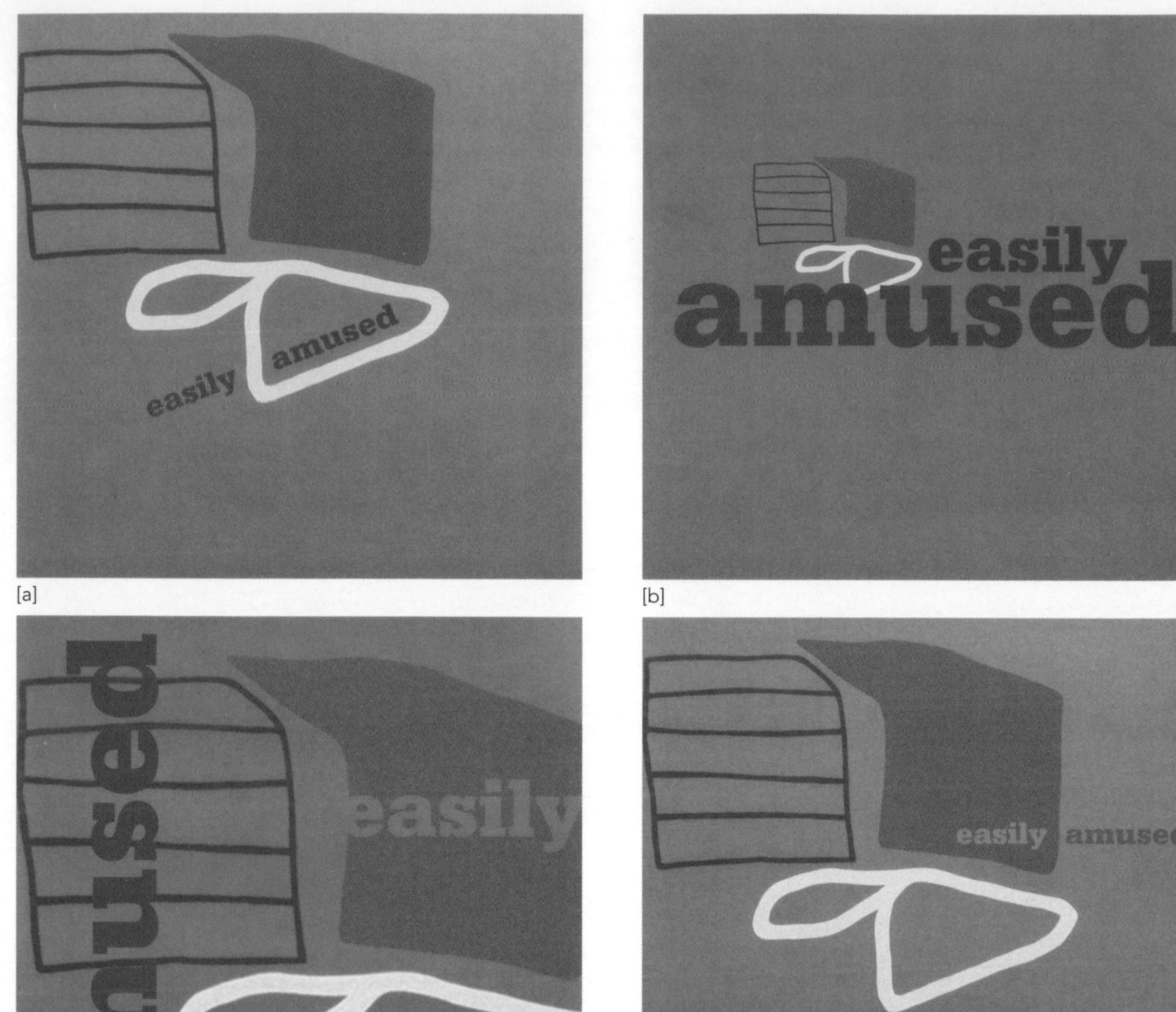

[a] [b] [c] [d]

[1.4a to d] It is sometimes helpful to think of design elements as actors on a stage, with the designer determining which element will lead and which elements will support the lead. These examples are composed of four major players: the primary typographic message, "easily amused," a solid purple shape, and two line-drawn elements.

In 1.4a, all three elements are similar in size but the looped linear element is dominant due to its pastel yellow color. The type is "ganged" with the shapes, creating a triangular negative space that complements the shapes of the other elements.

The composition in 1.4b places emphasis on the type, which presents the dimension of depth with the size shift in the two words and the overlapping. Even though the shapes are small and subordinate, the pastel yellow loop element draws the eye and serves as a focal point. In 1.4c, the vertical placement and size of "amused" creates an entry point for the eye. This composition has small pockets of negative space as the scale of the elements dominates the space, pushing out to the edges making the "purple" shape seem larger than it is. The shapes in 1.4d are the same as 1.4a but the arrangement seems more vertical and horizontal in 1.4a and more diagonal in 1.4b because of the placement of the type. How does the placement of the type change the negative space in the bottom one-third of each composition? Which of the four compositions seems physically larger? Of the four, which one attracts your eye first?

Courtesy of Paige Williams.

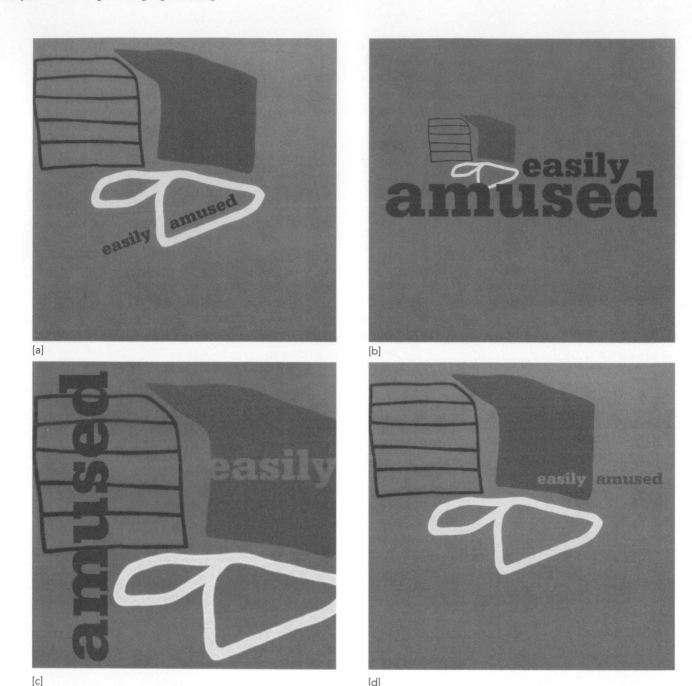

language is read. In Western cultures, people read from left to right and top to bottom. Most Arab and Semitic writing is read from right to left, but numbers are read left to right. Hieroglyphics, pictographic writings that preceded alphabets, are read in different directions. Traditional Chinese calligraphy is read top to bottom and right to left, but modern Chinese newspapers and books are read left to right. Depending on the concept, most graphic design can be read from middle to top, from bottom to top, up a side, or down a side. The designer is in control of how a designed image is read by managing visual hierarchy, **1.4a, 1.4b, 1.4c,** and **1.4d**.

Proportion

Proportion refers to the size relationships within a composition. Those relationships serve as a transparent, underlying structure for the surface design. The outer dimensions determine the form of a two-dimensional design and are its most basic proportion. A square, a vertical rectangle, and a horizontal rectangle are all formats with unique proportions that affect particular qualities of a design **1.5a, 1.5b,** and **1.5c**. The outer proportions or dimensions of a design have an important relationship to the internal divisions and alignments. As shown in 1.5a, 1.5b, and 1.5c, outer dimensions affect the orientation of the viewer and are often dictated by the nature of the design venue.

Designers and illustrators must work with numerous proportional formats. Books and posters tend to be vertical in orientation, CD covers are square, billboards are horizontal, mobile phones rotate between horizontal and vertical, and three-dimensional surface graphics can assume many forms. Whether the format proportions are a given or are determined by the designer, they are one of the first important considerations in a design plan. The relationship between outer dimensions and internal divisions can provide a system for managing design decisions. Some proportional systems have been

[a]

[b]

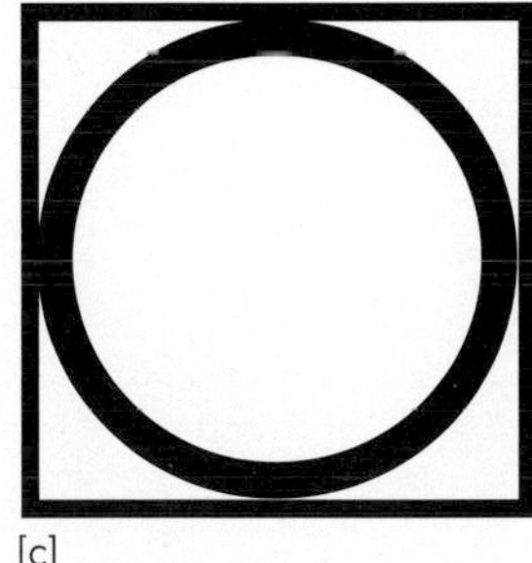

[c]

[1.5a to c] One of the first decisions a designer makes is to determine a design composition's overall dimensions. Because the internal relationships of the design composition depend on the proportions of the outer dimensions, the overall dimension should not be an arbitrary decision. The shape of a design format also possesses associative meaning. (a) A vertical rectangle in contemporary Western culture is associated with architectural metaphors such as a building, a window, or a door.

A vertical rectangle also can relate to the proportions of a standing human form. Magazines, books, print ads, and most poster designs use the rising presence that a vertical rectangle offers. (b) A horizontal rectangle (center) has a long-standing association with the landscape. In contemporary culture, movie screens, computer monitors, and televisions all make use of this panoramic format. (c) A square configuration offers a stable, neutral format that allows the designer, illustrator, or photographer to influence the overall composition by controlling the relationship of internal elements. The square can be a difficult format in which to design because it does not offer the proportional shift of a rectangle. The square has a proportional relationship to the circle and equilateral triangle. Those three shapes are considered primary shapes.

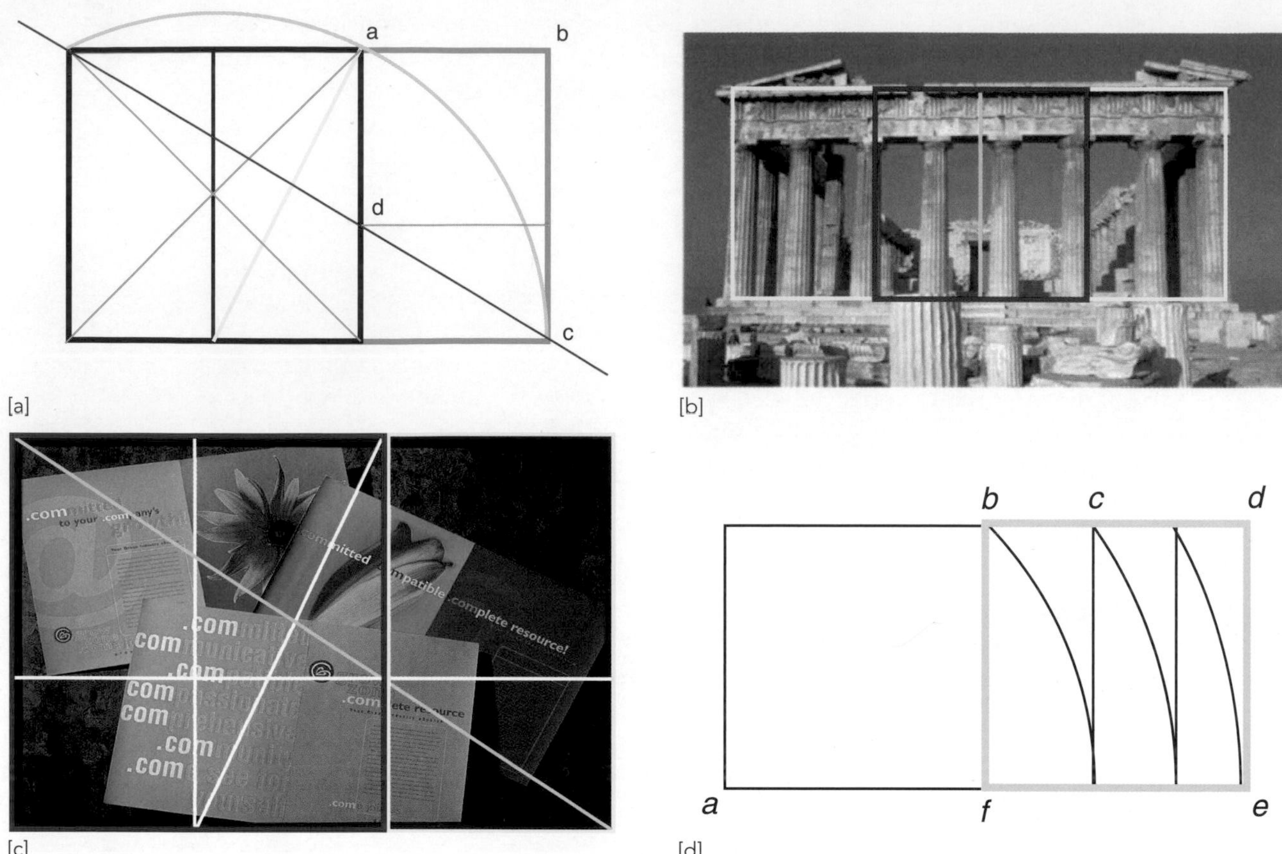

[1.6a] The Golden Rectangle You can construct a golden rectangle by starting with a square. Find the center of the square by drawing intersecting lines through opposite corners, as shown in the gray *X*. From there, draw a vertical line through the intersecting point of the *X*. Place the point of a compass where the centerline intersects the base of the square and scribe an arc that intersects the top right corner of the square (Point *a*) and extends to the square's baseline.

Complete the rectangle by extending the square to the point where the arc meets the baseline (Points *b* and *c*). You can form a second golden rectangle by drawing a diagonal line (shown in red) that extends across opposite corners of the rectangle and drawing a horizontal line from the point where that line intersects the original square (Point *d*). The second rectangle and its parts are proportional to the original rectangle and corresponding parts.
© Cengage Learning 2013.

[1.6b] The ancient Greeks found the proportions of the golden rectangle of great use in architectural design. Its proportions served them in the building of the Parthenon, contributing structural integrity in columns used to provided support for the entablature and pediment. The golden rectangle also possesses aesthetic beauty in the overall proportional relationships of all of the architectural components. The spacing of the columns related to their height and width and the relationship of the column height to the distributed number of columns and the supported entablature fit into two golden rectangles that share a common square.
© Cengage Learning 2013.

[1.6c] Today designers find the proportions of the golden rectangle useful for organizing and arranging elements in a composition, as in the design of this page from an ad campaign for Growzone.com. The intersecting construction lines used to build the golden rectangle serve as critical alignments and placement points in the layout. The random or casual arrangement as it appears was carefully planned.
Design by Erbe Design.

[1.6d] The dynamic rectangle, although not as elegant as the golden rectangle, also serves as a proportional device for organizing design elements. To construct it, begin with a square. Place a compass point in the corner of the square (Point *a*) and scribe an arc that intersects the opposite corner (Point *b*) down to the baseline of the rectangle. Draw a vertical line up to Point *c* and extend the rectangle. Continue by placing the compass point at Point *a* and scribe an arc through Point *c*. Extend the rectangle again. When you continue out to three extensions, you construct a new square. Extend out eight extensions to construct a third square.
© Cengage Learning 2013.

used for centuries in architecture, art, and design. Those systems are based on ratios—a comparison of one set of sizes or quantities with another. Although ratios are commonly expressed in mathematical terms, they also can be expressed as visual relationships. The golden section is a ratio that dates back to ancient Greeks. Its proportional **harmony** possesses both aesthetic beauty and structural integrity.

The ratio of the golden mean (expressed mathematically as 1:1.618) is used to construct the golden rectangle and is the same ratio found in the structure of plants and other life-forms. The spiral order of leaves growing from a branch, the seed pattern in the center of a sunflower, and the spiral of a nautilus shell can all be expressed in terms of the golden ratio. Building a golden rectangle using the ratio requires no calculations. The rectangle is constructed using a series of extended relationships as described in **1.6a**. Those relationships possess an inherent aesthetic harmony because the internal proportions relate in scale to the proportions of the original square and its extensions. The golden section can be extended to construct the golden rectangle, which was used by the Greeks as the basis for much of their architecture, including the Parthenon **1.6b**. Renaissance artists used the golden rectangle to create overall harmony and balance in works of painting and drawing, and contemporary graphic designers use the rectangle as a format for print and digital media **1.6c** and **1.6d**.

All of these proportional devices can work in conjunction with scale and perspective cues too establish pictorial depth. When a design is complex, proportion and scale give the viewer visual "touch points" to navigate the image and help to understand where the elements are relative to one another **1.7**.

Balance

Balance is the visual distribution of elements in a composition. There are four types of visual balance: **symmetrical**, **asymmetrical**, **radial**, and **crystallographic**. In *symmetrical balance*, elements are arranged the same or very similarly on either side of a central axis. The elements appear to be projecting a mirror image, like a landscape projected in a still lake **1.8a**. Symmetry also occurs as the halves of a circle and equilateral and isosceles triangles.

[1.7] The known constant in this image is established with human scale. The graphic simplification of the subject matter offers no textural or modeling detail as spatial cues. However, you can estimate the size of the trees and the crashing jet based on the presence of the human figures. Overlapping perspective and the cropping of the figures compress the space and help to balance the action that takes place in the background. The panoramic proportions of the image and the animated treatment of the content give this satiric social commentary a cinematic scale.
"Suburban Blight," Acrylic painting. © 2004 Kevin T. Kelly.

Asymmetric balance, sometimes referred to as *dynamic symmetry*, is the art of creating balance using uneven numbers, sizes, or kinds of elements. In the visual arts, dynamic symmetry can be achieved by changing the contrast relationship of value, shape, color, texture, size, placement, or even the kind of image such as type and photograph or illustration **1.8b**. *Radial balance* involves the arrangement of elements that radiate from a center point. The overall configuration is circular or concentric **1.8c**. *Crystallographic balance* is the even distribution of like elements over the surface of a design. Crystallographic motifs are often repetitive patterns where size and color offer variety **1.8d**. In all of these variations, the balance can be precise or approximate. Some forms of balance can function as hybrids of two or more of the four types of balance. Which of the examples 1.8a or 1.8b do you think function as precise balance and which as approximate?

Physical balance is a functional demand of three-dimensional design. Physical balance can be achieved with a base, as in a bottle of cologne, a lamp, or a computer monitor. It also can be designed through the use of legs or pods to support the central form, as in a chair, a freestanding kiosk, or a game machine **1.9**.

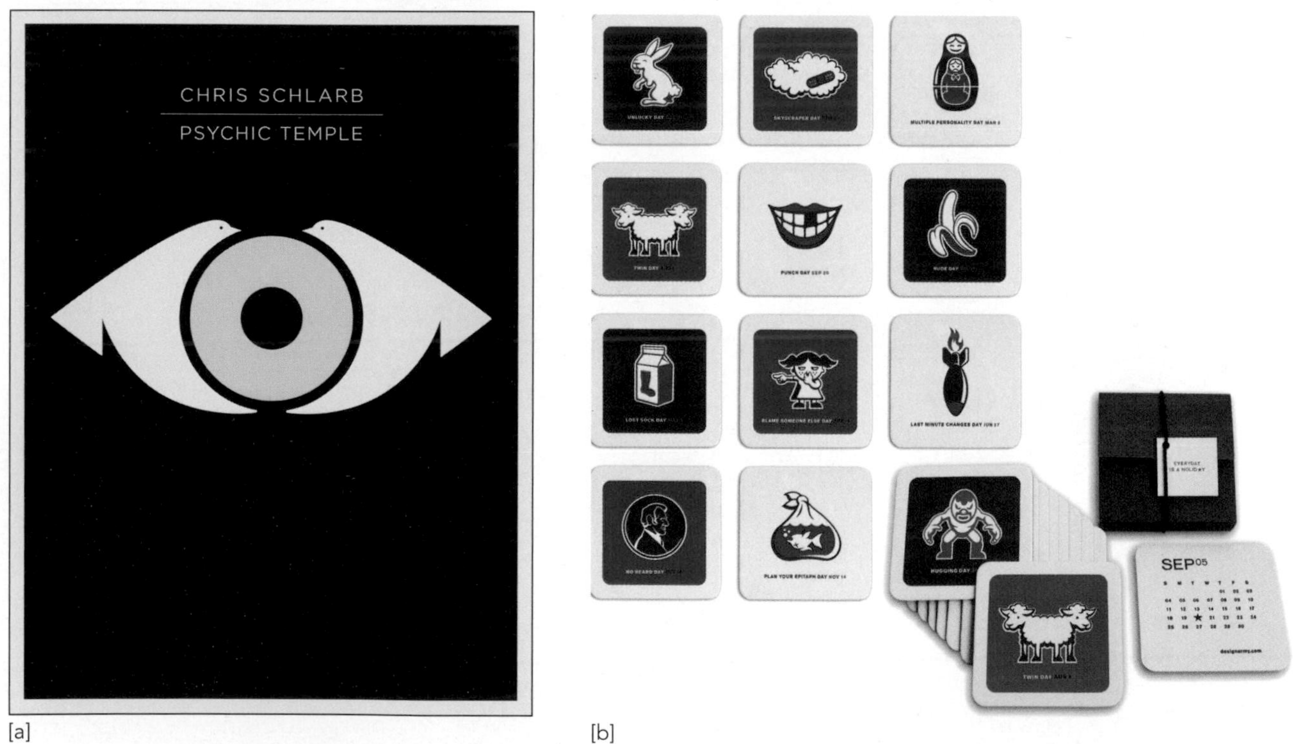

[a] [b]

[1.8a and b] Symmetrical balance is represented in both compositions.
(a) This poster design is also an example of bilateral symmetry where, if an imaginary axis were drawn down the center, one side would mirror the other.
Chris Schlarb/Psychic Temple—Design by Jason Munn.
(b) These calendar coasters were designed as a seasonal gift for clients. Each coaster presents a humorous illustrated image aligned with an obscure observance day. The rabbit (UNLUCKY DAY DECEMBER 31) is an example of an asymmetrical image. Can you determine which of these are examples of symmetry and asymmetry?
Design and illustrations by DESIGN ARMY.

[c]

[d]

[1.8c] This whimsical illustrated motif is the opening page for illustrator and artist Rina Donnersmarck's Web site. It utilizes hand-drawn concentric circles and relies on radial symmetry.
Courtesy of Rina Donnersmarck.

[1.8d] Navajo rug patterns are built from repeated shapes that create an even distribution of the geometric elements. Many primitive and native fiber arts use crystallographic balance as a result of the weaving process.
© Christie's Images / CORBIS.

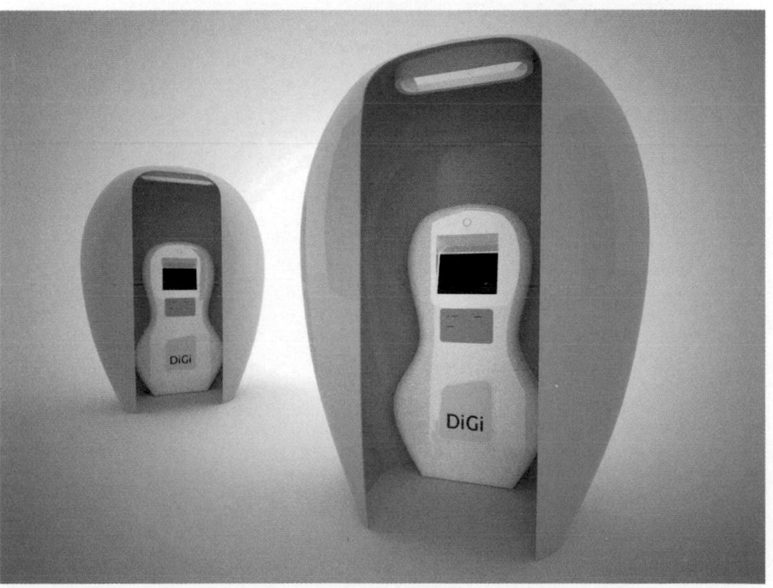

[1.9] The design of this kiosk is freestanding on the bottom edge of the main form, which wraps in a partial arch on the floor to offer structural stability or physical balance. The kiosk functions as a center providing mobile phone customers with a way to manage communication services.
Courtesy of Zarni Ko.

Support Principles

As stated, the support principles affect the interaction between elements and sometimes have a relationship with a primary principle. Scale and proportion are examples of support principles that have a direct relationship to a primary principle. Support principles help to establish visual organization in a composition.

None of the support or primary principles exist alone. In any composition, multiple principles are at work. However, you will see that in the arrangement of graphic elements, successful design tends to stress the use of one or two support principles.

Scale

Proportion and scale are related principles. **Proportion** refers to the size relationships of the design elements in a composition as an aspect of the space they occupy in a design composition as a whole. **Scale** refers to size comparisons of the internal parts of a composition, or a size relationship in the comparison of one design element to another. Size, distance, and configuration are often compared in the natural and constructed worlds. Comparisons based on a known constant provide a familiar orientation. The profile of a towering building or the mass of a mountain on the horizon can be difficult to judge in terms of size. However, when juxtaposed with a human figure, an automobile, or an animal, it becomes easy to establish a familiar comparison of size. Scale can be used to create variety and emphasis in a design and help establish visual hierarchy.

Emphasis

Elements in some designs have an arrangement that is evenly distributed over the surface. The elements create a **pattern** that gives equal importance to each element, as shown in the background area of 1.11. Textile designs such as quilts, rugs, tapestry, and fashion often rely on a repeated arrangement, or **design**, that is perceived as an overall pattern.

However, many designs use a point or points of visual interest that attract the viewer's eye, giving prominence to an element or to an arrangement of the elements. Emphasis is the use of a **focal point** to stress certain elements or to give special attention to an element. Without emphasis, the viewer's eye would wander around a design composition, with no purpose or direction. Emphasis can be achieved in a variety of ways: through size variation **1.12**, color 1.7, visual weight, density, or boldness, such as the bold black and patterned edge created in 1.11 or the shape and placement of the *R* in 1.10a.

Each of those examples results in a different kind of **contrast**: contrast of size, light and dark, color, shape or texture, and contrast of weight or density. They all function to create emphasis. Also notice in the examples that surrounding elements provide alignment or context for emphasis of the prominent elements.

Rhythm and Movement

The term *rhythm* is associated most often with music, defined as an alternating occurrence of sounds and silence.

Rhythm in the visual realm can be described the same way. When you replace sound and silence with form and space, the same description works for graphic design **1.10a** and **1.10b**. Creating a rhythm with visual elements is the choreography of graphic design. This choreography is the implied **movement** of the elements as manifested through the eye of the viewer. Rhythm gives shape to the movement in a composition. In 1.10a, rhythm is articulated through the descending size of the letters in each word. The subsequent movement takes the eye back into space on a curved trajectory in the word *Moon* and in a horizontal direction in the word *Rufe*. The line element offers a quiet contrasting rhythm.

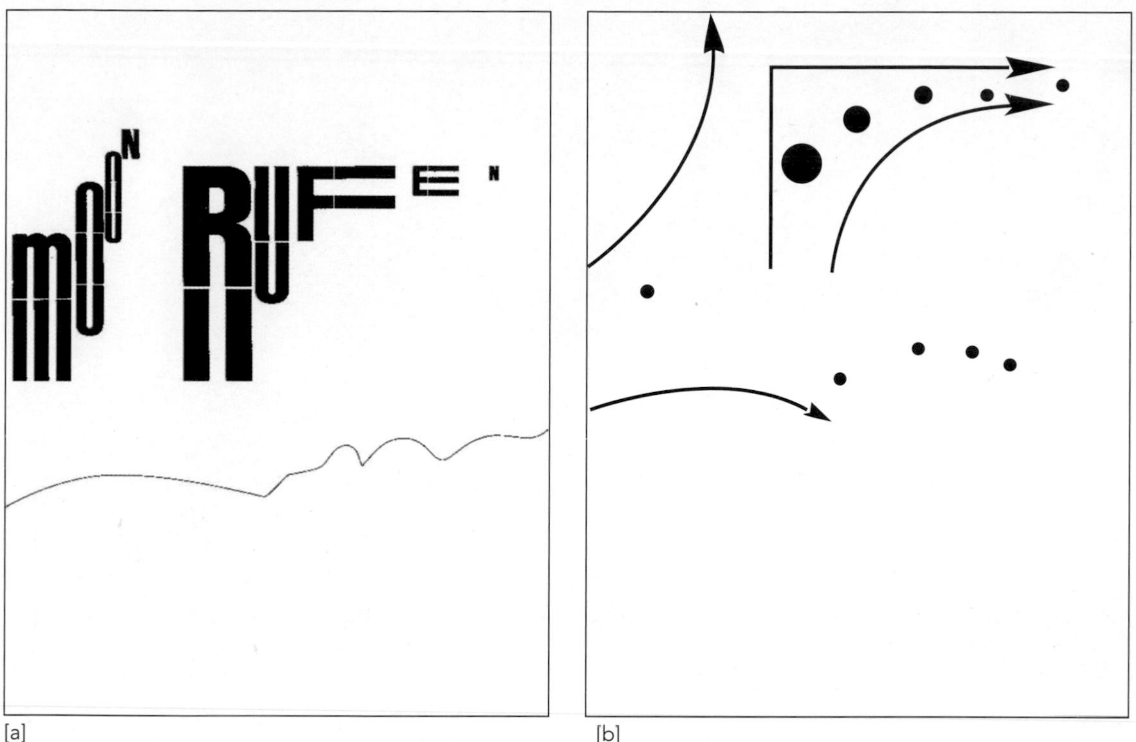

[a] [b]

[1.10a and b] (a) The rhythmic pattern that the typography establishes in this poster design is echoed in the treatment of the line below it.
Poster design by Wolfgang Weingart.
(b) A diagrammatic breakdown gives a more basic representation of this rhythm.
© Cengage Learning 2013.

In a sense, rhythm and movement are transparent to the design. They function with an implied presence defined through the arrangement and configuration (varying line, shape, size, and color) of graphic elements. Rhythm dictates the form of the arrangement, giving movement and natural flow to related elements in the composition. Rhythms can be regular and static **1.11** or pulsating and full of exaggerated gesture **1.12**.

Proximity and Repetition One of the most critical decisions a designer makes is where to place design elements. **Proximity** is the position and space given to the placement of elements in a composition. Proximity determines the placement of elements together and apart from one another. Controlling the relative size and distance from one element to another, based on common increments or shared attributes, also establishes visual continuity and aesthetic harmony. Proximity functions in two basic ways. First, **repetition** follows a regular pattern of related or juxtaposed elements 1.11. You also can repeat elements that vary in size, shape, color, texture, or orientation. The diagonal squares in 1.12 are related by shape, differ in size, and repeat in a varied manner to create both variety and unity. Second, counterpoint placement of elements is a dynamic arrangement of differing elements. In fact, most design is the art of achieving unity with a variety of different typographic and pictorial elements.

[1.11] In this turn-of-the-century poster, a regular rhythmic pattern is established to provide a backdrop for the typographic information. Each of the three areas—the solid black rectangle, the graphic background, and the type block—has differing density, which creates visual contrast, depth, and visual tension.
Vienna Workshop Poster by Josef Hoffmann © Austrian Archives/CORBIS.

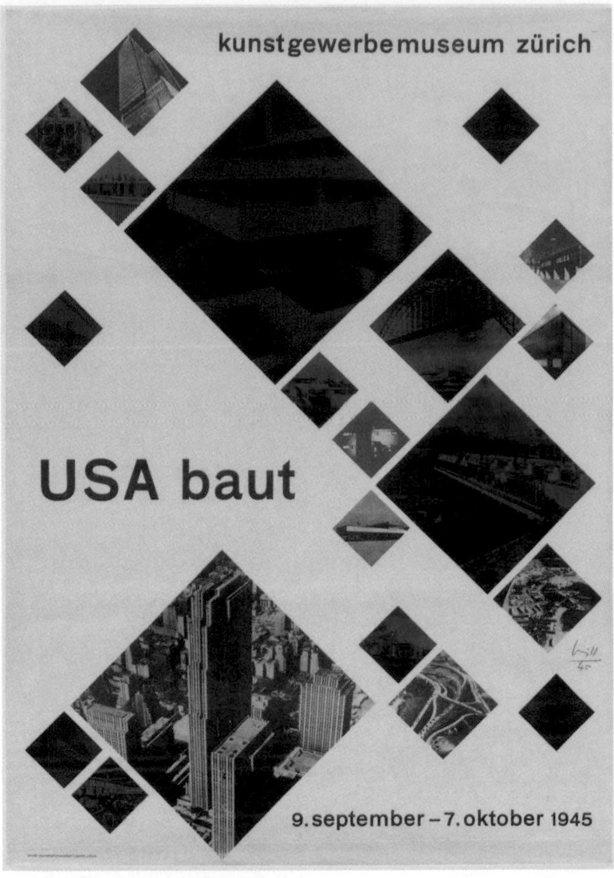

Digital Image ©2011 MoMA, N.Y.

[1.12] In this poster, scale and color shifting creates a pulsating effect. Placing the units on the diagonal results in a dynamic rhythm that moves in and out of space. S and Z configurations were used as compositional devices to create dynamic diagonal movement and structure.
'USA BAUT Poster' by Max Bill. ©2011 Artists Rights Society (ARS), New York/ProLitteris, Zürich.
Digital Image © The Museum of Modern Art/Licensed by SCALA/Art Resource, NY.

Designers look for ways to align images, text, and other graphic elements based on common attributes. **Grid** systems play an important role in determining placement, whether the message calls for regularity or for counterpoints to create visual interest **1.13** and **1.14**. An expanded discussion of grid systems is presented in Chapter 5.

The space between two or more elements affects their relationship. As they move together, a visual **tension** can result. When they touch, new hybrid shapes can form **1.15**. And at some point, as they move apart, they can become disassociated with one another. You can think of design as a conversation in which the elements talk to each other. The conversation can be quiet and understated, or it can be loud and chaotic.

The resulting dialogue is affected profoundly by the positioning of the design elements and their number in the composition **1.16a, 1.16b,** and **1.16c**. Proximity groupings can create patterns, a sense of rhythm, or other relationships that elicit a response from the viewer. Keep in

[1.13] With its *g* placed strategically in the bottom left portion of the circle, the asymmetrically balanced Gymboree logo demonstrates the importance of placement. Centering the *g* within the circle would have resulted in a static, predictable compositional relationship.
Design by Michael Osborne.

[1.14] A grid (shown in blue) serves as the underlying placement guide for the graphic elements on the cover and interior pages of this publication. From there, the alignment of common edges such as the number *2* and letter *U* on the cover, as well as other shared attributes, guided the designer in their design decisions.
Brochure design by Kinetik Communication Graphics Inc.

mind that the conversation must be in support of the communication goal or message. As a general rule, varied proximity of elements can result in a visual tension that brings dynamic interest to a composition. Equal and regular spacing between graphic elements of similar size can result in a static, uniform composition.

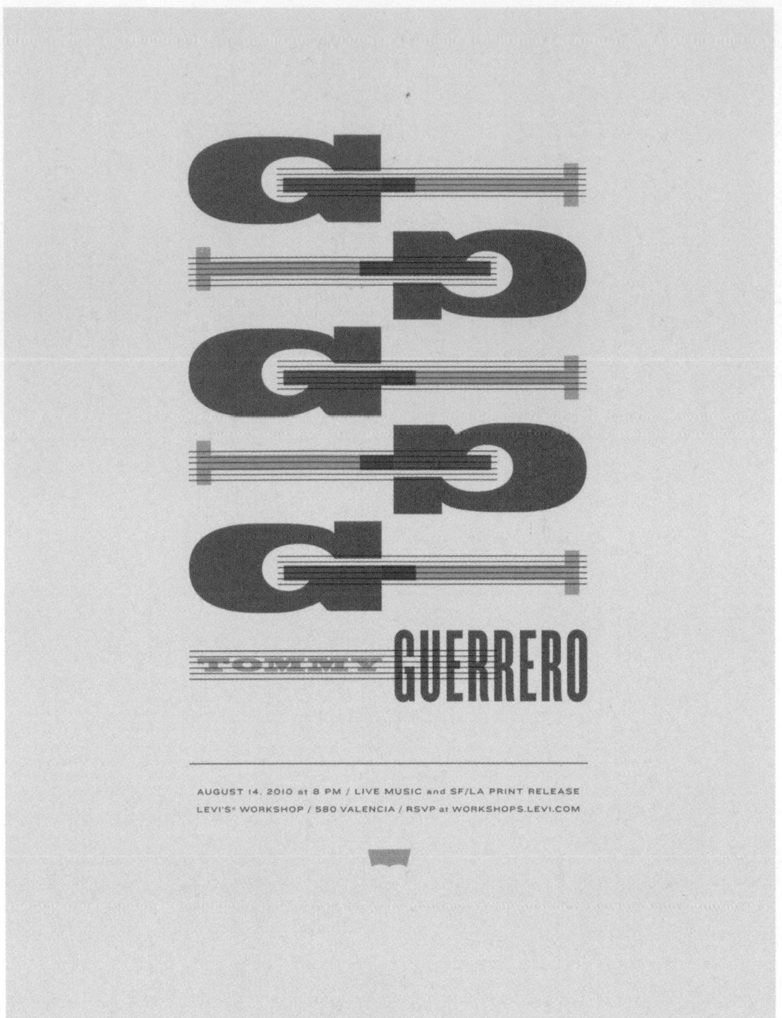

[1.15] The proximity of the inverted and evenly spaced elements here creates a rhythmic tension that mimics the tautness of stretched guitar strings. *Tommy Guerrero—Design by Dirk Fowler and Jason Munn.*

Elements of Design

The elements of design can be thought of as content—the design components. The elements discussed in this chapter are considered formal elements. Formal elements are general and abstract in nature—that is, they do not necessarily describe anything in specific terms. Formal elements can be used to represent or describe specific things. A line can represent a leaf, the human figure has shape, and a bowl of fruit has color. Described elements tend to be identified as what they represent, for example, a person rather than a shape. The elements are the visual vocabulary that gives voice to an image, allowing it to speak to the viewer. Study the vocabulary of elements in 1.26 and 1.27. Both rely on the use of circular elements, a single word form in black and white, and some shared colors. But the distinctive use of shapes and graphic treatment yield a very different feel and message. Studying the elements in formal, critical terms is helpful in understanding how the elements function as descriptive components in a design composition.

Shape, space, line, texture, and type are tangible elements (i.e., they have a physically defined presence). Color, value, size, and volume are examples of elements that are conditional. They exist as an embellishment or as a way of defining the tangible elements.

[a]

[b]

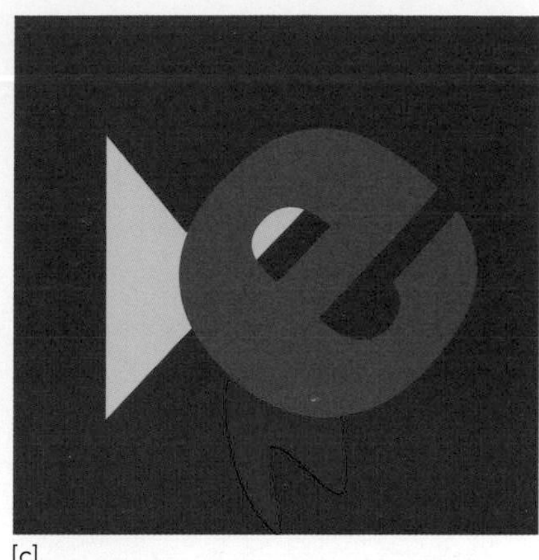
[c]

[1.16a to c] In these three designs, size, color, and orientation of each design element is the same for each composition. However, changing the position of the elements changes their relationship and the resulting conversation. In 1.16a, the elements are independent of each other, but each is touching the edge of the composition. In this somewhat aloof conversation, the shapes exist essentially independent form each other. 1.16b brings the elements together, touching in a precarious grouping where the elements are dependent on each other in a curious balancing act. The resulting conversation is playful and mutually supportive. The elements in 1.16c have been carefully aligned and overlapped to create new forms that have a three-dimensional quality. The full identity of the shape elements is partially concealed, transforming the identity of each one.

Shape and Space **Shape** can be defined as a figure or form. In two-dimensional design, shapes possess width and length. When shapes also possess depth, they move into the realm of three dimensions and are better described as mass. In either dimension, the configuration of the shape or mass determines its meaning. For example, a shape constructed of soft, curved edges could be described as sensual; a shape constructed of angular edges and points could be considered harsh. Shape configurations can be described on a basic level as geometric or organic **1.17a** and **1.17b**. Other ways of describing the overall configuration of shapes include figurative, mechanical, or natural.

Shapes must reflect the intent of the message. If your message is one of tranquil feelings, the use of harsh angular shapes would confuse the viewer. A sense of tranquility is more likely to be instilled by the use of flowing organic shapes.

Shapes exist as figures in or on a ground (background or space). Shapes are generally considered positive figures that displace space or impose themselves within a space. The interplay between figure and ground—positive shape and negative space—is a fundamental visual relationship. But in a curious way, space around figures has shape too. To orchestrate a harmonic balance of the parts of a design, it is critical to establish a purposeful relationship between the shapes of the design and the configuration of the space around the shapes. Experienced designers know the importance of paying equal attention to the shape of figures and the shape of their surrounding space or ground 1.17a.

In the most fundamental terms, space is an area activated by the other elements. Graphic design is a discipline concerned with the arrangement of elements in a given space. Artists tend to focus attention on the photograph, letterforms, or illustrated subjects in their design. But to present those graphic elements in a dynamic and visually effective way, artists also must

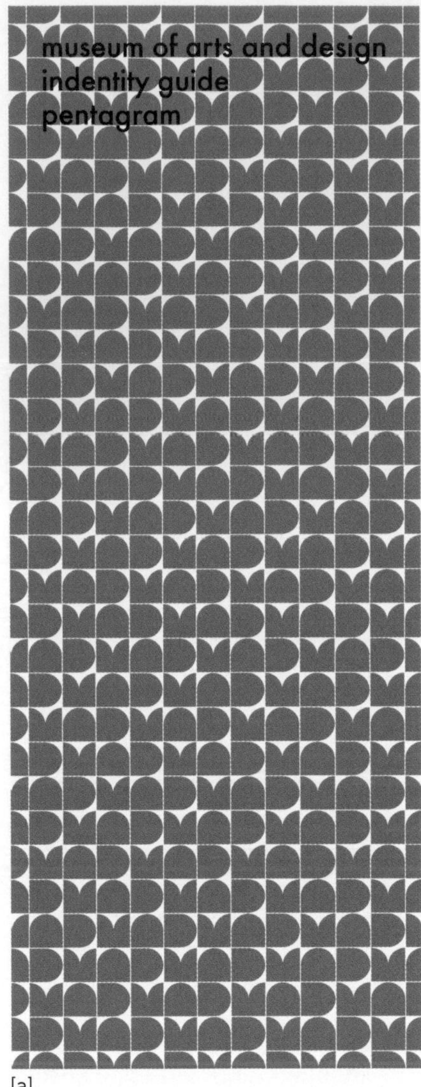

[a]

[1.17a] Shape is often used in support of a message. Within this identity guide, Pentagram uses repeated geometric shapes in a grid format to create a seamlessly continuous pattern that embodies the urban setting for the Museum of Art and Design in New York City.
Design by Michael Bierut/Pentagram.

[b]

[1.17b] The organic quality of the shapes, lines, and letterforms in this bakery's logo supports the natural ingredients and organic quality of its baked goods.
Design by Morris Creative.

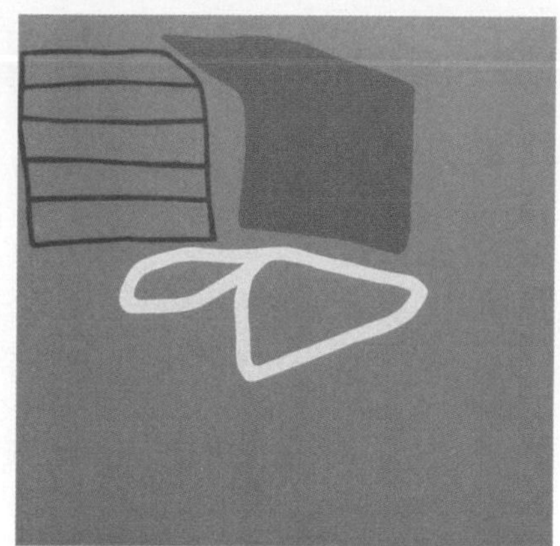

[1.18] Space is activated in this composition through the relationship of the outer shape of the three graphic elements to the square. The three elements roughly occupy a square space within the square composition. *Courtesy of Paige Williams.*

design the space around the elements. When a line or shape element is introduced into an area of space, it is said that the space is activated. Activating space can be attained subtly or overtly using line or shape **1.18**.

Beyond the formal considerations of space as an element, artists can create a particular kind of space for the viewer to experience. There are four ways that space can function.

- *Actual space* is the area that the design physically occupies. Some designs do not attempt to transform the actual space, but live in and on the space provided, as shown in 1.15. The guitar shapes and typography exist on the physical surface and occupy the space with respect to the rectangular edges.
- *Pictorial space* is the manipulation of a flat surface to create the sense of depth, movement, or direction. The depth in 1.25 is created through the use of overlapping perspective and is relatively compressed. A much deeper space is achieved in 1.26 using atmospheric perspective and diminishing size. Pictorial space relies on illusory devices that fool the viewer's eye.
- *Psychological space* presents an arrangement that influences the viewer's mind. Neither of the designed spaces in 1.27 or 1.28 represent spaces that potentially exist. Each in its own way, however, presents a space that evokes a strong emotive feeling. In the Wolfgang Weingart poster, the space is activated with a flurry of torn shapes, saturated color, scratched textures, and unique letterforms. The space presents an energy that can be associated with the excitement of learning. The space in the Carroll illustration is a kind of montage of soft dreamlike images that evoke an unsettling feeling. Carroll combines individual figures, the distant skyline and architectural forms, and scratched spirals and curves in his illustration. But he wants viewers to assemble their meaning. The result is a haunting feeling of desperation that is enhanced by the psychological space he creates.
- *Physical space* is the expanse of a three-dimensional area. Three-dimensional or environmental design must consider the function of space or environment and the aesthetics of designing within it. An example of the function of space is when design interfaces with the constructed environment. A signage system in an airport, the designed relationship of the parts of a coffeemaker, or the inherent restrictions imposed by a retail space on the design of a display or signage are examples of space function. How design visually interacts with space is an aesthetic and formal concern.

Line In formal terms, a **line** is the moving path of a point. The path determines the quality and character of the resulting line. The path can be straight, it can meander and curve across itself, or it can follow the precise arc of a circle segment. The resulting lines from those point paths give a specific character and meaning to a line. Another aspect of line quality is determined by the tool that makes it; for example, the sketched quality of a charcoal pencil line, the precision of a line drawn with a digital pen tool, or the organic quality of a line brushed with ink **1.19**. Lines of type can take the form of any shape just as a drawn line in pencil or ink **1.20**.

Another way to think of line is the idea of line as edge. A good example is a horizon line that exists as the line distinguishing land from sky. An edge line can exist along the side of any straight or curved shape or as the result of shapes sharing the same edge. You can see an example of line as edge in 1.12.

Line also can be implied, meaning it exists as the result of an alignment of shapes, edges, or even points. Implying the existence of a line in that way can be very engaging for the viewer. Implying lines can also activate compositional space 1.11.

Line functions in a variety of ways in design and art. Line can serve as the contour of an object or a human figure. It can exist purely to serve itself as a graphic element used to separate information, lead the eye in a particular direction, or imply alignment. The lines used in 1.20 function that way. The line in the same example functions symbolically, representing or describing an image of a "ten gallon" hat. Line also can exist as texture or pattern. The quality of a line can communicate the nature of what is being described, for example, delicate, precise, angular, architectural, mechanical, anatomical, fluid, or awkward.

Size Size serves scale and proportion. **Size** refers to the physical dimensions of an element or format. Determining the size of a typeface or a photograph or the dimensions of a poster or display is a basic decision that needs to be made within the context of the overall design objective. For some design venues such as CD packaging, magazines, billboards, and Web sites, size is a given. Where and how they will be viewed is a determinant of size. In packaging applications, the size or quantity of the product determines the size of the package **1.21**.

In other situations, the designer may determine the size of a work. Most design is first consumed through the eyes and then manipulated by hand. Books, magazines, other publications, and packaging and product design are good examples. In those instances, size is a function

[1.19] Lines can have different qualities depending on the tool used to create them. Shown here are five examples of lines drawn with (from left to right) compressed charcoal, a brush, soft charcoal, ink, and a digital pen tool. Note the different characteristics of each. The charcoal lines can be described as rough and gritty, the brushstroke line feels wet and streaked, and the digitally drawn line is clean and precise. *© Cengage Learning 2013. Design by Mark Thomas.*

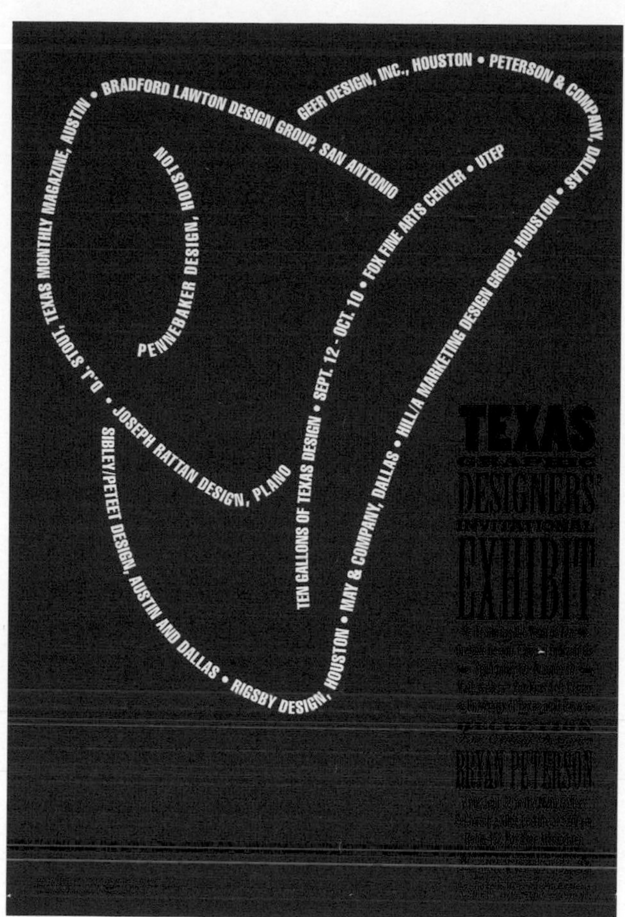

[1.20] Type also can function as line to describe a shape or form, as it does in this poster promoting a Texas design exhibition. The result is playful and has a memorable graphic impact. *Poster design by Mithoff Advertising.*

[1.21] In most food packaging the quantity of product dictates the size and volume of the package. How the product is packaged is primarily dependent on the material used for the package itself. Efficiency and environmental impact are serious considerations in package design. The "skin" of this product package is designed to reflect the brand name and the line, Jane Goodall organic dark chocolate, using a collage of photo imagery of Goodall interacting with chimps, an illustrated veil of colors, and the hand-rendered Theo brand logo. The resulting effect combines a boutique aesthetic within the illustrated elements with a historic documentary aesthetic in the memorable photos of Goodall. The result is graphically eclectic and unique. *Graphic Design by KittenChops.*

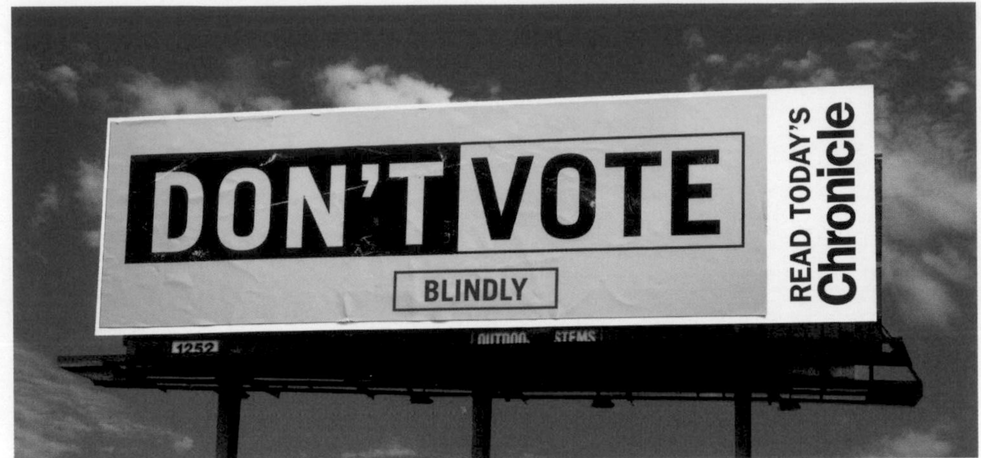

[1.22] Designed to be viewed at a distance, the large scale of a billboard does not necessarily mean more room for more information. Billboards usually contain relatively little text and imagery because they need to deliver a message that passing motorists and pedestrians can perceive at a glance. Enhancing the readability of the message is an effective graphic device of using high-contrast colors to reverse the type out of the background. *Billboard design by Rives Carlberg.*

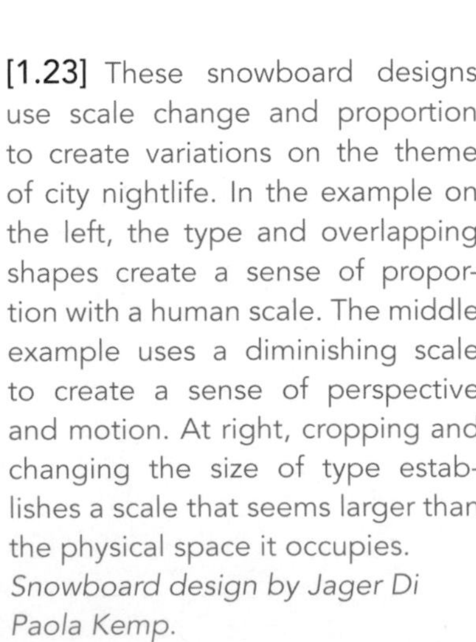

[1.23] These snowboard designs use scale change and proportion to create variations on the theme of city nightlife. In the example on the left, the type and overlapping shapes create a sense of proportion with a human scale. The middle example uses a diminishing scale to create a sense of perspective and motion. At right, cropping and changing the size of type establishes a scale that seems larger than the physical space it occupies. *Snowboard design by Jager Di Paola Kemp.*

of portability, ergonomics (the science of fitting products to the human form), and hand-eye manipulation. In other situations, viewing the message from a distance dictates the venue's size **1.22**. Even when size is open for consideration, designers are forced to work creatively within externally imposed constraints. A savvy designer uses the comparison of sizes (scale and proportion) to control how the viewer perceives relative size **1.23**.

Color

Color describes the intrinsic hues found in light and pigment. Hues are distinguished in common discourse by common color names such as blue, orange, brown, maroon, olive, yellow, and ochre. In industry, numerous systems have been designed to categorize, name, and classify color for various applications. As an element, color heightens the practical, cultural, psychological, and expressive dimensions of any visual image.

Color carries intrinsic meaning that communicates immediately without the aid of words or pictures **1.24**. Color also can convey an attitude or a mood. Color enhances compositional space by controlling color contrasts. Color can have a role in supporting all of the visual principles and can be applied to the other elements **1.25**. It can help create emphasis and variety, support an established hierarchy, and activate shapes and space. Chapter 4 is dedicated to a thorough discussion of color and its strategic and expressive role in design.

Texture

Texture refers to the quality and characteristic of a surface. Texture can be tactile (responsive to physical touch) and visual. Like color, texture cannot function as a design element on its own. It enhances the other elements, relying on shape and space to exist **1.26**. Texture provides designers with an opportunity to create variety and depth in a composition and helps to differentiate figure from ground when a design is complexly layered **1.27**.

[1.24] The color used in this package system conveys an immediate associative correlation to the flavors of product.
Courtesy of Ampro Design.

[1.25] Color can be used to manage hierarchy by establishing position in space, as exampled in this restaurant signage where the brightly colored lime jumps forward in space even though it is considerably smaller than the orange directly behind it.
Restaurant signage design by Sibley/Peteet.

[1.26] Combining drawn line and shape elements with the clean lines and shapes in the radial designs results in a rich contrast of visual texture. These motifs were successfully used to communicate the rich Mideastern flavor of the music within this compact disc packaging.
Package design by Sagmeister Inc.

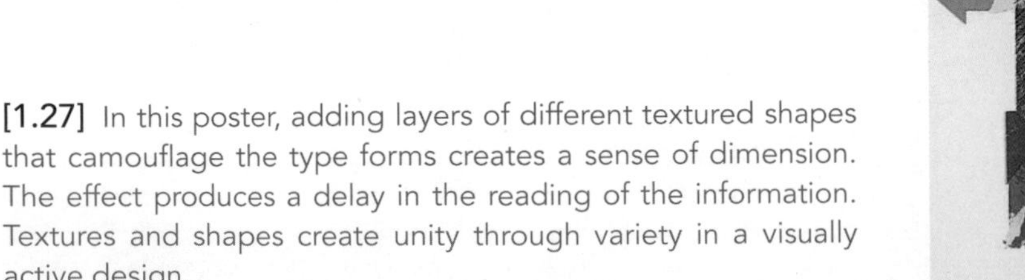

[1.27] In this poster, adding layers of different textured shapes that camouflage the type forms creates a sense of dimension. The effect produces a delay in the reading of the information. Textures and shapes create unity through variety in a visually active design.
Poster design by Wolfgang Weingart.

[1.28] Artist Jim Carroll's illustration technique combines photography, layers of type, and painted and scratchboard surfaces to create rich textural imagery.
Illustration by Jim Carroll.

Lines of text, painted surfaces, applications of dry media such as pencil or charcoal, or actual surfaces photographed or digitally scanned replicate actual texture but function as visual texture. Illustrators and photographers often make images that simulate real texture **1.28**.

There are instances in design in which texture is a tactile experience. Perhaps the most common example is the feel of paper surfaces within magazines and books or the paper used for business cards and letters as well as on packaging and other products that are designed to be handled. The paper surface specified by the designer plays an important role in the way the user interacts with the product. A variety of materials such as paper, plastic, metal, glass, and wood play an important role in determining the perception of quality and the function of the design. Texture can be arranged using its direction to create a pattern. Patterns of texture can be arranged to achieve visual tension and movement. Texture has an interesting function in interactive media. Most all of the devices that deliver a visual experience for the user, mobile phones, game devices, touch screen media, and computer keypads rely on remote, tactile interaction to function. However, the interaction with the imagery itself is completely a visual and virtual experience.

Typography **Typographic** forms are elements unique to communication design because they play a dual role. On a formal level, they function as shape, texture, point, and line **1.29**. But, of course, typographic forms also contain verbal meaning. Word forms must communicate a verbal message as well as function effectively as graphic elements in a composition.

When typographic elements are managed only with regard to their verbal meaning, the design can lack visual impact. When type is manipulated with a treatment that enhances its message, that message is perceived on a sensory as well as an intellectual level **1.30**.

In primary and secondary school, you related to typography as words in books that contained information for you to learn. You write letters to make words, sentences, and paragraphs that express your thoughts and ideas. That information is usually presented in horizontal lines

[1.29] The array of photographic texture in this design helps to distinguish the figure shapes and the negative shapes to create a distinctive foreground, middle ground, and background for this iconic travel poster.
© Todd Gipstein/CORBIS.

[1.30] This eclectic typographic and pictorial montage combines a Dadaist sensibility (*see the discussion in Chapter 2 about the influence of art movements on design*) with urban graffiti to produce a "skin" design for an Apple computer tower. The resulting design is a "noisy" and audacious aesthetic that appeals to a youth demographic.
Courtesy of THEOCY design (theocydesign.com). Designed by Brandon Ramirez & Mark Fankhauser.

that are stacked in columns that are arranged on a sequence of pages. After years of relating to type in that way, it is understandably challenging to think of type as a visual form that can assume other configurations and arrangements. Exercises that provide an opportunity to work with type in unusual and creative ways help reorient your thinking toward type as a potentially dynamic element in design composition. A further discussion of typography is presented in Chapter 2.

SUMMARY

The principles and elements of design function as a visual vocabulary. And in that sense, learning to use them is like learning a new language. It can be overwhelming to understand how to use all of them in your own designs. Study them individually at first and gradually learn to combine them in more complex ways. Also helpful is to study the work of contemporary designers and design through the twentieth century and contemporary design from the twenty-first century.

The exercises for this chapter stress one or two main principles, limiting the elements used to solve them. Once you have mastered the vocabulary of any language, you can effectively communicate in that "tongue." The visual language is complex and fluid. It is so because it is influenced by cultural, social, political, economic, and technological factors that can change on a daily basis. Using visual language is an ongoing learning process, but the principles and elements do not change. When you have gained a working knowledge of them, you possess the means to create powerful communication and the ability to provide reasons for your design decisions.

projects

LINE STUDY GRID

Objectives

- Gain control of hand-eye coordination in drawing.
- Work with control of line quality in a variety of tools.
- Work with a simple grid system to produce a composition.
- Engage in a process of visual decision making to create a design.
- Work with variety and contrast.

Description

Draw a series of line sets of equal line length (approximately 2½ inches long and 2½ inches wide) and at equal intervals from each other. Change the interval from tight to loose as you practice your control in each set. Generate 15 to 20 sets.

Cut the sets into 2-inch squares and arrange nine of them in a nine-unit grid. Strive for a variety of texture and value as you create this arrangement. Also explore variation in the character and quality of the lines as you draw them.

Drawing is a critical skill for all designers. This type of drawing can be used as a warm-up for brainstorm sketching or design drawing.

Limitations and Materials

Use a quality drawing paper or bristol board. Draw with fine to heavyweight markers, an ebony pencil, medium to soft charcoal pencil, and graphite sticks. Adhere the final 2-inch squares to a two-ply bristol board. Mount the final grid composition on a gray board with a 3-inch border.

Critique Discussion Points

How does the process serve the final design?

What different types of contrast did you achieve?

What role does texture play in the design?

How would you assess your control in the drawing?

Vocabulary

line, grid, composition, variety, contrast

References and Resources

Brice Marden, Willem DeKooning, Robert Motherwell, Jasper Johns, Louise Fishman, Eva Hesse, Louisa Chase, Franz Kline, Jackson Pollack, Susan Hauptman, Cy Twombly, Jean-Michel Basquiat, Stuart Davis, David Carson, Bradbury Thompson, Louise Fili, Ryan McGinness

Evaluation Criteria

Source Work and Research

Concept Development

Design and Composition

Craft and Execution

INTERRUPTED LINE STUDIES

Objectives

- Work with basic relationships of line and space.
- Expand critical visual judgment skills.
- Improve hand skills by using a studio knife and a straightedge, measuring, and cutting.
- Translate verbal criteria into visual form.
- Work with simple figure-ground relationships in a nonobjective design.

Description

Develop a series of five line studies that are spaced and arranged according to the following criteria:

1. Black and white are equal in a regularly spaced interval.
2. Black is constant to itself and white varies dramatically in an alternate spacing interval.
3. Black constantly increases, and white remains constant to itself.
4. Black increases as white decreases in width.
5. Black and white increase constantly, but at different rates.

Limitations and Materials

Use vertical parallel lines and use no more than seven lines per study.

Use black paper to cut strips (lines) and arrange them vertically on a white 5-inch by 5-inch piece of cover stock. Use a glue stick or rubber cement as an adhesive. Finish the studies by mounting them on a gray board with a 3-inch border.

Critique Discussion Points

Identify the figure-ground relationship in each study.

Identify any illusory effects caused by the high-contrast relationships.

What does each study describe or evoke?

Vocabulary

space, figure-ground, contrast, illusory, nonobjective, vertical, parallel

References and Resources

Brice Marden, Robert Motherwell, Louise Fishman, Eva Hesse, Louisa Chase, Franz Kline, Susan Hauptman, Cy Twombly, Jean-Michel Basquiat, Stuart Davis, Frank Stella, Bradbury Thompson, Lance Wyman, Malcolm Greer

Evaluation Criteria

Source Work and Research

Achievement of Criteria

Design and Composition

Craft and Execution

LINE, LEAF, LETTER

Objectives

- Work with an exploration of the design principles.
- Manage design decisions using basic elements from the designer's toolbox.
- Establish a hierarchy of elements that achieves unity.
- Explore visual relationships based on closure, balance, and proximity.

Description

Using a line, a leaf, and a letter, produce two contrasting compositions. You also may use up to three planes or divisions in the background. Decide beforehand how the two compositions will contrast by exploring various ideas. Do a group think session to explore visual possibilities. Use a notebook or journal to make note of the visual contrasts that you discussed and what possibilities you would like to explore for your own solution.

Work with the following issues as you explore solutions:

Scale changes between the line, letter, and leaf

Complementary or contrasting qualities in the compared compositions

Quality and character of the letter you chose

Effect of natural color

Control and management of visual hierarchy or dominance, proximity, scale, and closure

Limitations and Materials

Use any source of paper that is neutral in color (newspaper, cover stock, or other solid printed paper) for the planes. You can cut the line and the letter from source material, or you can create the line in drawing media. You can generate the letter from a computer or cut it from an existing source. You might want to press the leaf with an iron to flatten it. Work with an image area of 10 inches by 10 inches on two- or four-ply bristol board. Rubber cement works well as an adhesive, but a glue stick or high-quality adhesive paste is a good low-toxic option. Lay a clean sheet of paper over the design and roll a printer's brayer over the surface to press the paper to the adhesive. Trim the design and mount it on a piece of gray board with a 3-inch border. Depending on the color scheme in the design, black or white board may be better for mounting.

Critique Discussion Points

Which of the primary principles is dominant?

What is the function and relationship of the formal elements?

How did you manage the contrast concept in the compositions?

Discuss the form and function of line in the compositions.

Vocabulary

hierarchy, closure, balance, proximity, scale, dominance, two- or four-ply bristol board, brayer

References and Resources

Wolfgang Weingart, David Carson, Piet Zwart, Laszlo Moholy-Nagy, Josef Albers, Neville Brody, Bradbury Thompson, Robert Motherwell, Ben Nicholson, Jean Arp, Georges Braque, Jean Miro, Andy Goldsworthy

Evaluation Criteria

Source Work and Research

Concept Development

Design and Composition

Craft and Execution

in review

1. Which of the primary principles controls variety?
2. What is the distinction between proportion and scale?
3. What is the distinction between how the primary and support principles function?
4. What is the purpose of formal elements?
5. Which of the elements is unique to graphic design?
6. Which two elements can exist only in support of or as an enhancement to the other elements?
7. Discuss various forms that line can take.
8. What is similar about texture and color as they relate to the other elements?
9. Which principle deals with the placement and position of elements in space?
10. What is unique about tactile sensory experiences and interactive media?

Courtesy of Lance Wyman, Ltd.

"Today, more than any time that I've experienced, there's an overload of technology and data."

Lance Wyman

Lance Wyman is a widely recognized award-winning designer whose illustrious career encompasses designing graphics for a World's Fair exhibition, symbols for the U.S. National Zoo, and countless other logos, symbols, and identity systems for nonprofit and commercial agencies and institutions. He developed a high level of recognition early in his career with his designing of the graphics for the 1968 Mexico City Olympic Games where his multidimensional integration of logos, typography, and color developed for a multilingual audience set a precedent. This project has been cited by design historian Philip Meggs in *A History of Graphic Design* as "… one of the most successful in the evolution of visual identification." Other notable identity projects Wyman has designed include logo and symbol design for the American Museum of National History and the Washington Mall.

How did you get started in your career?

My first job was with General Motors in 1960. I designed the two-part circular logo and the packaging system for Delco United, the makers of General Motors auto parts.

What is your educational background?

After completing my first year at Pratt, the foundation year, I knew I wanted to do something that communicated visually but I wasn't interested in the courses available at that time (advertising, illustration and fine arts). Graphic design was not taught in undergraduate programs at that time. I chose Industrial Design because the department had interesting showcases of student work and probably because I built model planes when I was a kid. I have a bachelor's degree in Industrial Design from Pratt Institute in Brooklyn.

What made you decide to pursue the career path that you've chosen?

In 1959 I was chosen to represent the Pratt Industrial Design department at the first General Motors summer design program held in their new Tech Center. It was the summer between my Junior and Senior year and I had the chance to work with students from other U.S. design schools. I met a student who was studying Graphic Design at the graduate level at Yale. He was studying logo design under Paul Rand and when I saw the work he was doing I knew I wanted to design logos.

What has been your biggest challenge in your career?

My biggest challenge might have been getting into Pratt to study design. I was popular in high school, class president, four years of football, fraternity president, but my grades were terrible. I had to go to a community college for a year and maintain a B+ average to get in.

I did that at Fairleigh Dickenson College and was finally accepted at Pratt. Then the challenge was to stay in. I worked factory jobs in the summer (7 p.m. to 7 a.m. seven days a week) and did things like clean the cafeteria and run the shop in the ID department to pay tuition and expenses.

Your biggest achievement?

So far my biggest achievement is the design of the graphics for the 1968 Olympic Games held in Mexico.

What do you believe has been the biggest factor in your success?

Certainly one of the biggest factors in my success was an English course at Fairleigh Dickenson College. The instructor, Dick Holub, was an ex-professional basketball player and coached the Fairleigh Dickenson basketball team, as well as teaching English. We had no books in that course. Between classes the class assignment was to record examples where our English failed to communicate. We analyzed the results as a class, keeping in mind that English was just another form of communication. This was a major lesson for me that I apply to my graphic design work—if my intention doesn't come out the other end in a way that is understood, it is failed communication.

What advice would you give to recent graduates or others who are just getting started in a career in illustration or graphic design?

Today, more than any time that I've experienced, there's an overload of technology and data. I think of them as partners that can empower me and fool me. Here are some thoughts for recent graduates as well as for myself:

1. Use what's on the Web and take advantage of the latest technology, but don't be suckered into thinking they automatically make you better and smarter. Think of them as a resource for your work, not a solution.
2. Just show up. What I mean by that is to make your best effort to understand and evaluate your own experience. See what's happening in the world around you without making it up or projecting your own attitude. See what's happening in your inner world, that's one of your best clues as to how to create and apply your work.
3. Be sensitive to your objectives—they can be moving targets so you have to stay on your toes.
4. Stay active in the work you love—this enhances your opportunities to make it successful.
5. One project does not a career make—learn from your successes and your failures.

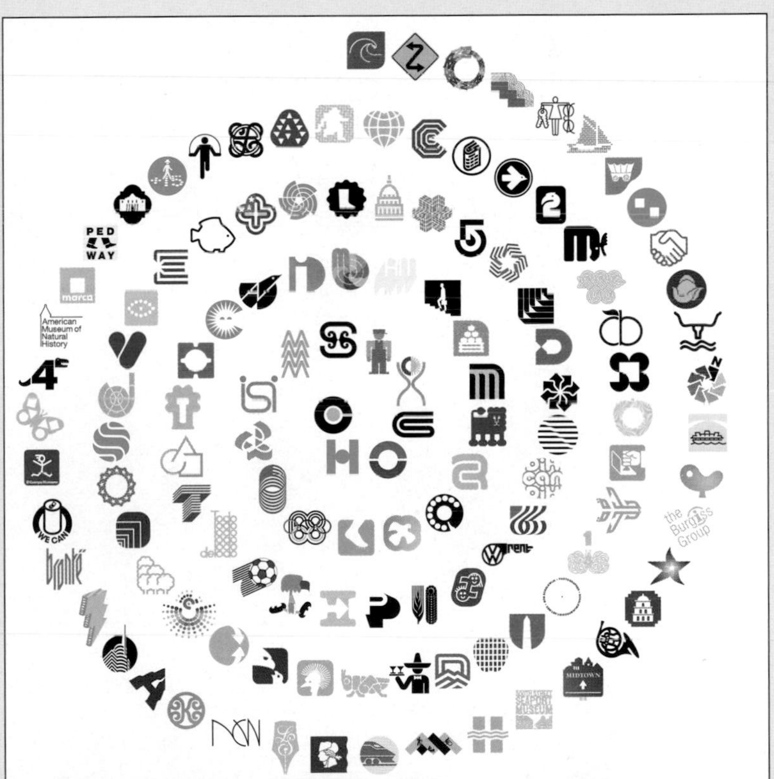

This spiral of logos and symbols Wyman has designed also acts as a timeline of career projects, starting at the center with icons he designed during his school days, and extending to more recent projects at the end. The spiral welcomes viewers on the home page of his Web site. When an icon is selected, it activates a window that includes a detailed explanation of the design project.
Courtesy of Lance Wyman Ltd.

two

Typography in Design

Photo courtesy of House Industries. Design by Bondé Prang. Art Direction by Andy Cruz.

2

introduction

You are surrounded by typographic information and communication. Every day you encounter it on billboards, in newspapers and magazines, on the Web, on social media, and in your mailbox. Although type allows you to communicate complicated messages to other people, there is no guarantee that the intended audience will notice, read, or respond to its content.

When you think about it, relatively few printed messages with which you are bombarded on a daily basis hit their mark and make a memorable impression. To a large extent, people's perception and comprehension of the printed word are influenced by how it is presented. Designers who know how to use type effectively use it to enhance the message embodied in the written text to engage an audience and create visual appeal while communicating the intended message in a clear and compelling manner.

Using type effectively requires an understanding of its communication and visual possibilities. Chapter 1 introduced some of those aspects by discussing how type can function as more than just a means of communicating content. Type can work to satisfy several design objectives at once, serving as text to be read and as a means of adding expression to a message while simultaneously functioning as a compositional element.

Some features of working with type addressed in Chapter 1 included how styling type or handling it in a certain way can enhance the meaning of a word or phrase. By presenting examples that demonstrated how typographic forms function as shape, line, or texture, Chapter 1 also showed how type works as a design element. This chapter discusses those aspects in more detail by analyzing additional examples and ways that type can work to support content and composition.

Knowledge of basic typographic terms and specifications is vital to understanding and working with type. Knowing these terms and rules and the

objectives

- Present a historical context for the evolution of typography.
- Define typographic terms and explain measurement systems.
- Explore how to select typefaces appropriate to a project's design and communication goals.
- Discuss the relationship between typographic design and technology.
- Explore ways that type can lend expression to a design.
- Examine harmonious combinations of type with imagery and other design elements.
- Investigate a variety of sources for type.
- Explore how to use type when legibility is a factor.
- Discuss typography and technology.

larger context of the history and use of typography provides an essential foundation for exploring its creative uses and applications. This chapter begins with a discussion of typographic origins and history and proceeds to introduce the basic terminology, standard rules, a perspective on typographic designers, and the technology that gave form to type.

THE EVOLUTION OF TYPOGRAPHY: CLAY TO PAPER TO PIXELS

As a child you may have used a stick or your finger to record impressions in sand at the beach or in the dirt in your backyard to count or keep score. The first forms of typography originated symbolically in the same way. Three thousand years ago the first symbolic impressions were pressed into clay slabs using fingers and eventually reeds to create lists or ledgers as a form of record keeping. These impressions are referred to as cuneiforms and originated in Sumer, a region located in the basins where the Tigris and Euphrates rivers empty into the Persian Gulf, a region where clay is abundant. As we explore this timeline, it is interesting to note the relationship between cultural influences, natural resources, technology, and need **2.1a** and **2.1b**.

The Egyptians invented a process of early papermaking using the papyrus plant. The plant is indigenous to the Nile delta region and strips from the stem were used to form flat sheets that functioned as a writing surface. The combination of the availability of the plant and the dry climate that served to provide a long life for the material made this invention possible and sustainable. The

[a]

[2.1a] Sumerian cuneiforms.
© Gianni Dagli Orti/CORBIS.

[b]

[2.1b] Assyrian cuneiforms.
© The Trustees of the British Museum.

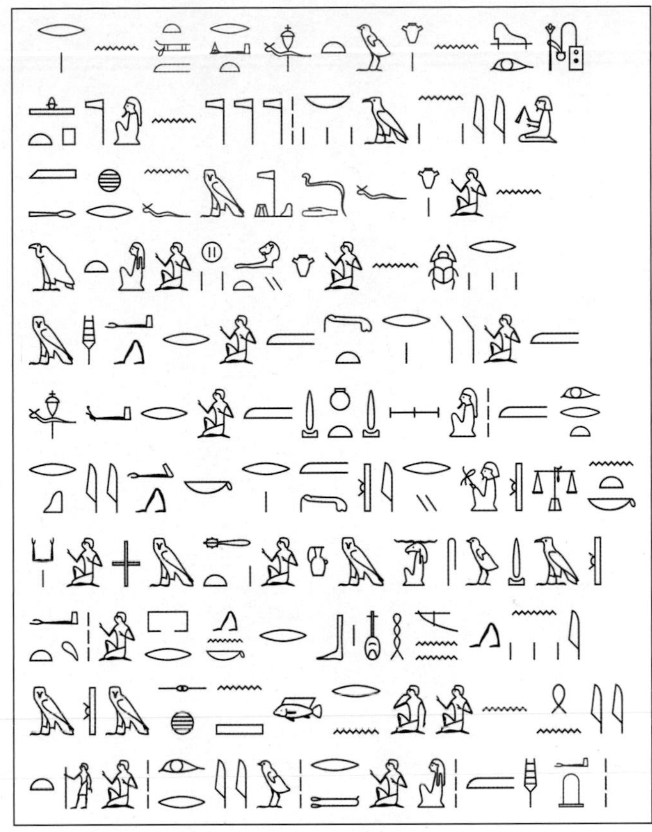

[2.2] These hieroglyphs from the *Book of the Dead* 1600 BCE were originally written by the Egyptians on papyrus. This is a beta version translated using Hierowriter Web-based writing tool.
Courtesy of Hieroglyphs.net.

Egyptians of this period used a form of writing called *hieroglyphs*, which evolved from the cuneiform. Hieroglyphs relied on a complicated combination of logographic and alphabetic elements and are considered an ancient form of alphabet. It was in use for over 2500 years **2.2**.

Cuneiforms, hieroglyphics, and early stone carvings represent the first writing systems. The first systematic alphabet, however, was developed in 1500 BCE by the Phoenicians, a Semitic people who lived in the eastern region of the Mediterranean Sea. This alphabet was 22 characters and was void of any vowels **2.3**. Some scholars clarify that without vowels, the consonants could not be pronounced, which limited the function of this alphabet. Because of their proximity to the sea, the Phoenicians spread the alphabet through trade and eventually the Greeks contributed vowels. In fact, the word *alphabet* is a compound of *alpha* and *beta*, the names of the first two vowels added by the Greeks.

Beginnings of writing using a flat pen occurred around 50 BCE as seen in Roman square capitals. Large capital letters known as *majuscules* were written on parchments and carved in stone. Carolingian *minuscules* or small letters were used in Europe around 800 CE **2.4**. These two terms were the precursors to small and capital letters that would eventually be referred to as upper and lowercase letters, the nomenclature for typography today.

In 868 CE, the earliest known printed book the *Diamond Sutra* was printed in China. Later, Johannes Gutenberg, inventor of the first movable type press, printing with both metal and wood type, was also credited with the first printed book—a Latin language bible printed in 1455 CE in Mainz, Germany. Arnold Pannartz and Conrad Sweynheym, two Germans who were contemporaries of Johannes Gutenberg, produced the earliest known type design. Their fonts were cast Greek type that reflected the aesthetic expectations of Italian buyers of Latin books. Other early font designs included Jenson, a Venetian roman typeface; Griffo, the first italic typeface; and Garamond, a roman font designed by Claude Garamond, a Parisian who was also a skilled punchcutter.

[2.3] The Phoenician alphabet as compared to modern consonants. *© Cengage Learning 2013.*

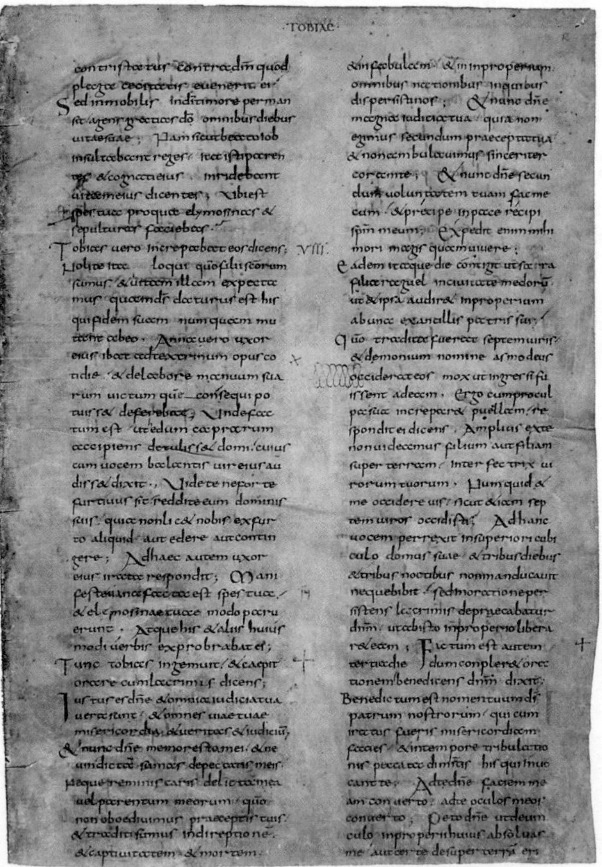

TOBIAE
MS 617
Bible: Tobit. Germany, ca. 800. Early Carolingian minuscule

[2.4] *Courtesy of The Schøyen Collection, MS 617.*

In 1529 CE, Geoffroy Tory, printer, engraver, publisher, and the author of *Champ Fleury* (*Flowery Fields*), explored the relationship between letterforms and the human body. The relationship is a study of proportion and scale and utilizes an arithmetic grid, the golden rectangle, and perspective (discussed in Chapter 1) to discover the classical common relationships between human and typographic anatomy. The result is both an analytic and poetic treatment of Tory's ideal concept of letters as presented through his personal experiences **2.5a** and **2.5b**.

In the mid-nineteenth century, the invention of a mechanical router to produce wood type supported a sustained interest in the printing of posters, handbills, and broadsides. James Edward Hamilton began producing wood type in the 1880s in Wisconsin and became the

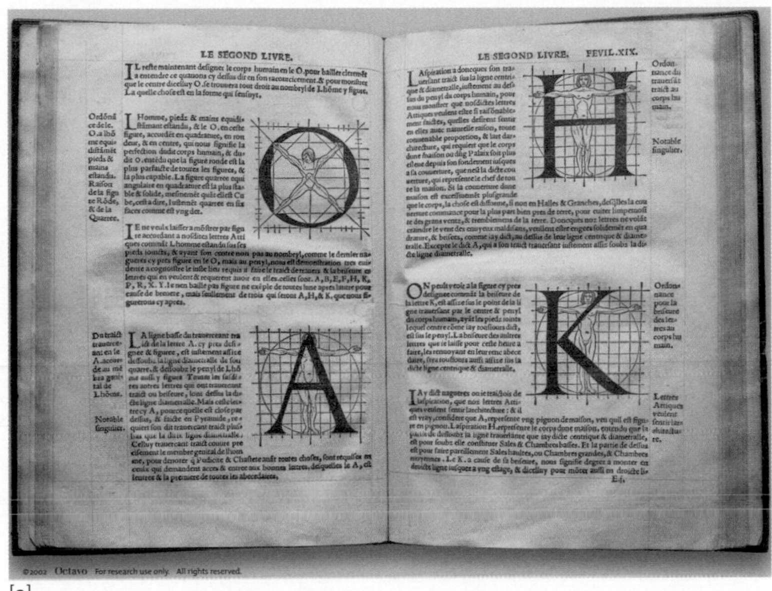

[a]

[2.5a] *Courtesy of Octavo and The Library of Congress, Rare Book and Special Collections Division.*

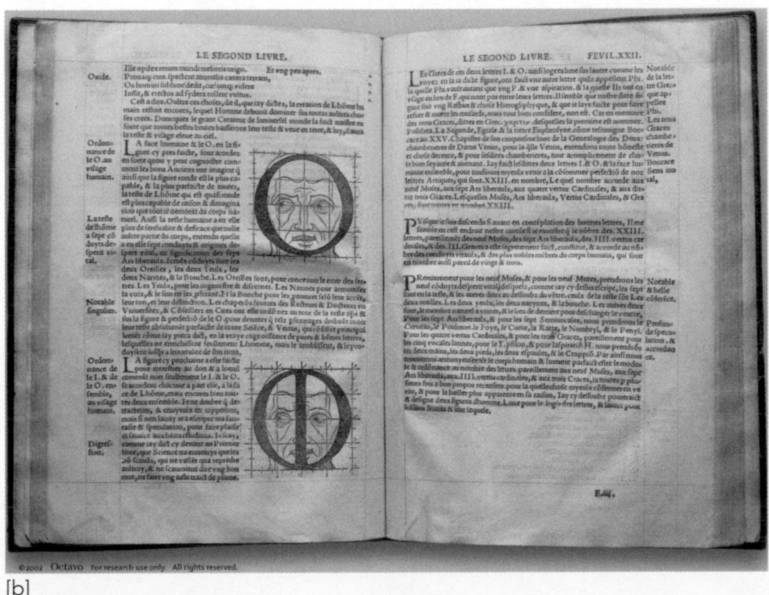

[b]

[2.5b] *Courtesy of Octavo and The Library of Congress, Rare Book and Special Collections Division.*

largest supplier and print foundry in the United States at the time. Hamilton employed printers, typesetters, and artisans who routed wood type, called *pantographers*, who used a tool connected to a router to scale sizes of wood type to be cut. Wood type could be set in small text sizes and as large as 4 feet for each letter **2.6a** and **2.6b**.

[a]

[2.6a] Wood type arranged in an easel is placed on a press for printing.
Photo courtesy of Nick Sherman/Hamilton Wood Type & Printing Museum.

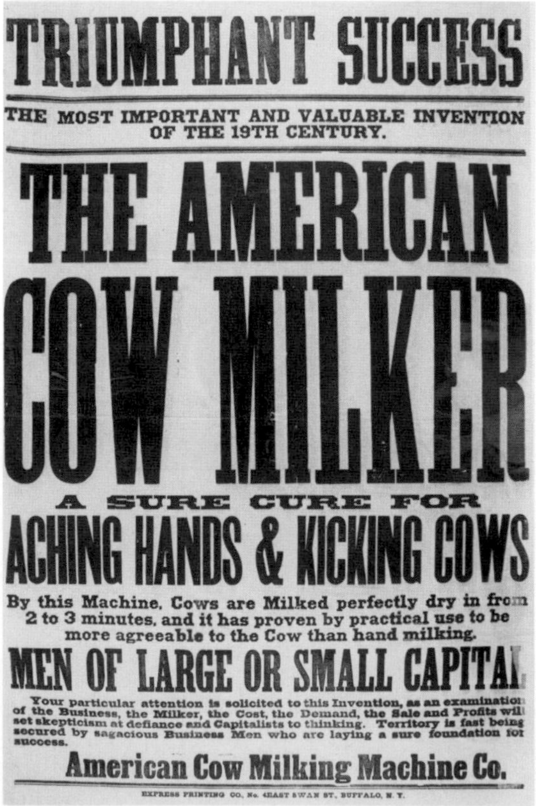

TRIUMPHANT SUCCESS
THE MOST IMPORTANT AND VALUABLE INVENTION OF THE 19TH CENTURY.
THE AMERICAN
COW MILKER
A SURE CURE FOR
ACHING HANDS & KICKING COWS
By this Machine, Cows are Milked perfectly dry in fro
2 to 3 minutes, and it has proven by practical use to be
more agreeable to the Cow than hand milking.
MEN OF LARGE OR SMALL CAPITA
Your particular attention is solicited to this Invention, as an examinatio
of the Business, the Milker, the Cost, the Demand, the Sale and Profits wil
set skepticism at defiance and Capitalists to thinking. Territory is fast being
secured by sagacious Business Men who are laying a sure foundation fo
success.
American Cow Milking Machine Co.
EXPRESS PRINTING CO., No. 4 EAST SWAN ST., BUFFALO, N. Y.

[b]

[2.6b] Farmers relied on posted information in the late 1800s to keep informed. This advertisement is actually a broadside printed with wood type that is selling a cow milking machine.
Courtesy of New York State Historical Association Library, Special Collections, Cooperstown, NY.

ART MOVEMENT INFLUENCES ON TYPOGRAPHY

At the onset of the twentieth century, typography was influenced by a series of movements in the art and design world. Most of these movements were a counterresponse to the ornate and classical notions of art that existed in the nineteenth century. In 1910 the German block letters (sans serif) were developed to reflect the "new" industrial aesthetic.

Art movements, such as the Futurists, embraced the technology of the day, which included speed, industrial inventions, and concepts of the future. These ideas were explored by artists and designers in film and in literature. Dadaism was a revolutionary movement interested in a rejection of established standards in politics, art, and social culture. It involved many disciplines including design **2.7**. The De Stijl movement sought to reduce form to its essential parts and also seek a utopian order as reflected in the universal color scheme of black, white, and the primaries. Examples of artists working in this movement include Piet Mondrian, painter, Theo Van Doesburg designer, and Gerrit Rietveld, architect **2.8**.

[2.7] The Dadaists vigorously challenged established moirés in all aspects of the culture in which they lived. This design demonstrates the anarchist attitudes of the Dada movement. It is titled, *Small DaDa Soiree* and is a promotional poster for a DaDa tour of the Netherlands in 1923.

While it appears chaotic and unmanaged, it is in fact, a carefully designed, non-hierarchical and unorthodox composition that reflects the untamed and physical aesthetics of Dadaist design. *Digital Image © The Museum of Modern Art / Licensed by SCALA / Art Resource, NY*

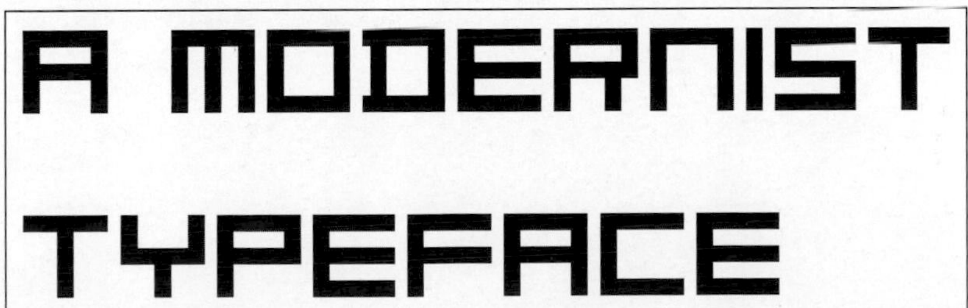

[2.8] Reducing the structural elements of this square alphabet (1919) to single consistent strokes and linear right angles is based on the concept of a square subdivided into a raster of 5 by 5. Theo Van Doesburg achieved in this alphabet the ideals sought by artists of the De Stijl movement, which he founded in 1917. *© Cengage Learning 2013.*

Other movements that profoundly affected typography in the twentieth century included the Bauhaus, Art Deco, Surrealism, Cubism, Expressionism, and Pop Art. These movements were influenced by "modernist thinking," which was pervasive throughout most of the twentieth century and embraced the refutation of established values in the arts, in favor of abstraction. In the last quarter of the twentieth century, modernism became the established aesthetic and postmodern ideas a counteraction to it **2.9a** and **2.9b**.

All of these movements combined with social changes and rapid developments in all areas of technology profoundly affected the look and function of typography in the twentieth century. Typographic communication in the first decade of the twenty-first century continues to be impacted and transformed by advances in technology, but also a changing relationship

[a]

[2.9a] A classic modernist typographic composition, this poster design by Jan Tschichold utilizes two san serif typefaces—a simplified presentation and a grid structure for organizing the placement of the type elements. Also common in modernist design is a limited color palette of black, white, and red, which is used to support the typographic hierarchy.
Type specimen of the font Iwan Reschniev from fonts.info.

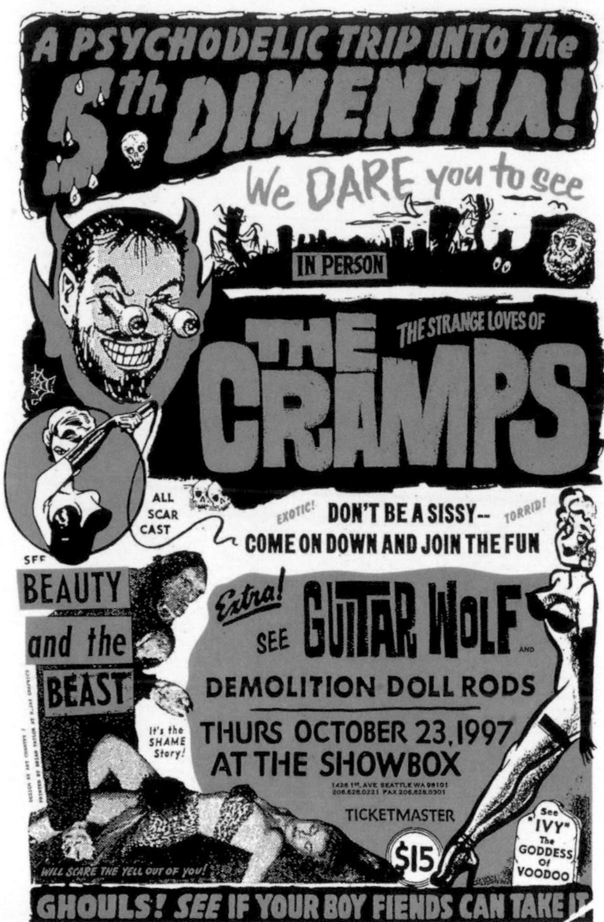

[b]

[2.9b] Art Chantry broke the rules established by modernist design, mixing and using different sizes of type within words and throughout the design, mixing upper- and lowercase letters in the same word, presenting type that touches in awkward alignment, and crowding type with imagery, making reading a disjointed experience. But this was Chantry's intent in this poster design, which communicated to the audience—a youthful and rebellious-minded rock culture—that expected an counterculture design aesthetic.
Design by Art Chantry.

between design and global "economic health, social equity, environmental protection, and cultural vitality."[1]

TYPOGRAPHIC MACHINES AND INVENTIONS

1450 The Letterpress—Movable lead and wood type. Johannes Gutenberg

1796 Planography/Lithography—Printing on a flat surface and based on the chemical repellence of oil and water. Alois Senefelder

1818 Chromolithography—Multicolored printing on stone surfaces. Alois Senefelder

Typographus. Der Buchdrucker.

ARte mea reliquas illuſtro Typographus artes,
Imprimo dum varios ære micante libros.
Quæ prius aucta ſitu, quæ puluere plena iacebant,
Vidimus obſcura nocte ſepulta premi.

Hæc veterum renouo neglecta volumina Patrum
Atq; ſcolis curo publica facta legi.
Artem prima nouam reperiſſe Moguntia fertur,
Vrbs grauis, & multis ingenioſa modis.
Qua nihil vtilius videt, aut precioſius orbis,
Vix melius quicquam ſecla futura dabunt.

C 3 Char-

[2.10] *Courtesy of Erich Lessing / Art Resource, NY.*

[1] These ethical guidelines are part of the "Living Principles" work of the AIGA Center for Sustainable Design. A more in-depth discussion of sustainable design is in Chapter 6. To join the ongoing conversation on sustainable practices, visit livingprinciples.org.

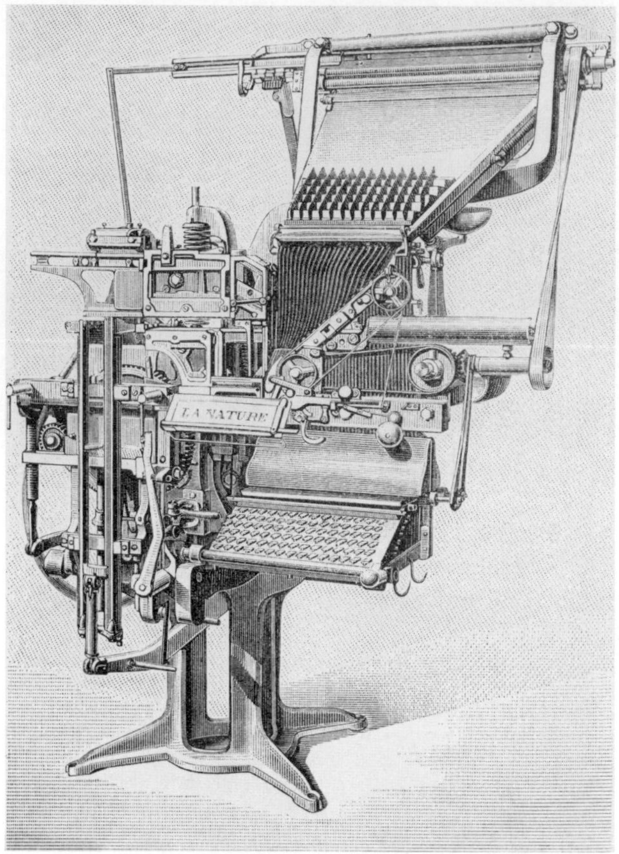

[2.11] Nineteenth-Century Linotype Machine
© Bettmann/CORBIS.

1887 Linotype—Machinery that produces type one line at a time from a keyboard. Ottmar Mergenthaler

1904 Offset Lithography—A flat, planographic process that transfers the reverse image to a rubber cylinder from which a "right" reading or direct impression is printed. Prior to offset, designers and printers worked with imagery that was backwards. Ira S. Rubel

1937 Electrophotography (1960 Photocopier)—A dry printing process based on electrically charging a heated drum, which attracts toner and transfers it to paper. Chester Carlson

1947 Phototypesetting—A photomechanical process in which type is developed onto sheets of photo paper. Designers cut and pasted the sheets by hand into a design layout that was then transferred to metal lithographic plates for printing. Rene Alphonse Higonnet and Louis Marius Moyroud

1969 Laser Printer—Similar to the photocopy process, which is analog, laser printing is a process where the image is scanned by a laser beam converting it into digital information that is used to produce an impression onto paper using toner. The first machine marketed in 1979 was the IBM 3800. Gary Starkweather

1988 Inkjet Printer—A digital process that converts computer-generated imagery into small, sprayed drops of ink onto paper. Hewlett-Packard Deskjet

[2.12] *Courtesy of Heidelberg.*

DESIGN AND TYPOGRAPHY

In a design composition, type works as a design element, just as shape, line, color, and texture serve as design elements. So all of the principles that guide decision making in a design composition also apply to typography. How to style type, what typeface to use, and what size and color the type are all dictated by the primary principles of hierarchy and dominance, unity and variety, balance, and proportion. The secondary principles of scale, emphasis, rhythm, movement, proximity, and repetition apply as well.

When designers begin a project, they are given a message (typically verbal content) to communicate. The designer's job is to determine what kind of typographic form this content will assume and how it will be handled relative to the other elements in the composition.

Hierarchy

Many designers find it helpful to start by determining the hierarchy, or most important element, in a composition. From there, they organize type and other elements around that focal point. Often the quality of an image, nature of the message, or overall concept determines whether imagery or type will play a leading or supporting role in a design composition.

Imagery and type should be combined in a synergistic manner. It is up to the designer to determine what the hierarchy and balance will be between these elements, as well as other design elements.

The designer also manages the treatment and placement of the elements in a way that controls how the viewer's eye will travel from image to text and travel around a design composition. Even if the most prominent element in a composition is a photograph or another image, type still needs to be organized and assigned a hierarchical role so the viewer is led through a design composition in a way that supports the message's intent and its ability to be understood. This allows the viewer to take in all of the design's visual information **2.13**.

When typographic hierarchy is assigned, the most important part of the verbal content or message is given the most prominence. When you examine a Web or printed page that is composed entirely of type, you can see how the headlines assume a dominant role and how subheads and other smaller text play a secondary or subordinate role in a design composition. Depending on the venue, the verbal content receiving the most prominence could be a headline, title, compelling sentence, word, or phrase. Once the viewer is visually engaged, the most prominent content is followed by information of secondary or supplementary importance **2.14**.

As with other design elements, size, color, and surrounding negative space all affect the degree of prominence a typographic focal point will assume. Relative size or scale is often used to control hierarchy in a design composition. Words, phrases, or sentences that are larger than surrounding text will be more dominant. Type that is a different color than that of surrounding text or its background also will assume prominence by standing out in contrast. Type, even if it is small, will stand out if it is surrounded by large amounts of negative space **2.15**.

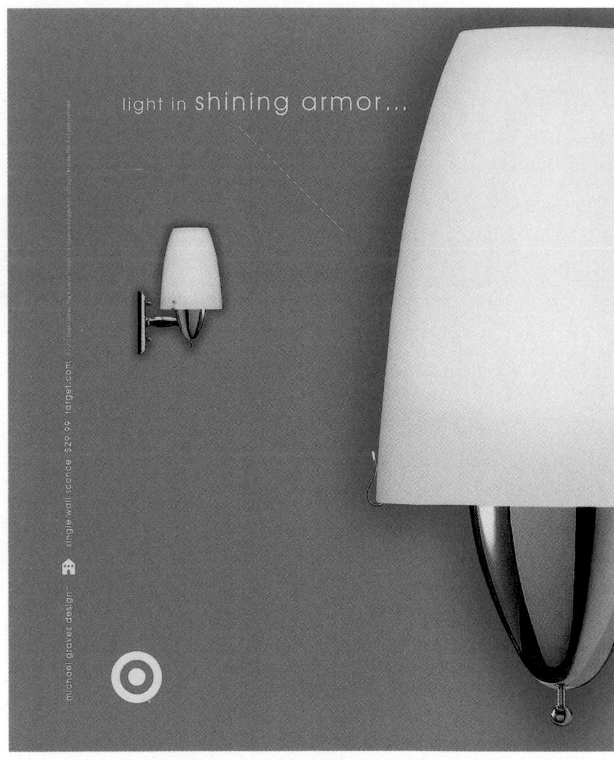

[2.13] This ad for Target uses type as a linear element to guide the viewer's eye from the large lamp at the right, across the top of the ad, and down the left side so the eye loops around the entire composition, taking in all of its visual components.
Design by Design Guys.

[2.14] In this modernist poster design, a clear hierarchy is established with the size and prominence of the type. To catch the viewer's attention, the word *Landing* is largest and most prominent. From there, the viewer's eye is drawn to the image and then to the supplementary information. *Design by Kees van der Laan.*
Design by Kees van der Laan. Courtesy of the Minneapolis Art Institute, the Modernism Collection, gift of Norwest Bank Minnesota.

[2.15] Even though the type in this example is quite small, the surrounding negative space draws your attention to it. The small type gets noticed because it stands alone in a sea of black.
© Cengage Learning 2013. Design by Mark Thomas.

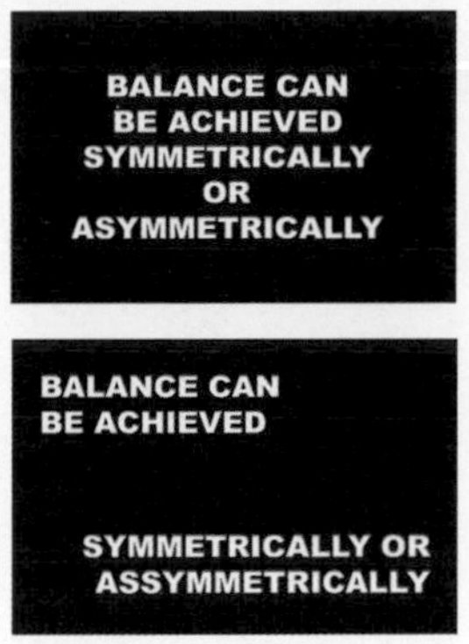

[2.16] In these examples, the type size and format of the rectangle are identical. However, the top example shows a symmetric arrangement where type is equally distributed on either side of a central axis. The bottom example demonstrates how an asymmetric arrangement balances positive and negative space.
© Cengage Learning 2013. Design by Mark Thomas.

Balance

After hierarchy has been assigned, balance determines the visual distribution of type and how it will appear in relation to the other visual elements in a composition. As you learned in Chapter 1, there are four types of visual balance: symmetric, asymmetric, radial and crystallographic. Type in symmetric balance is arranged so that it is equally distributed on either side of a central axis. Asymmetric balance is achieved when type is distributed unevenly on a page so that positive and negative space is in balance **2.16**. Radial balance presents type elements in a circular configuration or radiating from a central point **2.17**. Crystallographic balance is utilized when a uniform distribution of type elements is desired.

Use of Type to Create Theme and Variation

The design principles of unity and variety also apply to type. Type can play an important role in unifying a composition or creating variety within it. When various visual elements need to

[2.17] The use of five concentric circles represent the three "C's" and spaces offering a symbolic, radial symmetry to present the logotype for this organization.
Courtesy of Colorado Contemporary Arts Collaboration.

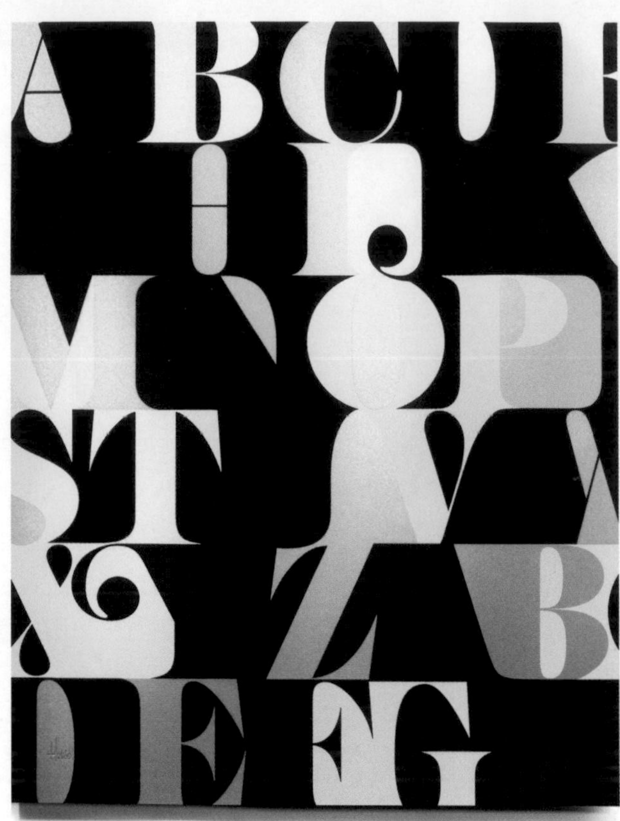

[2.18] Varying stroke weights of the font Caslon and a playful use of the figure-ground relationship add variety and interest to this typographic composition. Rhythm and repetition also play an important role in the success of the design.
Photo courtesy of House Industries. Design by Bondé Prang. Art Direction by Andy Cruz.

[2.19] A mix of typefaces lends character with an inventive combination of old and new to create this letterpress paper swatch book for Crane paper. Although in this case the combination is effective, mixing several typefaces in this manner requires an expert eye.
Design by Michael Osborne Design. Client: Crane Paper.

be incorporated into a cohesive visual scheme, using the same typeface helps to create unity. That can be an important factor in web, magazine and brochure design where visual continuity needs to be established over many pages. Applying a single typeface family ensures a rhythm as well as theme and variation. **2.18.**

Although using a single typeface family in a design is an effective way to achieve typographic harmony, in some instances, however, too much of the same thing can result in a design that is repetitive and predictable. Sometimes a mix of typefaces is more appropriate to the theme or message of a design and may be necessary to achieving graphic interest or an even richer sense of theme and variation. However, care should be taken to combine typefaces in a way that is harmonious and appropriate to the message or theme. **2.19.**

Proportional Systems and the Grid

When considering proportional relationships within a composition, it is useful to think of type as a design element that is aligned or confined to columns within a grid. As discussed in Chapter 1, a grid is a modular compositional structure made of relational units that divide a

Mixing Typefaces Effectively

The strategy to mixing typefaces is to make the differences look obvious and purposeful by using opposites—typefaces that have different but complementary characteristics or that are radically different. In the top example shown in **2.20**, a sans serif typeface (Futura, extra bold, 36 pt.) is contrasted with a serif typeface (Goudy Old Style Standard, bold italic, 33 pt.). The second example contrasts two versions of the same typeface (Modula). Setting one word in "black" all caps and the other in "bold" all lowercase provides visual interest and variation. The third example contrasts a delicate, elegant typeface set in upper- and lowercase (Palatino, light italic, 36 pt.) with a more masculine typeface (Gill Sans, bold, 36 pt.) set in all caps. The difference in the weight of the stroke and shift in axis supports the interplay between the two words. Avoid combinations that use similar typefaces, such as the pairing shown in the bottom example of (Frutiger 75, black, 36 pt., and Futura Heavy, 36 pt.). Mixing typefaces that are close but not quite alike can have a confounding effect on viewers who sense, rather than see, the subtle disagreements.

What dissonant relationships can you describe in the bottom example?

TYPE
logic

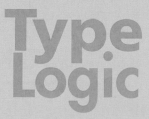

Type
LOGIC

Type
Logic

[2.20] *© Cengage Learning 2013. Design by Mark Thomas.*

composition into a proportional format. In compositions that conform to a page, the proportional grids typically consist of columns of type. The negative area of space surrounding the columns of type is called the *margin area.*

An underlying grid structure helps to maintain clarity, legibility, balance, and unity—aspects that are especially important in web and publication design where consistency needs to be established over many pages. In addition to serving as a unifying element and a means of organizing text and visuals, a grid automatically sets up a system that creates blocks of text that can be easily arranged as elements in a composition **2.21**.

Type Alignment Arranging type so that it conforms to a grid requires aligning it to the imaginary axes that form the grid structure. Arranging or styling type that way is called *type alignment.* Type alignment options that designers frequently use are as follows:

- Flush left/ragged right—text or lines of type aligned to a left vertical axis that is uneven on the right side
- Flush right/ragged left—text or lines of type aligned to a right vertical axis that is uneven on the left side
- Justified—text or lines of type aligned to both left and right sides
- Centered—text or lines of type centered on a central vertical axis **2.22**.

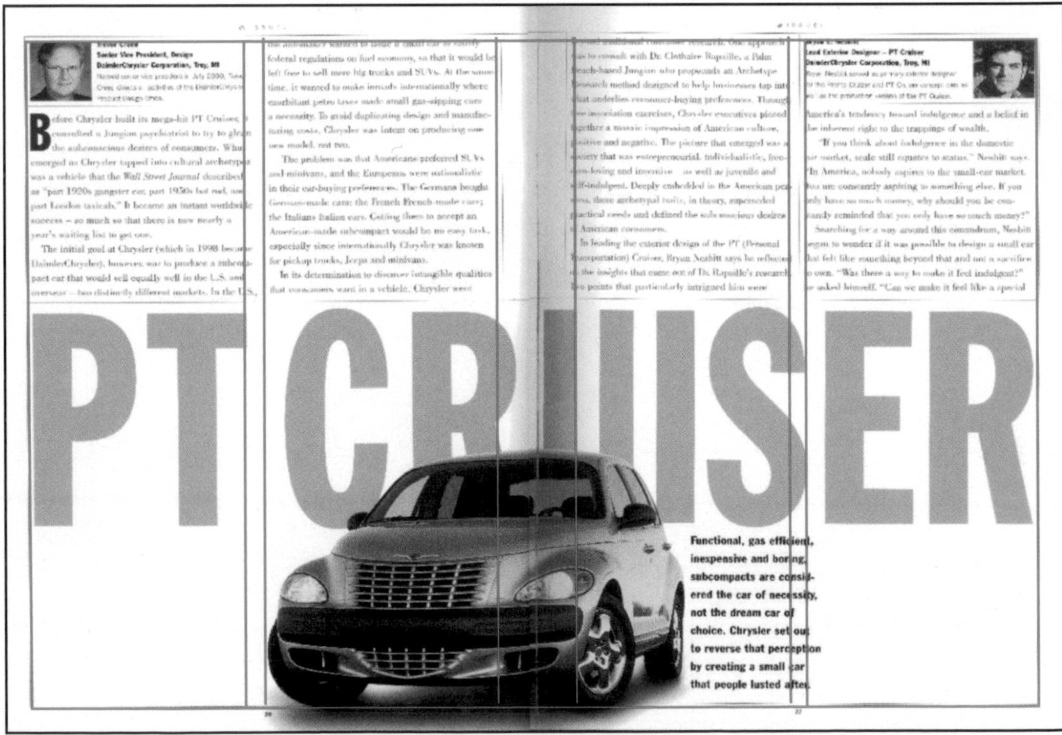

[2.21] The underlying structure for this spread is a two-column grid. All of the spread's text is aligned to this format as well as its photos.
Page layout from @ issue: Design by Kit Hinrichs, Pentagram, San Francisco.

flush left, ragged right

Towards thee I roll, thou all-destroying
but unconquering whale; to the last I grapple
with thee; from hell's heart I stab at thee; for
hate's sake I spit my last breath at thee.

centered

Towards thee I roll, thou all-destroying
but unconquering whale; to the last I grapple
with thee; from hell's heart I stab at thee; for
hate's sake I spit my last breath at thee.

flush right, ragged left

Towards thee I roll, thou all-destroying
but unconquering whale; to the last I grapple
with thee; from hell's heart I stab at thee; for
hate's sake I spit my last breath at thee.

justified

Towards thee I roll, thou all-destroying
but unconquering whale; to the last I grapple
with thee; from hell's heart I stab at thee;
for hate's sake I spit my last breath at thee.

[2.22] *© Cengage Learning 2013. Design by Mark Thomas.*

TYPE AS A DESIGN ELEMENT

As you learned in Chapter 1, type functions as a design element, adding shape, line, pattern, or texture in a design composition, in addition to functioning as verbal content.

Type as Line

When type is produced on a computer or by other means, it takes the form of a linear set of characters (letters in the alphabet, numerals, and punctuation marks) that are read from left to right in Western culture. As a result, designers often rely on individual lines of type to function as linear elements in a design composition. When a line of type works as a linear element, it can be used to guide a viewer's eye through a composition or to connect elements in a composition by the linear direction it assumes. Lines of type can be straight or curvilinear depending on how they need to function in a design **2.23**.

Type as Shape

Typographic forms also can serve as shapes in a design composition. The letterforms of a well-designed typeface have an inherent beauty and a sense of balance and proportion that

[2.23] Type does double duty in this ad, providing content and serving as a link between the graduate and the cap she has tossed in the air.
Design by Clarity Coverdale Fury.

can be utilized in a design composition, often adding interesting positive and negative relationships to the design. Enlarged letterforms or numerals can serve as the basis for a dynamic composition **2.24**.

In addition to the shapes that occur when letterforms are enlarged, blocks of smaller type called *text* also create shapes in a design composition. Text type can be formatted to rectangular

[2.24] In this CD design, the letterforms of the names and the negative space between them are all that is necessary to create a dynamic composition.
Rage CD design by Aimee Macauley, Sony Music Creative Services.

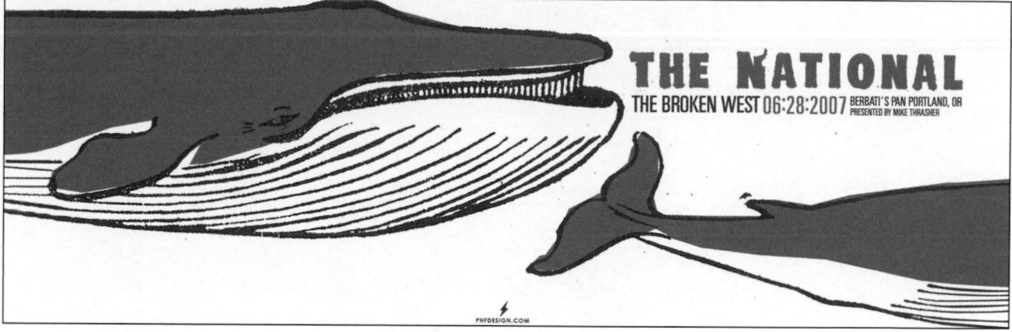

[2.25] The type in this two-color screen-printed poster suggests the surface of the ocean and supports the horizontal movement of the format and composition.
Design by Powerhouse Factories Design.

columns and be made to conform to more contrived shapes that support a design composition's communication message or content theme **2.25**.

Type as Texture

Just as large-scale type and letterforms and blocks or columns of text serve as shapes in a composition, small-scale type lends textural richness to a composition. The perception of texture is largely controlled by the weight or variety of weights of the typefaces used and the degree of negative space interjected into the text through line or letter spacing as well as layering **2.26**.

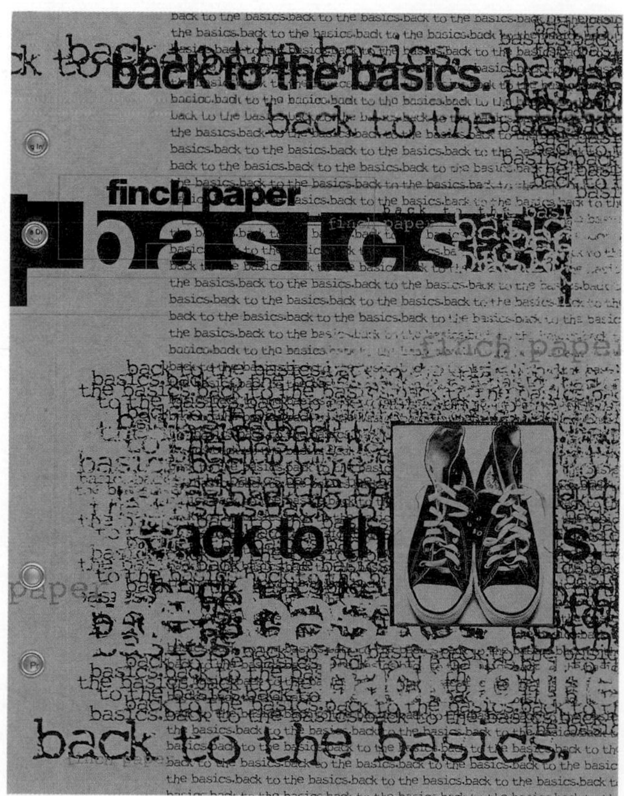

[2.26] A variety of sizes and weights and layering create typographic texture in this cover for a paper promotion.
Design by Robert DeLuke, Finch Paper.

Again, contrast, balance, and scale and the manipulation of graphic space to create illusion dictate how type is handled relative to other design elements in a composition. It is possible to use type alone to create an exciting composition where all of those factors come into play. Exploiting these aspects can yield results with a timeless quality **2.27**.

TYPOGRAPHIC CONVENTIONS

Type is measured and described in a language that is unique to the world of the printed word. In fact, many of the typographic terms and conventions in use today have their roots in the days of Gutenberg, when type was set in metal. Because designers, graphic arts professionals, and the equipment and computer programs they use employ this unique terminology and measurement system, it is important to understand their meaning. To start, typographic nomenclature can be divided into two categories: terms that identify type and typographic forms and terms associated with sizing and adjusting type.

Terms That Identify Type and Typographic Forms

Character—Individual letterforms, numerals, punctuation marks, and other units that are part of a font.

Drop Cap—A text treatment in which the first letter of a paragraph is set larger usually aligned even with the cap height to indicate the beginning of a section of text.

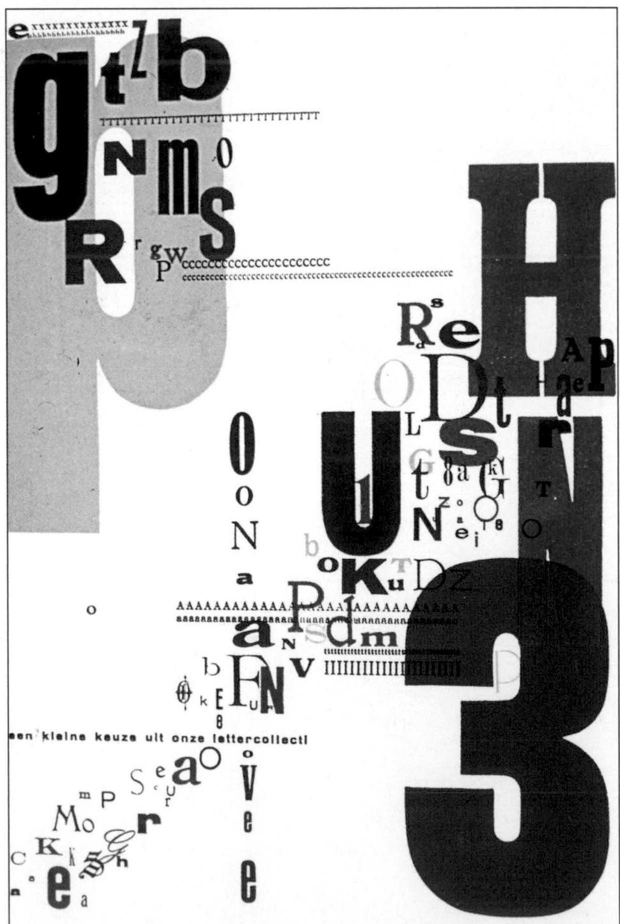

[2.27] This page from a type specimen book, design by Piet Zwart in 1930, demonstrates how type alone can be scaled, colored, and arranged to create a sense of depth and movement in a dynamic composition. The results look just as fresh by today's design standards, as they did when this page was first created. Good design is timeless.

Photo courtesy of the Merrill C. Berman Collection.

Glyph—A basic building block in typesetting that includes individual letters, numbers, and symbols. Groups of glyphs combined are referred to as a font.

Letterform—The particular style and form of each individual letter in an alphabet.

Ligature—Pairs or groupings of letters that are physically joined together for the purpose of improving their aesthetic appearance.

Lowercase—Smaller letters, as opposed to capital letters, of a type font 2.29.

Multiple Master—Digital fonts containing two or more original master styles, allowing the designer the ability to insert variations between the masters to create an additional range of styles without compromising integrity.

Open Type—Cross platform fonts that contain thousands of glyphs forming character sets that provide the designer with special characters and languages.

Tracking—The same as letter spacing or the average space between letters in a text block.

Typeface—The design of a single set of letterforms, numerals, and punctuation marks unified by consistent visual properties. Typeface designs are identified by name, such as Helvetica and Garamond.

Type Family—A range of style variations based on a single typeface design **2.28**.

Type Font—A complete set of letterforms (uppercase and lowercase), numerals, and punctuation marks in a particular typeface that allows for typesetting by keystroke on a computer or another means of typographic composition.

Type Style—Modifications in a typeface that create design variety while maintaining the visual character of the typeface. These include variations in weight (light, medium, or bold), width (condensed or extended), or angle (italic or slanted versus roman or upright).

Uppercase—Capital or larger letters of a type font (A, B, C, etc.) **2.29**.

Helvetica Medium

Helvetica Bold

Helvetica Bold Italic

Helvetica Narrow

Helvetica Extended

[2.28] *In a type family such as Helvetica, style variations based on the design include (from top to bottom) medium, bold, bold italic, narrow, and extended versions. © Cengage Learning 2013.*

Terms Associated with Sizing and Adjusting Type

Interline Spacing/Leading—The amount of space between lines of type, measured in points. The term is derived from metal type where strips of lead were inserted between lines of type (alternative terms: *line spacing* and *interline spacing*) as illustrated in the line spacing in **2.30**.

Letter Spacing/Kerning—The distance between characters in a word or number and between words and punctuation in a line of type **2.31**.

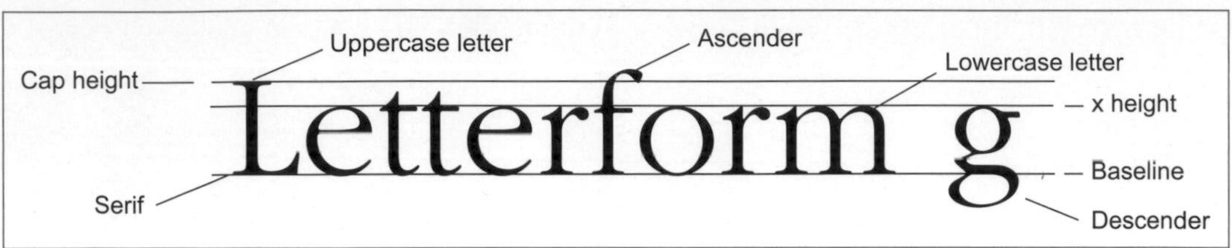

[2.29] Terms associated with letterforms include *uppercase* (which describes capital letters) and *lowercase* (used to describe small letters). The height of a typeface's lowercase letters is called its *x-height*. *Ascender* refers to the parts of a lowercase letterform that ascend the typeface's x-height, and *descender* refers to the parts of a letter that fall below the baseline.
© Cengage Learning 2013.

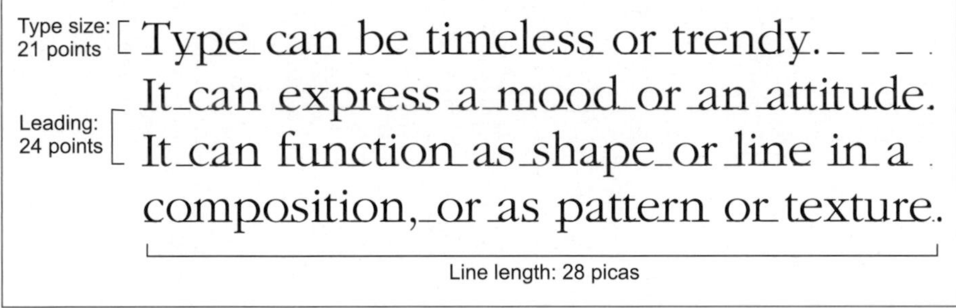

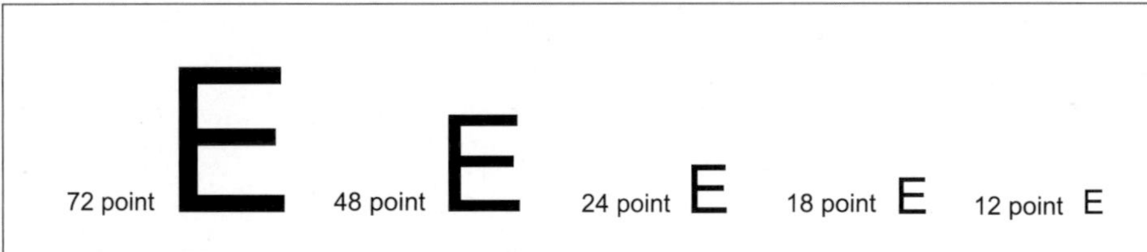

[2.30] Points are used to measure the height of type and leading, the vertical distance between lines of type. The horizontal length of a line of type is measured in picas or inches.
© Cengage Learning 2013.

LETTER SPACING

L E T T E R   S P A C I N G

[2.31] Letter spacing refers to the distance between characters and words in a line of type.
© Cengage Learning 2013.

Line Length—The horizontal length of a line of type, traditionally measured in picas, but also in inches.

Pica—Equal to 12 points, approximately one-sixth of an inch.

Point—A unit for measuring the height of type and vertical distance between lines of type 2.30.

Production Tip

When kerning or adjusting the spaces between letters in a word, it often helps to turn the word upside down. Getting a fresh perspective makes it easier to quickly see where spacing is uneven.

Selective Letter Spacing

When words are produced as type on a computer, the letter spacing that occurs between letterforms is not always even. That uneveness is usually not noticeable when type is small; however, type often appears uneven in headlines or other large type applications. Seasoned designers know it is their responsibility to manually adjust, or *kern*, the letter spacing in those instances.

That can be especially important in situations where certain letters come together, such as in the before and after examples of the word *WILLOWY* shown in **2.32**. After space is adjusted between the *W*, *I*, and *L* and between the *W* and *Y*, the spacing between the letters appears to be more balanced.

LEGIBILITY VERSUS EXPRESSION

You probably have noticed that typefaces come in a broad range of styles. Some are easy to read, whereas others present a challenge. Glancing at a newspaper will likely reveal examples of both. Because it is important to get time-sensitive, newsworthy information to readers as quickly as possible, most newspapers use typefaces that are bold, clear, and highly legible for articles and headlines. However, a newspaper's masthead or logotype may be set in a typeface that is not quite as easy to read. In the presentation of a newspaper's name, sometimes it is more important for the typeface to project an attitude or image that readers will associate with the newspaper. When making an impression is important, legibility is sometimes sacrificed for the sake of expression **2.33**.

Another factor designers take into consideration when weighing legibility versus expression is the length of the text. In the case of a company or product name, legibility is not such an important factor, because reading a few words at a glance is far less taxing to the eye than reading long passages of text.

[2.32] © Cengage Learning 2013.

LATE SCORES INSIDE — THE NATION'S NEWSPAPER — $1.00

6th French Open win for Nadal

Record-tying victory for the king of clay brings him 10th Grand Slam title, 1C

USA TODAY

A GANNETT COMPANY

Selena Gomez: Actress arrives for broadcast.

MTV Movie Awards

Show bestows honors in a variety of out-of-the-box film categories, 3D

Newsline

MONDAY, JUNE 6, 2011

Arizona fire forces thousands to flee as 144,000 acres burn

Aggressive Wallow Fire is third-worst in state history; still uncontained, 3A

Miami's Game 3 win gives Heat a 2-1 lead in NBA finals

Dallas rally falls short as Nowitzki's jump shot at the buzzer fails to drop; Game 4 is Tuesday. 1C.

Video game battle is joined between consoles and mobile

At Electronic Entertainment Expo, opening Tuesday, console hardware makers will announce strategies to make games more versatile. 1B.

Advocates say pool-safety law isn't working to save lives

The recent recall – just before Memorial Day – of pool drain covers is the latest of many setbacks for the authors of the 2007 law. 3A.

New hope in cancer battle

There's a new focus on drugs that prevent breast cancer and excitement over a drug that prolongs life for patients with metastatic melanoma. 4D.

Internet coupon sites make finding deals the new cool

The modern coupon is relatively hassle- and pain-free – and just a website away. 1D.

China shows N. Korea's Kim how it transformed economy

China showed off its economic strengths during Kim Jong Il's recent visit, but analysts say it's unlikely China's model will work in N. Korea. 5A.

See news photos of the day on your smartphone

Download the Microsoft TagReader app at http://gettag.mobi and capture a photo of today's tag.

Crossword, Sudoku 5D · Editorial/Forum 8-9A · Monthly mutuals 4-5B · Marketplace Today 5D · State-by-state 9A · TV listings 6D

COPYRIGHT 2011 USA TODAY, a division of Gannett Co., Inc.
Subscriptions, customer service
1-800-USA-0001
www.usatodayservice.com

USA TODAY Snapshots®

Money secrets among couples

Bought something partner didn't agree with	57%
Hid purchases	42%
Misrepresented amount of purchase	39%
Secret account or card	27%
Did not disclose debt	26%
Not forthcoming about credit score	12%

JOBS HEALTH CARE IRAQ THE DEFICIT HOME PRICES JOBS IMMIGRATION JOBS AFGHANISTAN DEBT LIMIT

What comes after HOPE?

Obama seeks reshaped image for 2012 effort

By Susan Page
USA TODAY

WASHINGTON —The Obama Brand in 2008 was pretty simple: Hope and change.

Then things got complicated.

The jobless rate on Friday ticked above 9% again. The housing market nationwide continues to fall. Gas prices are straining family's summertime budgets. President Obama's signature health care law to expand insurance coverage doesn't command majority support more than a year after it was signed into law. Washington negotiations on reducing the budget deficit are as polarized as ever.

Now, preparing for next year's re-election campaign, Obama is moving to refurbish a political brand that has been defined for the worst by his Republican opponents, dented by the realities of governing and battered by a faltering economy. He is going on the road to Americans' workplaces to argue he has made tough decisions that will pay off over time.

COVER STORY

Even so, good news that has boosted the president's standing in USA TODAY/Gallup Polls – the military operation that killed Osama bin Laden and the controversial GOP plan to overhaul Medicare – haven't been enough to offset the impact of bad news about the economy.

Please see COVER STORY next page ▸

Cyberattacks target smartphones

Google, Apple urged to act

By Byron Acohido
USA TODAY

Cyberattacks that commonly had targeted computers are zapping smartphones and tablets, prompting security experts to urge Google and Apple to do more to slow their spread.

"The drive to push new tech products out the door has always trumped security, and now that mind-set has moved to the mobile platforms," says John Pironti, an adviser at ISACA, a group for information systems professionals.

After a recent attack, Google last week removed 25 corrupted applications from its Android Market, but not before up to 125,000 Android users downloaded the bad apps, says Kevin Mahaffey, chief technical officer of Lookout Mobile Security.

On each Android phone with these apps, the attacker can connect to a remote server when a voice call is received, then download other malicious programs to the phone, Mahaffey says.

Mikko Hypponen, chief researcher at Finnish anti-virus firm F-Secure, says he has monitored "several dozen cases targeting Android over the past 12 months."

Apple's App Store for iPhones and iPads has been only lightly probed by hackers – showing a difference in its security approach, experts say.

Google has made it easy for any developer to post an app in Android Market and relies on users to supply feedback about security problems.

"Their market is very open and lightly vetted, if at all," says Kurt Baumgartner, senior researcher at Kaspersky Lab. "When there are enough complaints … Google has the ability to pull the apps, which it has sparingly done."

"If Google allows it into their app store, then they should take some responsibility for the integrity and security of the code," says ISACA's Pironti, who is also president of IP Architects.

Google should also step up efforts to streamline its cumbersome process for pushing out Android security patches, Mahaffey says. "Many Android handsets are not patched against the latest security flaws." Google spokesman Randall Sarafa declined to comment.

Apple, by comparison, keeps tight control over its App Store. "Apple performs its work quietly and without discussion," Baumgartner says. "But malicious apps have appeared and are pulled as well, so their process of vetting is not perfect."

Another Apple shortcoming: To get security patches, iPhone users must sync handsets to iTunes on a Mac or PC.

"It's only a matter of time before iPhones and iPads become more of a target," Pironti predicts.

Apple also declined to comment.

Homes that cost less hit hardest

Prices rose faster and fell the most

By Julie Schmit
USA TODAY

The housing bust has been kinder to higher-priced homes than to lower-priced ones.

Nationwide, top-tier homes have lost 38% of their value since prices peaked in 2006, while prices for bottom-tier homes have dropped 63% since peaking in 2007, says real estate website Zillow.com.

The disparity is consistent across larger cities, according to a study on the state of the U.S. housing market to be released today by the Joint Center for Housing Studies of Harvard University.

In Atlanta, for instance, prices of high-end homes fell 23% from their 2007 peak to December 2010. But low-end Atlanta homes fell 50%, the study says. In San Francisco, the most-expensive homes dropped 24% from their peak vs. 54% for the least-expensive ones, says the study, which analyzed Standard & Poor's/Case-Shiller home price data.

Prices range widely in major markets. Atlanta's low-tier homes are under $122,533, and the high tier starts above $221,679, according to S&P's latest definition based on March data. For San Francisco, S&P's ranges are under $312,546 and over $573,577.

In many cites, lower-priced homes appreciated more before they peaked, so they've fallen further, too, says Daniel McCue, senior research analyst for the Joint Center.

In San Francisco, for instance, low-end homes almost tripled in price before peaking, while high-end homes didn't even double before they peaked, the data show. Before the housing crash, lenders made loans more available to lower-income households, which stoked demand and prices for the less-expensive homes, McCue says.

Also, higher-income homeowners tend to have more resources to ride out a recession. "They don't need to sell their homes in a bad market," says Stan Humphries, Zillow chief economist.

Low-income areas have also been hit harder by foreclosures, which can pull down prices. The average rate last year for completed foreclosures in low-income neighborhoods was more than twice that of high-income neighborhoods, the Joint Center for Housing Studies estimates.

High-end homes in some places may face price pressure starting Oct. 1, when Fannie Mae and Freddie Mac are scheduled to lower the size of loans they buy from lenders. Their purchases help finance mortgages by providing a market for lenders to sell the loans they make, instead of holding them. The limits on Fannie and Freddie loan purchases were raised in late 2008 amid the financial crisis to stimulate mortgage lending in high-cost markets. In many such areas, the limits will go from $729,750 to $625,000. They'll drop more sharply in some areas, including Monterey, Calif., and Monroe County, Fla., which includes the Florida Keys, and less in other places.

As a result, lenders may charge higher rates on loans they can't sell to Fannie and Freddie. That could affect what homes people buy, says Cameron Findlay, LendingTree economist.

Falling prices

Change in home prices in some metro areas in December from peak prices in 2006 or 2007:

	Low-priced	High-priced
Boston	-27%	-11%
L.A.	-52%	-28%
N.Y.	-30%	-18%
Miami	-65%	-44%
Seattle	-33%	-25%

[2.33] *USA TODAY* is a good example of a newspaper that relies on easy-to-read fonts from the headline to the finer print. The daily publication is packed with stories and information and relies on a four-column grid to organize heads, subheads, and text type in a visually accessible format. Creating a contrast of scale helps to establish a visual hierarchy for the reader to navigate the pages.
© 2011, USA TODAY. Reprinted with permission.

Reader-Friendly Type

In addition to selecting a legible typeface, other considerations guide designers in sizing and styling type so the typeface is easy to read **2.34**, **2.35**, and **2.36**.

WAYS OF CATEGORIZING TYPEFACES

Over many years, designers and others who work with type have developed several ways of breaking down and organizing typefaces into categories based on style and practical application. Because designers need to differentiate between legibility and expression, it is helpful to think of type as falling into two basic categories. In fact, font manufacturers often make this distinction by sorting their typefaces into two groups: text and display.

IT MAY SEEM AS THOUGH ALL UPPERCASE OR CAPITAL LETTERS WOULD BE LIKELY TO CATCH A READER'S ATTENTION, BUT ITS LACK OF LEGIBILITY IS MORE LIKELY TO ALIENATE THAN ATTRACT READERS.

It may seem as though all uppercase or capital letters would be likely to catch a reader's attention, but its lack of legibility is more likely to alienate than attract readers.

[2.34] You can see how much easier it is to read this text when it is set in upper- and lowercase. That is because the eye reads words at a glance more easily when upper- and lowercase letters are used. All capital letters are best reserved for short passages of text.
© Cengage Learning 2013.

This Can Work for Short Lines of Text

But excessive letterspacing can cause problems in long passages of text where word groupings become harder to separate from surrounding space.

[2.35] Wide letter spacing in short lines of type can create an interesting graphic effect but can affect legibility when applied to a block of text. Adjusting the space between letterforms may be necessary in logo design and other applications that involve large-scale type.
© Cengage Learning 2013.

Short lines of text are hard to read, be-cause they create un-necessary hy-phenation and awkward line breaks.

Long lines of text are hard to read because they cause the eye to track back to the beginning of the next line. Readers forced to read long lines of text often find them-selves starting to read the line of text they have just read, instead of tracking down to the next line. Sometimes designers compensate for this factor by increasing the amount of leading between lines of text. Although adding space can help the eye to differentiate one line from the next, this option may be impractical when space needs to be saved. To save space and ensure reader-friendly text, set up a column width that allows for no more than fifty characters per line.

Above sample set in Garamond 8/10 at 25 picas.

Sample at left set in Garamond 18/21 at 10 picas.

[2.36] Long lines of text are hard to read, because the eye has difficulty tracking back to the beginning of the next line. Short lines of text are hard to read and often unsightly, because they can result in a great deal of hyphenation and awkward rags in a ragged-right configuration. For best legibility, line lengths should be approximately fifty characters.
© Cengage Learning 2013.

Text Typefaces

These typefaces are used where legibility is an issue—typically for small print and long passages of text. Text typefaces are easy to read and easy on the eye when a great deal of reading is involved. Newspapers, magazines, and books use text typefaces for the bulk of the content on their pages—this textbook is a good example **2.37**. Although text typefaces are known for their reader friendliness, they work equally well in large-scale applications.

Display Typefaces

Display typefaces, used when projecting a mood or an attitude is important, are selected for their expressive quality. Display typefaces are typically used for names, logos, titles, headlines, Web graphics, and other short passages of text **2.38**. Display typefaces come in a wide range of styles, all having a distinctive and unique character or personality. Later in this chapter, you will learn more about how display typefaces can be used expressively. There are very few situations in which a display typeface should be used to set lengthy content. Inappropriate use of a display font as a text application is likely to discourage, not encourage, fluid reading **2.39**.

Additional Typeface Classifications

There are literally thousands of typefaces from which to choose. Selecting a typeface from the vast array of possibilities may seem like a daunting task if you do not have a clue as to what

Ariel
Garamond
Times New Roman

[2.37] Text typefaces are used for long passages of text and other situations where legibility is a factor.
© Cengage Learning 2013.

Bauhaus
COPPERPLATE
Serifa

[2.38] Display typefaces are used when projecting a mood or an attitude is important. Each of these typefaces has a distinctive expressive quality.
© Cengage Learning 2013. Design by Mark Thomas.

Towards thee I roll, thou all-destroying but unconquering whale; to the last I grapple with thee; from hell's heart I stab at thee; for hate's sake I spit my last breath at thee.

Towards thee I roll, thou all-destroying but unconquering whale; to the last I grapple with thee; from hell's heart I stab at thee; for hate's sake I spit my last breath at thee.

[2.39] When you compare a text passage set in Brush Script, a display typeface (top), and Times New Roman, a text typeface (bottom), you can see the importance of choosing a typeface with effective legibility.
© Cengage Learning 2013. Design by Mark Thomas.

distinguishes one typeface from another. Fortunately, there are ways to help designers narrow their selection.

To help in organizing and choosing typefaces, designers and typographers have identified characteristics that typefaces have in common and have grouped the typefaces accordingly. For instance, most text typefaces can be classified as either serif or sans serif. Serif typefaces originated with the Romans, who identified their stone shrines and public buildings with chisel-cut letterforms. To hide the ragged ends of the letterforms, the Romans would cut a short, extra stroke on the ends of their letters. That extra cut was called a *serif*, a term still in use today.

Sans serif literally means "without serif." These typefaces originated in the early twentieth century in response to the Industrial Revolution. As a result, sans serif typefaces project a more streamlined and contemporary aesthetic **2.40**.

Serif Sans serif

[2.40] Serif typefaces such as Garamond (left) are characterized by short strokes or serifs at their ends. They tend to convey a traditional look. Sans serif typefaces such as Helvetica (right) tend to project a more industrial look.
© Cengage Learning 2013.

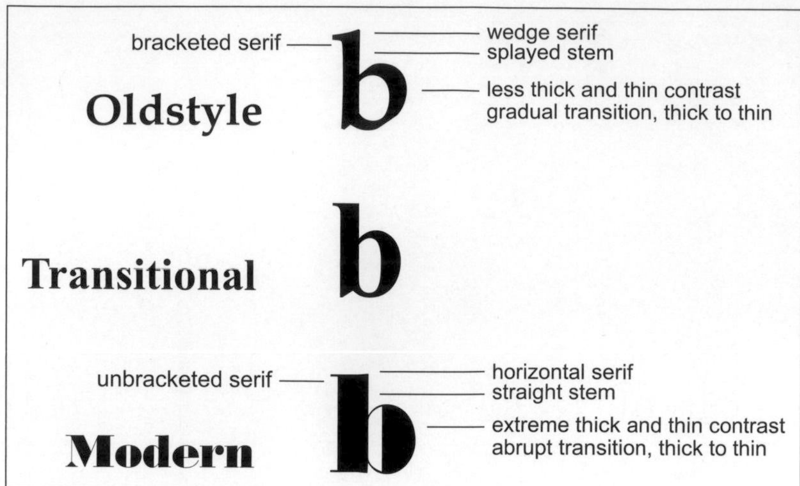

[2.41] Old style typefaces (top) are direct descendants of the chisel-edge Roman letterforms. They are characterized by angled and bracketed serifs and less thick and thin contrast. Examples: Times Roman, Garamond, and Caslon. Modern typefaces (bottom) are a style of Roman type characterized by extreme thick and thin contrast and straight, unbracketed serifs. Examples: Bodoni and Caledonia. Transitional typefaces (center) exhibit characteristics of both modern and old style typefaces. Examples: Baskerville and Century Schoolbook. *© Cengage Learning 2013.*

Beyond serif and sans serif typefaces, designers and typographers have traditionally relied on other typeface classifications to help them organize typefaces. Old style, transitional, and modern—these style categories refer specifically to serif typefaces and reflect modifications that have taken place over time from the original Roman or old style serif letterforms **2.41**.

Brush

Zaph Chancery

Serifa

Lubalin Graph

Capone

[2.42] Script typefaces such as Brush can resemble hand-painted signage or, in the case of Zaph Chancery, calligraphy. Egyptian or slab serif typefaces such as Serifa and Lubalin Graph are characterized by slablike serifs. Other typefaces that are highly stylized and suitable only for display use fall into the decorative category. These typefaces include period looks such as Capone, which resembles typography of the 1930s. *© Cengage Learning 2013.*

Script—These typefaces most resemble handwriting and run the gamut from elegant to casual.

Egyptian or Slab Serif—These typefaces (also called square serifs) are characterized by heavy, slab like serifs.

Decorative—Many typefaces, by default, fall into this category. Most are highly stylized and suitable only for display use **2.42**.

DESIGNING TYPOGRAPHY

In addition to graphic designers, there are designers who specialize in type design. These typeface designers (also called *typographers*) design the typefaces manufactured as fonts based on the technology of the day. Today fonts exist electronically as software and are installed on computers. Those fonts allow designers to set and style type as they choose.

Many of today's more traditional typefaces have been in use for more than a hundred years, whereas others are fairly recent. Although today's digital fonts seem like free-use design tools, they are creative intellectual property that are protected by copyright and trademark laws. Make sure you have the right to use a typeface by purchasing a license. Even though it is tempting to share fonts with friends or colleagues, this is considered unethical practice. It would be no different than using an illustration or photograph created by another artist in your design. Think of it as "recognizing the value of another colleague's work, to respect the practice of another designer and to uphold the integrity of the design profession."[2]

Typographic Design and Technology

Throughout the history of typography there has been a natural relationship between typographic design, printing technology, and related inventions. As discussed in the section *Evolution of Typography*, individuals in specific cultures advanced the sophistication and functional use of typographic communication based on the raw materials at hand. The ability to fashion wood, metal, and stone combined with oil-based inks and paper manufacturing made it possible to develop the letterpress, planographic or lithographic printing, and chromolithography. Offset lithography, phototypesetting, and digital printing processes relied on electricity, photography, and eventually computer technology to produce modern machines that print with high speed and graphic integrity 2.11 and 2.12.

In the digital age, typography is designed to become both printed and digital communication. Literally, all mass-produced design is converted to digital form whether printed or used electronically. The principles and elements are applicable in the same way to all of these applications. One distinct difference between typography in print and interactive digital design, film, and video is the dimension of *type in motion.* Designers who work with motion graphics rely on storyboards, computer sketches, and sophisticated software tools to manipulate and produce interactive typographic messages.

Throughout the history of typography, though, it is the typographers who brought the printed page to life with their unique designs of typefaces and fonts (see the section *Typographic Conventions* on page 000). Each typeface was created with a specific function in mind. Early Roman letters evolved from the limitations of the tools used to carve them into stone.

[2] AIGA guide book "Use of Software".

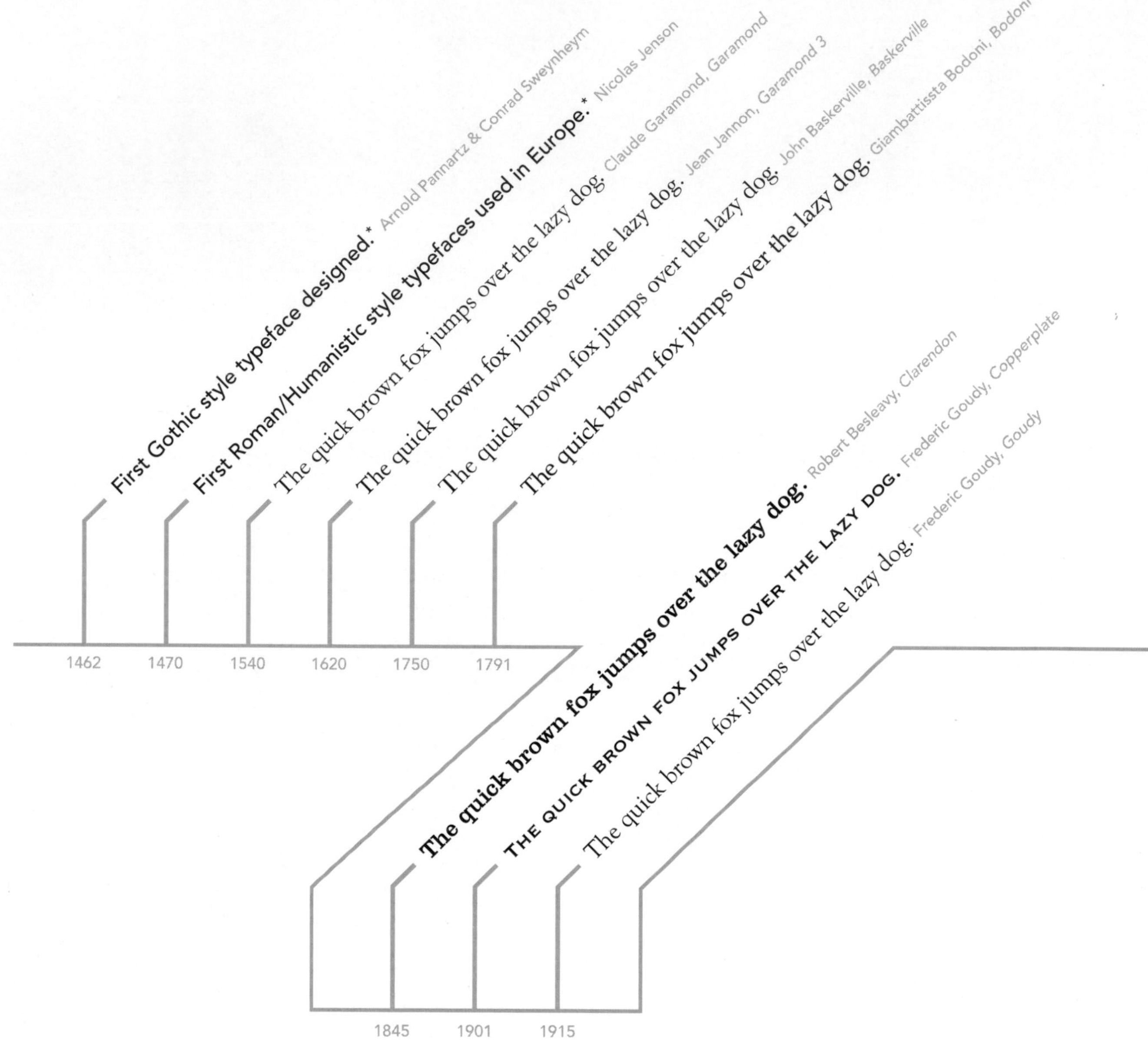

A Highlighted Typographer's Timeline

Each of the designers in this timeline has made a significant contribution to the history of typographic design. The designer is listed with the typeface(s) to which they are attributed and the specimen line, *the quick brown fox jumps over the lazy dog*, is set in the typeface. The specimen line is a pangram, which means that it uses every letter in the alphabet. How many of these fonts have you used? What are some of the aesthetic similarities and differences between typefaces over the past 500 years?

* Electronic font sample not available.

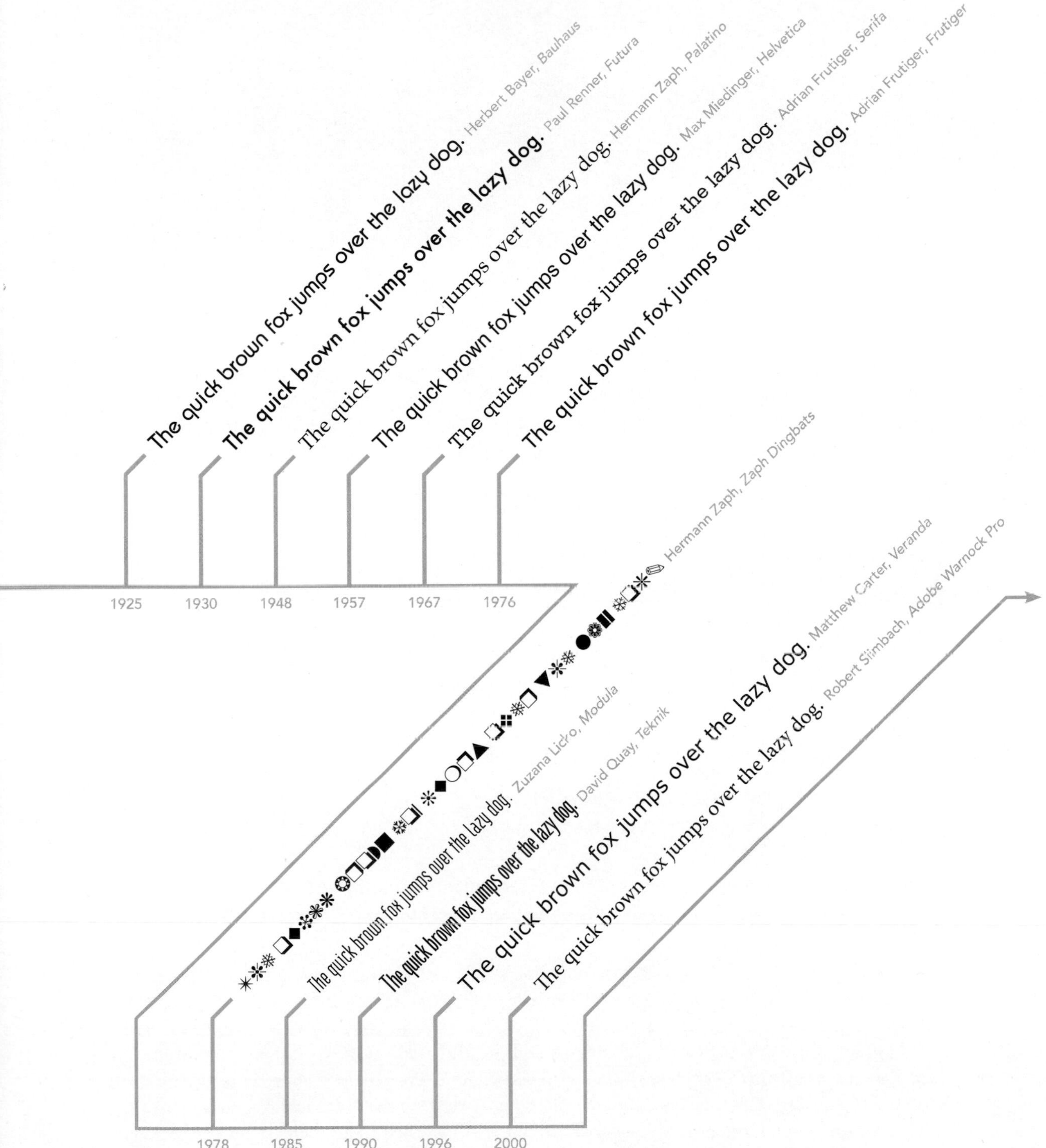

© Cengage Learning 2013. Design by Libby Sillis.

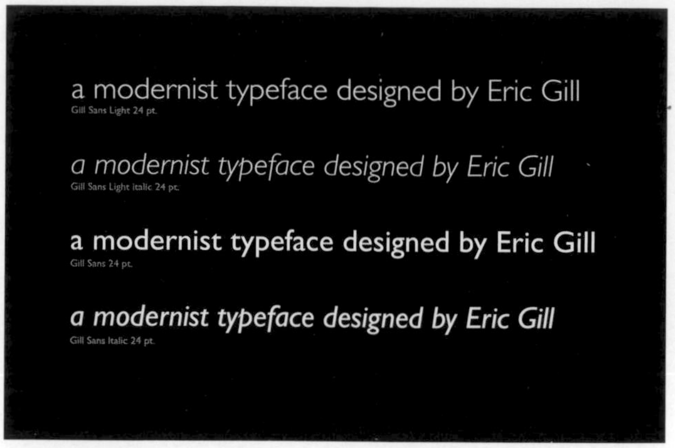

a modernist typeface designed by Eric Gill
Gill Sans Light 24 pt.

a modernist typeface designed by Eric Gill
Gill Sans Light Italic 24 pt.

a modernist typeface designed by Eric Gill
Gill Sans 24 pt.

a modernist typeface designed by Eric Gill
Gill Sans Italic 24 pt.

[2.43] Four style variations of Gill Sans illustrate its versatility and inherent beauty. It endures today as one of the most popular typefaces over the past century.
© Cengage Learning 2013. Design by Mark Thomas.

Later Roman typefaces that were hand-rendered and punched into individual lead letters reflected the aesthetic of the original carved versions. Roman letters and other early forms of type still adopt the same names and conventions of their technologically advanced counterparts today. Throughout the evolution of printing and design, typographers have designed type with a traditional respect and awareness of the history that influenced their work **2.43**.

Media, Form, and Type

Most of the discussion and typographic examples presented in this book were produced digitally. The type was converted from electronic form to film, to press plates, and finally to the inked typographic impressions you are reading. For most book design and printed material, this is the media that gives form to text type. Working with type on a computer or as a page printed from an ink-jet printer is the way that most people experience type. But type can be experienced in many forms and designers work with type in a variety ways with a variety of media.

Sometimes the media choice and form the designer gives type in a design is conventional like a letterpress poster, offset lithography book, desktop laser print, public transportation signage, a menu, or a text message on your mobile phone. In each of these cases, the media and processes were chosen to deliver readable and legible words **2.44**.

Sometimes a design needs more impact to communicate the message and designers will explore creative possibilities to give form to type. Creative solutions can be achieved through unusual use of materials, manipulation of typographic elements, or creatively combining media **2.45a** and **2.45b**.

To achieve creative and inventive typographic solutions, you must engage in creative brainstorming and visual thinking (see *Visual Thinking Is a Process* and *What Is Risk Taking* sidebars in Chapter 6). Learning a variety of media processes can expand your repertoire of skills. Painting, drawing, sewing, woodworking, screen printing, calligraphy, carpentry, and photography are a few art processes and skills that could provide creative possibilities for generating typographic design. Can you imagine making type by writing the words with ketchup, arranging stones to form letters, or weaving straw in a chain-link fence? These ideas could prove very effective and appropriate ways to communicate a typographic message.

The point of this discussion is that you never know where your solution will come from. Stay open-minded about the creative possibilities. Question routine ways of working. Consider your audience, the design objective, and delivery as you consider the media and form the type in your design will assume.

[2.44] Color and scale support the vertical alignment and straightforward presentation of the type in this moniker yielding high legibility. Note that the color scheme of the type is responsive to the illustration.
Design by Bruce Holdeman/601 Design Inc.

[a]

[2.45a] This hand-stitched interpretation of the identity for the documentary film *Handmade Nation* presents a creative approach for promoting this film about the crafts movement in America.
Design by Kate Bingaman Burt, embroidery by Jenny Hart.

[b]

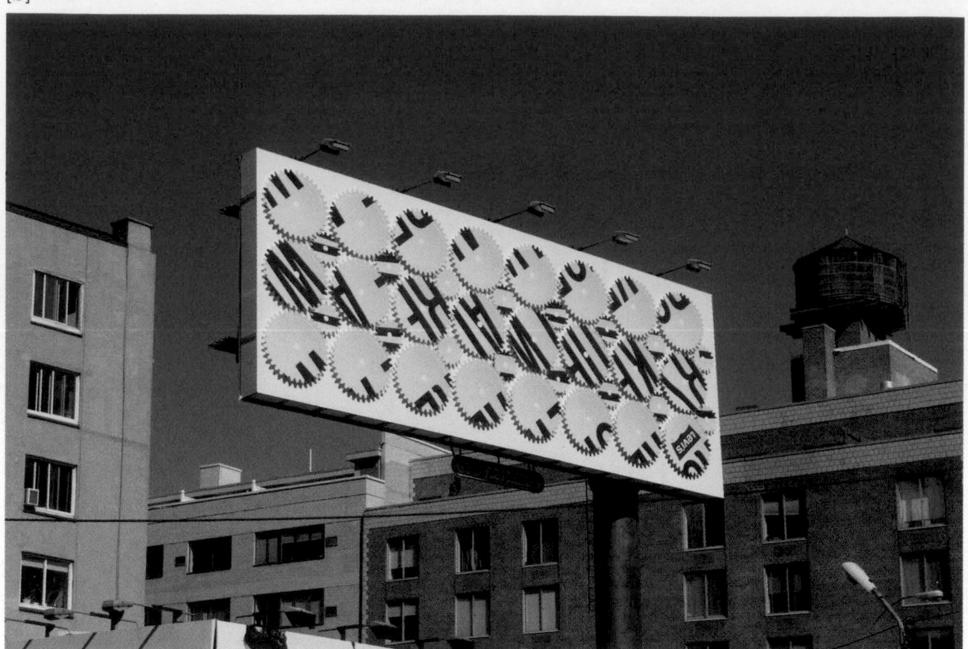

[2.45b] Stefan Sagmeister is sought after for his inventive and compelling approach to visual thinking. This Levi billboard is based on 24 rotating wheels containing type fragments. When the wheels align, they form a promotional text message, "We are workers." *Courtesy of Sagmeister, Inc.*

USING TYPE EXPRESSIVELY

Typefaces, like people, have character, personality, and voice. Typefaces can be exciting or bland. Some are playful, whereas others are serious. The physical characteristics of a typeface have much to do with its character. Typefaces with hard edges tend to project a more serious or industrial mood and look more authoritative. Those that are curvilinear, flowing, or organic in form tend to be associated with graceful characteristics **2.46**.

Typefaces convey period looks as well as ethnic or cultural sensibilities. They can express a broad range of moods **2.47**. Choosing a typeface with an attitude that enhances the message you are trying to convey is one of the most important considerations of effective typography **2.48**.

Type can be altered to express an attitude or a concept as well. Computers make it possible to configure type so that it suggests an image or a shape **2.49**.

[2.46] *© Cengage Learning 2013. Design by Mark Thomas.*

Type Sources and Resources

MyFonts: http://www.myfonts.com/

Ascender Fonts: http://www.ascenderfonts.com/

Fonts.com: http://www.fonts.com/

FontShop: http://www.fontshop.com/

Linotype Library: http://www.linotype.com/

Veer: http://www.veer.com/

ITC: http://www.itcfonts.com/fonts/

Letraset: http://www.letraset.com/

Émigré: http://www.emigre.com/fonts.php

Web Designer Depot: www.webdesignerdepot.com

Creative Pro: www.creativepro.com

Typophile: www.typophile.com

IDSGN, a design blog: www.idsgn.org

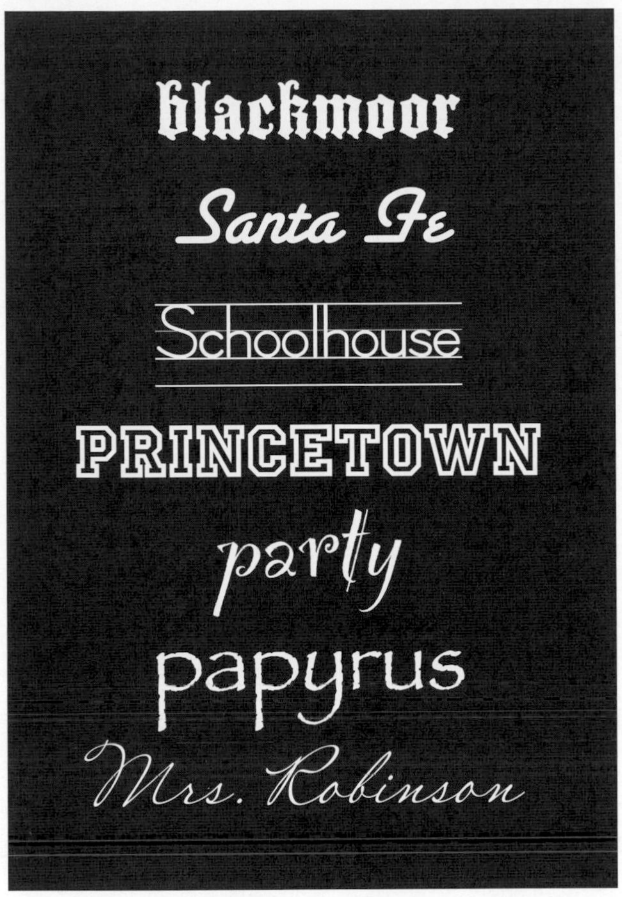

[2.47] Many typefaces have "voice" and can express a broad range of attitudes and cultural sensibilities. If you want to project a certain attitude or emotion, chances are good that you will find a typeface that captures it. *© Cengage Learning 2013. Design by Mark Thomas.*

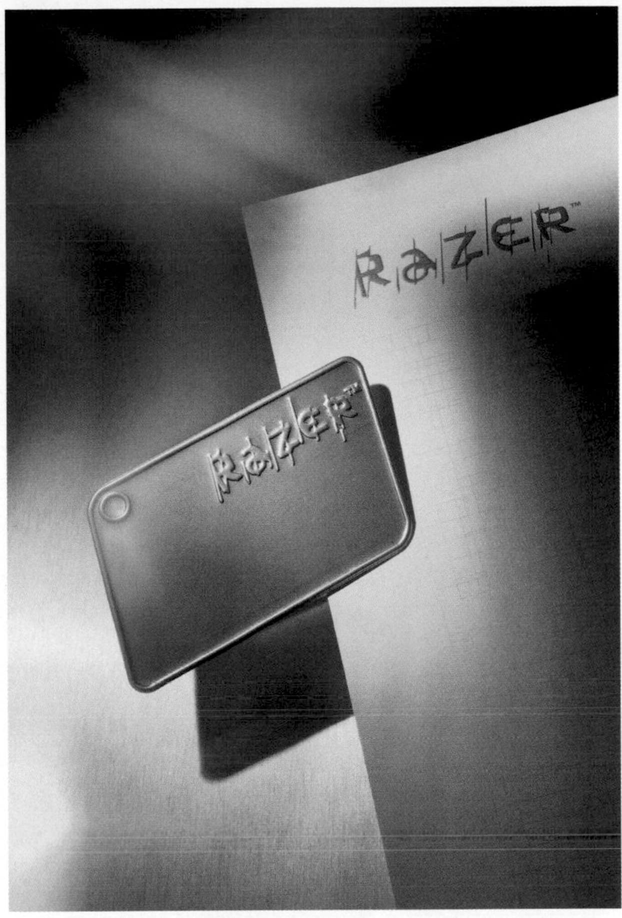

[2.48] Razer is the brand name for a highly sensitive computer mouse that is marketed to hard-core gamers. The slashed and degenerated look of the typography used for its logotype suggests an aggressive, cutting-edge attitude appropriate to the product and its market. *Courtesy of Dr. Nita Rollins.*

Type can also be distressed or manipulated to convey movement or motion. It can be layered or otherwise configured to suggest a sense of depth or perspective. Physically manipulating type is one of the easiest and most profound ways of adding expression to your typographic message **2.50**.

Creative Typography

Keep in mind that it is important to know the conventions of typographic design, so you understand how to work with them and against them. Throughout the history of typography, especially in the twentieth century as we have learned, some of the most exciting and inspiring design has challenged the status quo. To challenge is to offer a response to "what is," so you must study the history and, more important, the relevance of current design. Make an assessment of the design that you encounter on a daily basis. Decide if it is breaking rules or satisfied to respect conventional approaches. Good design can do either **2.51a** and **2.51b**.

And, just because a design is shocking or defiant does not make it automatically good. As you experiment with type treatments and even media, consider the communication objective and the overall design strategy. The use of type can be strategically responsive and creatively engaging at the same time.

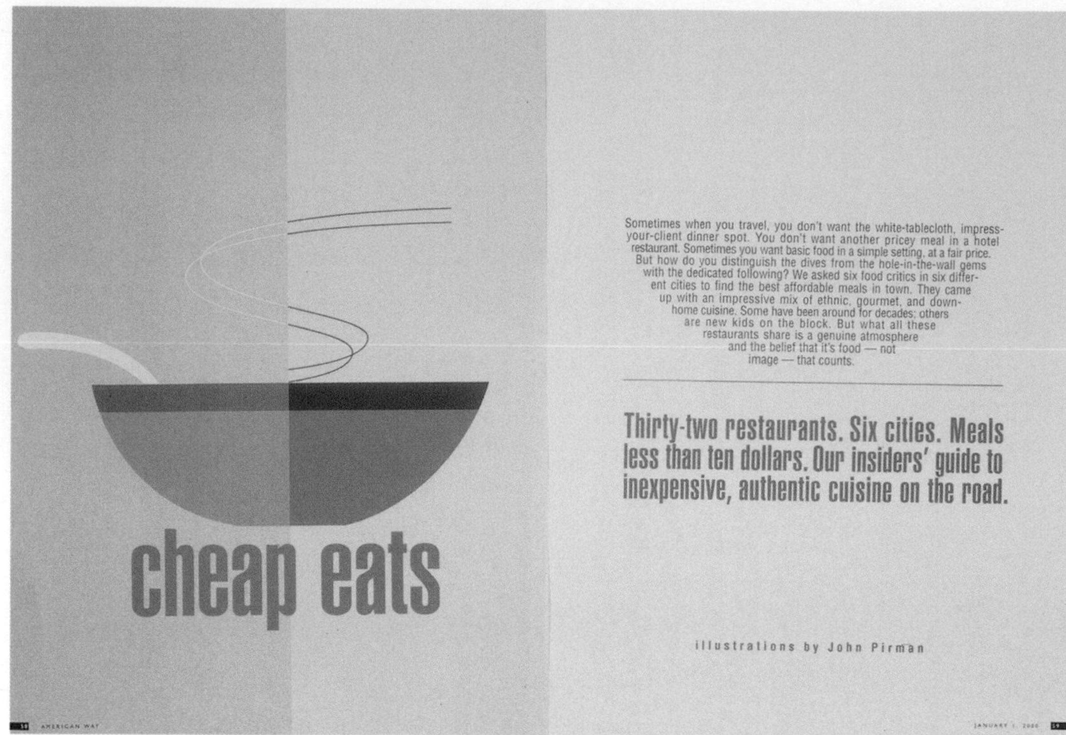

[2.49] This article about dining out on a shoestring uses text formatted in the shape of a half circle to echo the image of the bowl on the opposite page. The formatted text not only reinforces the article's message but also serves as a strong compositional element in the layout of the page. *Design by Charles Stone and Melanie Fowler, American Airlines Publishing.*

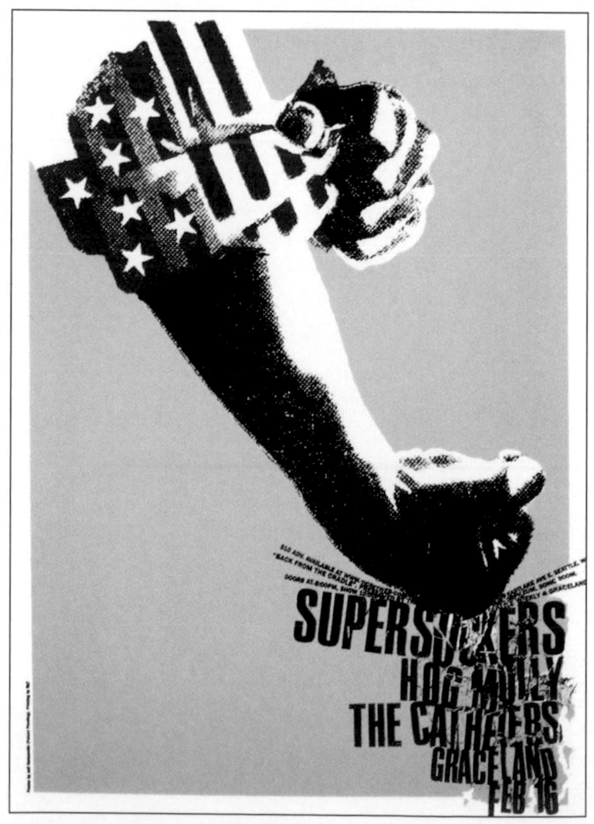

[2.50] Distressing the type on this poster adds clout to the message by helping viewers imagine the potential impact of the fist. *Design by Jeff Kleinsmith (Patent Pending). Printed by Patent Pending Industries.*

[a]

[2.51a] The typography and image for "*Ink Bleeds 3*," an exhibition of screen printed Rock Posters, work together stylistically. The typeface used for the show title mimics the line quality used in the illustration. Neltner and Warnick frequently collaborate on such projects, blending their illustration style and sense of type to produce inventive and striking designs for modern rock poster prints.
Poster Design by Keith Neltner and Rob Warnick.

[b]

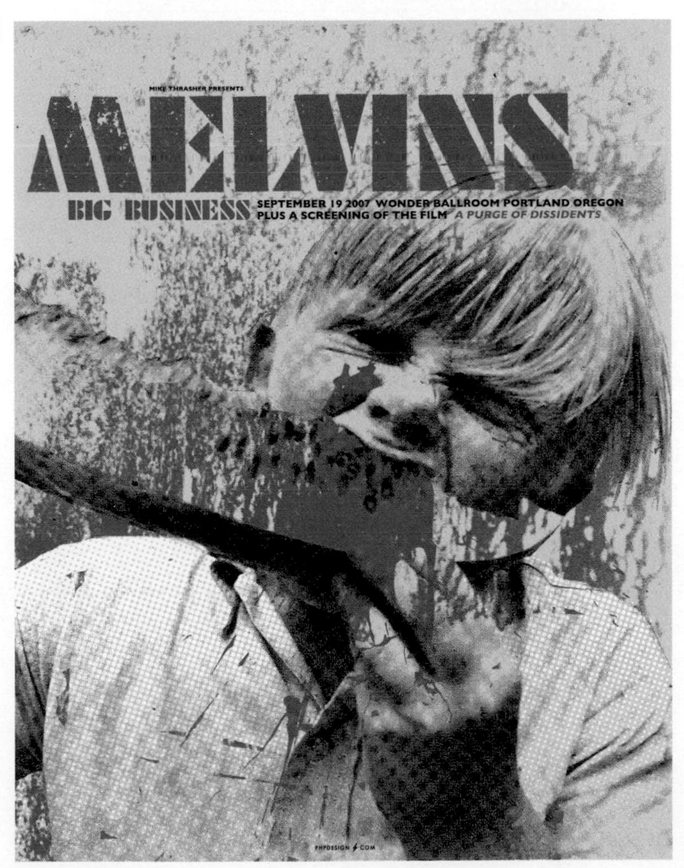

[2.51b] This poster design works with layered imagery and a hierarchy of limited typographic information. In this composition the photo-based imagery relies on diagonals, and the type is presented on a more conventional horizontal baseline. The splattered use of color ties the typography to the image. While the rock poster genre uses type in bold, physical and sometimes outrageous treatments, the designers that create them rely on conventional principles to manage visual unity in the design.
Design by Powerhouse Factories Design.

CASE STUDY: Designing a Logotype

As you learned earlier in this chapter, designers select a typeface to enhance the communication message of a design. In the case of a book title or a headline, an existing typeface usually suffices. However, a company or product name typically needs a more proprietary look. In those cases, a designer is often hired to hand-letter or otherwise develop a logotype that is unique and different from an existing typeface or font.

In the case of Blisscotti frozen desserts, Hornall Anderson Design Works was contracted to develop a logotype that would be clearly legible on packaging and would appeal to the product's audience of upscale consumers. After considerable research, the design firm determined that the aesthetic it needed to develop should project a high-quality, hand-crafted look, a sense of European romance, and simple elegance. In addition, the logotype had to be highly legible and look high-end but approachable.

One of the initial approaches the Hornall Anderson design team explored was pencil sketches of logotype ideas. According to firm's principal, Larry Anderson, the renderings were a way of quickly putting down an idea on paper that captured the look and feel of the attitude the team wanted to convey **2.52**. Other approaches the team explored included letterforms with obvious embellishments **2.53**. Computer renderings of logotype ideas also were developed and presented to the client, along with the hand-rendered logotype designs. The design that was ultimately chosen combined the best of all of the examples submitted—high legibility with a hand-crafted look **2.54**. Additional refinements were made to the final design to produce a logotype with custom letterforms and an even more proprietary look **2.54** and **2.55**.

Blisscotti

BLISSCÓTTI

[2.52] From the onset, the Hornall Anderson team developed ideas that allowed the letter *L* to run beneath the *I* and *SS* as a way of underscoring the word *Bliss* in *Blisscotti*.
Design Firm: Hornall Anderson Design Works.
Client: Cold Standard.

[2.53] To achieve an old-world sensibility, many of the ideas that were developed incorporated romantic flourishes and other embellishments that gave the logotype a hand-tooled look.
Design Firm: Hornall Anderson Design Works.
Client: Cold Standard.

BLiSSCOTTi

[2.54] Although the type for these concepts was generated on the computer, letter spacing and individual letterforms were tweaked to give the logotype a custom look and feel.
Design Firm: Hornall Anderson Design Works.
Client: Cold Standard.

[2.55] The design that was chosen combines a custom-designed *L* with the high legibility of Gotham, a sans serif typeface. Filigree is suggested by the tiny dots that surround the Blisscotti name.
Design Firm: Hornall Anderson Design Works.
Client: Cold Standard.

"MAD": A Typographic Identity

When Michael Bierut of Pentagram Design was faced with creating an identity for New York City's Museum of Art and Design (MAD), he drew his inspiration from the museum's site. The building's square shape and its location at Columbus Circle served as a starting point for a concept based on combining circles and squares to create a series of letterforms to express the monogram "MAD," the museum's acronym **2.56**.

The initial concept of the monogram as a geometric configuration spun off the creation of a typeface based on circles and squares and the development of an entire alphabet and numerals. The typography drove an identity system and promotional campaign for the museum that conveys a message of inventiveness and surprise consistent with the museum's focus on the exploration of interpreting traditional forms in unique ways. Slogans such as "Go MAD" and "New York City is MAD" set in the unconventional, proprietary typeface piqued curiosity, while its emphasis on geometric shapes supported the museum's focus on form and design **2.57**.

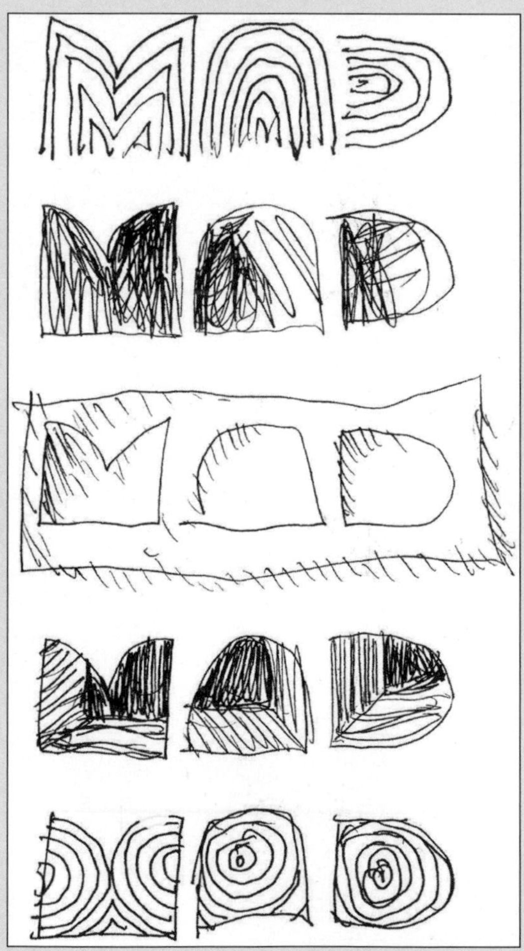

[2.56] Bierut explored a variety of rough concepts for the MAD logo that combined circles and squares in various configurations.
Design by Michael Bierut/Pentagram.

[2.57] The Museum of Art and Design's promotional campaign made use of MAD's proprietary typeface through its use of slogans that played on the word *mad* and incorporated the MAD logo.
Design by Michael Bierut/Pentagram.

In addition to promotional slogans to kick off the museum's redesign and reopening, MAD's proprietary typeface serves the museum well in identity applications such as promotional postcards and on merchandise and packaging **2.58a** and **2.58b**. Bierut and his design team selected Futura as a supporting typeface to be used where high legibility is absolutely necessary. The typeface echoes the geometric forms of MAD's proprietary typeface in its circular interpretation of letterforms, particularly the letter "O" **2.59a** and **2.59b**.

[a]

[b]

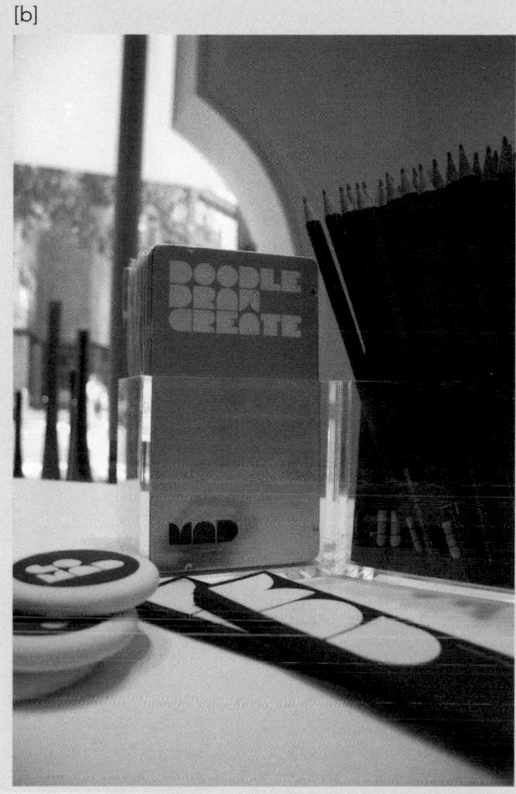

[2.58a and b] MAD's proprietary typeface worked well when applied to slogans on the museum's postcards. The typeface's geometric lines also made it easy to apply the identity's aesthetic to museum merchandise and packaging. *Design by Michael Bierut/Pentagram.*

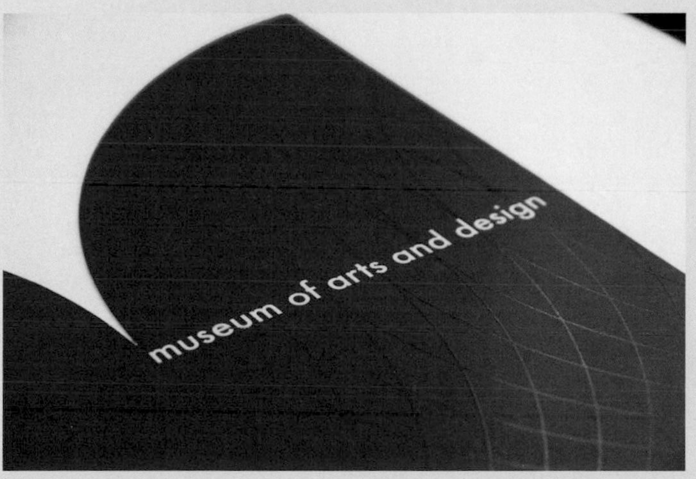

[a]

[b]

[2.59a and b] For applications where legibility is important, Bierut and his design team chose the typeface Futura. The circularity of the typeface's letterforms complemented the geometric look of the MAD logo and typeface. *Design by Michael Bierut/Pentagram.*

SUMMARY

The role of type in design is communicating content, but type also can add expression to a design and function as a compositional element. To work with type, you need to understand its history, basic type terminology, and the typographic systems designers and other graphic arts professionals use when working with and classifying typefaces. Expressive typography can add emotional emphasis to a design's message but may interfere with legibility. When choosing typefaces, designers must make discerning choices between type that is legible and type that is expressive. The role type plays in a design involves determining hierarchy and using type so that it works synergistically with imagery and other design elements. Type needs to work effectively as an integral visual element in a design composition by functioning as shape, line, or texture. It can serve as a unifying element in a composition, as well as a means of adding theme and variation.

projects

LETTERFORM GRID

Objectives

- Make compositional decisions using letterforms as design elements.
- Study type as shape.
- Work with a variety of high-contrast typographic relationships.
- Manage a variety of figure-ground relationships in the same composition.

Description

Begin by generating 20 to 25 studies, 3 inch by 3 inch and in black and white, using a variety of single letterforms (one letter per square). Variety is the key—while limited to one typeface, seek variety through scale changes, figure-ground relationships, orientation, and proximity in the small compositions. Variety can also be achieved through the use of "style" variations in the font—plain text, bold, black, italic, and demi bold, for example. Cut the small studies carefully into 3-inch squares. Create a new, larger composition using nine of the small studies arranged in a nine-unit grid, three studies across by three studies down. Work to create overall continuity or "good gestalt" and rhythm in the arrangement of units.

Hint: Partially obscure the identity of some of the letterforms through cropping, rotating, or reversing them within the small compositions. This will offer variety and visual interest. Make and use a 3-inch by 3-inch cardboard viewfinder to crop and frame the grid units

Limitations and Materials

Generate type from a computer or photocopy from printed sources. For the final, use clean good-quality laser prints or photocopies. Use a studio knife and metal straightedge to cut small studies. Glue the nine studies in a square grid arrangement on a study surface and trim flush. Use glue stick, spray adhesive, and so forth.

Use any one of the following fonts:

Garamond
Gill Sans
Futura
Helvetica
Bodoni
Serifa
Minion
Warnock Pro

Critique Discussion Points

Describe the kind of rhythm and eye movement created in the arrangement.

How does the use of negative space complement the arrangement of the letterforms?

Can you identify a point or points of emphasis?

What qualities does the composition communicate?

Vocabulary

plain text, bold, black, italic, demi bold, font, grid, figure-ground, Gestalt

References and Resources

Herbert Bayer, Piet Zwart, Wolfgang Weingart, Herb Lubalin, Paula Scher, David Carson, Eric Gill, Hermann Zapf) Neville Brody, Jan Tschichold, Theo Van Doesburg

Evaluation Criteria

Source Work and Research
Achievement of Criteria
Design and Composition
Craft and Execution

WORD AND TYPE MIX AND MATCH

Objectives

- Practice finding typefaces that support a mood or attitude.
- Discuss how the physical characteristics of a typeface support its character or mood-conveying attributes.
- Explain how type can enhance the meaning of a word or phrase.

Description

For each of the following words, set the word in a typeface that expresses its meaning.

Print each out on one 8.5-inch by 11-inch sheet of computer paper. You may use upper- and lowercase, all caps, or all lowercase. You may also use any variation of the font, that is, italic, bold, plain, light, and so on, to affect the expression.

ancient

organic

fancy

old-world

casual

Limitations and Materials

notepaper or scrap paper, digital font library, Adobe Illustrator or InDesign,

laser prints or ink-jet prints

Critique Discussion Points

Which typeface did you pick for each of the terms?

What physical characteristics of each typeface supported your choice?

How do your choices compare with those of your classmates?

Vocabulary

display type, script, sans serif

References and Resources

House Industries, Matthew Carter, Hermann Zapf Edward Benguiat, Herb Lubalin, Zuzana Licko

Evaluation Criteria

Source Work and Research

Achievement of Criteria

Design and Composition

Craft and Execution

EXPRESSIVE TYPE AND DESIGN

Objectives

- Gain practice at selecting typography that enhances meaning.
- Experiment with type manipulation to enhance meaning.
- Explore type possibilities by browsing font libraries and other typographic resources.
- Manage design decisions using basic elements.
- Practice using type as a compositional design element.
- Study letterform as a shape.
- Continue to explore design principles.

Description

Select a typeface that is expressive of each of the following words and manipulate the typeface to further enhance the meaning of the word.

austere

crush

ornate

precarious

Select one of the words you manipulated and incorporate it into a black-and-white design composition that includes shapes or linear elements that support the meaning of the word. Apply the principles you learned in chapter one such as repetition, rhythm, and scale, to create a dynamic composition.

Limitations and Materials

Use a computer or magazines or other printed materials to serve as a source for finding type. A computer, a photocopier, or other tools can be used to distress or otherwise manipulate the type. Cutting, painting, or embellishing the type with pen or pencil or other drawing tools is an appropriate means of modifying the type you have chosen if it is used in a way that supports a word's meaning.

Limit your black-and-white design composition to a 10-inch by 10-inch format. Explore various design possibilities before you settle on a final solution. Use the computer, gouache, or acrylic paints to create your final composition. Incorporate different values of gray, if you like, to create a dynamic composition.

Discussion Points

Of the typefaces you chose, which one does the best job of supporting the meaning of each word?

What physical characteristics does each typeface possess to support the word's meaning?

How was the type manipulated or changed in a way that further supports each word's meaning?

What physical characteristics does the manipulated type possess to support the word's meaning?

How does type function as a design element in the final composition?

Which element in the composition has the most emphasis?

How does the type relate to other elements in the composition?

What design principles are at work in the composition?

Identify the figure-ground relationships in the composition.

Vocabulary

hierarchy, dominance, closure, proximity, scale, figure-ground, script, serif, sans serif

References and Resources

Wolfgang Weingart, David Carson, Neville Brody, Bradbury Thompson, Alexey Brodovitch, Otto Storch, Émigré

Evaluation Criteria

Source Work and Research

Achievement of Criteria

Design and Composition

Craft and Execution

TYPE COLLAGE

Objectives

- Discuss how type can function as a purely compositional element.
- Experiment with type as a design element by using it as a means of creating line, shape, and texture.
- Work with basic relationships between shape, line, and space.

Description

Make three collages composed entirely of black-and-white type using type cut from magazines or other printed materials. Each composition should be well balanced and in a square format.

Compose each design to show how type can function in each of the following roles:

As line

As shape

As texture

Limitations and Materials

Use a 5-inch by 5-inch piece of cover stock or bristol board for each composition. Limit your selection of type to black and white or values of gray. Use a photocopier or another means of reproducing the type to scale or create multiples of the type you have chosen. Use scissors or a utility knife to cut the type and rubber cement, a glue stick, or another appropriate adhesive to adhere the type to the bristol board. If you want, make a photocopy of each final composition so each is a seamless design.

Discussion Points

How successfully does each composition satisfy the listed objectives?

What physical characteristics (shape and size) of the typography help it function as shape, line, or texture?

How does line function as a composition element?

Where does rhythm, repetition, or pattern occur?

How does type style, leading, or letter spacing affect the texture of type?

Vocabulary

rhythm, repetition, pattern, scale, linear, curvilinear, parallel, text type, display type, serif, sans serif, leading, letter spacing, type style

References and Resources

Émigré, Rudy VanderLans, Piet Zwart, Laszlo Moholy-Nagy, Herbert Bayer

Evaluation Criteria

Source Work and Research

Achievement of Criteria

Design and Composition

Craft and Execution

in review

1. What is the difference between a typeface and a type family?
2. What do the terms *uppercase* and *lowercase* mean?
3. What units are used for measuring the height of type and the vertical distance between lines of type?
4. What does the term *leading* mean?
5. When is it appropriate to use a display typeface? When is it appropriate to use a text typeface?
6. What is the difference between a serif typeface and a sans serif typeface?
7. How does type work to unify a composition?
8. What does the term *alignment* mean? What types of alignment options are there?
9. What is a cuneiform?
10. Describe how offset lithographic printing process works.
11. What is a ligature?
12. What is a multiple master?

Courtesy of Bondé Prang.

"Focus on learning the fundamentals of design before you get hung up on technology."

Bondé Prang

Bondé Prang is a graphic designer at House Industries, a type foundry, illustration studio and a design firm that markets unique fonts. As House Industries' graphic designer, Prang's promotional concepts are instrumental in the marketing of House's fonts and other design products. Prang is also an award-winning designer with work selected for inclusion of the Type Directors Club's typography annual. She has also been featured in *Print* magazine as one of 20 emerging designers, illustrators, and photographers under 30.

How did you end up choosing design and illustration as a career path?

It might have been because I was young and impressionable, but I was sold on graphic design the first day of my high school Visual Communications class. After I learned about what a graphic designer does, I became a full-blown design nerd: finishing my projects before anyone in the class; making sketches for the following week's project on the bus ride home; having trouble falling asleep at night due to the excitement of the next day's project. That said, I wouldn't have been nearly as excited about graphic design if I hadn't had a phenomenal teacher to encourage me. Kathleen Piretti invested a lot of time and energy in her students, especially the ones who showed interest and potential. Along with my hard work, her guidance helped prepare me for a career in graphic design. After I had built up a strong portfolio and won a state-wide design competition judged by House Industries two years in a row, I was offered an internship at House.

How did you end up choosing the schools you attended?

The local public high school I was assigned to in New Castle, Delaware, did not have a very good reputation, and my parents wanted me to learn a trade, in case they couldn't send me to college. My mother knew I was interested in art, so she had me apply to a local technical high school that offered a good visual communications program. I initially protested attending a school that none of my friends were going to, but I soon learned that my mother had actually made a very good decision. When the time came to go to college, I had already been interning at House Industries for a few months. I was a stubborn, know-it-all teenager and I told my parents that I had made up my mind that I wasn't going to art school. I told them I had already learned the basics of graphic design in my high school design classes, and they would just be wasting their money. They sent me to the local art school anyway. Drawing and illustration classes were a nice change of pace from sitting in front of a computer, but I still knew that all I wanted to do was graphic design. Besides, I was working at House Industries part-time, so when I wasn't in school I felt I was being schooled by the masters and I was getting paid for it, too. (As a teenage design nerd, I felt like I was holding the key to the holy grail!) When House Industries finally offered me a full-time position before my second year of art school started, I went home after work and told my parents I was quitting school. This made them very unhappy and even made my mom cry! However, they forgave me after not too long.

What has your career path been since you finished school?

I have been employed by House Industries since I was 17 years old. For the first couple of years, I did mostly production work, but had my hands in a little bit of everything. Now, after having worked there for seven years, I design most of House's type catalogs, promotional materials, accessories, and Web sites.

bondé prang

Prang says she draws much of her inspiration from the pop culture of the 1960s and 1970s. Her ability to incorporate the aesthetic sensibility of this era into her catalog design complements and enhances the nostalgic look of many of the type foundry's fonts.
From House Industries. Design by Bondé Prang. Art Direction by Andy Cruz.

I have considered freelancing, but to be honest, the thought of it seems very overwhelming to me at the moment! I'm quite shy and introverted and not really used to working directly with clients, so that will be something I'll have to overcome. Like anything else, I think I'll get better at it with practice, but for now I'm sticking to working on fun, small, stress-free projects for friends and family.

What do you think has been the most important factor in your success?

I know that it sounds cliché, but my father raised me to believe that hard work pays off. Admittedly, I wasn't even the best designer in my high school Visual Communications class, but because I worked hard and applied myself I was able to consistently produce good-quality work that distinguished me from my peers and eventually led to a job at House Industries.

What advice would you give to students?

Just a few pieces of advice that students may find useful: First, I recommend keeping a folder of reference material—it can be very helpful if you're stuck on a design project. I would recommend using source material that you've found yourself such as old ads, packaging and book covers at libraries, flea markets and thrift stores, instead of using the same regurgitated material seen on art and design "tumblr" sites and blogs. My second piece of advice is to save yourself from future embarrassment and learn the difference between lettering and type. I'm not sure why this is, but many students and professionals in the design community alike don't seem to know the difference. People will respect you more if you know what you are talking about. Finally, I think it's good to remember that software and computers are only design tools. I've met people who equate being a graphic designer with owning design software and knowing tricks. Anyone can learn software "tricknology," but learning how to use software to support your own concepts and aesthetic is what makes someone a good designer. Focus on learning the fundamentals of design before you get hung up on technology.

bondé prang

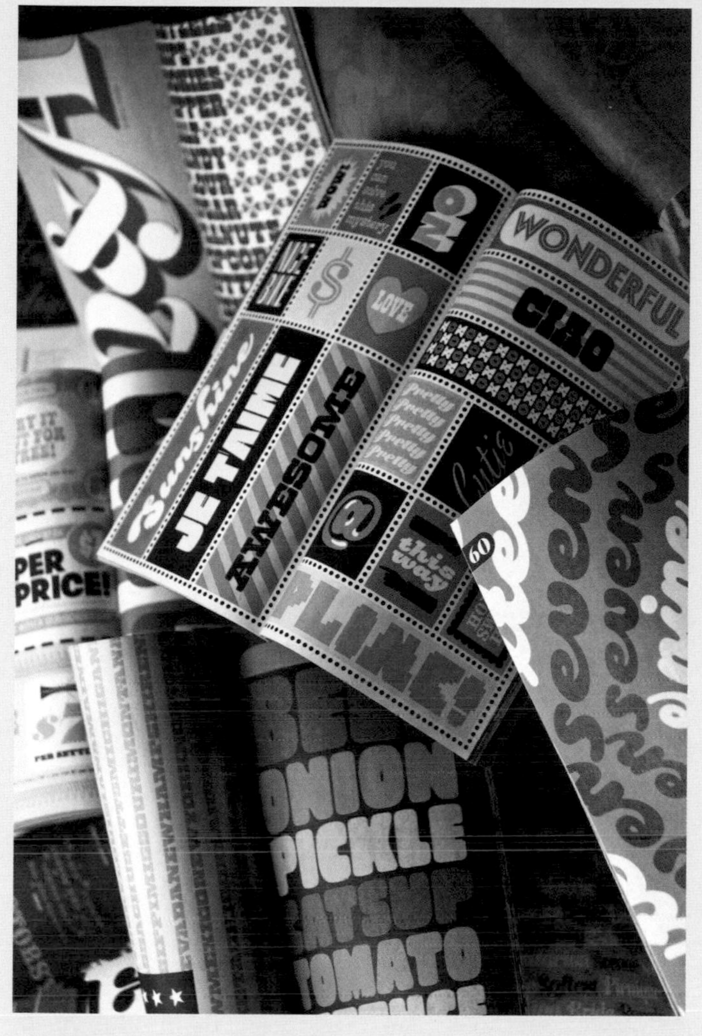

From House Industries. Design by Bondé Prang. Art Direction by Andy Cruz.

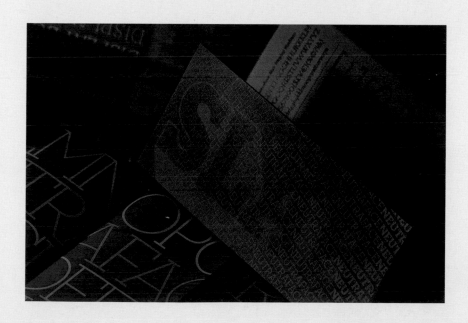

From House Industries. Design by Bondé Prang. Art Direction by Andy Cruz.

three

Imagery in Design

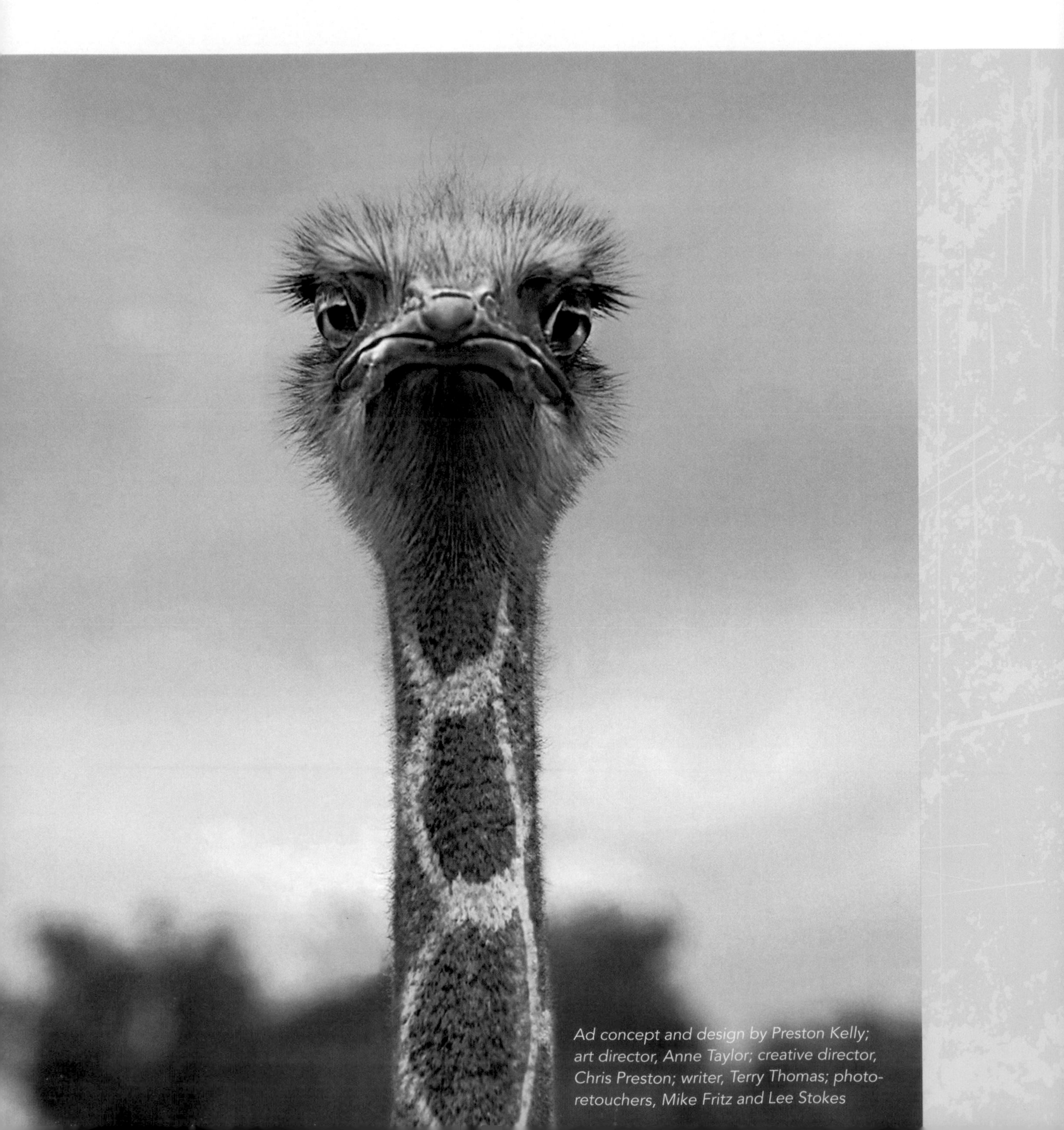

Ad concept and design by Preston Kelly; art director, Anne Taylor; creative director, Chris Preston; writer, Terry Thomas; photo-retouchers, Mike Fritz and Lee Stokes

3

introduction

You have no doubt had the experience of thumbing through a magazine and becoming immersed in an article because an arresting photograph or illustration caught your eye. Everyone has had that experience, as well as similar ones such as being drawn to an image on a billboard or poster. Because "a picture is worth a thousand words," designers often use imagery to grab an audience's attention and to establish an immediate connection with the audience.

Representational imagery such as photographs and illustrations do a good job of arousing curiosity, luring a viewer, and eliciting an emotional response. However, a photograph or an illustration is often too complex to serve as an effective means of communicating universally understood information at a quick glance. Airport signage, for instance, guides travelers with simple iconography or symbols that are understood by all individuals, regardless of language or culture.

Simple iconographic symbols, called *logos*, also are used in the marketplace to identify products and services. Think of a product brand you have grown to trust. If you are like most consumers, you associate that brand's symbol or logo with quality and consistency. So when you consider purchasing a new product or service, you are more likely to look for one bearing that brand's logo than to choose one with which you are unfamiliar.

In the design process, it is important to distinguish between different image types and to produce or select appropriate imagery for each application. The right image can help you connect and communicate with members of your intended audience, whereas the wrong image can confuse and alienate them.

objectives

- Explain the differences between symbols, logos, and representational and informational imagery and describe the ways they function in design and communication.
- Explain the differences between photographs and illustrations and describe the ways they can be fully exploited to best serve and enhance a communication message.
- Explain how iconographic symbols differ from other types of imagery and how they communicate visual information at a glance.
- Discuss how logos are designed and how they identify brands in the marketplace.
- Examine ways in which identity and wayfinding systems are developed.
- Develop a knowledge of the basic types of charts and graphs and the way they put statistical information into a visual context.

REPRESENTATIONAL IMAGERY

Think of how a picture of a sunny tropical beach can transcend you into a more relaxed state of mind. That is probably because, on some level, you are experiencing what it is like to be on that beach. Representational images rely on creating the illusion of a reality that exists only in the mind's eye.

When designers want to communicate a mood or affect viewers on an emotional level, nothing speaks more clearly than a photograph or an illustration. In the case of the tropical beach scene, part of its appeal lies in seeing the blue sky, sunny beach, and water and imagining how that feels. Being able to see details such as tropical foliage helps distinguish this beach from one in a more northerly climate. The realism in a representational image is what helps to convince audience members that what they are seeing is or could be within the realm of their experience.

Photography

Because most people assume the camera never lies, photographs are generally regarded as the most credible type of imagery. This visual assumption sets up a situation in which the viewer is likely to accept a photograph as being real, without question—a premise that supports the visual power of photography. Photographs are often used in a photojournalistic way to support newsworthy editorials or to document informative content. They also are used when accuracy or recognition is important **3.1**.

[3.1] The pair of photographs in this *National Geographic* article give visual credibility to the story of an Afghanistan woman who left her native land for a refugee camp in Pakistan. The earlier photograph appeared on the cover of the June 1985 *National Geographic* with a cover note that read: "Haunting eyes and a tattered garment tell the plight of a girl who fled her native Afghanistan." Photographer Steve McCurry made a second photograph of her 17 years later after the fall of the Taliban to support the article's focus on how little the country has changed.
© Steve McCurry and Magnum Photos.

Food manufacturers and retailers are well aware of how a photograph with strong appetite appeal can prompt a purchase. In fact, the temptation to alter a photograph of a product to enhance its appeal prompted legislation that now requires all food manufacturers to use unaltered product photographs on product packaging.

Practically everyone has had the experience of purchasing a food or beverage because a photograph of it made the product seem irresistible. Photographs of food and beverages are often used at the point of purchase to promote food products and food service establishments. They also are used in advertising and other promotional venues, such as consumer Web sites **3.2**.

Photographs also can be extremely effective at eliciting an emotional response or at helping the viewer visualize himself in a specific situation. Photographs are frequently used in advertising to portray scenarios where the viewer can easily identify with the individuals or setting that is depicted **3.3**.

In addition to advertising, photography is an important component of editorial design, annual reports, corporate literature, and other types of publication design. In those situations, designers often commission commercial photographers, working with them in the creation of photographs that support the designers' design and communication needs. Commercial photographers have years of training and experience when it comes to understanding lighting, composition, and other aspects of the photographic process that are beyond most designers' expertise. Commercial photographers also can offer studio space, professional lighting, and other equipment necessary for producing high-quality results.

Designers often use stock agencies that grant limited rights for the use of their photographs. Stock agencies feature the work of professional photographers and allow potential customers to browse through the agencies' Web sites, searching for the relevant subject matter. When a suitable photograph is found, the customer pays for the image and downloads it from the Web site. Photographs purchased through these agencies are typically contracted for a usage-based fee, typically for one-time use.

[3.2] The appetite appeal of this ice cream brand is highlighted with photographs of ice cream cones featured on a Web site for Graeter's ice cream. Seeing the real product helps convince the audience of the dessert's cool, creamy sweetness. *Courtesy of Graeter's Inc. Web site design by LPK.*

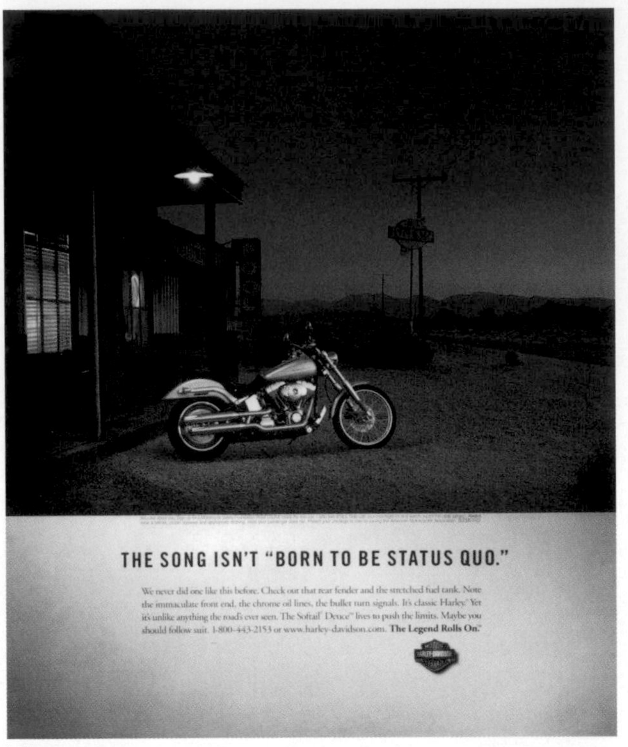

[a]

[3.3a and b] The realism of photography helps the reader identify with a situation or setting, as well as clearly identifying a product. In this case, the romance of the road calls to motorcycle enthusiasts as well as those who would like to imagine themselves engaging in the lifestyle of a motorcyclist.
Courtesy of Harley Davidson. Ad concept and design by Carmichael Lynch; photographs by Paul Wakefield and Chris Wimpey.

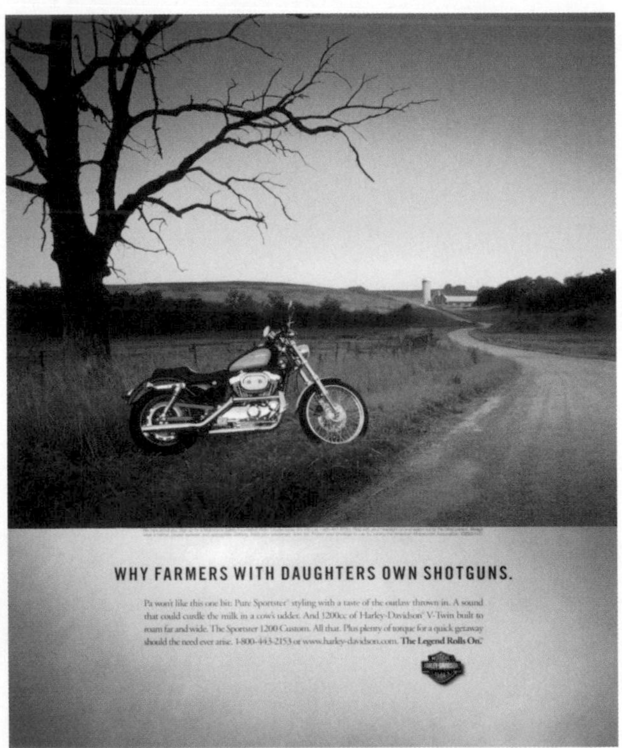

[b]

Judicious Cropping

When you are in a position to take your own photographs or commission them from a professional photographer, you may have control over how an image is framed and what the composition of the final photograph will be. However, designers must often work with supplied photographs that are less than perfect. They may also want to make adjustments to their own photographs to produce the best possible image. These are occasions when understanding how to crop a photo is important.

Beginners often overlook the need to crop a photo, assuming they should use all of a photograph, including its entire background. However, seasoned designers understand that removing portions of a photograph that detract or distract the viewer's attention from its central focal point can draw attention to what is most meaningful about the photograph. Knowing where and how to crop an image involves studying it and singling out its best part **3.4a** and **3.4b**.

Cropping should also take into account the most interesting portion of an image and the shape the final image will assume in a composition. When dealing with human subjects, cropping close on a subject's face puts more focus on the individual as opposed to his clothing, gesture, or activity in which he is engaged **3.5a, 3.5b,** and **3.5c**.

[a]

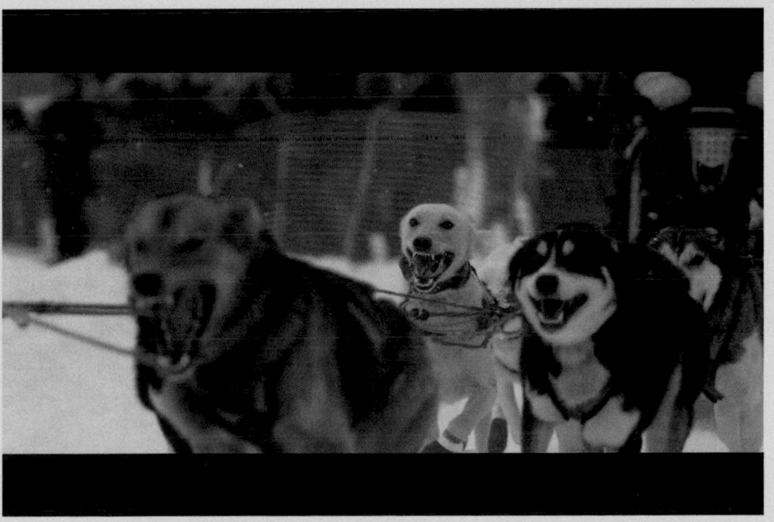

[b]

[3.4a and b] The original photograph of the sled dog–racing team is good, but the most expressive and interesting portion of the photograph is the area that contains the sled dogs. The cropped version also highlights the expression on the face of the dog that is in sharp focus, yielding a much more dynamic image. *Photos by Evan MacVeigh.*

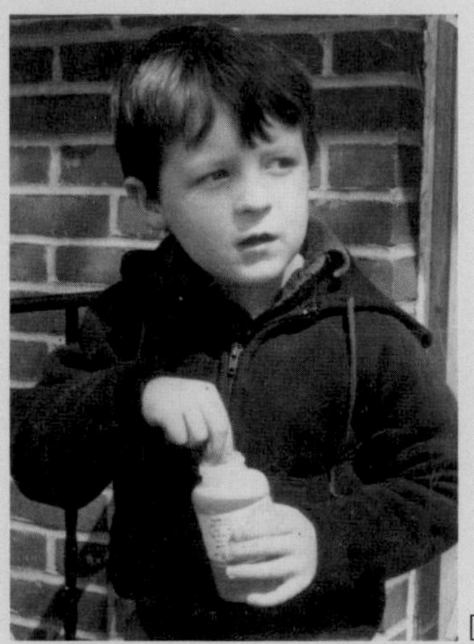

[a]

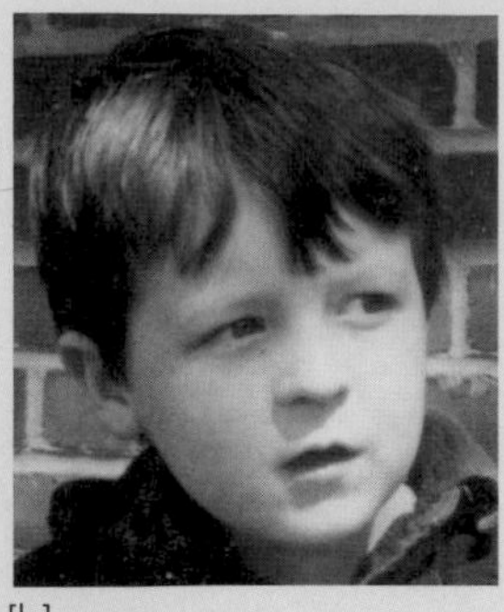

[b]

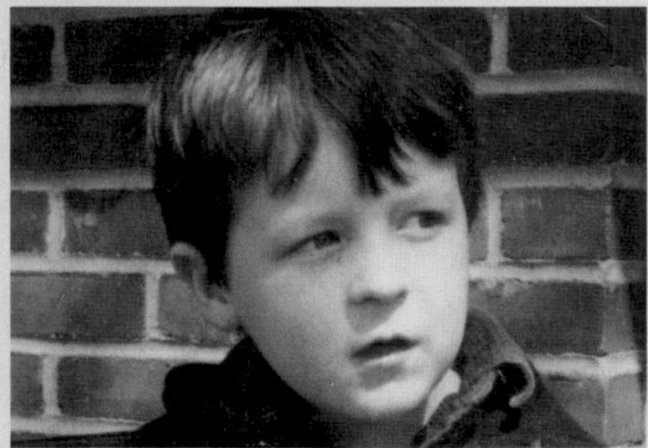

[c]

[3.5a, b and c] (a) The original photograph shows a child engaged in an activity. (b) A closer crop puts more emphasis on the face. (c) This crop focuses even more on features. Its horizontal format can assume a different role in a composition than the vertical thrust of the original photograph or the square format in the second version.
© Cengage Learning 2013.

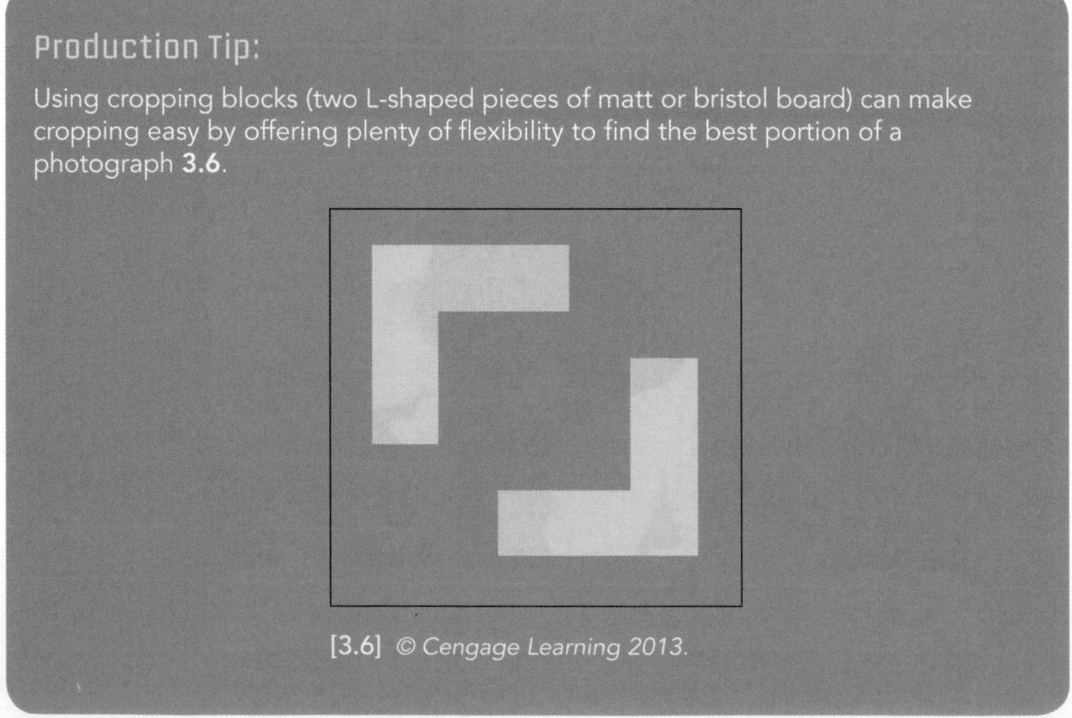

Production Tip:

Using cropping blocks (two L-shaped pieces of matt or bristol board) can make cropping easy by offering plenty of flexibility to find the best portion of a photograph **3.6**.

[3.6] *© Cengage Learning 2013.*

There may be occasions when a photograph's central image should be featured without any background. Isolating a subject from its background is called *outlining* or *silhouetting*. This technique may be your only option if the photograph is poorly composed or if the background is so distracting that it needs to be removed. Outlining or silhouetting also is appropriate and used frequently when an image works well as a compositional element **3.7a** and **3.7b**.

[a]

[b]

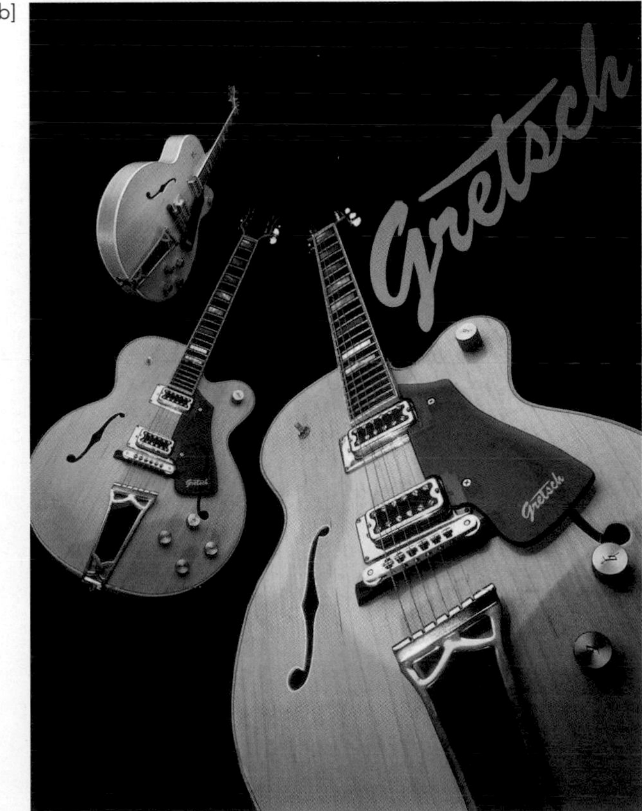

[3.7a and b] In this poster, photographs of guitars were isolated from their background so that they appear to be floating in space in the final design.
Poster design and photography by David Steinbrunner.

Production Tip

Keep in mind that images will lose quality if they are not the right size or resolution when printed or featured online. When creating an image, sizing or cropping it for reproduction, first determine the size that it needs to be for your design. Next consider its application. Images that are used in printed media should be between 250 and 300 dpi (dots per inch) or ppi (pixels per inch) for reproduction at their original size (100 percent). Images that are intended for the Web should be 72 dpi or ppi for reproduction at 100 percent.

Digitally Altered Photographs Cropping a photograph or removing a photograph from its background is a simple way of making alterations that are easily accomplished with a photo-editing program such as Photoshop. Photo-editing programs can also give the user opportunities to creatively manipulate original photographs by adjusting color, by applying filters, or through other means. Users new to these programs often take advantage of how easy it is to manipulate a photograph in a way that instantly creates a distortion of the original. However, the best results are often achieved when a strong concept is behind a digital manipulation of a photograph. Remarkable effects can be achieved when photographs are seamlessly combined so that a familiar image is treated in an unexpected way **3.8a** and **3.8b**.

Use a Photograph That Supports Your Design Concept The old saying "A picture is worth a 1,000 words" is true when you consider that the right photograph can sometimes communicate an idea more effectively than a few words. When a designer starts with a solid image-based concept and creates or commissions a high-quality photograph to support his or her idea, the results can be powerful **3.9**.

However, novice designers sometimes find photographs when browsing online and then incorporate these images into a design concept. Sometimes this approach can work if it inspires a great concept and the photograph is appropriate and the right size and reproduction quality. But no matter how great the concept, a photograph of marginal quality will always yield second-rate or poor results. Consider the following when choosing and working with photographs:

- Determine whether or not your concept is better expressed typographically or supported by a photograph. Does it have emotional content that a photograph can support?
- Make sure that the size and quality of the photograph you have chosen will work for your design concept. Does the photo have a full range of tones? Is it in good focus? (See the *Production Tip* in this chapter for information on image resolution and size standards.)
- If cropping is necessary, section off the best part of the photo. Use cropping blocks to help determine the best part of the image and then determine how the design will best work with the cropped image.
- Do not try to enlarge a photograph of marginal quality to make it fit your design. The quality of the photograph should determine its size, not the size of the area you have chosen for the photograph in your design.
- Give good photographs the attention they deserve by displaying them prominently in your design. Photographs with strong emotional or aesthetic appeal deserve first-class treatment.

Illustration

The expressive quality of illustrations makes them valuable when a mood or feeling needs to be enhanced. A case in point is romance novels, which for years have depicted posed models on their covers in illustrations, but rarely in photographs. That is because illustration is the more expressive than photographs **3.10**.

The mood projected in an illustration is largely controlled and dictated by illustration technique as well as the medium. For black-and-white illustration, pen and ink, scratchboard, and digital drawing programs are just some of the media possibilities available. Each medium has a unique look and sensibility and, in the hands of different artists, can convey additional nuance and feeling, depending on the artist's technique and visual interpretation **3.11a**, **3.11b**, and **3.11c**.

[a]

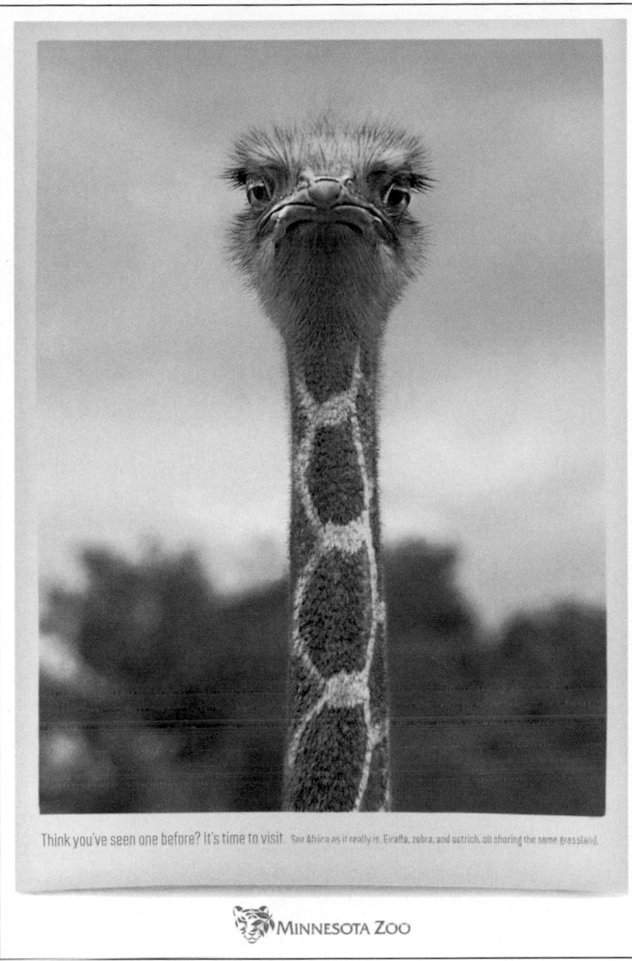

[b]

If you can name this animal, it's time to visit.
See Africa as it really is. Giraffe, zebra, and ostrich, all sharing the same grassland.
MINNESOTA ZOO

[3.8a and b] This series of magazine ads for the Minneapolis Zoo had viewers taking a second glance when encountering unexpected fur patterns of the zoo animals featured in each ad. The images were created using a photo-editing program to combine various stock photographs into a single image. *(a) Ad concept and design by Preston Kelly; art director, Anne Taylor; creative director, Chris Preston; writer, Terry Thomas; photo-retouchers, Mike Fritz and Lee Stokes. (b) © Gerry Ellis/Digital Vision/Getty Images.*

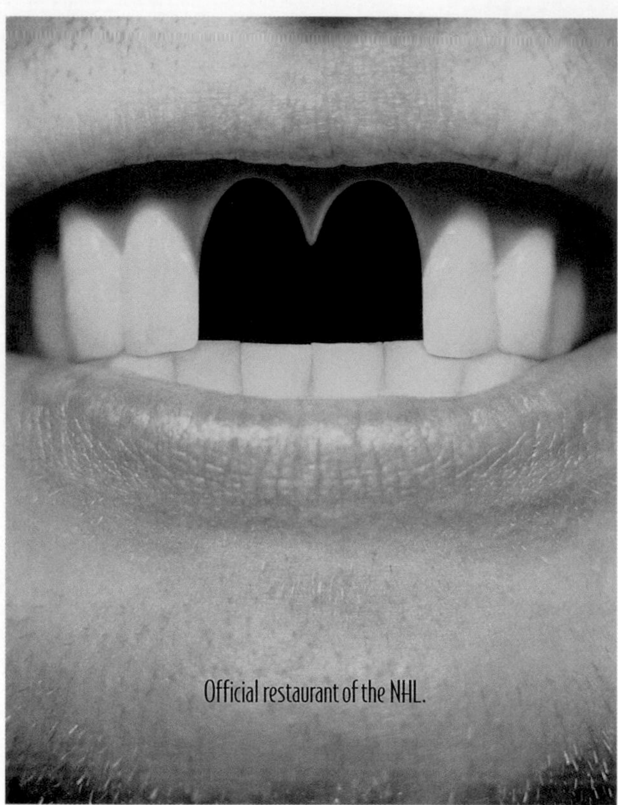

Official restaurant of the NHL.

[3.9] Few words are needed to make the point in this ad. The photograph, manipulated to show a toothless gap echoing the shape of McDonald's golden arches, clearly communicates its intended message.
Design by Palmer Jarvis DDB.

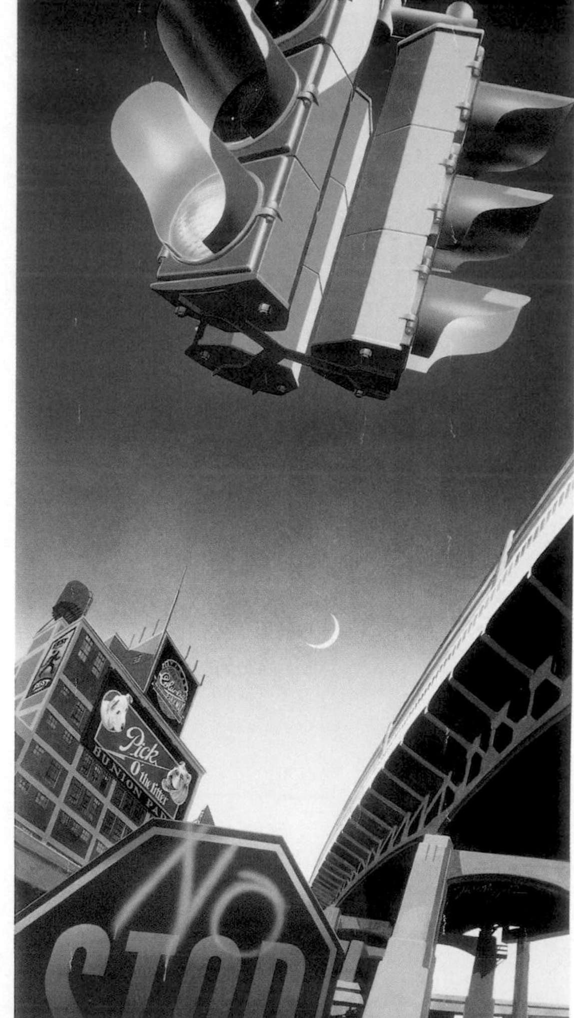

Humana ChoiceCare Heart Mini-Marathon 24
Saturday and Sunday, March 24 & 25, 2001
15K Mini-Marathon • 5K HeartRun • 5K and 10K Walk • 2K Kids' Mini-MaraFun

[3.10] Although the media and rendering technique in this poster illustration promoting a road race makes it appear as photographic, its unusual lighting, vantage point, and exaggerated perspective have resulted in an image that is more surreal than real.
Illustration by John Maggard; poster design by Cliff Schwandner.

[a]

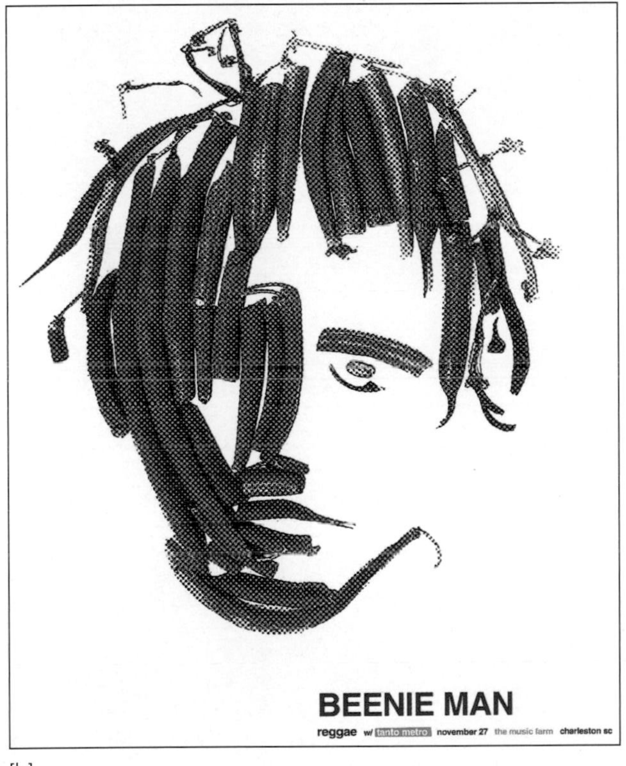

[b]

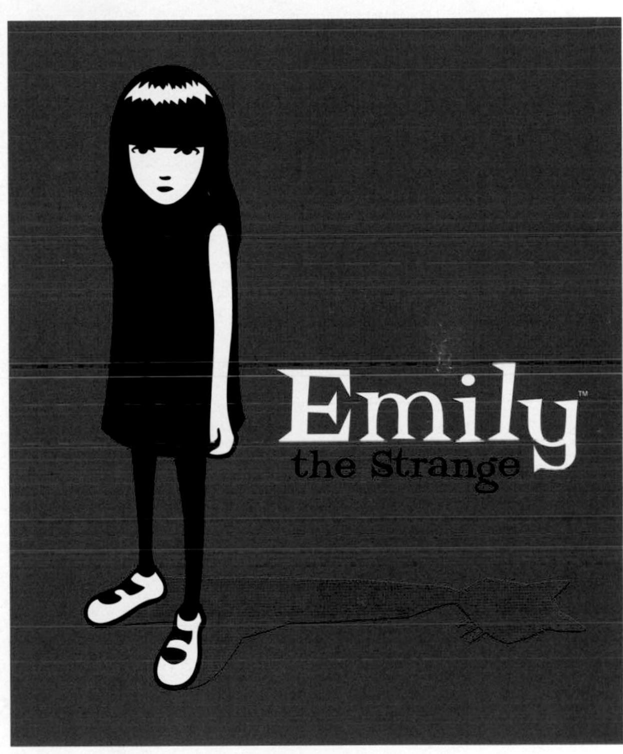

[c]

[3.11a, b and c] Black-and-white illustrations include a range of media possibilities. Shown here are (a) a scratchboard illustration by Greg Dearth, (b) a charcoal rendering by Mark Lawrence of Gil Schuler Graphic Design, and (c) a digital rendering by Cosmic Debris for Chronicle Books.
(a) Courtesy of Gregory M. Dearth. (b) Courtesy of Mark Lawrence. (c) Courtesy of Chronicle Books.

Illustration also allows flexibility of interpretation. The artist is free to be selective in the amount of detail rendered and the degree of abstraction, heightening the emotional or evocative content of the subject matter by exaggerating gestures or other details, including and color and texture **3.12**.

Illustrations also can help an audience visualize something that cannot be seen or help an audience better understand a complex concept. For instance, medical illustrations give those who study medicine a fuller understanding of how the body works. Diagrammatic illustrations help technicians assemble or maintain complex equipment.

[a]

[b]

[c]

[3.12] Three artistic interpretations of the same image yields three very different impressions. The first illustration is a vector drawing done in Illustrator. The hard edges of this rendering technique make the image seem unnatural and impersonal. The second illustration was created in Photoshop. Its warm and vivid color palette and decorative embellishments add a sense of excitement and movement to the image. The third illustration, done in soft pastels, is the most realistic of the renderings and the most honest in its expressiveness.
Copyright 2011, Ken Henson.

Illustrations, like photographs, are usually chosen or commissioned with output in mind. It is important to select or commission black-and-white media for output in black and white, as opposed to converting a color illustration to black and white.

Sources for Imagery

Many designers generate their own imagery, shooting photographs or creating drawings, paintings, or digital art for their designs. However, if you are not able to generate your own imagery, the following resources are commonly used:

- Royalty-free collections—Collections of illustrations and photographs with no limitations on their usage can be purchased on CD-ROM or downloaded from commercial Web sites as an inexpensive source of imagery. Their only drawback is that some of the images have a generic look. Because they are available to anyone willing to purchase them, there's always the chance that an image from a royalty-free collection may appear (or may have already appeared) someplace else.
- Stock agencies—These agencies grant limited rights use of their photographs and illustrations for a fee. The drawbacks are similar to royalty-free collections in that there is no guarantee that an image has not or will not appear elsewhere.
- Commissioned—Hiring a photographer or an illustrator will yield an original piece of art. Professional photographs and illustrations typically, but not always, cost more than stock or royalty-free collections.
- Fonts—Some typeface companies offer symbol or picture fonts. These images are very simple and often iconic, so they are legible in small as well as large sizes and typically come in themed collections. They function just like fonts, with each image accessible by a keystroke, and can be purchased the same way that fonts are purchased.

Storyboarding: Giving Visual Form to Concepts

Storyboarding is a type of illustration that gives visual form to concepts for video presentations, movies, television ads, and animations and is an important component in taking an initial concept to final form. After a script is developed, a storyboard illustration shows the sequence of events as they take place in the script **3.13**. Storyboard artists produce rough pencil or marker sketches of the concept as a means of communicating an idea to the production team, client, or others involved in the funding or development of a project. In an era in which the computer has increasingly become a means of producing finished illustrations, the hand-rendered look of marker and pencil illustration sends a message that the concept is fresh and "on the drawing board" for discussion and revision. Storyboards for high-tech gaming and animation can involve "digital sketching" with sophisticated tools to produce more technically and conceptually finished sequential images.

[3.13] *Courtesy of Justin Coro Kaufman, Massive Black Inc.*

- Found imagery—Small or flat objects such as leaves and coins can be directly scanned and incorporated into designs **3.14**.

Uncredited illustrations and photographs found in printed materials or work created by individuals whose copyright has expired can often be used. These images that are copyright free fall into a category called *public domain*, meaning they are no longer protected by copyright **3.15**.

[3.14] Flat objects such as this leaf can be photographed by placing them on a scanner.
© Cengage Learning 2013.

[3.15] Uncredited photographs and illustrations that are at least 75 years old, such as the one on this matchbook, are no longer protected by copyright laws and can be freely incorporated into designs and layouts.
Public Domain

Image Terminology for Production Bringing an image into the design and production process requires digitizing or scanning so it can be printed in a way that will result in the best possible reproduction of the original. To determine the best way of scanning an image, it is important to know how prepress houses and scanning manufacturers classify imagery and the terminology they use.

- **continuous tone**—A photograph or an illustrated image that is composed of a series of gray or color tones with gradations from one tone or color to the next, as opposed to color or tonal areas that are flat and distinct from one another.
- **grayscale**—A continuous-tone black-and-white image.
- **halftone**—A method of reproducing a continuous-tone image by photographing it through a fine screen to convert the image into a series of dots. A color image is called a *CMYK halftone.*
- **line art**—Refers to a black-and-white image that does not have continuous tones, such as a logo, a graphically reduced image, or a pen-and-ink illustration. If created on the computer, this can be a *vector* or *bitmap* image.

SYMBOLS AND LOGOS

Because they need to be easily and often universally understood as well as recognizable in both small- and large-scale applications, symbols and logos are images or words that have been stripped down to their simplest form. The process of simplifying an image and emphasizing its most salient points could be described as turning it into an **icon** or a "sign." The study of icons and what they represent is called *semiology.*

Understanding how to simplify an image and making it symbolic is based on many of the design principles you have already learned. Creating a well-balanced design with pleasing proportions is important, particularly in a logo design in which the character or essence of a brand or business must be communicated.

Graphically Reducing an Image

Taking an image down to its simplest form while preserving its ability to be recognized is called making a *graphic reduction.* The simplicity and legibility of a graphically reduced image makes it especially suitable for pictograms or logos.

Graphic reduction is a process of image translation. Most often the translation is an edited, simplified version of the original subject. Logos, symbols, marks, pictograms, and ideograms need to be deciphered quickly if they are to communicate successfully. Reducing subjects to their essential parts yields images that fulfill this requirement **3.16**.

[3.16] In this example, a photograph of a pencil (left) is converted from a continuous-tone, grayscale image to black-and-white icons. In the process of graphically reducing this image, important attributes were retained, including the pencil's basic shape, the contours of its edges, and its black lead point.

To achieve unity and harmony, the visual attributes of a graphically reduced image must have a structural as well as aesthetic relationship. Through the process of editing and translating, careful consideration must be applied as the subject is drawn and redrawn. Working toward a final graphic translation of the original subject requires visually aligning and tuning the feature parts. Width, length, and sizes of visual attributes can be based on a constant unit of measure.

The transformation of a continuous-tone image to a graphic reduction can be accomplished in many ways: describing the contours of an image with an outline, converting the basic form of an object to a silhouette or simple shape, interpreting shadowed contours of a form into a series of shapes, or using a combination of those methods. To successfully reduce an image, the designer should concentrate on emphasizing essential qualities—a process that involves retaining some details of the image while eliminating others. Contours may be converted to simple curves. The designer's role in the process is one of judicious decision maker—deciding what features of an image will go, what will stay, and how the elements that are retained will take on new meaning within a new, more simplified context.

Simple Image Terminology

The following terms will help you differentiate among the different types of simple image applications:

- **ideogram** or **ideograph**—A pictorial image or symbol that represents an idea or a concept, for instance, a representation of a lightning bolt to symbolize a thunderstorm warning.
- **logo**—A logotype or mark or a combination of the two used symbolically to represent a product, brand, company, or group.
- **logotype**—Letters, words, or a name formed in a distinctive way and used symbolically to represent a product, brand, company, or group.
- **mark**—A symbol used to represent a product, brand, company, or group.
- **pictogram** or **pictograph**—A pictorial image that depicts a simplified representation of an object or activity.
- **symbol**—A letter or sign that represents an activity, idea, or object that can be used within a cultural or commercial context. Effective symbols are universally understood and transcend language and cultural boundaries.

Logos and Trademarks

If you are shopping for athletic wear, spotting the logo of a well-known brand helps you immediately identify the price range and quality of the merchandise. When you are loyal to a brand, you are more likely to look for and buy merchandise bearing that logo. The term *logo* is used describe whatever symbol a company uses to identify its brand in the marketplace.

A logo can be more than a symbol or a mark. As you learned in Chapter 2, a logo can be a distinctive typographic treatment of a company name, called a *logotype.* Or, it can be a combination of a mark and logotype. A logo that includes both offers a degree of versatility. A name and mark work well together, but they can function independently of each other if necessary **3.17a**, **3.17b**, **3.17c**, and **3.17d**.

[3.17a, b, c and d] This combination of mark and logotype allowed for flexibility in the development of a corporate identity system for the OneWorld Challenge team that competed for America's Cup. The two components work well together on letterhead and packaging but function equally as well independent of each other.
Identity design by Hornall Anderson Design Works.

[a]

[b]

[c]

[d]

Manufacturers recognize the importance of consumer loyalty and brand devotion and work hard to develop a logo that captures and communicates the spirit or essence of their brand. If they are successful, their logo is a unique identifying mark that cannot be confused with any other logo. In fact, logos are so important to brand recognition that most manufacturers trademark their brand's logo, a process of legally registering it with the government's trademark registry. When a logo becomes a registered trademark, it is the exclusive property of the trademark holder. No other company can apply that logo to its product or merchandise without suffering legal consequences.

In addition to a design expressing the character of a company or brand, another important factor of a logo's design is its ability to be easily recognized in many applications. Because logos often appear on apparel labels, in newspaper ads, and in other situations where there is little control over the size and color of the logos' reproduction, the design is typically clean and simple so they can be recognized and understood easily regardless of scale or color.

Make Images Part of a Logotype Logotypes and images are typically paired so they can work together or apart from each other to identify a firm or an organization. However, images also can take the place of a letterform or become part of a letterform in a logotype, as demonstrated in **3.18**. Images also can be incorporated into numerals, as demonstrated in **3.19**. Graphically reducing an image to its simplest form makes the melding process between image and letterform or numeral much easier.

Logos and Identity Systems

Once an organization's logo has been determined, business materials such as stationery, shipping labels, and business cards are designed bearing the logo. Beyond those basic identity needs, most companies have other situations where their logo needs to appear, such as on their Web site, promotional literature, merchandise, packaging, and signage and for vehicle and uniform applications.

Although it may seem as though identity applications would require little more than scaling and positioning a logo, an organization's identity is often based on more than just its logo. A distinctive color palette and typography as well as other identifying elements also may be involved in the identity. To provide a means of applying those elements across a broad range of materials, designers develop what is called an *identity system*. The overall

[3.18] The Kazi Beverage Company logo uses a silhouette of a martini glass to fill in the open area of the A. *Design by Hornall Anderson Design Works.*

[3.19] These numerals, representing floors in the American Museum of Natural History, signify where visitors can find areas of interest. The animal forms that are combined with the numerals derive their inspiration from the fossils and scenes that appear on each floor.
Icon design by Lance Wyman.

goal in designing an identity system is to provide a unified presentation based on the image established with the logo. Identity systems are often sophisticated, modular schemes that provide a flexible means of applying recognizable features of a company's identity to a variety of design venues.

To ensure that a company's identity is applied consistently across the board, designers often develop graphics standards manuals to serve as a guide for others in implementing an identity system. With a graphic standards manual, the arrangement and application of the logo in a variety of situations is assured, as is consistency in the use of the identity's colors and typographic requirements.

Stationery and Business Card Design

Any individual or organization doing business needs to produce correspondence on stationery bearing its identity. Business stationery includes important contact information such as the business address, phone and fax numbers, and e-mail and/or Web site address. The business's logo is typically placed at the top of the letterhead, but any arrangement is acceptable as long as enough space is left for the correspondence. The letterhead design should not overpower the message it contains. Because postal regulations limit the amount of space on an envelope that can include a design, an organization's logo, return address, and other identity elements containing imagery or type should be confined to the upper left corner of the envelope.

Business cards are handed out when professionals want to exchange contact information. That is why the name of the individual needs to be featured prominently on the card along with

The Making of a Museum Identity

New York City's Museum of Art and Design (MAD) explores the integration of contemporary art, design, and craft. Its collections and exhibitions feature work by artists and designers who transform materials through processes ranging from the artisanal to the digital.

Working with the MAD acronym, Michael Bierut of Pentagram Design developed a logo and identity system for the museum that captures its focus on materials and processes. MAD's location, in New York City's Columbus Circle, and the building's square shape served as an inspiration **3.20a**. By combining squares and circles, Bierut explored a number of geometric possibilities before arriving at a monogram that is unique and proprietary **3.20b**. Once the logo had been designed, an entire alphabet of letterforms and numbers was created based on this concept. (See Chapter 2, for more information on this aspect of the identity.)

The logo and identity system also needed to be inventive and surprising, so that it could appear in different ways on different occasions. The idea of transformation and surprise ties in with the museum's focus on artists who take typical forms such as vessels or chairs and transform them or interpret them differently. The logo's solid, bold geometric shapes translated easily into different interpretations **3.20c**.

The identity's flexibility comes from applying MAD's proprietary alphabet to its promotional messages **3.20d**. In addition to the consistency of the alphabet's geometric shapes, a distinctive color palette of bold, saturated colors was added to a palette of textures and patterns to ensure unity

[a]

[3.20a] The Museum's location at Columbus Circle and on the corner of a square block in New York City's grid configuration of streets and avenues served as the starting point for the MAD identity.
Photo courtesy of Pentagram.

[b]

[3.20b] Bierut explored configurations of circles and squares and developed a monogram based on the MAD acronym. This monogram became the museum's logo.
Design by Michael Bierut/Pentagram.

[c]

[3.20c] The logo adapts easily to interpretations that include various colors, textures, and patterns that comprise the MAD identity palette.
Design by Michael Bierut/Pentagram.

and consistency in all of MAD's merchandise, promotional materials, and other identity applications **3.20e**. (See Chapter 4 for more information on developing the color palette for this identity.) Pentagram developed a graphics standards manual to guide museum personnel in their application of the identity system.

[d]

[3.20d] Promotional messages echo the logo's geometric configuration of circles and squares through the use of a MAD's typeface based on the logo design.
Design by Michael Bierut/Pentagram.

[e]

[3.20e] Merchandise such as T-shirts bear the MAD aesthetic and promote the museum.
Design by Michael Bierut/Pentagram.

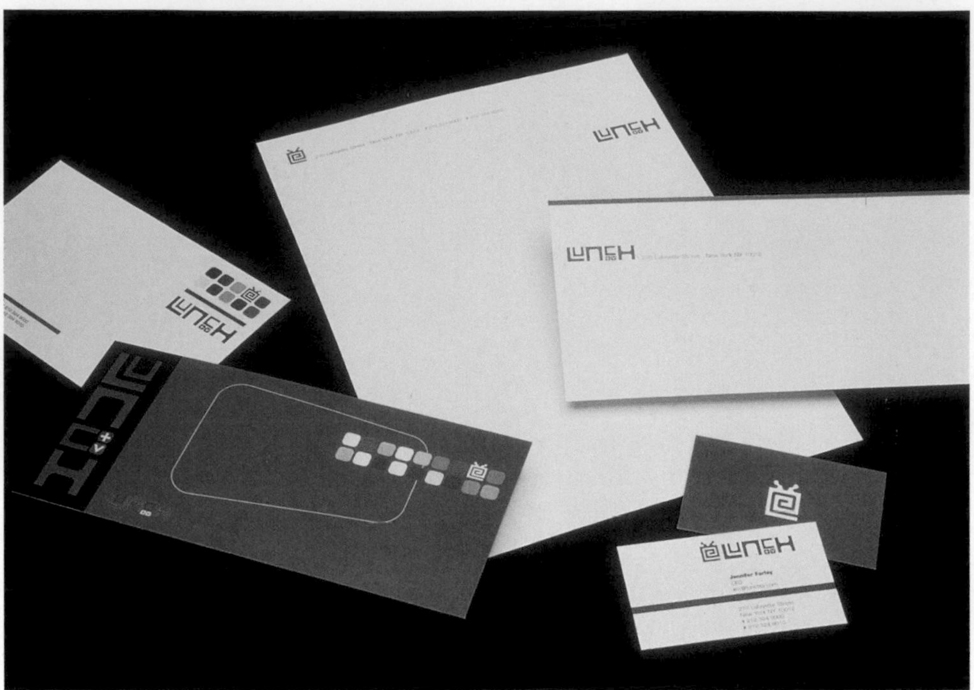

[3.21] This suite of business materials for Lunch TV, a television and video production company, features a logotype and mark that work well as a team and independent of each other. Other unifying elements of the Lunch TV identity include a palette of red, blue, and violet hues and round-cornered squares that mimic a television screen. All of the identity elements work together in a modular way that allows for a variety of design options. Even the logotype is modular, with letterforms that work just as well stacked vertically as they do horizontally.
Design by Stoltze Design.

the business name and contact information that appears on the letterhead. The business card should be visually coordinated with the stationery system, using the same typefaces, color palette, and other identity elements to ensure a unified presentation **3.21**.

Because stationery and business cards are handled and require close inspection, the tactile qualities of the paper that is used play an important role. Many paper companies manufacture paper lines in a variety of textures and colors that include standard letterhead and business card weights as well as coordinated envelopes.

INFORMATIONAL IMAGERY

Informational imagery guides and informs people in situations where words do not do an adequate job. Maps, for instance, help people find their way in unfamiliar situations. Diagrammatic illustrations, such as those used in textbooks, enable people to better understand how things work by showing them what they cannot see or easily visualize. Instructional diagrams often help individuals operate, maintain, assemble, or install complex or unfamiliar equipment or technology.

Beyond those needs, designers are often involved in creating sophisticated wayfinding systems composed of directional symbols and pictograms that can be universally understood. Designers also work with charts, giving informational data visual form so it can be more easily understood. This section discusses each of those design applications in more detail.

Symbols and Wayfinding Systems

If you have ever flown to a destination where you are unfamiliar with the native language, you know how important symbols can be when finding your way around an airport. Signs with pictograms of luggage direct you to the baggage claim area. Other symbols guide you to places where you can exchange money and find ground transportation. And if you are totally confused and need help finding your way around, chances are you will be looking for signs bearing the ? symbol.

Pictograms and symbols convey information that is universally understood. They are especially helpful to anyone navigating unfamiliar territory and are often incorporated into the design of wayfinding systems—a configuration of symbols, typographic applications, and signage that help to guide visitors in parks, airports, museums, and other situations that accommodate a cross-cultural audience. For instance, when developing the symbols and wayfinding system for a zoo, a designer typically becomes involved in developing pictograms that involve reducing an image of an animal species or family to its simplest and most recognizable form and making it part of a visually unified system. Those pictograms are combined with directional symbols such as arrows and are strategically placed at path intersections and other places in the zoo to help guide visitors **3.22**.

Designers often need to incorporate a wayfinding system and its symbols as well as other informational graphics into a broader identity scheme so that visitors receive an overall impression that is conveyed in everything they see and experience. For instance, the symbols used to guide visitors in a zoo are more likely to be rendered with a more casual or playful spirit than those used in an airport. A well-coordinated and unified wayfinding system will be stylistically in tune with other aspects of an identity system and will make use of the same color palette.

Charts and Graphs

Nothing seems as boring and can alienate a reader more quickly than a page of statistics. That is where charts can help. Charts are more likely to engage a viewer's attention. They also help readers visualize how the numbers look in a more meaningful and visually dynamic way.

Although there are many ways of plotting information, pie charts, bar charts, and graphs are most commonly used. Pie charts demonstrate how a population segment or lump sum can be broken down into portions. Pie charts work well for showing how a group voted or how the

[a]

[3.22] Brooklyn's Prospect Park Wildlife Center uses an identity and wayfinding system based on colorful animal cutouts. The animal iconography, which appears on signage throughout the park, helps visitors immediately identify areas of interest.
Design by Russell Design Associates.

[b]

[c]

group is composed in terms of demographics or opinions, how budget money was allocated, or where funds came from to arrive at a total **3.23**.

Bar charts work well for comparing data. Whether the data involves sales or snow, bar charts show how things literally stack up when what happened in one defined period is compared with another period. The bars in bar charts can run vertically or horizontally. They are often represented as stacks of coins, as pictograms, or as other symbols.

Graphs do a good job of plotting trends. They are particularly effective when showing dramatic growth or when comparing growth in several areas. They can be dressed up with pictorial representations or can become eye-catching visual additions to a layout when color is applied to their lines **3.24**.

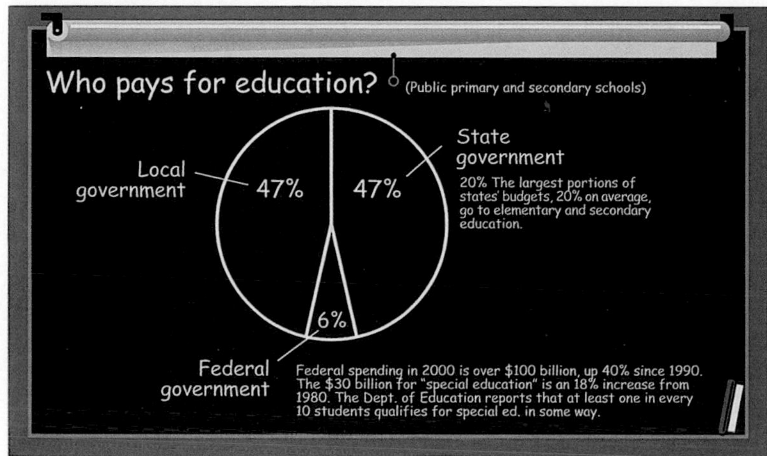
Who pays for education?
(Public primary and secondary schools)
Local government
47%
47%
State government
20% The largest portions of states' budgets, 20% on average, go to elementary and secondary education.
6%
Federal government
Federal spending in 2000 is over $100 billion, up 40% since 1990. The $30 billion for "special education" is an 18% increase from 1980. The Dept. of Education reports that at least one in every 10 students qualifies for special ed. in some way.

[3.23] Pie charts show how a total is a sum of its parts or how the total can be broken down into portions. This example shows what portion of public education is funded by state, local, and federal governments.
Design by Nigel Holmes, From "Understanding USA" 2000.

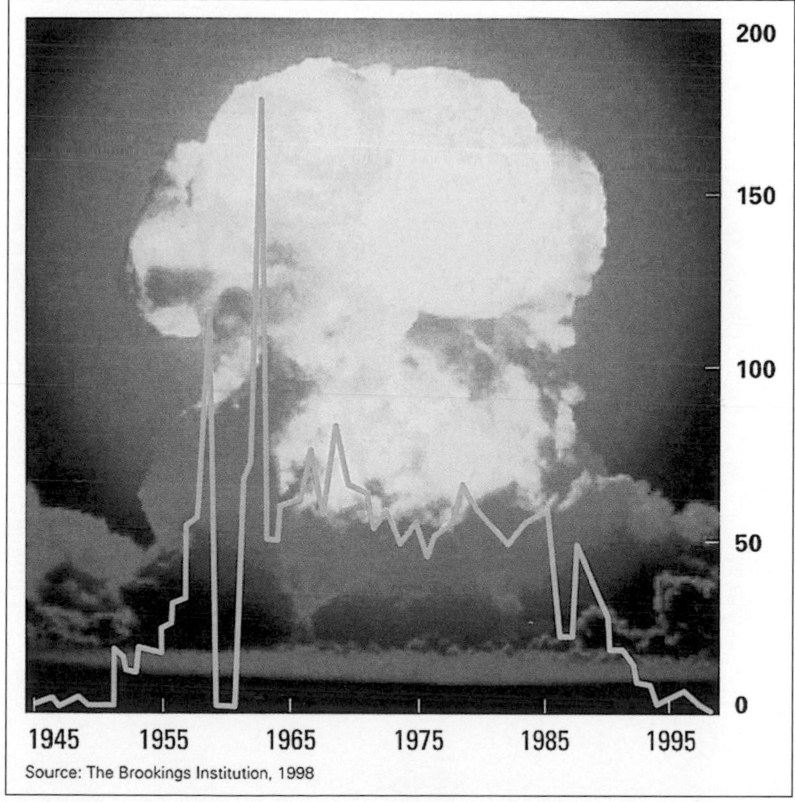
200
150
100
50
0
1945
1955
1965
1975
1985
1995
Source: The Brookings Institution, 1998

[3.24] Graph charts help readers visualize trends. This chart plots, over a 50-year period, the number of nuclear weapons detonated since 1945 and when most occurrences took place.
Courtesy of Brookings Institute.

SUMMARY

Representational imagery can enhance a message and helps draw attention to content. It is important to use photographs when recognition, documentation, and accuracy are important. Illustration offers a range of looks and media possibilities and can lend expressiveness to representational imagery. Graphically reduced images are images that are visually represented in the simplest possible way. They work well as universal symbols and in logo applications and are often used as trademarks for identifying brands. Logos and trademarks are typically extended to a broader context where they serve as part of a visual scheme of coordinated color, typography, and other graphic elements that constitute an identity system. Identity systems are applied to stationery, business materials, products, product packaging, architecture, signage, and other situations that need to display a company's name and identity. Symbols and visual themes also are used in an informative way as environmental graphics that guide individuals who are in unfamiliar situations. Charts and graphs are another means of informative imagery and are used to make statistics more visually engaging.

projects

GRAPHIC ANIMAL

Objectives

- Study from observation to produce a visual analysis.
- Study the process of form reduction.
- Demonstrate design drawing ability.
- Refine and achieve an appropriate level of craft.
- Apply the use of mechanical tools to produce finished work.
- Make a connection between graphic reduction and logo and pictographic design.

Description

Choose an animal or insect and research its behavior, anatomy, and physical characteristics. Before you begin, do a physical analysis and study of the animal from photographs. Look at it from a variety of viewpoints. Count the number of features and anatomical parts and describe the individual attributes in diagrammatic drawings. Do a series of 10 to 15 studies to refine the composition. Refine and translate a chosen drawing into a final black-and-white study that is a graphic reduction or an object simplification of the original. Keep only the attributes that describe the object.

Limitations and Materials

Produce pencil sketches that are thumbnail or small-scale studies that are confined to an area no larger than 4 inches by 4 inches. Working on tracing paper will allow you to trace over parts of a drawing you like in order to generate refinements. When you arrive at a final drawing, enlarge it on a photocopier so it measures 8 inches by 8 inches. Transfer the final drawing to illustration board with 4H pencil. Ink with fine-point black pens and markers or a ruling pen and black gouache. Touch up your image if necessary with white gouache or acrylic paint. Use a ruler, triangle, and template for precise drawing.

Critique Discussion Points

Does the final simplified image maintain the essence of the original object? Why or why not?

What did you learn about the object from the physical analysis?

What did you find most challenging about this assignment?

What pleases you most about the final image?

Vocabulary

graphic reduction, symbol, icon, pictogram, value, gray-scale, continuous tone

References and Resources

Lance Wyman, Ryan McGinness, Malcolm Grear, Luba Lukova, Paul Rand, Otl Aicher

NAME LOGO

Objectives

- Use typography in a meaningful way.
- Design a symbol that supports a message.
- Combine typography and a symbol in a simple icon that is easily read and understood.
- Demonstrate design drawing ability.
- Refine and achieve an appropriate level of craft.
- Combine traditional media with digital and electronic tools to produce finished work.

Description

Make a logo of your name. Start by researching typefaces through online type libraries as well as the font library that is already installed on an available computer system. Find several typefaces for your name that you believe convey an attitude appropriate to who you are and combine your name (in one of the typefaces) with a symbol that does the same. Use the technique you learned for graphically reducing an image in the previous project to develop an appropriate symbol. Limiting yourself to black-and-white media, experiment with different ways of combining the symbol and your name using layering, scale changes, and other ways of combining the elements in a harmonious manner. Consider figure-ground relationships with a combination of image and type and apply the design principles you have learned to combine them in a synergistic manner. Keep your design simple so it can be read and understood easily on small- as well as large-scale applications.

Limitations and Materials

Use a computer to generate at least six variations of your name, each time making use of a different typeface or stylistic treatment. You can distort the type on the computer with a drawing or photo-editing program or manually distress the type. Use pencils, pens, and black-and-white media as described in the previous project to develop an image icon that can be combined with your name. Use pencil sketches and tracing paper to trace and refine the visual ideas you are developing and combine your image icon with the typographic treatment of your name. Use a photocopier to reduce and enlarge or make copies of the elements of your design. You also may use a scanner to scan your drawings or photocopies and trace over them with a digital drawing program. The computer also is a useful tool for combining type with an icon as well as for further refining your final design.

Critique Discussion Points

How is the typography you used expressive of you and your personality?

What physical attributes does the typeface possess that give it its character?

How does the image icon that you chose express you and/or your personality?

What design principles influenced your design decisions when you were combining type with iconography?

What types of refinements did you make to produce the final design?

Vocabulary

typeface, type style, graphic reduction, symbol, icon, pictogram, figure-ground, logo, logotype, synergistic

PHOTO CROP

Objectives

- Determine which portions of a photograph are worth salvaging and which are not worth saving.
- Develop a judicious eye for photographic composition.
- Practice cropping techniques.

Description

Find two photographs that can be improved through cropping. Find the best portion of each photograph and crop it so the viewer's eye is redirected to a portion of the photo.

Limitations and Materials

Locate a poorly composed photograph, or one that could be cropped so that attention is drawn to a different portion of the original image. Locate a second photograph of a human or animal subject that contains the head and all or part of the body. Make cropping blocks from two L-shaped pieces cut from black poster board or construction paper. Use a T square to ensure that the edges are square and cut at right angles. Crop each photo by positioning the cropping blocks so that the areas of the photo that do not improve the composition are eliminated and the best portion of the photograph is preserved. With the photograph or the human or animal, concentrate on cropping it so that the focus is on the head or face. When you have found a crop that works, tape the L-shaped pieces together and mark off and trim your final selections.

Critique Discussion Points

How successfully does each crop work?

How is cropping an improvement to the original?

What unnecessary components in the original have been eliminated through cropping?

How has the focal point in each photo changed or been improved?

Are the cropped images compositionally well balanced?

Vocabulary

crop or cropping, cropping blocks, focal point, hierarchy, balance

References and Resources

Man Ray, Richard Avedon, Ansel Adams, Henry Wolf, Annie Leibovitz, Otto Storch, Fred Woodward, DJ Stout

in review

1. When is it more appropriate to use an illustration as opposed to a photograph?
2. How is a graphically reduced image different from a continuous-tone image?
3. What are the differences between a mark, logotype, logo, and trademark?
4. What is a graphics standards manual? How is it used?
5. Why are symbols an important part of designing wayfinding systems?
6. What are the differences between a pie chart, a bar chart, and a graph? How is each one used?

© Luba Lukova.

"We face so many challenges—how to get better in what we do, how to keep our work fresh, passionate, and honest."

Luba Lukova

Luba Lukova is an award-winning freelance artist, illustrator, and designer based in New York City. A native of Bulgaria, Lukova grew up under communist rule. Her career in this country began in 1991 shortly after the Berlin Wall came down. She was invited to participate in the International Poster Exhibition in Fort Collins, Colorado, and after the show, she visited New York City where she landed an illustration assignment at *The New York Times*. More assignments came and Lukova decided to make her home here. Now a U.S. citizen, Lukova continues to create illustration and design for a wide range of national and international clients. She is also a fine artist whose work often focuses on social issues such as peace, censorship, immigration, ecology, hunger, and corruption. Her award-winning work is exhibited around the world and is included in the permanent art collections of MoMA in New York, The Library of Congress, and The World Bank. She has published a collection of posters that express her passion for social justice.

How did you get started in your career? What is your educational background?

I became interested in art from a very early age. My grandmother was a painter and she was my earliest influence. As a kid I took many art classes and eventually graduated with a master's degree in graphic design and poster art from the National Academy of Fine Art in Sofia, Bulgaria. Immediately after my graduation I began work as a graphic designer for a theater company. This was a great experience because it put me in touch with other creative people and gave me the opportunity right after school to see my work displayed in a public space.

What made you decide to pursue the career path that you've chosen?

I really don't know. This was not a decision but a conviction, from the age of 5 probably, that becoming an artist is the only thing I wanted to be.

What has been your biggest challenge in your career? Your biggest achievement?

There have been always challenges, I would say external and internal. My parents did not want me to pursue the career of an artist. I was good at math and they thought that being an engineer is a better profession. It was very difficult to convince them that my decision was right. This was probably the earliest challenge. Then in our everyday practice we face so many challenges—how to get better in what we do, how to keep our work fresh, passionate, and honest. Each new project is a new challenge. About my biggest achievement, I'm not sure. I guess the viewers have to decide on that.

What do you believe has been the biggest factor in your success?

Probably hard work, and faith that art can make a difference in people's lives.

What advice would you give to recent graduates or others who are just getting started in a career in illustration or graphic design?

Don't give up your dreams.

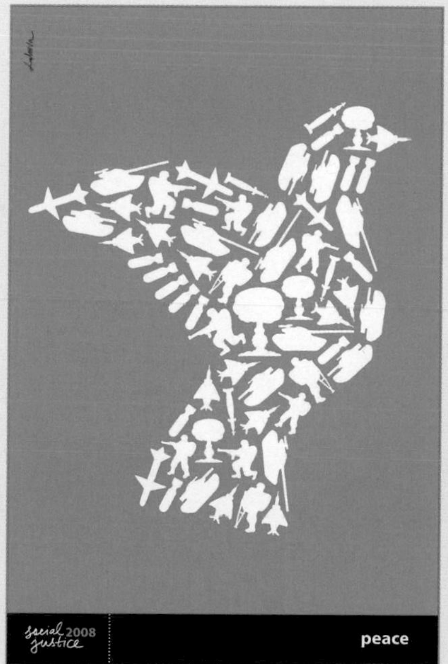

These illustrations are part of a collection of images from *Social Justice 2008, 12 Posters by Luba Lukova*. The book is an extension of Lukova's focus on issues such as censorship, peace, hunger, and corruption.

four

Color and Design

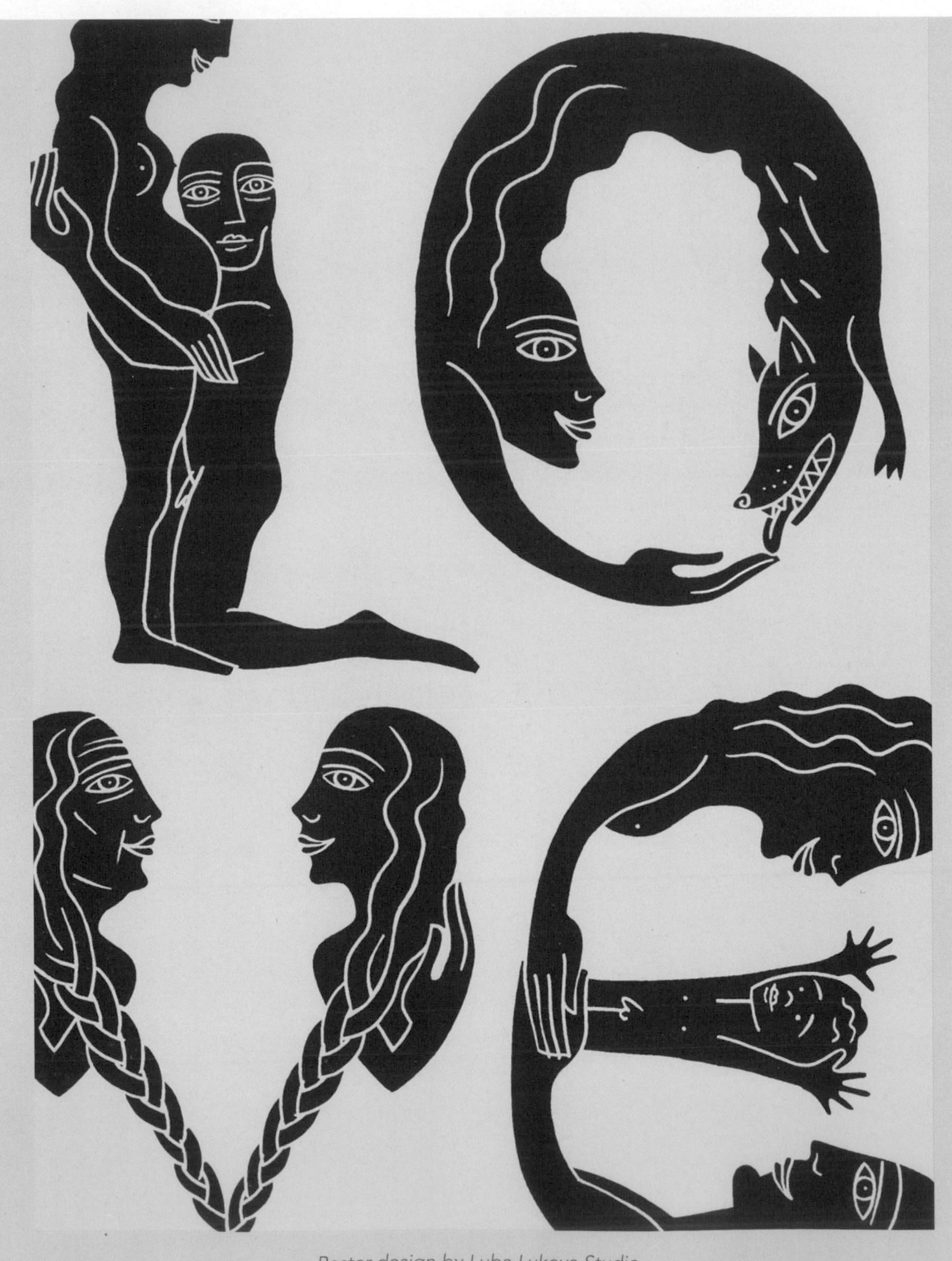

Poster design by Luba Lukova Studio.

4

introduction

The role of color in visual communication is complex. It is undoubtedly the most researched, the most visually powerful, and since the advent of computers, the most technical of all of the elements of design. It enhances the viewer's response on a variety of levels; it heightens the viewer's perception and intensifies emotional and psychological reaction. To become proficient with color, you must spend time studying it and working with it.

This chapter examines the fundamental dimensions of color related to science, theory, language, and practice. Crucial components of color, an exploration of color relationships, and ways of applying this knowledge to the practice of design will be presented.

objectives

- Explore the dimensions of color related to issues of visual communication.
- Explain how color is perceived and processed by the eye and brain.
- Identify key color systems and describe their relevance to graphic art.
- Define color terminology using visual examples.
- Present significant color theories that are useful in contemporary design.
- Investigate color psychology, symbolism, and cultural influences as they affect your understanding and use of them.
- Reveal strategies for choosing color schemes.
- Discuss the impact of color in composition.

COLOR SYSTEMS

Numerous color systems have been developed that attempt to order color so it can be comprehended more easily. Some of the systems are relatively simple, while others are technical. Some systems, such as the color wheel, are theory-based, demonstrating the order and relationships between purely saturated color hues. Other systems, such as Albert H. Munsell's color solid, were designed based on human perception as a standard for organizing color for industry and education.[1] His model was the first widely accepted color order system and along with others, influenced the 1931 Commission Internationale de l'Eclairage (CIE; International Commission of Illumination) in the development of a global color standard for science and industry.

The result was the CIE chromaticity model, which is used to measure hue, value, and chroma. The model also serves as the basis for computer color. Other color systems function as tools for specifying color as ink formulas for the printing industry. This chapter will discuss those systems and others, but first you need to understand how color is perceived at the source.

Color Perception

Color perception is a complex physiological function. Artists do not have to be proficient in their knowledge of human physiology, but they should have a basic understanding of eye and brain functions in the perception of light and form. The retina, the light-sensitive surface lining on the back of the eye, can be compared to film in a movie camera. Within the tissue of the retina are receptors, referred to as rods and cones. Rods detect lightness and darkness, or tones; cones detect color sensations, or hues **4.1**.

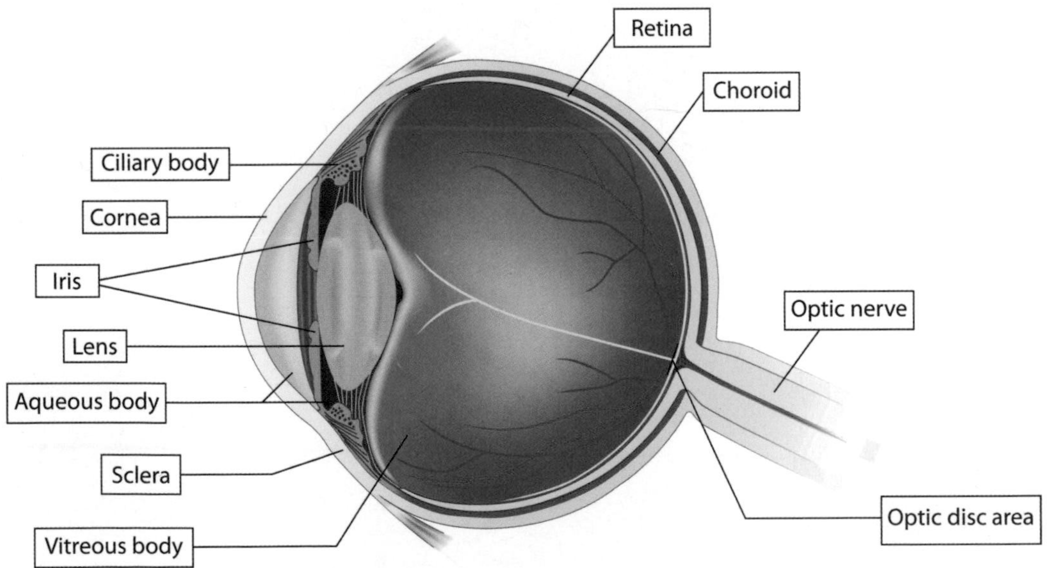

[4.1] The eye sends visual information to the brain for processing via the optic nerve. Some of the features in this diagram are larger than actual scale to illustrate their appearance.
Illustration by Miro Kovacevic/Veer.

[1]See A. H. Munsell, *A Color Notation*, 12th ed. (New Windsor, NY: Munsell Color Co., 1975).

Rays of light illuminate objects in the world of vision and reflect them back to the eye. The eye functions like a lens, which perceives the light information that is then carried to the brain via the optic nerve. Hundreds of thousands of light messages are sent through the optic nerve at the same time. The brain processes the messages to provide you with an apparently seamless view of the world. It is remarkable that the color you perceive on objects is not tangiBle. That is, what you see is not actually color, but vibrating wavelengths that are emitted from the surface of every object. For example, a red ball is reflecting red wavelengths and absorbing all other wavelengths. In fact, the wavelengths being absorbed can be thought of as the perfect light complement to the color wavelength being reflected.

Wavelengths are a form of energy that makes up the visible spectrum. They are part of the electromagnetic field, which also produces microwaves, radio waves, infrared radiation, and X-rays. Each color hue has its own wavelength. Wavelengths also determine a color's intensity, which is dependent on the amount of available light **4.2**. You can observe the intensity of a color diminish in an object by watching it during a sunset or by dimming artificial light.

Additive System

Having discussed how the human eye perceives light, it is appropriate now to introduce the **additive color system**, which is dependent on light **4.3**. The additive system makes all colors visible. It is the color system of white light. The light necessary to see color can come from the sun, from a natural source, or from artificial sources such as incandescent, fluorescent, and halogen light. Artists and designers must pay attention to the source of light in which they work. The different light sources can significantly change the effect of color in a design image.

Isaac Newton may have been the first person to study light. He performed an experiment in 1666 using a prism and a ray of light to discover, in essence, the additive color system. He discovered that white light is composed of a blend of red, green, and blue primary hues. Mixing any two of those colors will yield a secondary hue. Blue and green yield cyan, the complement of red. Blue and red yield magenta, the complement of green. Red and green yield yellow, the complement of blue. Therefore, the secondary hues in the additive system are cyan, magenta, and yellow **4.4**.

Some of the principles of the additive system (for example, green and red mixing to make yellow) run counter to people's intuitive sense of how color works, that is, because they first learned about color in grade school, mixing paint and crayons, which is color pigment.

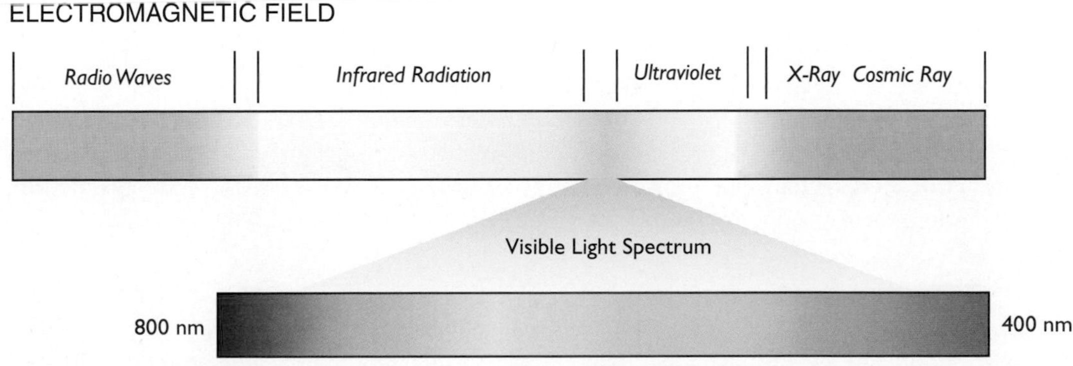

[4.2] The visible light spectrum is a narrow band in the electromagnetic field.
© Cengage Learning 2013.

[4.3] The spectral blended color scheme used for this CD package is transparent, which heightens the effect of color light. The banded color simulates the visual effect of light projected through a prism. It also mimics the design look experienced when visiting the Web site for the Pleats Please clothing line.
Jewel case design by Sayuri Shoji; Client: Issey Miyake, USA.

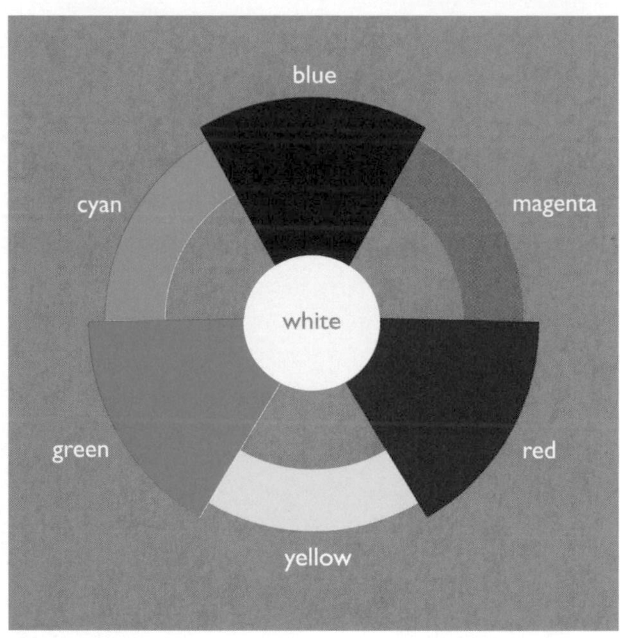

[4.4] Mixing the three primary colors in the additive system yields white (white light). The colors seen here are not as vibrant or luminous as when viewed on a computer monitor.
© Cengage Learning 2013.

Remember that the medium for the additive system is light. It is the system that forms the basis for color photography, film and video, computer imaging, and television. The principle behind all of those media is the projection of a fine blend of red, green, and blue light. Varying the amount of each primary hue projected yields a varying intensity, which re-creates the full spectrum of color in your eye. You can see that effect by looking closely at the edge of a TV screen **4.5**.

Subtractive System

The **subtractive color system** is based on mixing color pigments. As colors are mixed, they render a subtracting effect, which essentially filters the light striking the new color's surface. When two colors are mixed, a new color is created because the mixing has changed its wavelength.

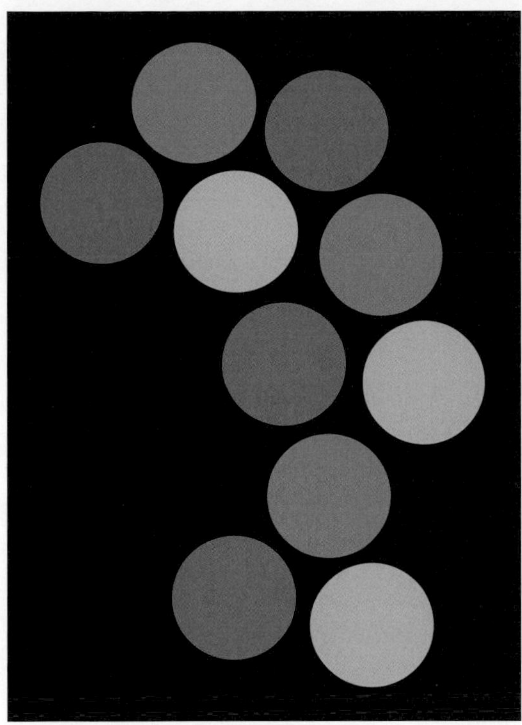

[4.5] Television screens and computer monitors display three separate patterns of red, green, and blue dots called pixels. The pixels form a lattice of individual colors emitting points of light that creates a full color picture. *© Cengage Learning 2013.*

The additive and subtractive systems are interdependent. The secondary hues of the additive system are the primary hues of the subtractive system. Cyan (blue), magenta (red), and yellow are the subtractive primaries. In color printing, cyan, magenta, and yellow are referred to as process primary colors. As they are recombined on a printing press, with the addition of black to enhance value, they re-create the colors known in the visible, natural world. A trip to a printing press facility early in your study of design is a valuable experience that will help you understand these processes and their application to design. In the world of mixing paint and other forms of pigment, the blue and red that are considered primary hues differ from the hues cyan and magenta. Cyan is lighter and leans more toward a blue-green than the primary blue you learned about in school. Magenta is lighter and more pink than the rich reds achieved in most pigments. Yellow is slightly lighter and brighter. Keep in mind that there are many hue shifts within each hue and between sets of hues **4.6**.

Traditional color wheels have been used for centuries to explain and illustrate subtractive color relationships. Johann Wolfgang von Goethe is responsible for developing the first color wheel using blue, red, and yellow as *primary* hues and purple, green, and orange as *secondary* hues **4.7**. Models such as Goethe's are valuable for understanding color relationships.

[4.6] This blend from blue to orange illustrates the many colors that exist between the two hues. Because these hues cross the color wheel, the colors seen in the middle area approach neutral gray. *© Cengage Learning 2013.*

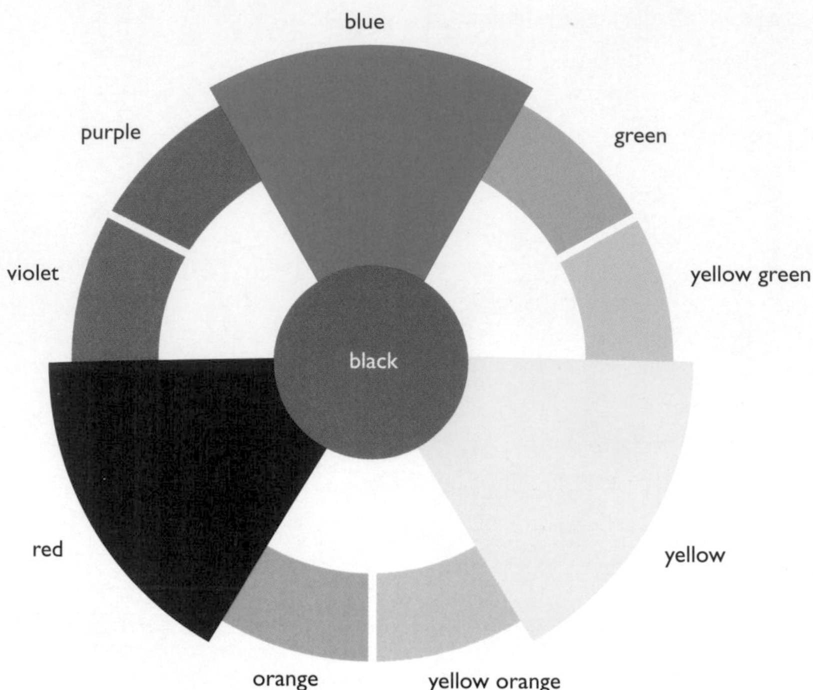

[4.7] This color wheel identifies primary, secondary, and tertiary hues. The black is actually an equal mix of 50 percent cyan, magenta, and yellow.
© Cengage Learning 2013.

But the theory on which the models are based does not always translate well into the practice of mixing color. In Goethe's model, for example, when blue, red, and yellow are mixed together, the result is supposed to yield black. But you know from experience that mixing the primaries makes a grayish-brown color.

The secondary hues of mixing pigments are purple, green, and orange. The purple, green, and orange you get depend on the parent hues used to mix them **4.8**.

Hues found between primary and secondary are called **tertiary**. Red-purple, yellow-orange, and blue-green are examples. In addition to tertiary colors, intermediate hues can be made by mixing secondary and tertiary hues to achieve, theoretically, all of the colors in a spectrum.

Any two primary hues and the colors between them are called **analogous hues**. All primary, secondary, tertiary, and intermediate hues are fully saturated pure color—they are pure in the sense that they contain no white, black, or gray.

Other models have been developed that use a variation of color groupings as primary and secondary hues. Most of the models do a poor job of representing the full color range between

[4.8] Purple on the left and violet on the right are mixed from the same two parent colors—blue and red. Purple has slightly more blue, and violet has slightly more red.
© Cengage Learning 2013.

any set of hues. They present a limited window of the many hues that exist between two colors. That is evident in 4.8, which represents only nine of the limitless number of hues that exist between the primaries. Continuous blends, achieved electronically, better illustrate the range between any two colors **4.9**.

Other aspects of the color wheel limit your comprehension of color relationships. You learn, for example, that the complements are blue and orange, purple and yellow, and red and green, and so they are. But many other hue relationships can be complementary. Turquoise, similar to cyan, and red-orange have a complementary relationship, as does yellow-orange and blue-purple and infinite opposite pairs found on a color wheel.

Color systems such as the color pyramid in **4.10** have added black and white as primary colors.

[4.9] The top color study presents five intermittent steps from green to orange as compared with a continuous blend of the hues below.
© Cengage Learning 2013.

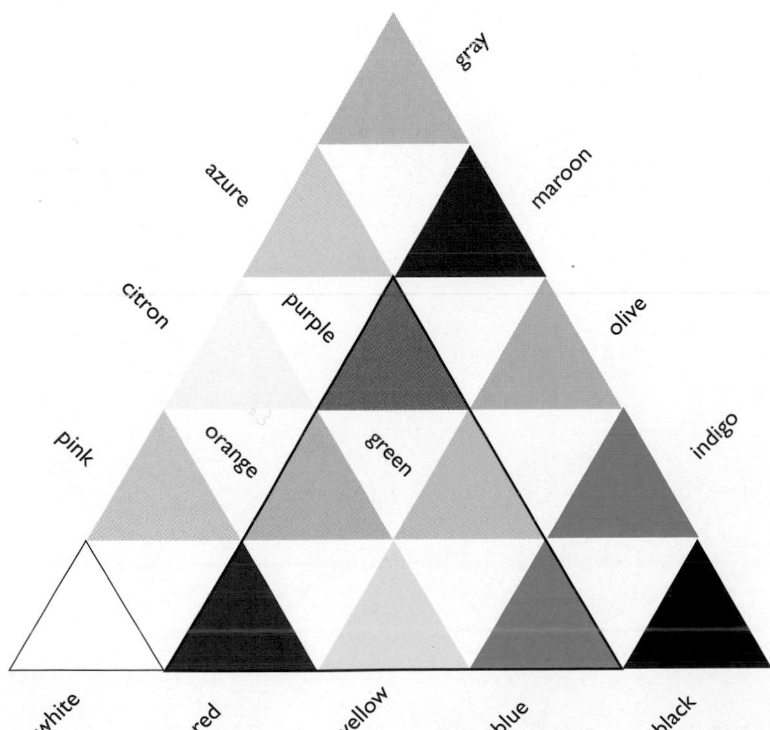

[4.10] The result of this model yields color mixes with expanded color names that are more useful than the simple generic names you probably learned in grade school. Any two colors on the bottom row can be followed diagonally to the color swatch they make. The inner triangle contains the basic primary and secondary hues.
© Cengage Learning 2013.

Remember that simple color names such as blue and green are arbitrary when attempting to specify colors. What one person has in mind when thinking of blue is likely different from another person's perception of blue. That is why color is specified in design by precise systems or by the comparison of color swatches or pigment samples.

Specification Systems Choosing the right color or color scheme is a process of narrowing a general idea of color to more precise color specifications. Designers use a variety of color specification systems from early ideation to final production. A designer may begin with an intuitive idea for a color scheme (for example, yellow, ochre, and blue) as a general concept. Early in the development of the design, markers or cut paper swatches may be used to visualize color for the design. But when it is time to prepare the design for electronic or print production, more accurate color specifications are necessary. Graphic design software offers a variety of color systems that are integrated with the printing industry and digital multimedia design. The electronic color systems can be cross-referenced to swatch books of printed color to ensure color accuracy in print design. Now you will examine the color specification systems individually, beginning with those used in the printing industry.

Printing is based on two types of color systems, CMYK and match systems. **CMYK** is cyan (blue), magenta, yellow, and black. (The K, which stands for key, is used for black, which also distinguishes it from blue.) CMYK is more often referred to as process color or four-color process. Digital or conventional reflective art is prepared by breaking down or separating it into each of the four colors. The separation process filters the cyan, magenta, yellow, and black, one at a time. Then each separation is converted to a dot pattern that is recorded onto metal plates.

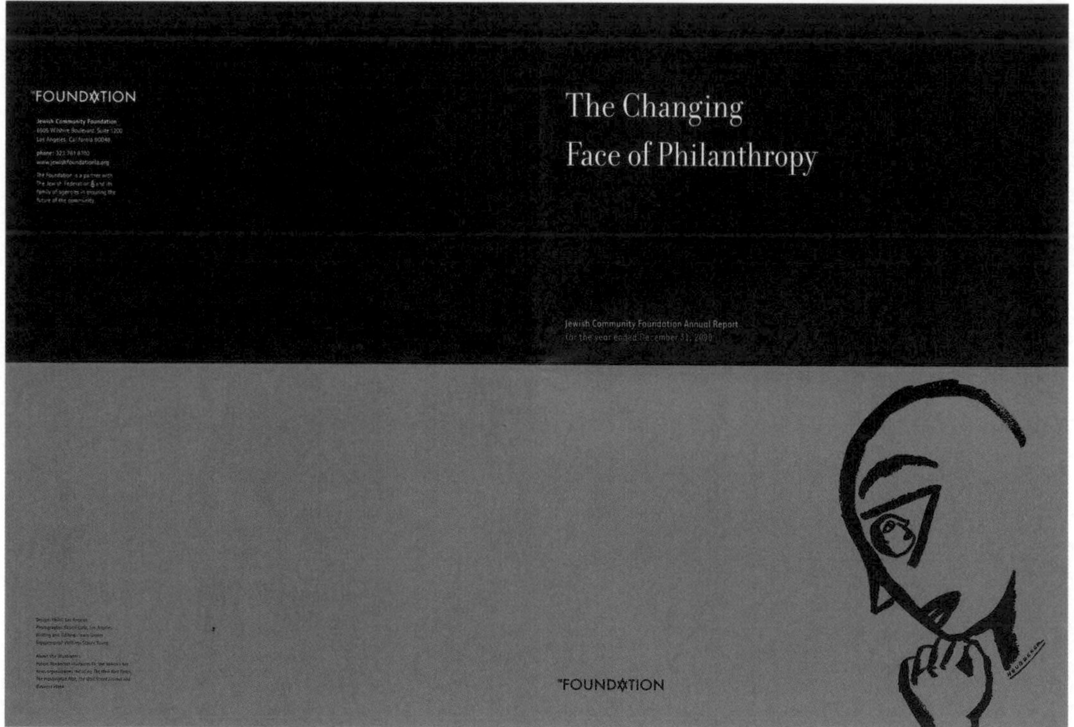

[4.11] Two match colors, orange and black, constitute the printed color in this annual report design. The white type is the color of the paper. When one color is printed in the area of another, it is referred to as reversed out or knocked out. The black creates a sense of confinement to the lower half of the composition.
Annual report design by KBDA.

The four plates are then fastened to drums located at four separate stations on a four-color printing press. Sheets of paper are run through the press, receiving an impression of ink from the plate at each station. The four colors are printed on top of each other, recombined to reproduce the color in the original design. Four-color process is used when the original art is continuous or blended tones.

Match systems are used when the color is solid and isolated within shapes or backgrounds **4.11**. As the name suggests, desired color areas in the original design are matched to an ink formula. Those formulas are selected from a book that presents a printed swatch accompanied by a number. The number is provided to a printer, and the corresponding ink formula is used to print only those areas specified. The color numbering system that is the worldwide industry standard is the PANTONE MATCHING SYSTEM (PMS) **4.12**. Other systems include TRUMATCH, TOYO, and Focaltone. Those and other similar systems work the same way PANTONE does **4.13**. All of the color systems are generally available for specifying color in electronic media. You may be familiar with some of the systems if you have used graphic software.

PANTONE®

PANTONE 7457 C ::
3 pts PANTONE Pro. Blue 1.2
⅝ pts PANTONE Ref. Blue .25
⅛ pts PANTONE Black .05
246¼ pts PANTONE Trans.Wt. 98.5

PANTONE 7458 C ::
1⅝ pts PANTONE Pro. Blue 9.0
⅜ pts PANTONE Ref. Blue 2.1
¼ pts PANTONE Black 1.4
15⅝ pts PANTONE Trans.Wt. 87.5

PANTONE 7459 C ::
4⅞ pts PANTONE Pro. Blue 18.0
1⅛ pts PANTONE Ref. Blue 4.2
¾ pt PANTONE Black 2.8
20¼ pts PANTONE Trans.Wt. 75.0

PANTONE 7460 C ::
15⅝ pts PANTONE Pro. Blue 90.6
1⅝ pts PANTONE Green 9.4

PANTONE 7461 C ::
2⅞ pts PANTONE Ref. blue 8.5
4⅛ pts PANTONE Pro. Blue 16.5
¼ pt PANTONE Black 1.0
18½ pts PANTONE Trans.Wt. 74.0

PANTONE 7462 C ::
2¾ pts PANTONE Yellow 6.2
1⅞ pts PANTONE Rub. Red 4.2
15⅞ pts PANTONE Ref. Blue 35.5
24⅛ pts PANTONE Trans.Wt. 54.1

PANTONE 7463 C ::
2¼ pts PANTONE Yellow 5.0
26⅜ pts PANTONE Ref. Blue 58.0
7¾ pts PANTONE Black 17.0
9⅛ pts PANTONE Trans.Wt. 20.0

pt(s) = part(s)
C = Coated Paper
:: = Achievable in CMYK

100 C

[4.12] Match color, also called a special color, can be specified for area color fill in typography, graphic elements, and borders. Each swatch provides the color number (the *u* indicates uncoated paper) and the ink formula prepared by a printer.
© Cengage Learning 2013.

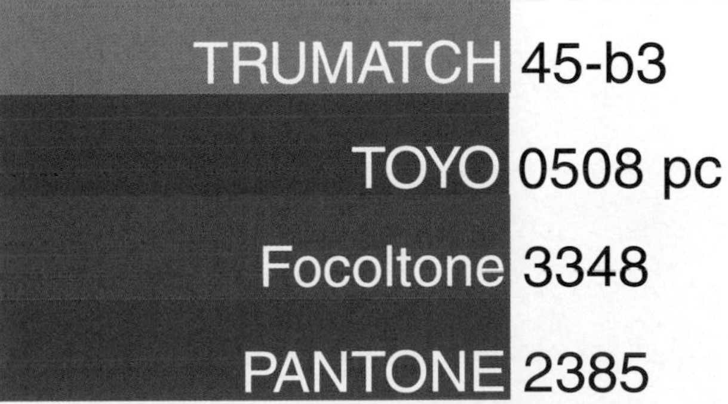

[4.13] These four violet-purple hues were specified from swatch libraries in Adobe Illustrator.
© Cengage Learning 2013.

> **Production Tip**
>
> The match color system most commonly used in offset printing is the PANTONE system. Specifying a PANTONE match color by its number (PMS XXXX) ensures that a printer will achieve an exact match to the swatch book color. Choosing a PANTONE match color is appropriate when an exact match is essential, such as a corporate color for a logo. Because printing four-color jobs generally costs more than running one to three colors on press, PANTONE match colors are also used when printing one- to three-color jobs.

Design and imagery that are created and produced digitally can be prepared in any of the systems mentioned previously. Most design software provides the CMYK system by default.

Colors often appear different on a computer monitor compared to when they are printed. That is because they differ in the way they are viewed. Colors can be specified and cross-referenced to a printed swatch to ensure color integrity when converted from digital to printed form.

It is important to note that match colors are more vibrant than CMYK process color because there are limits to what the CMYK mixes can achieve. It is particularly evident in blues and purples, some deep reds, and, of course, fluorescent colors. But for the most part, CMYK does a good job of re-creating a full color range. To clarify, CMYK and match systems are used in printing. Both systems are available in digital software and in printed swatch books for specifying color.

Color used for multimedia design or Web design requires the red, green, and blue (RGB) system. RGB is the primary hue system of light. Any media venue that relies on projected light, such as photography, DVD, video games, computer and television monitors, and film, depends on RGB. The RGB system is the default palette for most photo- and multimedia-based graphic software. Each hue—red, green, and blue—can be adjusted in 1-point increments of brightness from 0 to 255. Because there is no translation of color from digital light to printed ink, what is seen on the screen is generally what you get. The variance occurs between the designer's monitor and the user's monitor or projection screens.

Designing for the Web has a specific color limitation. Web graphics are often designed on Mac systems and consumed on PC systems. For the color to be consistent from one platform to another, the hexadecimal system was developed. There are 216 common colors derived from the system that constitute the Web palette. Most Web software provides the colors from the hexadecimal system. RGB colors can be used and converted to this system **4.14**. RGB colors are brighter than CMYK colors—projected light is luminous; pigments are reflective.

You can see the difference by converting color from RGB to CMYK in electronic design. Most software provides an option to convert color in a document from one color system to another and from color to gray scale.

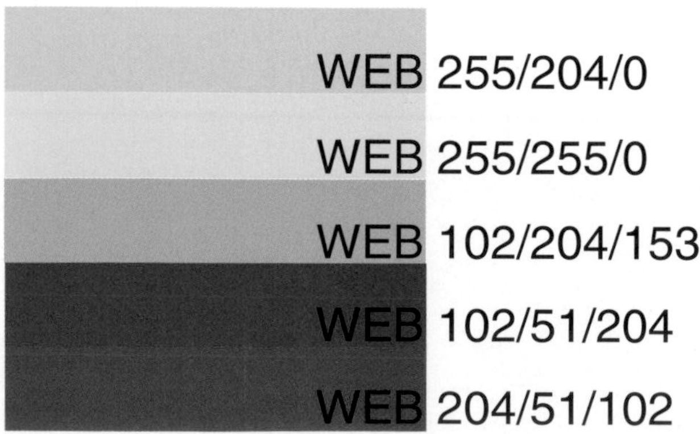

[4.14] The hexadecimal color system is intended specifically for Web design. The range of color choices seems limited but actually provides a decent palette. By limiting the palette, the amount of digital information to be processed is manageable, which allows Web pages to open more quickly. This system is set up in increments of 51 units each of RGB. *© Cengage Learning 2013.*

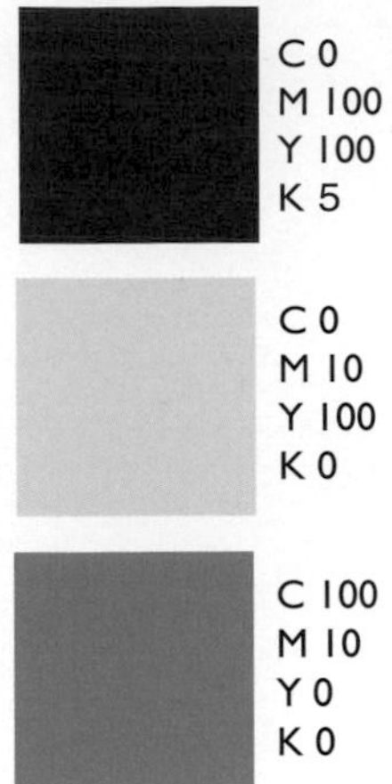

[4.15] Versions of the subtractive primary hues are accompanied by the CMYK percentages for each.

THE LANGUAGE OF COLOR

The language of color has evolved from research in theory, technology, and the practice of design. Sometimes the terms speak about specific aspects of color; sometimes color speaks its own language—with symbolic, cultural, and psychological meaning. This section will explore and define color terminology in words and images by offering color analyses of professional design.

Color Terminology

Hue is the same as color. It is the inherent color referred to by a name or formula. You should learn as many color names as possible. You also would find it beneficial to learn which CMYK percentages are used to build basic primary and secondary hues **4.15**.

Saturation refers to the purity of a color. Pure hues that are fully saturated are at their highest level of intensity **4.16**. Intensity corresponds approximately to the value of primary and secondary hues. The lighter hues, yellow and orange, are more intense than the darker hues, blue and purple. Red and green have similar values and fall in between.

Adding black, white, or midtones contaminates a pure hue and affects the intensity level **4.17**. When black or gray is introduced, pure hues immediately lose their brilliance. The smallest amount of black mixed with yellow dulls the impact of yellow, changing it to a somber green. Black has a similar effect with each of the primary and secondary hues—it changes their color name: red to maroon, green to olive drab, blue to indigo, orange to sienna, and purple to puce. Gray is not as profound but has a similar effect, making the hues murky. White has a lively effect on blue and purple as it brings them out of the dark value range.

Chroma is similar to saturation. Munsell describes chroma as the amount of colorant present in a pigment.[2] The more colorant, the more saturated the hue. There is a subtle distinction between saturation and chroma. The former is about dulling a pure hue by adding gray tones, and the latter is about the presence of hue in a pigment. The CMYK tool selector in graphics software illustrates the concept of chroma. The lower the percentage, the less color presence; the higher the percentage, the higher the color presence. It is not really a matter of adding white at all.

[2] Ibid.

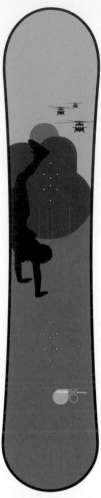

[4.16] In these snowboard graphics, orange is the brightest of the colors. The figure in the board on the left is silhouetted by the red and blue background areas that are more saturated; that is, they contain more of their inherent hue but are not as bright. The somber green in the right board has lost a significant amount of saturation, because of the presence of black in the color.
Graphics by Jager Di Paola Kemp.

[4.17] The photographic imagery in this design is practically colorless umber tones. They lend an eclectic, retro look to the design and exist in stark contrast to the highly saturated red-orange colors in the type and border graphics.
Self promotion design by Brian Murray.

Value is lightness or darkness. Value can exist without color in grays, black, and white; but it also is present in colors. Each hue has a value that can be compared with gray tones **4.18a**. Knowing the value of the basic hues can help in choosing a color scheme. The complements, for example, offer interesting value relationships. Red and green are very similar in value, so they contrast only in their hue. Purple and yellow have the highest value contrast of any set of complements **4.18b**.

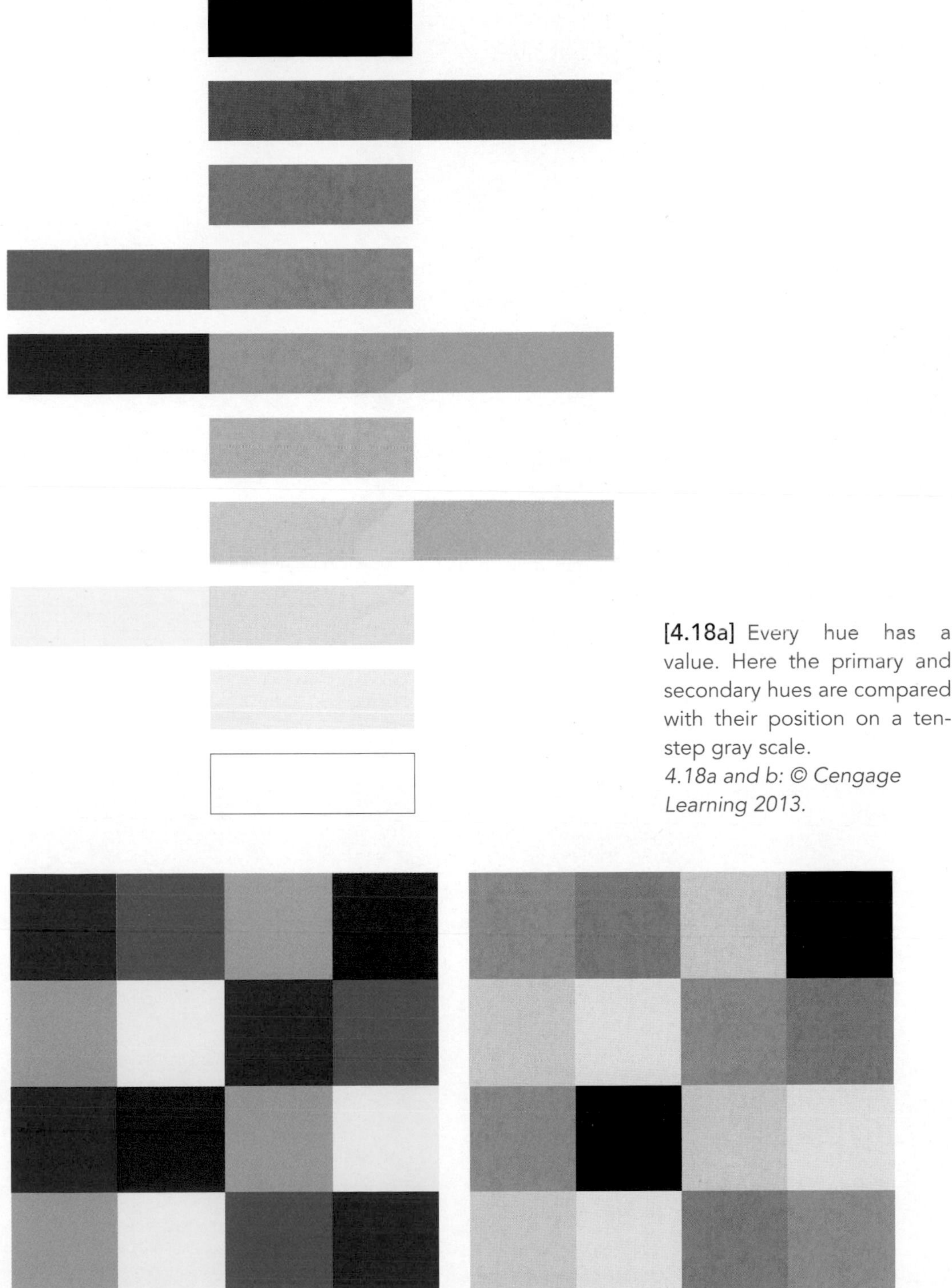

[4.18a] Every hue has a value. Here the primary and secondary hues are compared with their position on a ten-step gray scale.
4.18a and b: © Cengage Learning 2013.

[4.18b] A checkerboard arrangement of four colors is translated to corresponding gray values.

Tint is adding white to a pure hue. As most hues are tinted or lightened with white, they also are made brighter. White yields new color names when mixed with red, purple, yellow, and blue. The results are pink, lavender, citron, and azure, respectively **4.19**. Orange and green are made brighter as more white is added to each, but they hold their color integrity. A high ratio of white added to the hues yields a category of colors referred to as pastels **4.20**.

Shade is the mix of black with a color. The term *shade* is often misused to describe hue. A shade of blue is a mix of blue and black, not a variation in its hue. Adding black to the hues yields dramatic color changes. In small amounts, black has an insidious effect on yellow and

[4.19] The arrangement of cups glazed in tinted colors dominates this photo design. These tints are deeper in color than pastels, which produces an appetizing and festive color scheme. *Exhibition catalog by Chronicle Books.*

C/0
M/10
Y/5
K/0

C /0
M/10
Y/15
K/0

C/0
M/0
Y/25
K/0

C/15
M/0
Y/25
K/0

C/20
M/0
Y/0
K/0

C/12
M/12
Y/0
K/0

[4.20] This arrangement of primary and secondary hues is tinted to pastels. CMYK percentages indicate the negligible quantities of actual color in each.
© Cengage Learning 2013.

orange. But in higher proportions, black produces handsome, deep earth tones in these hues. Blue, green, and purple seem to be most compatible with black, holding their color identity as they are mixed **4.21**.

Tones are grays, also referred to as midtones. **Achromatic gray** is mixed from black and white and is the same as a tone. Tones run the range from light to dark values in the gray scale. Grays deaden the brilliance of pure hues. Darker grays have a similar effect on hues as black, and lighter grays have a similar effect on hues as white. Tones mixed with yellow produce rich, colorful earth browns that resemble ochre and umber. When tones are added to hues that match them in value, you can observe an absolute shift in saturation without a shift in value **4.22**.

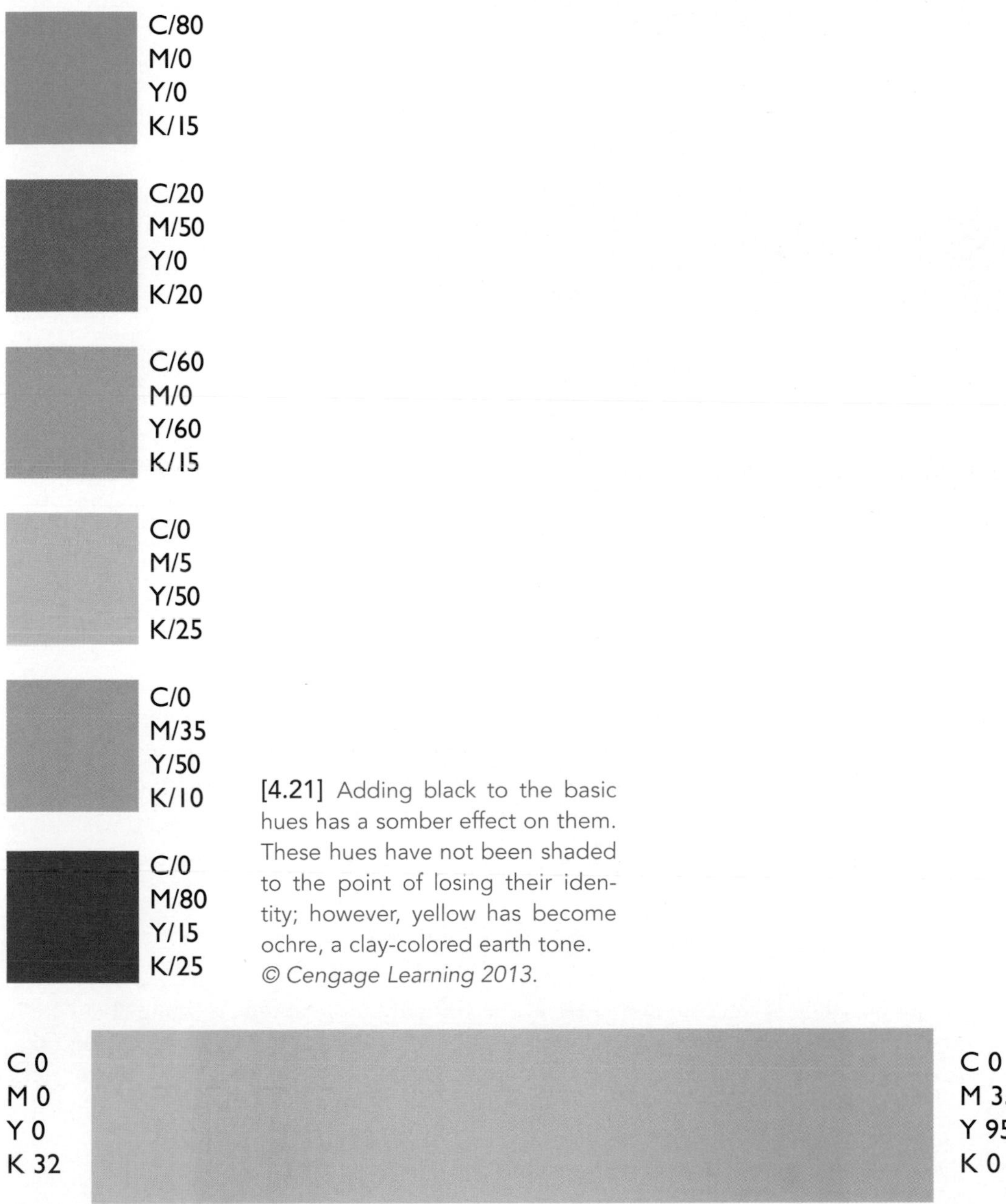

[4.21] Adding black to the basic hues has a somber effect on them. These hues have not been shaded to the point of losing their identity; however, yellow has become ochre, a clay-colored earth tone.
© Cengage Learning 2013.

[4.22] The orange and gray match in value, demonstrating the effect of a midtone as it blends to a pure hue.
© Cengage Learning 2013.

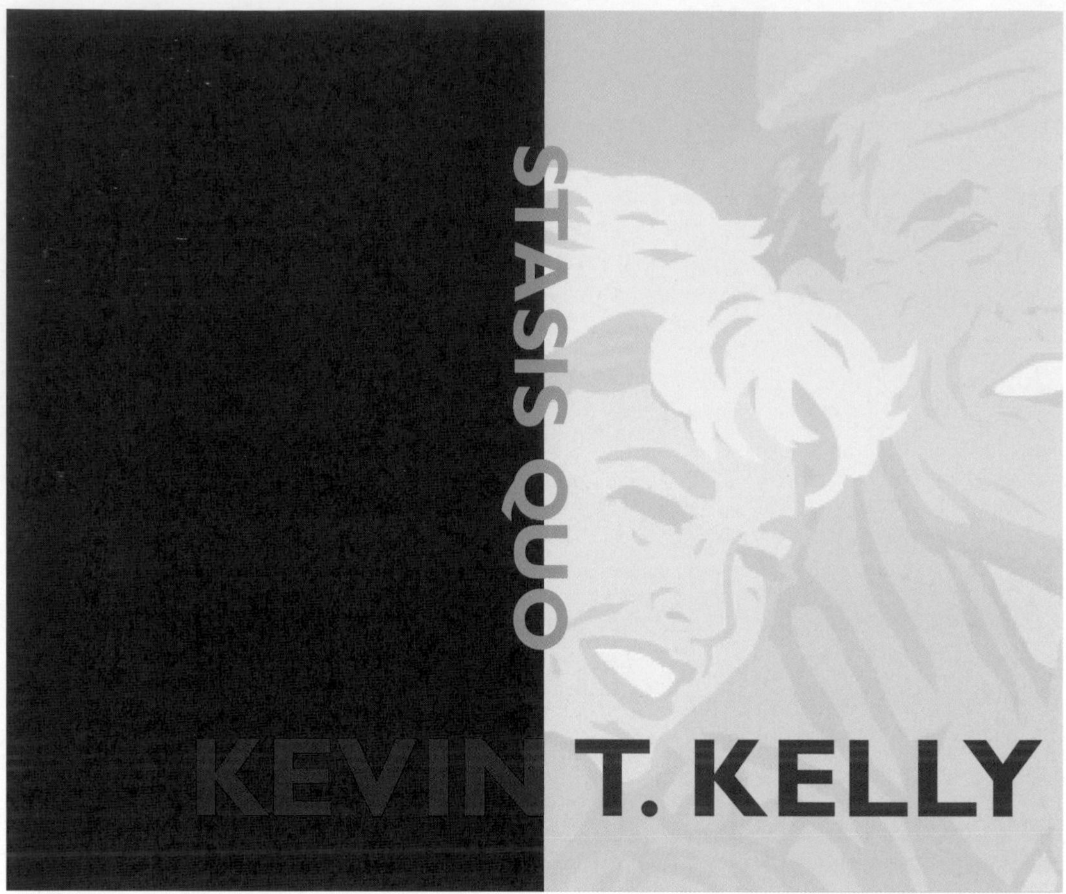

[4.23] The graphic image used on the right half of this cover is a detail from a larger work by the artist whose work is featured in the catalog. The monochromatic image was cropped from the original full-color image and digitally converted from full color using a duotone filter.
Exhibition catalog cover by Mark Thomas.

Monochromatic is a single color mixed with tints, shades, or tones. In printing, a monochromatic color scheme can be attained with a process called *duotone*, which is a gray scale and one hue. Monochromatic color schemes can effectively simulate the presence of other hues by virtue of the effect that tints, shades, and tones have on individual colors **4.23**.

THEORY AND INTERACTION

Anyone serious about a career in the visual arts needs to invest some time learning about color theories and understanding their impact on practical application. Of all of the color concepts, two theories profoundly and commonly affect the color decisions that designers make every day. Knowing those two theories and their applications will help you order and manage color decisions artistically and intellectually.

The first theory is that color can be examined with regard to a set of contrasts. In particular are the seven contrasts explored and defined by Johannes Itten.[3] The second theory advances the idea that the appearance of a color depends on the influence or interaction it has with

[3]See J. Itten, *The Elements of Color* (New York: John Wiley & Sons, 1970).

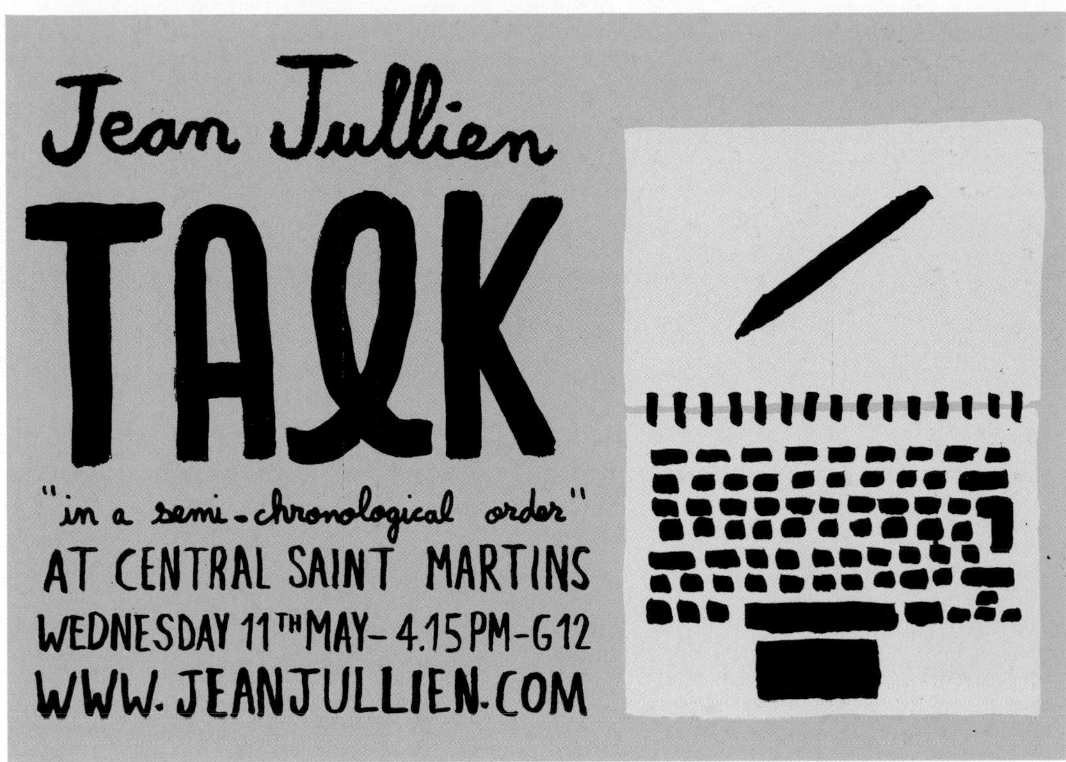

[4.24] The spontaneous, handwritten quality of the type in this poster communicates a sense of personal expression and immediacy. The black-and-yellow color scheme gives it a high degree of visibility. *Poster design by Jean Jullien.*

surrounding or adjacent colors. That theory is thoroughly explored by Josef Albers.[4] This chapter will examine both theories and their application to design.

Much of what has already been presented about color in this chapter lays the groundwork for a discussion of Itten's seven contrasts: value, hue, saturation, complement, temperature, size, and simultaneous contrast.

Contrast of value is the most basic color relationship. Designers often work in black and white by necessity or aesthetic choice. Black-and-white imagery offers a high degree of contrast surpassed for legibility contrast only by Black and yellow, the color choice for many publications and signs **4.24**.

As has been discussed, each of the hues has a value. Some combinations of pure hues have little value contrast. For example, orange, green, and red are very similar, whereas purple, yellow, and green have a broader value range. Contrast of hue is what distinguishes one color from another **4.25**. Often logos, advertisements, and brands need to function in black and white and in color. When a color image relies exclusively on contrast of hue, it is ineffective when translated to black and white.

Contrast of saturation is a juxtaposition of hues with varying purity. Adjusting the value of pure hues can be done by adding only white, black, or gray. To make purple lighter, you need to add white or light gray. In doing so, you lighten the color and weaken its saturation. Saturated colors tend to appear closer compared with weak colors, which recede. Using a color scheme of saturated to weaker hues creates depth through the effect of atmospheric perspective **4.26**.

[4]See J. Albers, *Interaction of Color* (New Haven, CT: Yale University Press, 1963).

[4.25] The immediate response to this illustrated design is the bold use of color. The bold energy is achieved by using a variety of saturated, contrasting hues. The playful quality of the illustration is supported by the variety of colors.
Phone card design by Metzler & Associates.

[4.26] Landscape photographs are good examples of aerial perspective. Colors weaken or become less saturated as they recede into space, losing their contrast to surrounding shapes.
Photograph by Evan MacVeigh.

A **complementary** contrast is based on any two hues directly opposed on the color wheel. In some ways, true complements exist only in theory, especially with regard to pigments.

The requirements for a true, perfect complement is that, when mixed, they produce an absolute neutral **4.27**.

A complement is composed of a precise mix of two primaries in opposition to the remaining primary; for example, green (yellow and blue) and red. Complementary contrast is the simplest relationship for the basis of a color scheme. The relationship is curious because complements are vivid opposites that, when placed adjacent to one another, bring out the full potential of each **4.28**.

Contrast of temperature is the relative warm-cold relationship between hues. Color temperature is psychologically linked to conditions in nature—the hot yellow-orange of the sun, the cool green grass, the cold blue sky, or the warm reds and oranges of autumn leaves. It is

[4.27] A complementary blend of blue-purple and yellow illustrates the difficulty in achieving a true complementary relationship in pigments. The area in the center of the blend (chromatic gray) is influenced by the parent colors, making it difficult to identify an absolute neutral.
© Cengage Learning 2013.

[4.28] Complements such as this orange-red/blue-purple color scheme produce a high-contrast energy that is fitting for the subject.
Magazine spread design by Barbara Reyes and Peter Yates; illustration by Phil Mucci.

generally accepted that red, orange, and yellow are warm colors and blue, green, and purple are cool colors.

Warm colors advance and cool colors recede, again taking their cues from nature. Within any hue range of analogous colors, a relative shift between warm and cool can be observed **4.29**. It is worth noting that most color pairs contain aspects of more than one contrast effect.

[4.29] All of the colors in this study are considered warm. But when the parent colors are compared, a relative shift in temperature can be seen. The magenta-red is relatively cooler than the orange. *© Cengage Learning 2013.*

Blue and orange are complements. They differ in value and present a warm-cool contrast. If you want to limit the coexistence of contrasts, adjust colors with regard to their complementary nature, value, or temperature **4.30**.

Contrast of extension is the comparison of quantities of color. It is a judgment of how much of one color compared to another color is needed to achieve harmony or balance. In the contrast in **4.31**, the design mantra coined by Mies van der Rohe, "less is more," can be vividly observed.

Often the impact and intensity of smaller color elements are more profound than larger elements. Certain color combinations cause color vibrations because of a combination of their size and value. The visual effect causes certain colors to expand beyond their edges **4.32**.

Other color relationships cause hues to remain contained within their edges; for example, a black square in a yellow color field.

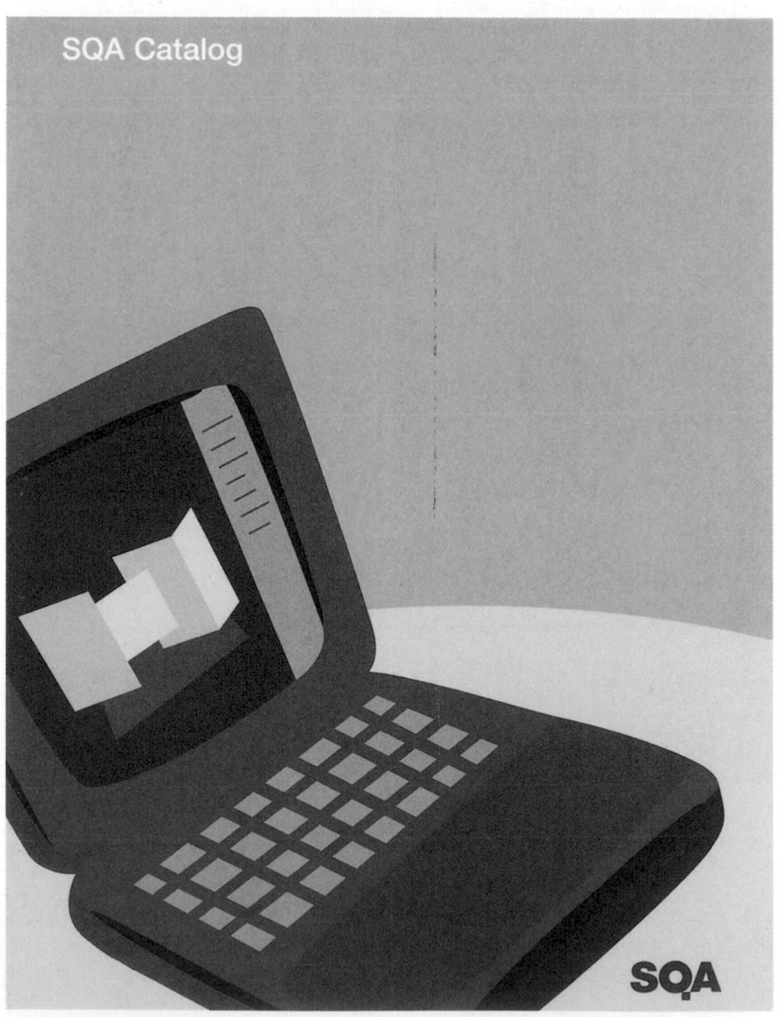

[4.30] The blue-orange color scheme is both complementary and contrasting in temperature. *Image courtesy of Herman Miller Inc.*

[4.31] The smaller percentage of the green area, contrasted by the reds and oranges, reinforces the scale of the dinosaur in the foreground, helping the dinosaur to dominate the composition.
Poster design by Ames Design.

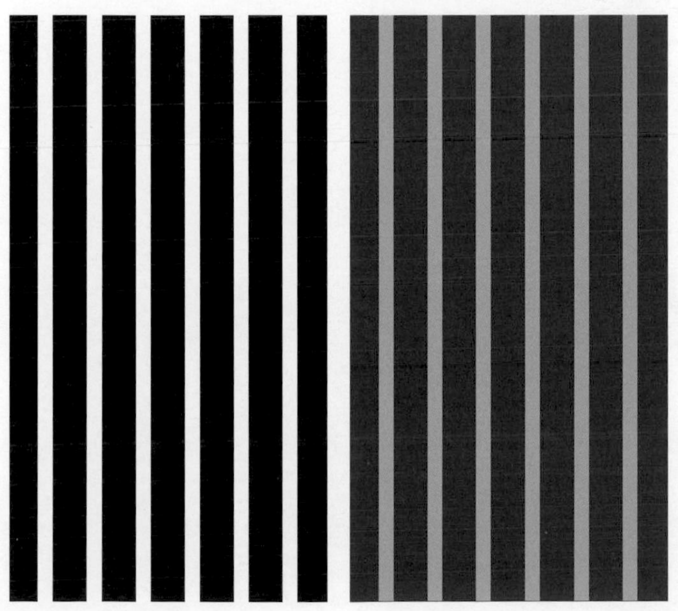

[4.32] In this figure, the black and red stripes are physically equal in size, as are the white and green stripes. Yet the black appears wider than the red, and the white appears wider than the green. This optical effect is due to the nature of the color relationships. The red-green study shows a relationship in which the edges dissolve because the colors are complements that have a similar value. Black strives optically to stay contained within its edges, and white tends to expand optically outside its edges.
© Cengage Learning 2013.

Simultaneous contrast is perhaps the most subtle and subjective of the seven contrasts—no doubt because the phenomenon is dependent literally on the "eye of the beholder." The eye is ever searching for color harmony through color complements. When a complement is not present, the eye physically attempts to provide one. That occurs as an optical illusion, but it affects the way individuals process color. There are numerous figures that effectively illustrate this phenomenon.

It can be experienced by staring at a color that "burns" itself onto the retina of the eye. Looking away at a neutral or white space produces the sensations of the opposing complement **4.33**. Simultaneous contrast also occurs in color relationships in which the interaction of colors affects how people perceive them **4.34**.

No color can exist in nature or visual art in a vacuum. As just discussed, gazing at a single color field or a deep blue sky finds the eye compulsively searching for complementary resolution.

[4.33] Stare at the center of the illustration for 30 seconds. Move your eye over to the dot to the right and blink quickly. You should see the black and white reversed and flashes of cyan in the red areas.
Card announcement design by Kathleen Burch and Michael Bortolos.

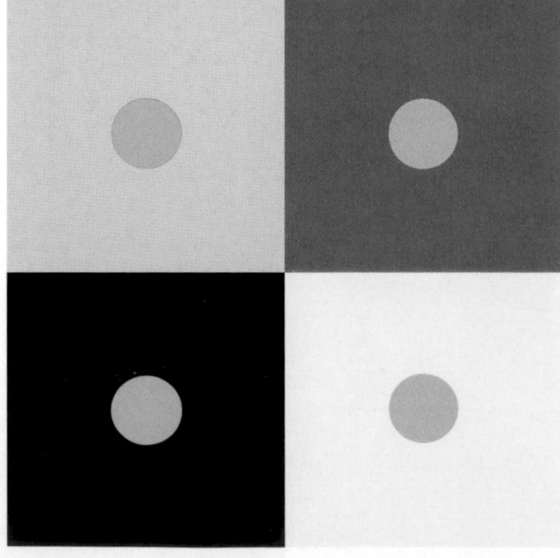

[4.34] Notice the significant change in the green circle as it is influenced by the four different-colored squares.
© Cengage Learning 2013.

No one has advanced the understanding of color influences and optical deception more than Albers.[5] His work is an illustrated application of the seven contrasts as they interact, producing remarkable effects. Albers conducted most of his investigations using painted color and screen prints. Geometric figures and shapes are arranged in studies that function as basic design compositions. They lend themselves naturally to electronic media. The studies can be easily replicated and worked using digital color.

The premise for the studies is that color creates a context and that controlling the color environment affects the perception of the color. To make green look greener, place it in a red color field. To make a color appear darker, place it in a lighter context.

Effective color decisions in design are critically dependent on managing color interaction. The essence of the color interactions demonstrates how one color can change its complexion to appear as two, how two colors can be independently influenced to appear as the same, or how color identity can be affected by surrounding colors **4.35**.

The ability to achieve the effect depends on the color choices and the size or amount of color undergoing change. At some point, as the size area of a color increases, it exerts its identity over the influence of its surroundings **4.36**.

Applying the knowledge found in color contrasts and color interaction can enhance figure-ground relationships, make type more legible, create harmony and balance, and enhance visual depth in design compositions **4.37**.

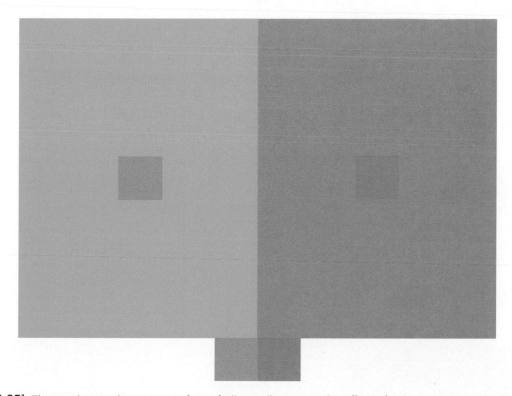

[4.35] This study is in the manner of Josef Albers, illustrating the effect of color interaction, making two different colors appear as the same color due to the influence of the background color fields.

[5]Ibid.

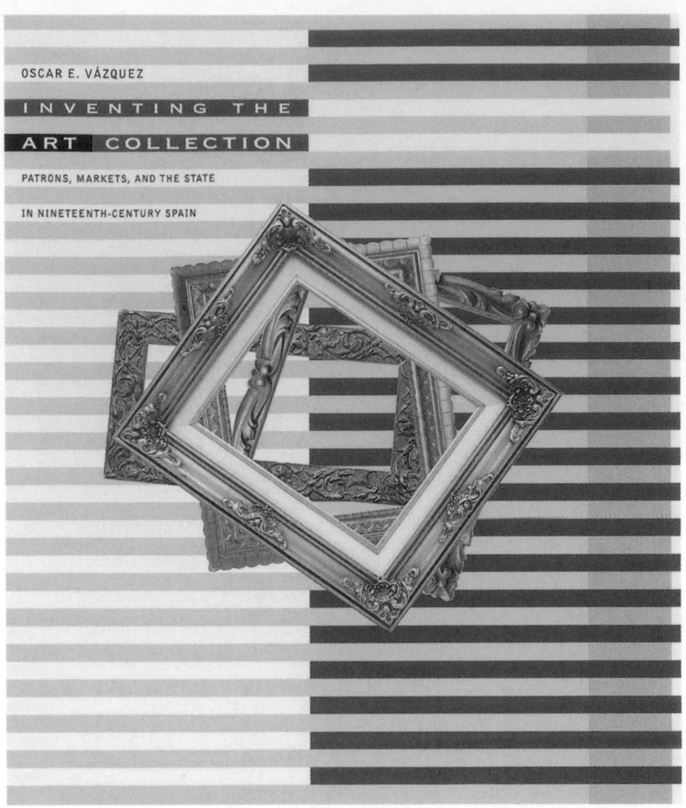

[4.36] The complexion of the yellow in this design is profoundly different since white and red independently influence it.
Book jacket design by Jennifer Norton, Jerry King Musser.

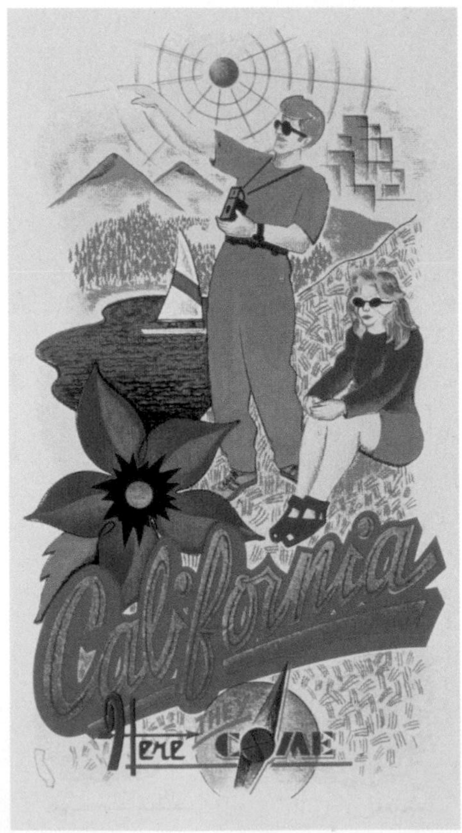

[4.37] The visual hierarchy and communication in this poster are enhanced by the color scheme. It contains some classic color devices, such as warm colors advancing and cool colors receding. It uses a complementary palette and strives for high legibility in the type, using effective color contrast.
Poster design by Sayles Graphic Design.

COLOR PSYCHOLOGY

Psychology plays an essential role in deciphering the meaning of color in visual communication. Color psychology involves the affective nature of color—how color makes a person feel. This is a powerful dimension of color in all of the visual arts. Color psychology encompasses symbolic and cultural associations that also affect how individuals feel about certain colors **4.38**. Color has been associated with the sounds of musical instruments, the energy centers of the body, basic shapes, musical notes, and basic emotional responses. Color is more emotional and subjective than intellectual and objective. In fact, the standard color wheel was developed more from views of human perception and psychological response to color than any scientific theory.

The trick is to learn how to use color psychology as a determinant in making effective color decisions. Each of the basic colors embodies a distinctive set of associations that can be translated into words. Knowing those associations will inform your color choices. Now you will examine some of the basic hues with regard to their universal meanings.

Purple is royal, sophisticated, and cultivated; because of its deep value, it has an enigmatic quality **4.39**. It is associated with valor, as in the Purple Heart. It is a hue that is associated with distinctive aromas derived from fruits such as plums, grapes, and berries. Purple can have ominous qualities especially when mixed with gray or black.

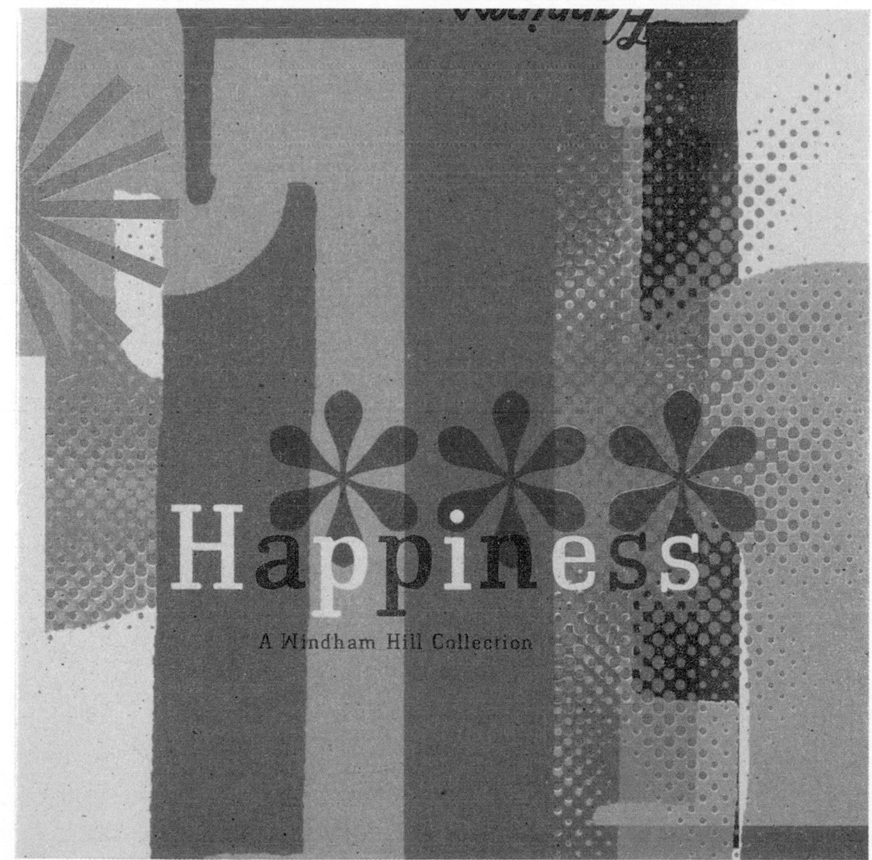

[4.38] The vibrant, whimsical color scheme in this CD design communicates the same message with the color as it does in word.
CD designs by Stoltze Design.

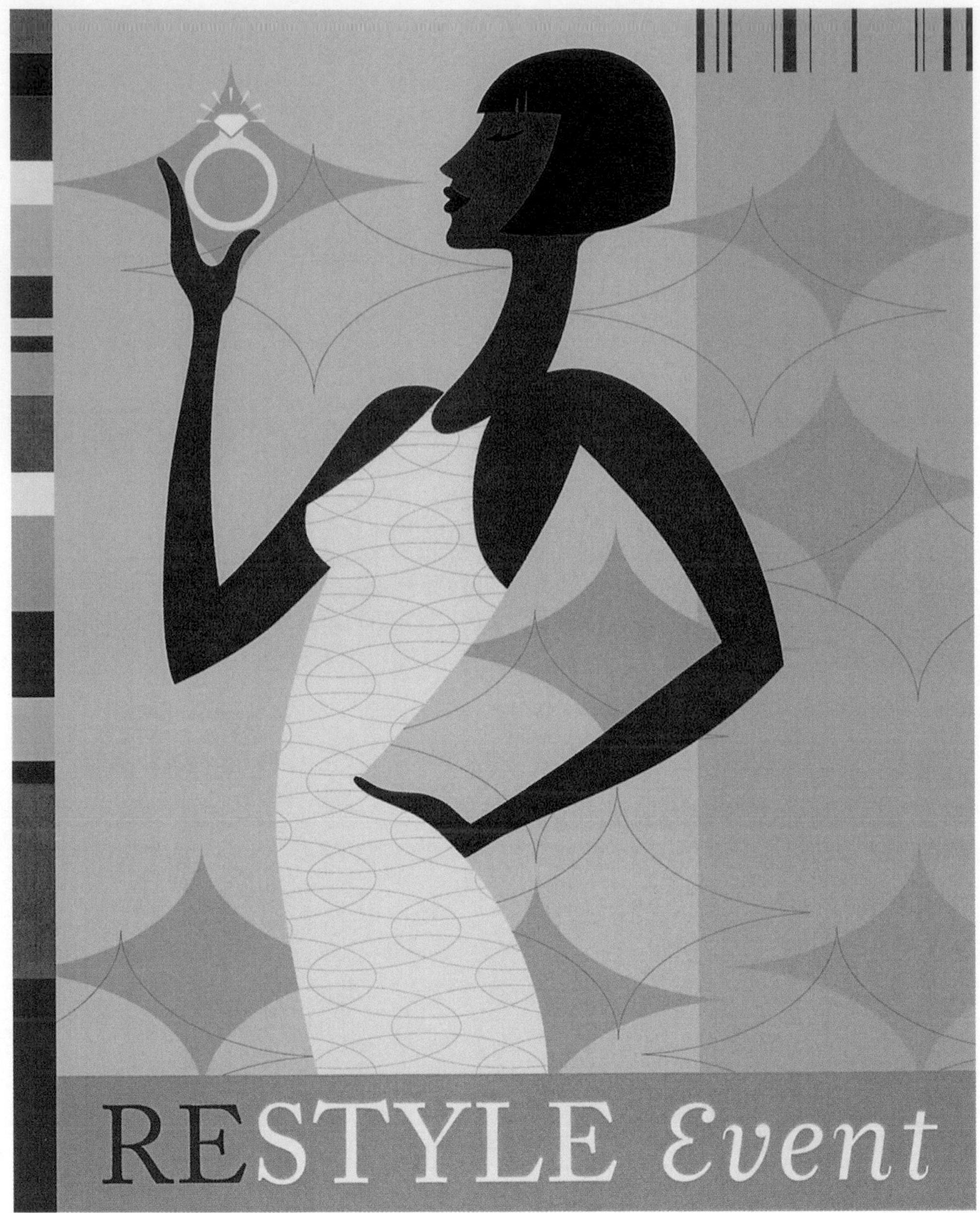

[4.39] *Poster design by Design Ranch.*

Blue is expansive, serene, and reliable, as in "true blue." It is used extensively in business as a color for banks and brokerage firms. In the financial marketplace, blue conveys a sense of reliability and trust to consumers. The sky and water are the color's most familiar associations. Psychologically speaking, when a person is blue, she is sad, lonely, or depressed **4.40**. In most surveys, blue is the top pick for favorite color.

[4.40] *Poster design by Mires Design.*

Green is growth, nature, and life-giving. Forests, fields, and farms are dominated by green. On the other hand, it also is the color of money, as in greenback. Green has been studied as the easiest of all colors to live with, especially as a shade or a tint. When it leans toward blue, it becomes aqua, the color of the sea in tropical environments **4.41**.

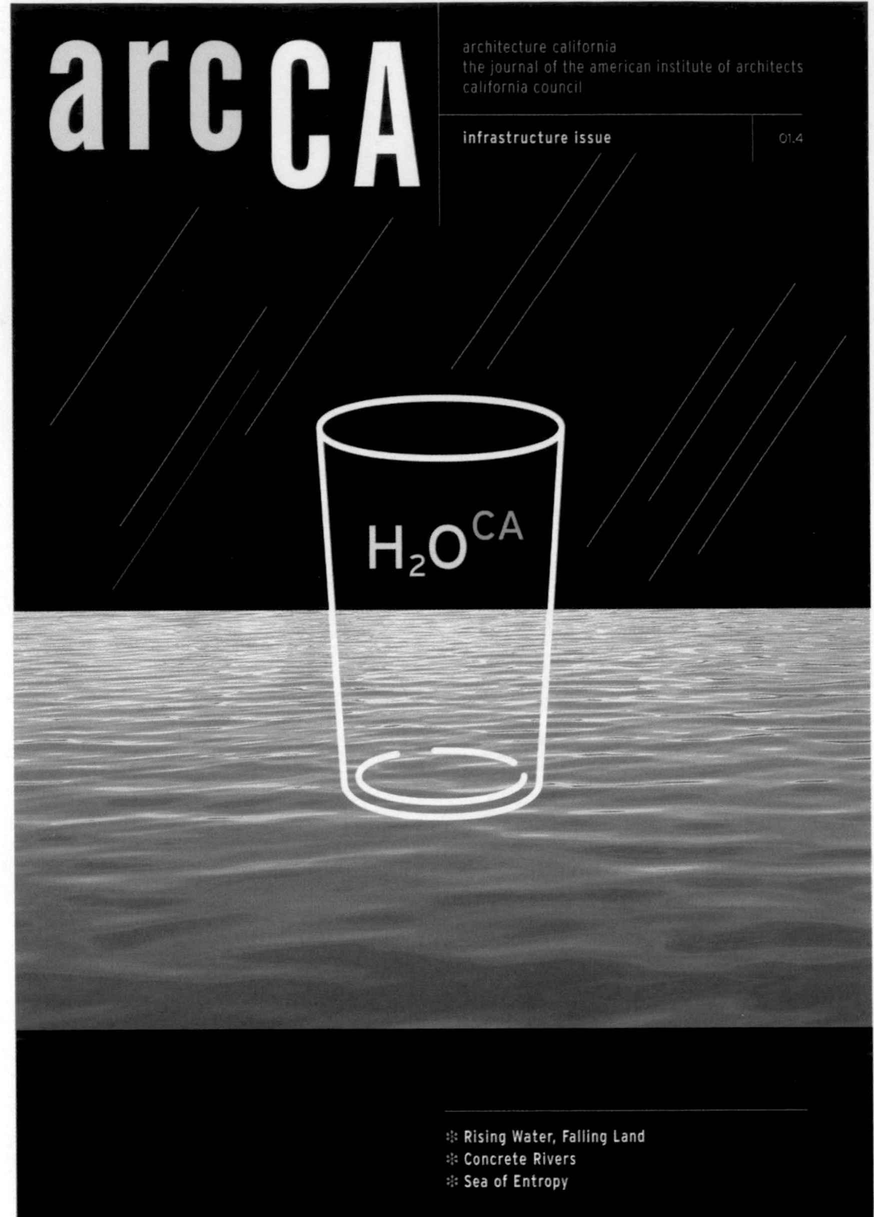

[4.41] *Design by Bob Aufuldish, Aufuldish & Warinner.*

Yellow is sunlight, citrus, and energy. It is often associated with gold and, subsequently, wealth. It suggests intelligence and reason. As was mentioned earlier, yellow and black are the highest color contrast combination. Yellow can be acidic in its pure form, but appealing with the addition of a small amount of red. It is a fragile color. Small amounts of any other hue, black or gray, have a significant effect on yellow **4.42**.

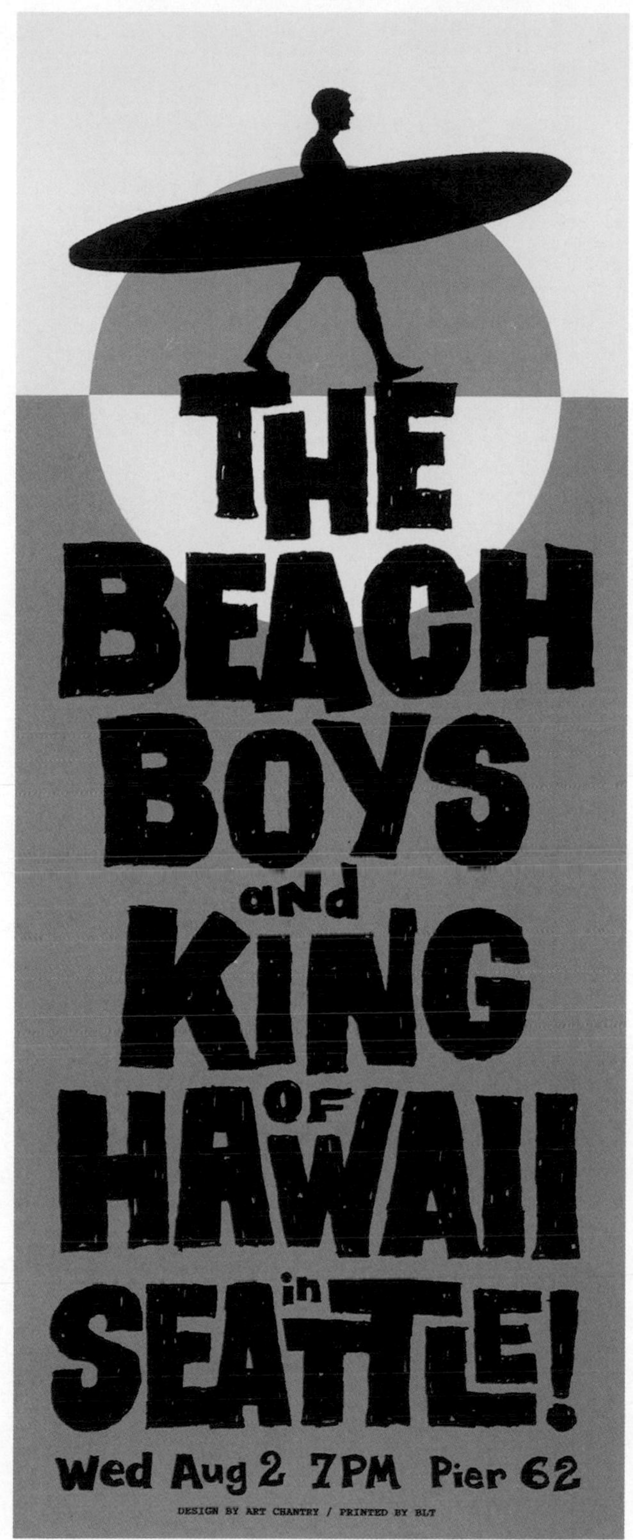

[4.42] *Poster design by Art Chantry.*

[4.43] *Product/package design by Turner Duckworth.*

Orange is active, appetizing, and hot. It is made from two warm colors that result in a transitional color associated with sunsets and the seasonal changes of autumn. It has a diverse association with smells that come mostly from sweet, tangy, and hot foods and spices. Many exotic foods are orange, such as mangoes, melons, papayas, seafood, peppers, and yams **4.43**.

Red is festive, exuberant, and romantic; it is associated with danger, blood, and imagination. Although red covers a range of seemingly contrasting associations (festive and danger), all of its suggestive qualities can be described with the word *passion.* Red is used extensively in packaging and advertising because it brings unrestrained attention to itself **4.44**.

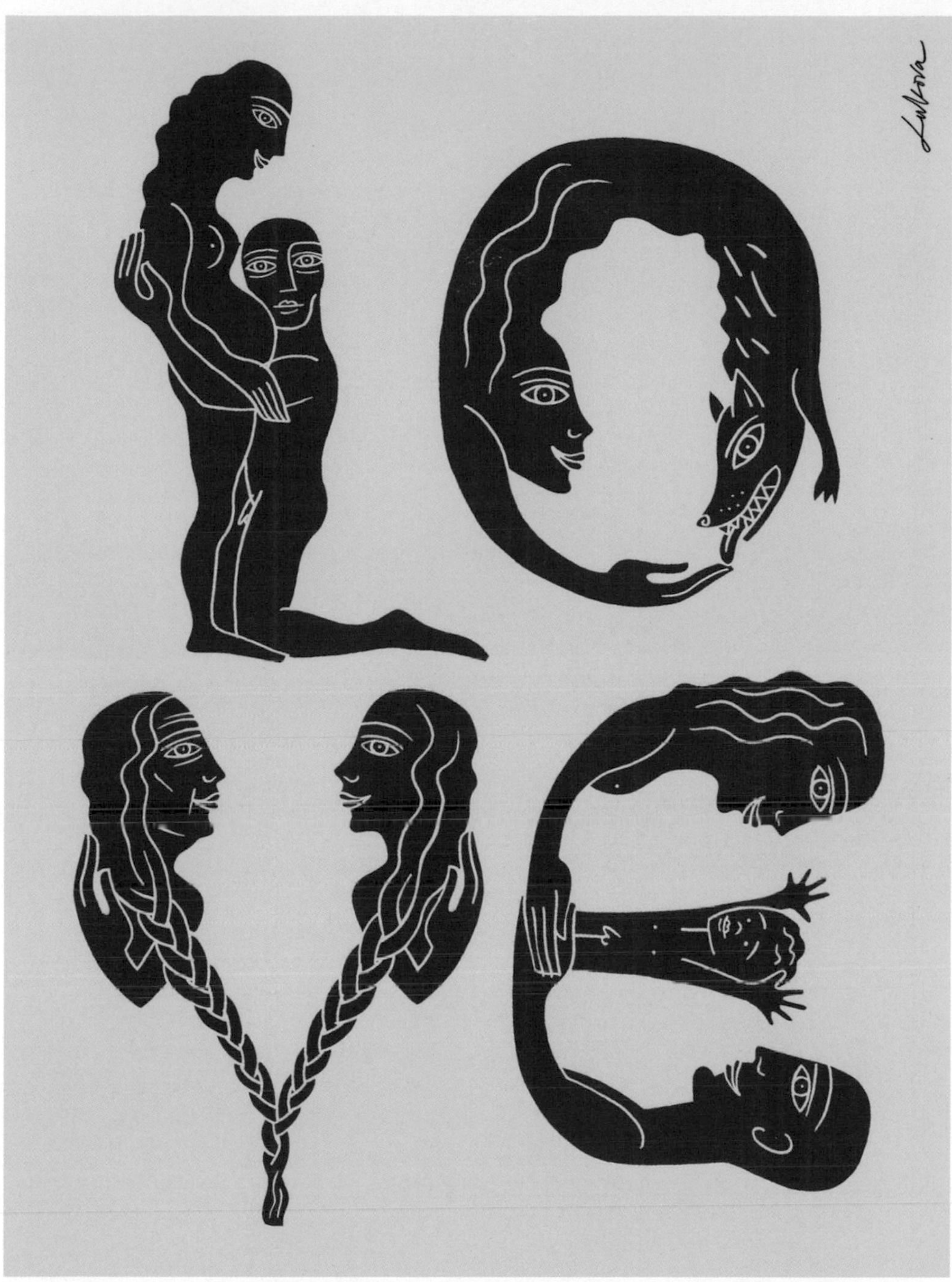

[4.44] *Poster design by Luba Lukova Studio.*

Color My World

Richard Palatini

Richard Palatini is senior vice president and associate creative director at Gianettino Meredith Advertising. Palatini also is an instructor of Visual Communication at Kean University in New Jersey.

People are affected and influenced by color in many obvious and not-so-obvious ways. We use color to describe feelings: "I'm in a blue mood," "She's green with envy," and "He's got me seeing red." It's used to identify everything from military organizations (navy blue), to businesses (IBM, "Big Blue"), to life stages (baby blue). Beyond words and images, color communicates instantly and powerfully. A world without color would be a world without emotion.

1 THE "LIFE" OF COLORS

People develop feelings about color that change and evolve as they reach different life stages and they also relate to color in different ways during each stage. For example, red and blue are colors to which young children are most responsive. Adolescents are drawn to colors that are most outrageous, intense, and used in unusual ways (think green catsup!). The same red that children are drawn to is the color that adults perceive as danger.

2 THE WIDE WORLD OF COLORS

When considering use of a color, we also need to understand how well it "travels." And, more specifically, how does a specific culture perceive a color or color combination? Historically, white has been associated with mourning by the Chinese, yet, in America, white is the color of wedding gowns. Because each culture has its own color symbolism, perceptive designers I know will often research countries and regions of the world to more fully understand what specific colors represent to them.

Be aware that in today's mobile global society, people will bring their color "baggage" with them on their travels. Still, individuals can also seek to assimilate into their new societal environment by emulating the new colors they find there. It's most important to consider all these factors when making color decisions that have "international travel" on their itinerary.

3 COLOR WITH FEELING

Think of the emotional response you want to elicit from your audience. Is it serene, sensual, exciting, powerful? Whatever it is, there are colors and color combinations for each and every one. Using light to midtones of greens, lavenders or blues and in combination will communicate that peaceful, serene feeling.

Dense purples, deep reds, and intense pinks are sensually provocative. Combining them with black will only increase the sensation. And, while black is THE power color, combining it with another hue can be even more powerful, such as black with a regal purple or royal blue. Many colors can bring feelings of excitement, but these should be warm and vivid. If your audience is young, consider vibrant warms and cools from every color family especially in combination.

4 CRIMES OF COLOR

Sometimes, breaking the laws of color can be the right thing to do. In creating a distinct identity it's better to be different than to use the right symbolic color. Car rental companies are a perfect example of this. Hertz's color is yellow, Avis is red, and National is green. Each has created its own distinct, yet appropriate color personality. Remember, it's OK to be different but it must be with a clear purpose in mind.

Color can be the most direct and memorable way of making your communication, whatever it may be, effective and successful. Consider your audience, their emotions, and culture and life stage. Understand how colors communicate your message best, and when necessary, break the rules.

Color in Design

Because color appeals so strongly to emotions, people tend to choose colors based on preference.

In design, colors must be selected for their ability to enhance communication and composition **4.45**. Relying on an understanding of how color is perceived, color systems, color terms, theory, and psychology provides a basis for exploring options for application. Researching color from an informed stance results in a sound rationale for your color choices.

Palettes and Color Schemes

To establish a palette or color scheme, you must establish the theme and content of the design.

Color may be limited by budget or aesthetic concerns depending on whether you use process color or match color.

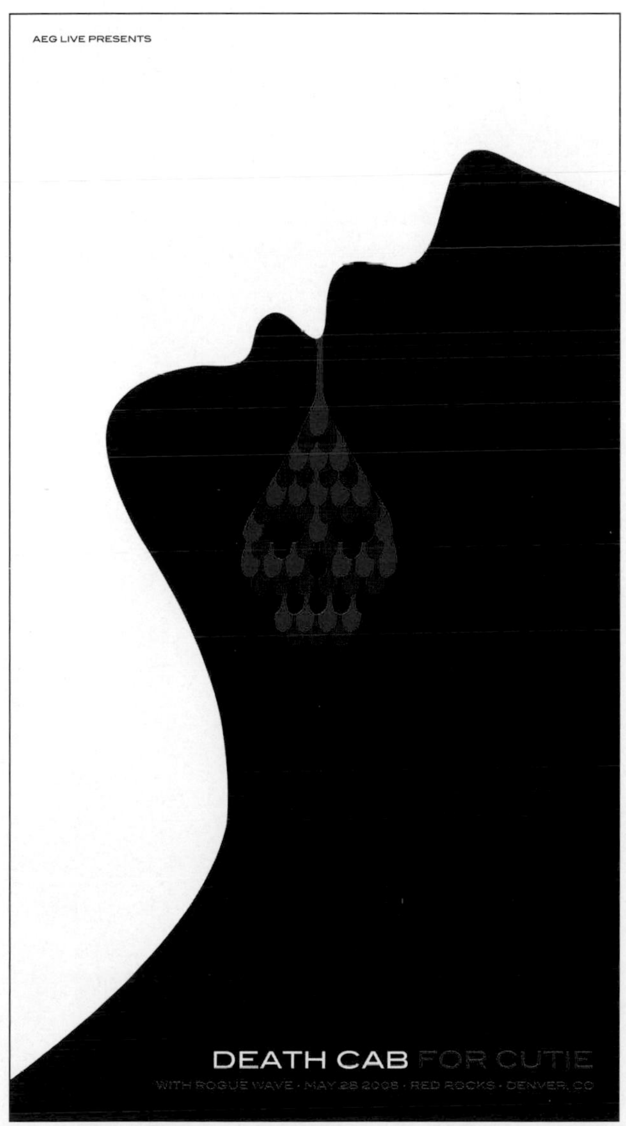

[4.45] The vivid red used in this poster draws the viewer's eye directly to the heart of its message. The impact is heightened by the red's contrast against the black background. The color of the type is harmonious with other aspects of the poster in that it echoes other colors that are used.
Poster design and illustration by Dan Stiles.

Color must support the communication message. Your goal is to determine what needs to be said and support it with an appropriate palette. Content determines color. Often designers must use supplied photographs or illustrations. Colors found within those subjects can enhance and unify other design elements such as type and other graphic elements.

If you are building a color scheme from scratch, work with a color triad. Triads should be built from two related colors, such as yellow and orange, and one contrasting color, such as blue **4.46**. As you explore your palette, adjust the contrast of the original colors using Itten's seven color contrasts as a guide.

Accents can be added to the triad depending on the nature of the design, but avoid having too many colors competing for identity in the design. Establish a hierarchy for color with regard to quantity and quality of its use **4.47**.

Color and Composition Most designs can function in black and white. Black and white can be the right aesthetic choice in some cases. The majority of design images, however, are produced in full color.

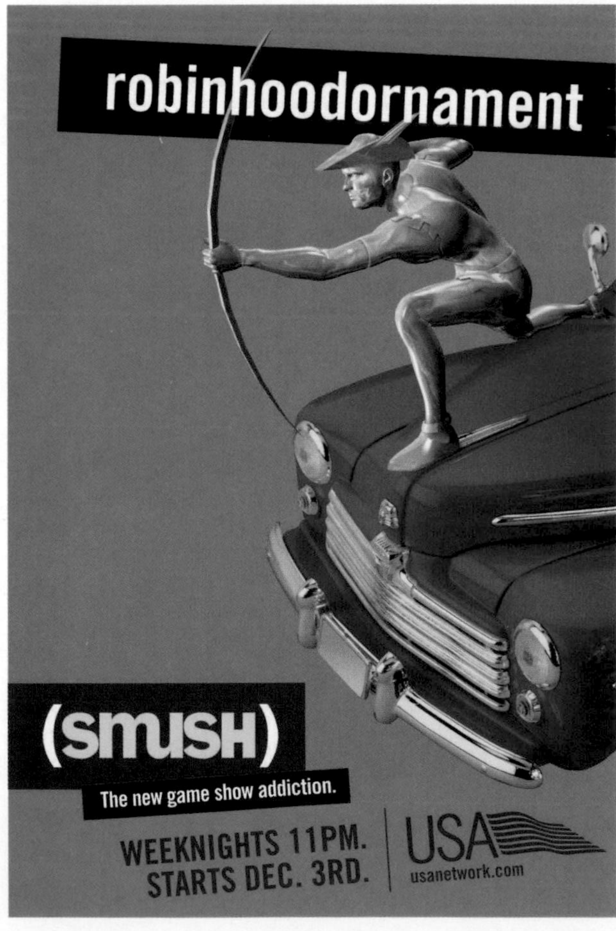

[4.46] The color triad of yellow, orange, and blue heightens the clean use of imagery and type.
Poster design by Bird Design.

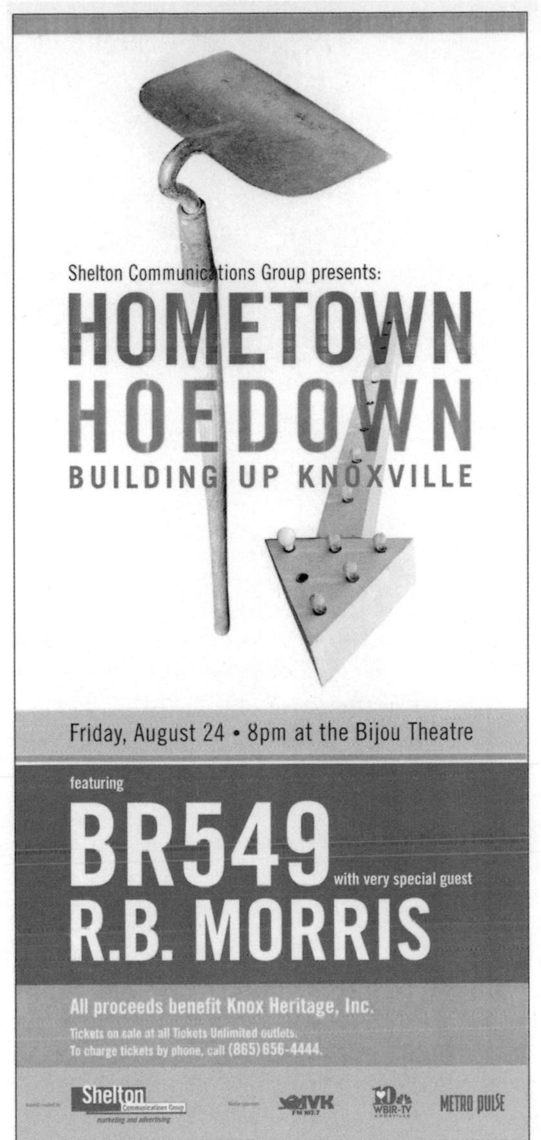

[4.47] This simple color scheme exemplifies the effective use of a color hierarchy. The color of typographic elements echoes the color of bands in the background. A thoughtful juxtaposition of colors found in the top and bottom creates strong unity and communication.
Poster design art direction by Stewart Pack.

Color intensifies and embellishes shape, line, texture, and type in a composition; color can enhance depth and help direct eye movement through a composition **4.48**.

Color is used to classify, identify, and code, helping to distinguish one thing from another **4.49**. Color also creates variety, supports balance, and establishes pattern, unifying all of the design elements, as shown in **4.50**.

A variety of ways to explore color use are available in the process of creating a design or graphic solution. Before beginning, it is helpful to select swatches for the color scheme you are contemplating. Swatches can be printed colors from the computer, PANTONE swatch chips, or swatches derived from other sources. Seeing how colors work together when they can be arranged and rearranged interchangeably is a good way to examine their effectiveness in support of your concept, as well as a means of coming up with a harmonious combination before you begin the design process.

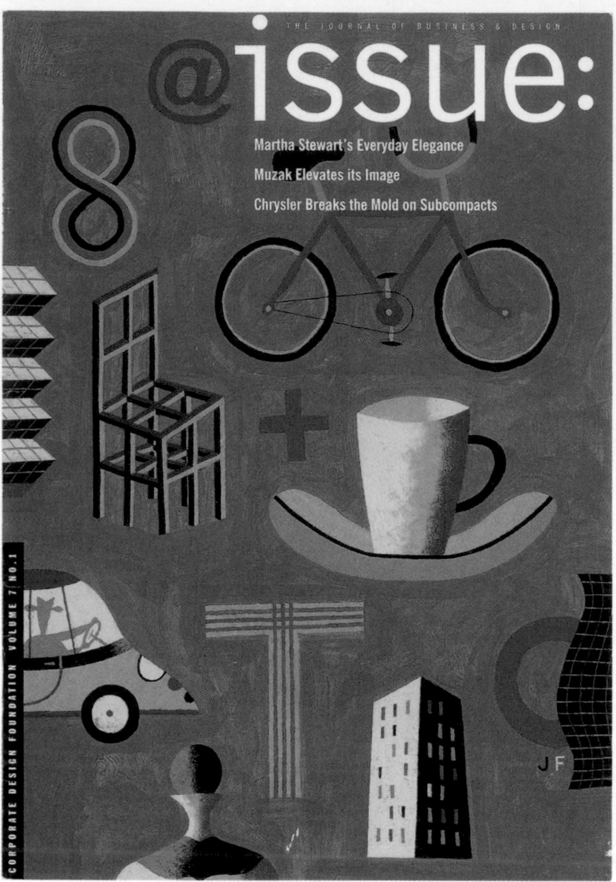

[4.48] The playful use of shapes and content is embellished by the curious color scheme that is dominated by deep earth tones and magenta hues. To offer additional contrast, modeled color, as in the cup and figure, is presented with flat color seen in the other subjects.
Cover design by Pentagram.

[4.49] The color of the product is visible through the transparent package and differentiates varieties of a line of bath soap. The word concepts for each variety correspond to a color association code.
Package design by Turner Duckworth.

[4.50] In this set of 24 compact discs, a recurring circle motif and bold, cropped type and imagery are supported by a rich color scheme of red, orange, black, white, and off-white. Color and graphic continuity have an equal hand in unifying the series.
CD design by Red Herring Design.

Professional designers often create theme or "mood" boards to present a concept. Those boards are a well-designed arrangement of textures, surfaces, photographs of content, and color swatches. (See the project, *Destination Theme Board*, in Chapter 6.) The color scheme represents a direction that the designer is thinking about and provides a visual example for everyone concerned to consider.

Illustrators and designers can explore color arrangements in imagery inexpensively by using a photocopier to duplicate line drawings for an illustration or a design. Once duplications are made, designer goauche, markers, or colored pencils can be used to do color media studies of compositions to investigate the effect of color schemes. Those studies can be digitally scanned to place into existing layouts for presentation purposes. Some brands of markers and colored pencils have corresponding PMS or Pantone numbers printed on the tool.

Photography is another medium used to explore color in composition. Digital cameras can be used to frame subjects or to explore a subject in depth with regard to color and composition. Once the photographs are digitally downloaded, color adjustments and changes can be easily achieved, providing a variety of color options.

Typically, though, the color determined in a preliminary design or motif board requires the designer's eye to convert the color to a digital color scheme to be used in finished designs.

Production Tip:

Keep a supply of printed color swatches in your toolbox. Color-aid paper has a high-quality pigment surface that is actually screen-printed ink. Those sets of color paper offer a broad range of hues that can be used to explore and specify a color scheme for an accompanying design.

Color in Support of an Identity

When designers create an identity concept, color is typically applied to the logo design. However, identity design requires the development of a more extensive color palette that is compatible with and enhances the logo color and can be applied to all aspects of the identity. In fact, determining this color palette and how it will be applied is a large component of the design process in identity and brand development.

In the case of the Museum of Arts and Design (MAD) in New York City, the museum's identity designers at Pentagram wanted the color palette to communicate a sense of energy and refinement. The color palette they developed communicates this sensibility by combining fully saturated colors that run the range from warm to cool, tempered by neutrals of Black, gray, and brown.

The designers chose a vivid red as one of the logo's colors. Other colors that were selected for the logo were a warm gray and Black **4.51a**. The designers referred to these as "primary" colors and selected six additional "secondary" colors to be used to complement the primary colors and to add variety in forming other color combinations in identity applications **4.51b**. An identity manual was developed with specific instructions for using the primary and secondary colors as well as suggestions for creating harmonious color combinations **4.51c**.

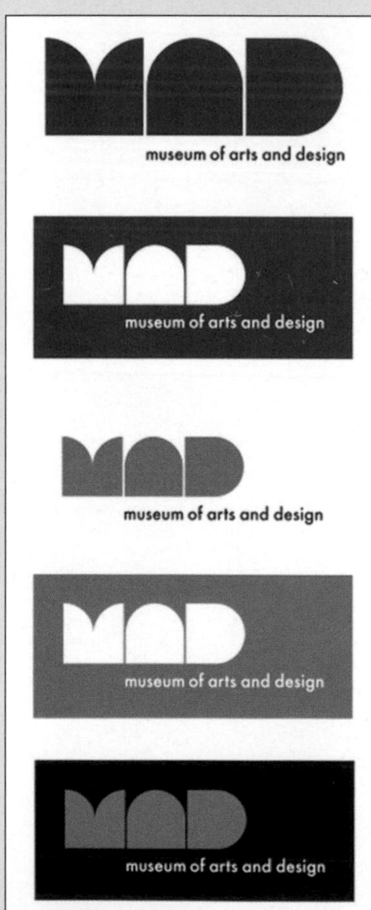

[4.51a] In addition to exploring how the MAD logo looked as a positive image against a white background, the designers also explored reversed applications of the logo as a negative image against a color field in each of the identity's primary colors. Each of these applications was presented as shown in the identity manual that Pentagram produced.
Courtesy of Michael Bierut/Pentagram.

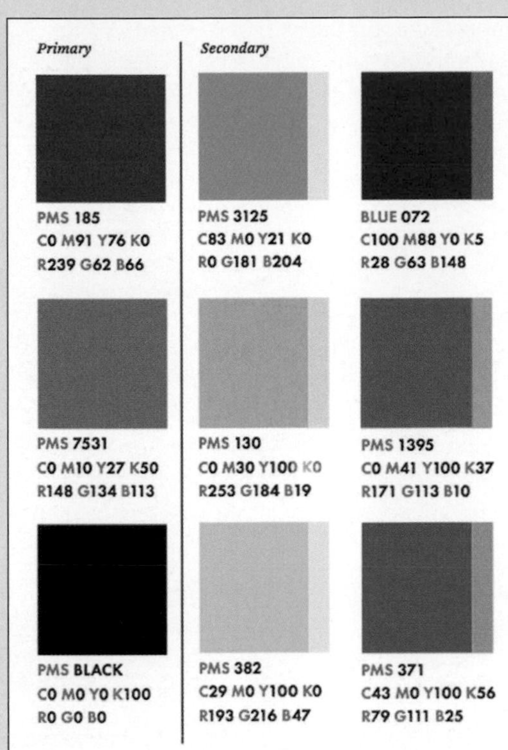

[4.51b] The primary and secondary colors that comprised the MAD identity color palette were specified in the museum's identity guide as PANTONE colors using the system's numerical code and were also referenced as combinations and percentages of CMYK colors for print applications as well as RGB combinations and percentages for Web, video, and interactive kiosk applications.
Courtesy of Michael Bierut/Pentagram.

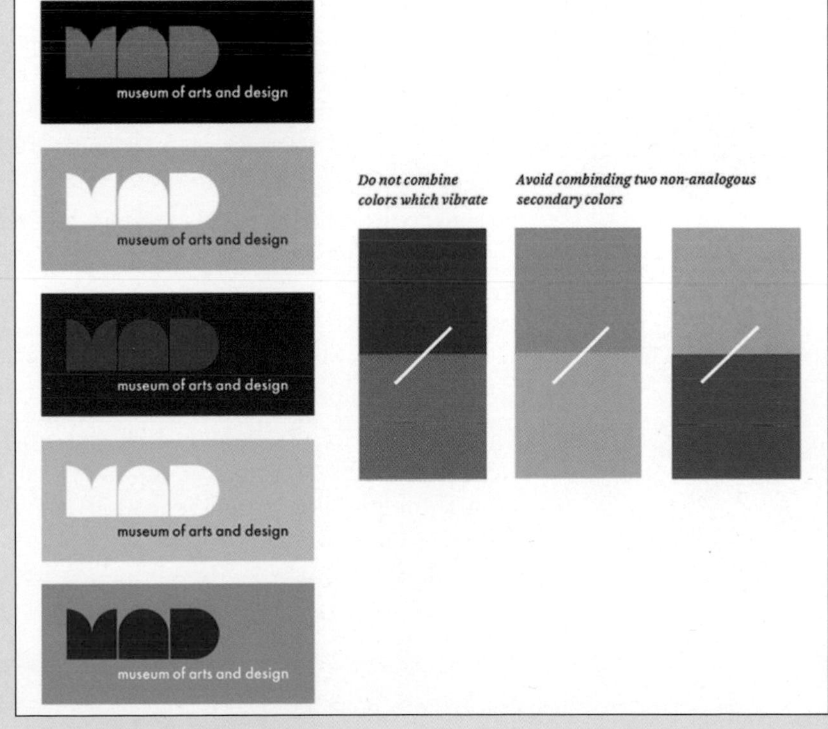

[4.51c] The identity manual includes examples of various combinations between the identity's palette of primary and secondary colors. The manual also includes guidelines on color pairings to avoid.
Courtesy of Michael Bierut/ Pentagram.

Production Tip:

On the computer, colors are created as percentages of RGB or CMYK. For example, purple when produced as a CMYK color could be a blend of 100 percent magenta and 50 percent cyan. As an RGB color, the same color would be a blend of 150 percent red, 40 percent green, and 140 percent blue. When creating colors, try to assign the percentages in whole numbers and even in values of five unless it is critical to refine digital color choices to within 1 percent increments. When you create a design or graphic images, create digital swatches of all of the colors you use. Save them in their own document so you can access them.

Keep in mind that color choices must support the communication message, psychological meaning, informational purpose, or local qualities of the imagery. Consider the audience as the receiver of the communicated message. Research your color strategy and ensure that it is integrated into the design for the benefit and visual interest of the audience.

SUMMARY

There is much to learn about color. This chapter serves as an orientation to essential building Blocks for continued study of color and its use. Although most of the information presented here is basic, it is the same information that experienced artists and designers use in their work. The accumulated knowledge of color systems, terminology, and theories changes very slowly. In fact, nothing significant has been added to the study of color in this regard for several decades. What does continue to change is people's attitudes about color as influenced by changing technologies and the evolving culture.

You have learned that color is the visual element that profoundly appeals to human emotion. But personal feelings must be tempered with good research when choosing color in design. The use of color in the images presented in this chapter appeals to you on an emotional level, but it does so through thoughtful design decision making. The color choices are carefully determined to support or enhance content, composition, and communication.

Color Tips

- Chromatic gray is a gray or neutral color achieved by mixing complements. You can determine the integrity of the parent color complements by seeing if, when mixed, they make a neutral gray or if the mix is a muddy, brownish color. Often to achieve a neutral gray, the parent colors need to be modified with magenta or cyan pigments.
- In some cases, a fully saturated complement is too strong for a design. You can dull complementary hues by adding Black or gray to achieve a more subtle, somber color scheme. Adjusting the hues in such a way is often necessary to strike an appropriate color balance.
- Consider using imperfect complements such as a green and purple, an orange earth tone with a violet, or a maroon with olive green as the basis for a color scheme.
- When mixing tints and shades, begin by adding Black or white in small amounts to the color. You will conserve paint and gain better control in achieving an accurate color mix.
- RGB digital color has a more expansive (millions) range of colors. CMYK has a more limited range of colors. When creating a project color scheme, generate a set of colors in RGB, copy the set, and convert the colors to CMYK to compare visually for your artistic preference and purposes.
- Work in RGB for the duration of a print project. Since you are working on a screen that is RGB, you will see more accurate color than if you set it up in CMYK. Once completed, print it for proofing purposes in RGB and then convert it to CMYK and print it again. Compare the two for color accuracy and to compare your expectation before you present the work. Sometimes the RGB print is more accurate.

projects

CHROMATIC METAMORPHOSIS

Objectives

- Research typefaces and fonts.
- Practice drawing lines and shapes from a variety of references.
- Work in small groups to present ideas and determine strategies.
- Produce a series of sequential sketches.
- Work with a grid to determine placement points.
- Research color theories, color schemes, and color uses.
- Develop a color strategy.
- Explore various color sources appropriate for completing the assignment.

Description

Design and produce a metamorphosis of elements that includes color in a series of five sequential painted compositions.

A metamorphosis is a gradual change of form. This phenomenon occurs most profoundly in nature. It is also a motif used in a variety of illustration applications and in film, animation, and graphic design. The challenge is to control the change through a series of frames or still images.

PHASE ONE

Use the first letter of your first or last name and a natural form for exploring and designing a metamorphosis in seven steps. *The change must be even and constant from step 1 to step 7.* Begin with drawing media to explore the metamorphosis of the letter and natural form individually. Each of the elements will change in five steps. Each changing element will ultimately be presented within a frame or compositional format of 6 inches by 6 inches. Frame 1 will be the illustrated letter; frame 7 will be the illustrated natural form. The five steps of metamorphosis will occur in between, for a total of seven steps.

Study letterforms by researching various typefaces and font styles. Avoid designer faces. Determine the natural element by browsing books and Web sites. You will work in small groups to present ideas and determine strategies.

PHASE TWO

Use your drawing to "design sketch" each of the steps. Start with the first and last compositions; then sketch the middle step. It should be a balanced Blend of the shape attributes, positions, and values of steps 1 and 7. Complete the design sketches of the other steps, applying the same strategy. Now you have a design sketch of the series in pencil. You will get feedback and direction at this stage in a progress critique. *Note*: Pay attention to the transitions between the actual steps. Work to control a fluid change through the steps. Avoid changes that are too gradual or too abrupt.

PHASE THREE

Execute the final metamorphosis. You can produce it as a hard-edged graphically reduced image or as a continuous tone with value. Any drawing or painting medium is acceptaBle, but choose a medium that is appropriate for your approach. Incorporate color into the final medium. It can be limited-use or full-color. Make sure the color morphs as well. The class will discuss strategies for color use.

Limitations and Materials

drawing tools, drawing paper and board, paint, colored pencils

Critique Discussion Points

How effective is the continuity in the seven steps?

Describe what is potentially happening between the steps.

How does the color element enhance the metamorphosis in a compositional sense?

Vocabulary

chromatic, metamorphosis, hard-edged, typefaces, font, value, continuous tone

Evaluation Criteria

Aesthetic Continuity

Achievement of Criteria

Craft and Execution

Control of the Continuity of Change

24 SHOTS

Objectives

- Produce a series of compositions directed by the principles of design.
- See and visually control figure-ground relationships that include simple, reversal, and ambiguous.
- Work to create engaging compositions through the use of color.
- Work to achieve a variety of tonal ranges—high-color contrast, low contrast, full tone, and local color.
- Use a camera as a tool for the imagery.
- Produce a series of images for a group dialogue of visual principles and composition.

Description

Begin with a think session of possible subjects, sites, and ways to interpret the list of design principles into interesting photographic content. Consider how composition, format, viewpoint, light and shadow, perspective, scale, and narrative can add to the descriptive-expressive impact of the picture.

Subject matter or content is open. But avoid overly familiar situations and redundancy. Strive to achieve a variety of color schemes as you interpret the set of design principles and strive to make each image different from the others. Variety is one of the main principles of design.

Purchase a 24-exposure color disposable camera or use your own camera. Select subjects interesting and unfamiliar to you and use 24 exposures to investigate your subjects with regard to the following list of formal visual principles:

Strive for UNITY through VARIETY as you explore color in composition.

Take the photographs in the following order:

3 frames—symmetrical balance

3 frames—asymmetrical balance

3 frames—dominance

3 frames—repetition

3 frames—scale change

3 frames—orientation (different points of view)

3 frames—rhythm or movement

3 frames—pattern

Limitations and Materials

24-exposure color disposable camera or your own camera, pushpins

Critique Discussion Points

Identify the set that uses color most effectively to enhance depth.

Which two or three images have the most saturated color?

Identify five of the seven color contrasts at work in your series.

Which photograph offered the most surprising color result? Why?

Vocabulary

format, viewpoint, light and shadow, perspective, scale, narrative, figure-ground reversal, figure ground ambiguity, local color, hue, high contrast

Evaluation Criteria

Attainment of Criteria

Formal Quality of Compositions

Effectiveness of Interpretation

Overall Depth of Concepts

COLOR AND SEASON

Objectives

- Work thematically with a color scheme.
- Explore different triadic color schemes that communicate a theme.
- Work with a palette that offers a variety of color contrasts.
- Arrive at a color scheme through a process of researching the subject.

Description

Design a color collage composition for one of the four seasons. Research the season and select a color scheme of a triad and one accent color. The design should consist of graphic elements that depict the season and the word name of the season.

The name can be incorporated with other graphic elements to create the essence of the chosen seasonal theme in the abstract design. Work with scale changes, economy, and directional changes to enhance the composition. Establish a visual hierarchy and use color to create depth.

Limitations and Materials

Select the color from sheets of high-quality color aid. Use the computer or any printed source for the type, but trace and transfer it to the color paper to be cut and incorporated into the collage. Cut or tear the paper for the appropriate visual effect. The final size is 11 inches by 14 inches. Mount the design on Black mat board with 3-inch borders.

Critique Discussion Points

Identify the dominant color contrast in your design and explain how it is working in the composition.

How does color create depth in the design?

Describe the visual hierarchy in your composition. How does it direct eye movement?

Vocabulary

color triad, palette, accent color, analogous, scale, economy, collage

Evaluation Criteria

Effective Use of Color to Communicate the Theme

Overall Composition

Effective Use of Elements to Communicate Seasonal Theme

Craft

in review

1. Colored light is the basis for what color system?
2. How are the additive and subtractive color systems interdependent?
3. What two terms describe the hues found between the primary and secondary colors?
4. What is the name of the industry standard for specifying match color?
5. What is the distinction between chroma and saturation?
6. What two color theories have profoundly affected designers' understanding and use of color in design?
7. Discuss the effects associated with contrast of extension and simultaneous contrast.
8. Define color triad and discuss how it is used in design to devise a color scheme.
9. Choose a color, describe its qualities, and present an analysis of its potential use in a design.
10. Which color system would you specify in graphic software for printing a design and which would you specify to view your design on screen?

Courtesy of Pum Lefebure.

"*We look for young designers who are not only talented, but they have something 'extra' like illustration, writing, or interactive skills.*"

Pum Lefebure, Design Army

Pum Lefebure is co-founder, with her husband Jake and creative director of Design Army, a Washington, D.C.–based design studio. Their work has been featured numerous times in *Communication Arts Magazine*, *Applied Arts*, *Gallery Magazine*, *Graphis*, *HOW Magazine*, *Print*, and Logolounge. They have won awards from One Show, Neenah Paper, STEP, Graphis, Mohawk Show, and Art Director's Club. The studio averages seven employees who manage dozens of projects per year from major clients that include: AIGA, GE, Adobe, PBS, Chronicle Books, Marriot International Inc., Washington Ballet, and ThinkFoodGroup.

How did you choose design as a career path?

My passion for design started from a very early age. Growing up in Bangkok, I was always artistic and I began drawing and painting since before I can remember. I always knew that I would end up being an artist. My parents were very supportive but they didn't want me to be a starving artist so they pointed me to fashion design and graphic design.

What has your career path been since you finished school?

Simple and focused. I had one job for eight years (started as an intern and ended up as a senior art director). Then I opened my own firm with my husband, Jake. In the years before we opened our firm, I learned what to do and what not to do.

What are some of the challenges managing your own studio?

I work all the time—not because I have to but I want to. I finally figured out there is really no such thing as balancing your work and personal life. So I integrated both. Finding enough time for each is always my biggest challenge.

What do you think has been the most important factor in your success?

1. Being determined to work harder than anyone else (including my employees). If you go home at 5:00 p.m. while others are working late, you'll never get respect from your team.
2. I'm lucky to have the most amazing business partner, Jake, who is both business- and design-savvy.

What are the two or three main qualities you look for when interviewing a young designer?

1. Passion. If you don't have passion, you just have a job. We want people who truly love design.

2. Idea person. Our studio focuses on concept first, execution later. That person has to know how to think conceptually, which is not easy to train. You either have it or you don't.
3. +1. We look for young designers who are not only talented, but they have something "extra"—like illustration, writing, or interactive skills. We are a small firm and you have to be able to handle a lot of different kinds of projects. So a candidate really stands out if they bring more expertise and versatility.

What do you see as the next significant change for the design industry?

To be able to design in the future, you have to approach the project from 360 degrees. The scope is bigger now. Clients want both print and multimedia. They also want to be involved behind the scenes because people are interested in how things are created. So designers have to be able to approach a project in a very systematic way.

Design Army combines a visually simple design concept with a "tongue in cheek" sense of humor for this accordion-fold moving announcement.
Courtesy of DESIGN ARMY.

Design studios often use the holidays as an opportunity to create a client gift that also functions as a self-promotion. Few are as creative, fun, and functional as this calendar design that doubles as a set of drink coasters. The palette is consistent with the Design Army brand and features exquisitely simple and entertaining illustrated graphics all packaged in a custom "mini" portfolio.
Courtesy of DESIGN ARMY.

An unusual and memorable announcement for a design exhibition series continues the use of the color brand, clean use of typography, and Design Army's brand of clever conceptually based humor.
Courtesy of DESIGN ARMY.

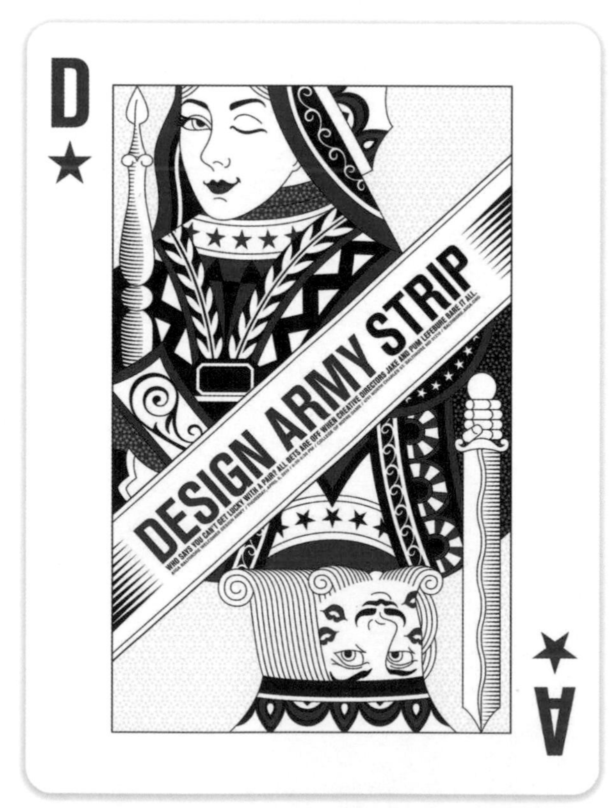

Design Army often creates effective design concepts based on equally witty verbal messages. This poster promotion for a speaking engagement for AIGA Baltimore utilizes an illustrated narrative with a double meaning to represent and distinguish themselves and the studio to an audience of designers.
Courtesy of DESIGN ARMY.

pum lefebure

A view of Design Army's studio in Washington, D.C.
Courtesy of DESIGN ARMY.

five

Managing Effective Design

Illustration by Chris Sickles, Red Nose Studios.

5

introduction

By definition, *design* is organization. Designers determine which elements to use and how to use them effectively to create visual interest and communicate an intended message. Managing visual organization is taking an active, informed role in the design process. This chapter will examine ways to manage the organization of design through the use of fundamental, universal strategies and techniques. You are now familiar with the principles and elements of design. You will learn what experienced artists and designers know about governing key visual and conceptual relationships that support effective design. This chapter will also introduce integral ways of using visual principles and relationships to establish visual organization and artistic control. Finally, we will examine the origins of design in the natural world to help you understand the structure of design, aesthetic references, and sources for inspiration.

objectives

- Discuss the role of organization and format as basic design issues.
- Present various grid systems for organizing compositions.
- Explain the functions of eye movement and strategies for controlling it.
- Identify and discuss key visual relationships that every designer must know.
- Present illusory phenomena that affect visual perception.
- Examine structures in nature and the constructed environment as sources for graphic designers.

VISUAL ORGANIZATION

Organization is central to good design. You must consider many factors to achieve visual organization; but primarily, you need to know how to manage the surface elements that are seen and the "hidden" structures that are transparent in the composition. Lines, shapes, and color are seen. Format, orientation, grids, eye movement, and theme are transparent or subliminal structures that achieve harmony in the "mind's" eye of the viewer. It also is important to know something about how the viewer experiences visual information.

The eye and brain work together to organize and make sense of the visual world as people see it. At the turn of the twentieth century, a group of German psychologists including Max Wertheimer, Kurt Koffka, and Wolfgang Kohler (whose work as a research psychologist is discussed in Chapter 6) studied the phenomenon of how humans perceive and organize the visual world. What these psychologists determined is that people tend to cluster shapes, colors, textures, and other visual elements in an attempt to process a "whole image."

In his 1890 publication *On Gestalt Qualities*, Christian von Ehrenfels was the first to use the term **gestalt**, which translates from German to mean "form" or "the way things come together." The group of psychologists coined a related phrase, "the whole is greater than the sum of the parts." It means that, when viewed together, the interaction of design elements is more dynamic than each of the elements are individually **5.1**.

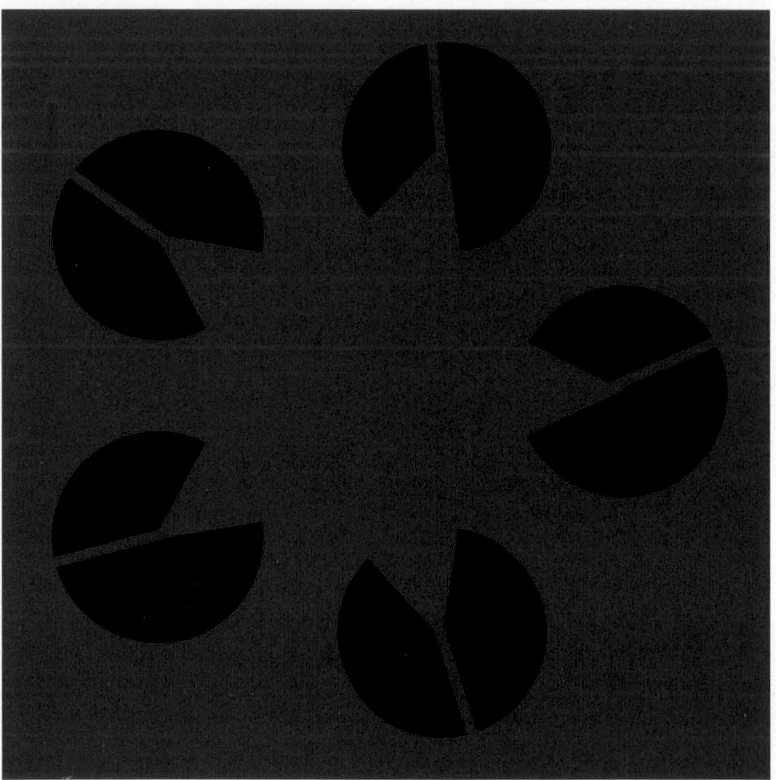

[5.1] The parts in this pictogram include five black circles and a star with lines projecting from its five points. The overlapping of the circles and star produces a new set of shapes and relationships. The positive and negative shapes have come together to create a whole image that transcends the presence of the individual parts. This graphic technique is often used to design logotypes and pictograms. Perceptual psychologists refer to this optical effect as subjective contour.

When looking at nature, people accept what they see as harmonious and "whole." Perhaps this is why nature has been such a popular subject for artists through the centuries. But when artists attempt to re-create nature in a painting or drawing, attaining visual harmony and wholeness is the result of arranging and rearranging the elements until a "good gestalt" is achieved. Here, good organization in design results from an informed decision-making process that involves creative thinking, combined with an understanding of how visual organization works. A good place to begin is to learn visual organization from the outside in.

Organization as a Whole

Overall organization involves four primary considerations:

- Format and orientation
- Underlying structure (grid systems)
- Eye movement
- Theme and motif

From ideation to execution, each design decision must be supported by a rationale or a set of reasons. Often choices are made intuitively because they "feel right." Although it is important to trust your instincts, it is equally important to test them. Testing your decisions is a matter of questioning the relevance of each decision with regard to the design objective. This is not always a linear, sequential process. Designers often work with components and elements that do not offer immediate resolution. But, by continually questioning and working the problem, designers find that the pieces ultimately fall into place.

Format and Orientation

In the design world, the term **format** is used two ways. It is the surface area that contains the design composition. The shape, size, and general makeup of the format is determined by the **venue** or kind of design—that is, packaging, publications, Web sites, posters, calendars, banners, and so forth. Venues are aligned and determined with the design objective in mind, which means that formats are often outside the control of a designer. Unconventional formats, however, offer creative design challenges **5.2**.

In print production, format refers to the arrangement of the design components as they will be printed, cut, scored, and assembled. The format for digital interactive media, mobile phones, CRT (cathode ray tube) and LCD (liquid crystal display) monitors, and digital projection varies by the dictates of the technology. All of the electronic formats are sized according to what is called *aspect ratio*. Aspect ratio is the relationship between the height and width (or the width divided by the height) of the screen. Conventional television CRT screens have an aspect ration of 4:3 (or 1.33:1) as do CRT computer monitors. This technology is practically being replaced by high-definition (HD) LCD and plasma screens that have an aspect ratio of 16:9 (or 1.78:1). The iPhone has an aspect ratio of 1.5:1 and other personal media devices (PMDs) vary in the format of the display screen **5.3**.

The point is that now, more than ever, designers encounter a multiplicity of media formats. It is important to consider the relationship and interrelationships between design formats and production formats from the beginning of the design process. Decisions that are made in a design are affected in the production stage. If they are not in tune with each other, the design will need to be reworked. A good practice is to consult production services early to avoid problems later. Even if you are not taking your design to full production, you should think ahead about format sizes and construct prototypes and comprehensives (comps) of your designs. Laser printers, large-format plotter printers, boards used for mounting, and other preparations for presentation of work are affected by formatting decisions that need to be considered early in the design process.

Orientation is the point of view determined by the designer, and it is the way the viewer is meant to relate visually to a design or an image. However, orientation begins with thinking about how the viewer relates to the world. Humans generally perceive the world standing or sitting perpendicular to the ground. This is a fundamental, stable viewpoint by which every nonperpendicular relationship is measured. The brain is so conditioned to this perpendicular relationship that even when people tilt their head to view any environment or image, their brain perceives it as perpendicular to the ground.

[5.2] Venue formats are often outside the control of the designer and can have a huge impact on a design. In this example, the designer was challenged to conceive and apply a cartoon character to the dynamic surface space of a watch face. *© TOKIDOKI, LLC. Designed by Simone Legno.*

[5.3] The wider panoramic format of the movie screen has a comfortable viewing proportion. Films that are presented on a conventional television (4:3 aspect ratio) lose action that occurs on the sides. The proportions of letterbox and Cinemascope are 2.35:1, although optically they appear different in this illustration because of the signature masking at the top and bottom. HDTV has a less panoramic proportion of 16:9.
© Cengage Learning 2013. Design by Mark Thomas.

[5.4] Architectural forms tend to be perceived as vertical rectangles. This perception serves as the basis for the logo design for *ArchitectureWeek*, where the rectangularity of the letter forms and their elongation, reminiscent of a skyline, reinforce the periodical's focus on architecture.
Design by Atelier Works.

A person's field of vision is an oval shape with the width roughly double the height. The film industry screen formats of Cinemascope and letterbox are designed to mimic the same proportions 5.3. Although people's field of vision is oval in nature, they tend to view the world in a rectangular frame. That tendency is culturally reinforced by the overwhelming use of the rectangle in architecture, art, design, and technology **5.4**.

The proportions and configuration of a format set up a psychological association that affects the way an image will be read. A horizontal format is associated with the horizon, nature, and serenity. Vertical suggests portrait and architectural proportions; a square implies a neutral, stable feel, 1.5a, 1.5b, and 1.5c in Chapter 1.

Grid Systems **Grids** have been used for centuries as a means of scaling smaller images to larger works or to break down the observed world into smaller, more manageable sections. For those same reasons, graphic artists today use the grid; but because design is more about arranging, grids also are used to help achieve good organization. Grids can be built from square (arithmetic), rectangular (geometric), triangular, and even varying-sized units. The square arithmetic grid is composed of equal-sized square units arranged in a series: 1, 2, 3, 4, and so on. The geometric grid is composed of units that are built using multiples. Units might be 1 × 2 or 1 × 1.5. Grids also can be built from arithmetic progressions such as 1, 3, 5, and 7. What makes that a progression is that the value between each number in the progression is constant. In these examples, the numeric values can be translated into a visual form used to build a grid **5.5a, 5.5b, 5.5c**, and **5.5d**.

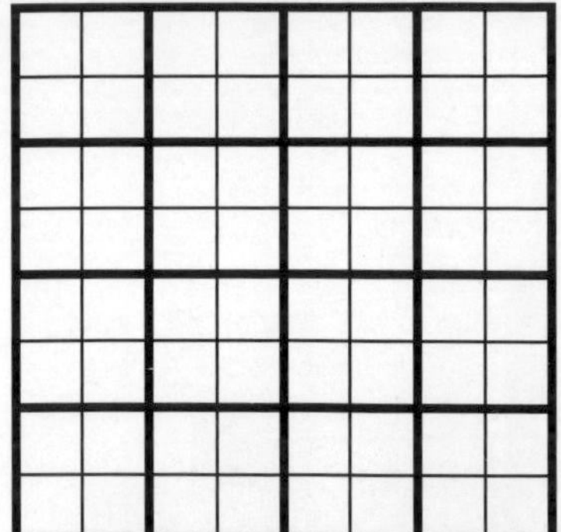

[5.5a] In this arithmetic grid, the 16 larger units have been subdivided into sets of four for a total of 64 smaller units. Subdividing grids identifies dominant and subordinate intersecting points to use for the placement of elements.
© Cengage Learning 2013. Design by Mark Thomas.

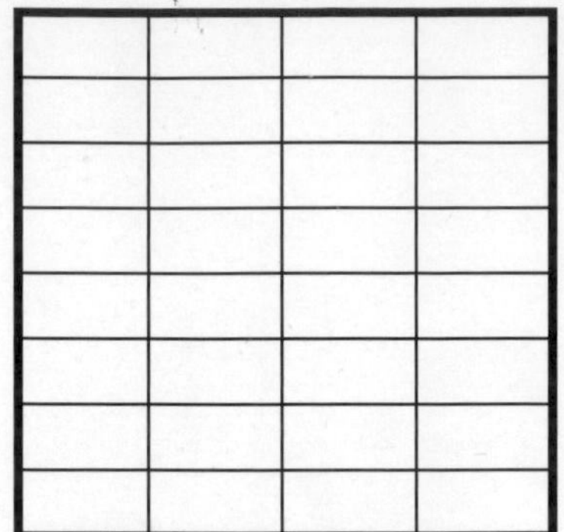

[5.5b] Geometric units are rectangular and in this case have a 1:2 proportion. This grid provides a different set of relationships from the arithmetic grid, suggesting an aesthetic distinction that would likely yield a different design. The alignment of intersecting points creates an angle that is more gradual than that of the arithmetic grid.
© Cengage Learning 2013. Design by Mark Thomas.

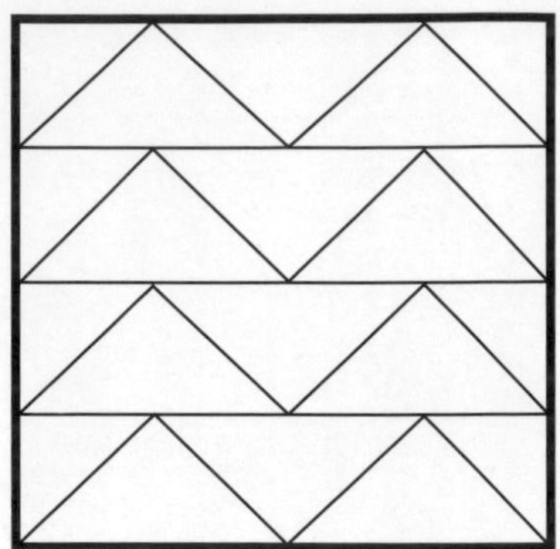

[5.5c] A grid built of triangles offers a departure from rectangular grids. Here the grid suggests a strong sense of overlap and depth with a bias toward diagonal alignments. The diagonals also create a repetitive movement that could profoundly influence the design on its surface.
© Cengage Learning 2013. Design by Mark Thomas.

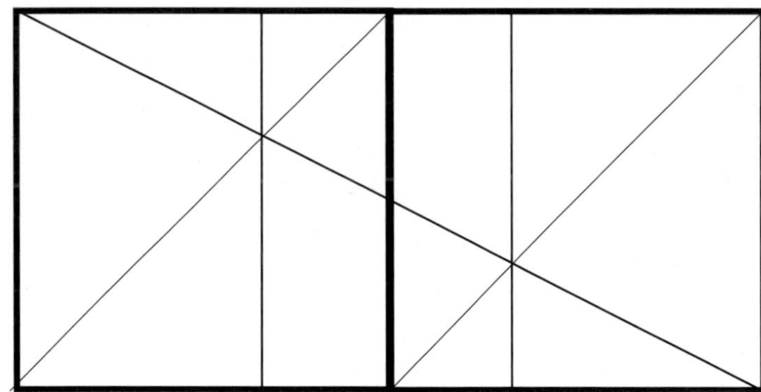

[5.5d] This grid is useful for page layout. It was built from a series of intersecting lines. Begin with two rectangles or squares, which in this example serve as pages for a publication. Draw a line diagonally through either set of opposing corners. Now draw a line through the corners of the individual rectangles. Draw a vertical line through each of the intersecting points created by the intersecting diagonals. The resulting vertical rectangles can be used as areas for the placement of text and images in publications.
© Cengage Learning 2013. Design by Mark Thomas.

Grids are useful for defining key alignments and intersecting points within a composition. They also provide a means of organizing and determining where to place graphic elements, imagery, and text; they also function as the underlying structure that is transparent to the eye **5.6**. A grid offers the designer a means for making efficient decisions. Using a grid is particularly useful when there are many elements and layers to organize.

Grid systems can also be combined to establish a hierarchy to manage both the outer proportions and internal placement of design elements. For example, a golden rectangle can be used in conjunction with a set of simple arithmetic and geometric grids that subdivide the squares and rectangles. The resulting grid hierarchy begins to suggest internal relationships and a direction for eye movement **5.7**.

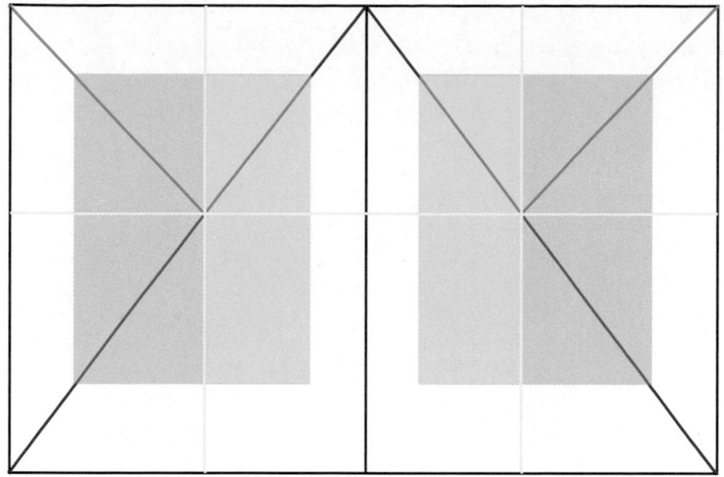

[5.6] There are infinite ways to invent grid structures for publications and book page layout. The first decision is to determine the trim size or the dimensions of the outer format. The trim size is a ratio of one dimension to another. This grid layout is based on an outer proportion of 3:4 and the inner rectangles devised from the intersection of the red diagonals and the yellow vertical and horizontal lines. The internal rectangle also has a proportion of 3:4 and using the intersection point as a vertical divider which yields a proportional two column grid for placing text and imagery. You can create your own page layout grid by exploring proportions, intersecting points, and the interposition of basic shapes. *© Cengage Learning 2013. Design by Mark Thomas.*

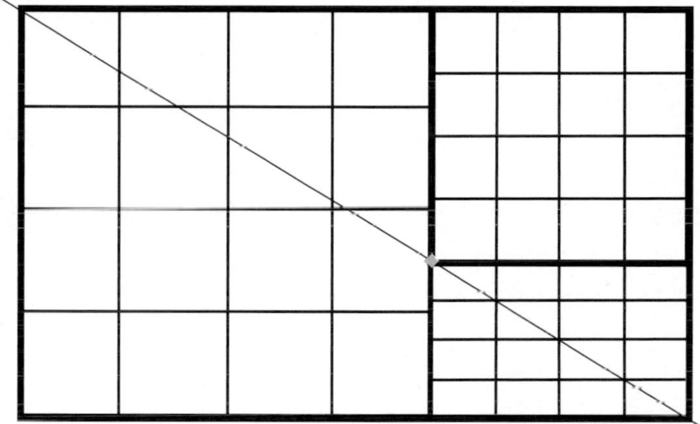

[5.7] Combining systems can suggest scale changes, movement, and emphasis, as in this grid, which begins with a golden rectangle and is further subdivided. The subdivided grids are two arithmetic systems and one geometric system. As the units decrease in size, a sense of spiraling movement is created, established around a pivoting focal point identified by the green diamond. *© Cengage Learning 2013. Design by Mark Thomas.*

Eye Movement The human eye is a wonderfully complex instrument. The eye works in conjunction with the brain to perceive the world. Physiologically, the eye provides people with neural impulses that are recorded on the brain's visual cortex. The best analogy is the one mentioned in Chapter 4—the eye and brain work like a movie camera. The lens works like the eye and the film is like the retina on the visual cortex of the brain, recording the world as it is perceived. One distinct difference between the eye and a camera lens is that the eye is continually moving or quivering, allowing the images that people perceive to be recorded on the retina 4.1.

This quivering or rapid scanning of the eye is a built-in survival feature of human physiology that helps people distinguish shape, pattern, and color. Therefore, it is difficult to maintain a fixed stare on any point within a picture. The tendency is for people to want to move their eyes around, scanning various features in an image. When people fix their eyes on a point on a picture, they perceive the rest of the image in their peripheral vision. The longer they stare, the more faded the images in the periphery become. Therefore, the bias is for the viewer's eye to want to scan and so it does. Controlling eye movement in a composition, then, is a matter of directing the natural scanning tendency of the viewer's eye.

But what kinds of arrangements, alignments, and shapes attract and move the eye? The eye tends to gravitate to areas of most complexity first. In pictures of people, the eye is always attracted to the face and particularly the eyes. The combination of the graphic complexity in a face and the fact that the face embodies the essence of human expression leads the eye to examine faces for clues about meaning **5.8**.

Light and dark contrasts create distinct shapes and line edges that attract the eye. Vertical and horizontal lines or edges are stable, functioning as constant axes. Angled lines, edges, and alignments that operate counter to the vertical and horizontal guide eye movement **5.9**. Isolated elements set in neutral areas away from more complex patterns or grouped elements also attract attention.

An effective strategy is to establish a visual hierarchy to direct eye movement. A rhythmic loop can be created that takes the eye on a journey over the surface and into the depths of the composition with built-in resting places, or white space. Textures and graphic details can offer the eye a reason to sustain interest, examining the picture again **5.10**.

Theme and Motif

Theme in design is a subject or topic being represented. It also can be thought of as the quality or character of a represented idea. As such, a visual theme determines the elements to use and the appropriate ways to use them. Theme serves as a conceptual scenario for making organizational decisions. Theme may be presented as the premise of a story, a symbolic association, or the use of a visual metaphor.

Motif is a concept related to theme. The appearance of the overall image in a design is referred to as *motif.* **Motif** is the inherent pattern or arrangement of the overall image. Descriptions of motif are often culturally referential, for example, an arabesque motif, a Navajo motif, a seasonal motif, or an urban motif. There are three general kinds of overall images: nonobjective, abstract, and realistic.

Nonobjective, or **nonrepresentational**, images have no resemblance to anything recognizable. These images are built from geometric and natural elements that make no attempt to depict the real world. Nonobjective images function mainly on a formal level,

[5.8] In this book jacket design, the viewer's eye is immediately drawn to the face, particularly the subject's eye, which is cast downward at the book jacket's title.
Design by Chip Kidd, photo by Geoff Spear.

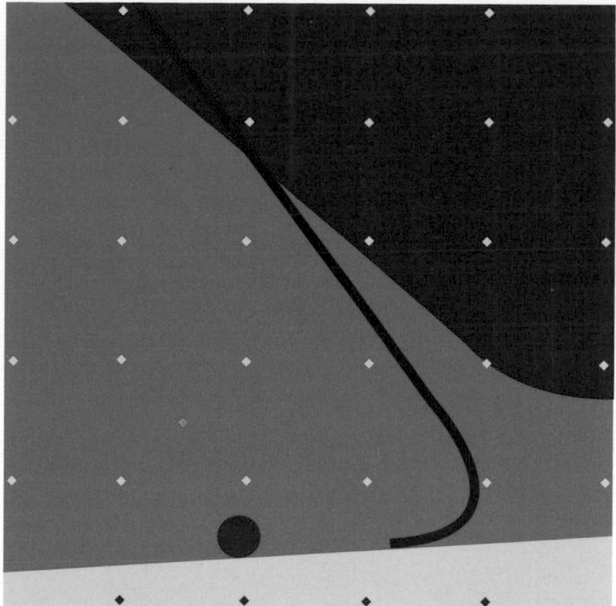

[5.9] In this composition, eye movement tends to follow the light blue line and the edges of the orange and yellow against the dark blue. The angles are countered by the regular placement of the yellow diamonds. The yellow diamonds and the dark blue area bring attention to the conspicuous circle and the isolated orange diamond. The grouped row of orange diamonds along the bottom edge of the composition call briefly for the viewer's attention.
© Cengage Learning 2013. Design by Mark Thomas.

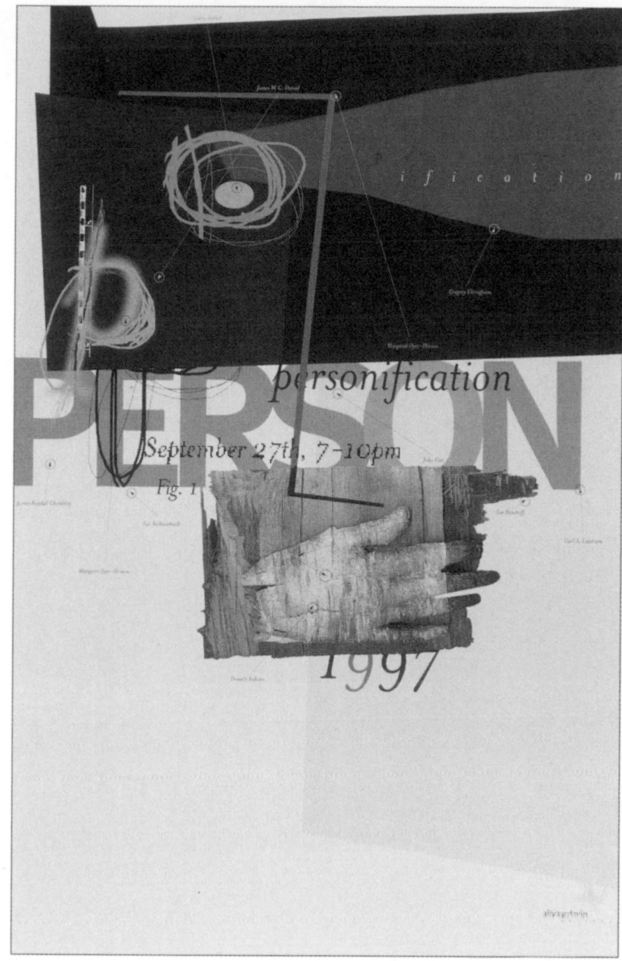

[5.10] This poster promoting the opening of a gallery exhibition features samples from work by each artist represented in the exhibition. This imagery and the typographic content about the opening and exhibition are strategically scaled and positioned to create a well-balanced composition, supported by neutral areas of black-and-white space that leads the viewer's eye from one design element to the next.
Design by The Partnership.

concerned with general relationships of basic elements. Conveying a theme with nonobjective imagery is conveying a quality or feeling that is interpreted rather than described **5.11**. **Abstract** images resemble the physical world but are a simplification or distortion of the things in it.

In theory, all images are abstract because they are re-creations of the physical world. But within the realm of the visual arts, images are classified by their degree of coherence to the world you see and live in **5.12**.

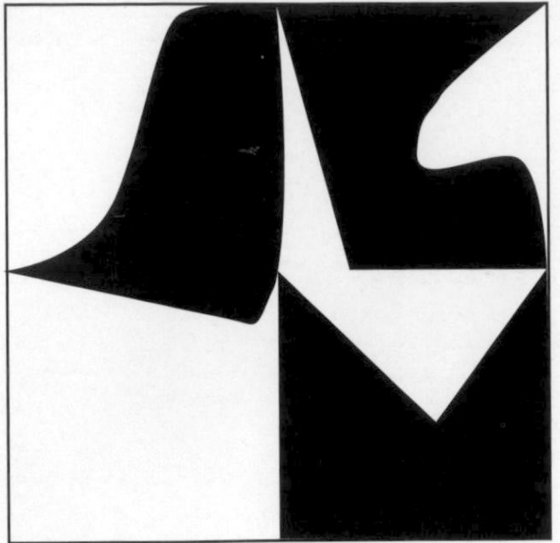

[5.11] Nonobjective imagery relies on shape relationships and a formal visual vocabulary to communicate. This composition is about the tension created between points and edges and the precarious balance of the shapes. The shapes also seem stuck in their position with no room to move. The prevailing feeling conveyed here in the relationship between the shapes is a sense of confinement and incompatibility.
© Cengage Learning 2013.

[a]

[b]

[5.12a and b] Every identity program created at Malcolm Grear Designers is the result of extensive research, conceptualization, and refinement leading to a specific and relevant design solution. The new identity for Vanderbilt, integrating the oak leaf and acorn within the *V* letterform, has symbolic (seed of knowledge, strength, and steadfastness) and historic references. Additionally, the form's incorporation of these elements reflects Vanderbilt's status as an active arboretum.
Courtesy of Vanderbilt University.

Realistic or **representational** imagery replicates the real world in a descriptive manner. Represented objects have defined and namable referents to the real world, although they may contain symbolic meaning **5.13**.

Theme and motif are used in design to create a graphic look that promotes the overall idea. Often the theme is given as part of the design problem, but it can sometimes be the job

[5.13] This illustration for the *New York Times* Book Review is an example of realism or representational imagery, which often involves exaggeration to project an editorial point of view, as in this caricature of Neil Young.
Illustration by C.F. Payne; Art direction by Steven Heller.

of a designer to determine a theme. In either case, a theme must be researched and developed so the imagery used to represent it is appropriate, accurate, and ultimately understood by the audience.

A theme is usually generated with a word concept that can be translated into graphic form. Some common thematic categories include animals, industry, music, seasons, places, sports, weather, holidays, culture, and historic periods. Narrowing a broad theme to a specific concept can provide more pointed communication. For example, winter might be narrowed to snow (and more specifically translated to snowflake) as a motif or symbol used to represent the broader original theme.

Design Criticism Model

The purpose of the Design Criticism Model is to expand your vocabulary and critical-thinking skills. It is adapted from a model developed by Edmund Feldman, *Varieties of Visual Experience*, and is directed toward a discussion of design imagery. You can use this model in critiques or in writing about your work or the work of others. Most of this discussion involves an examination of compositional organization and visual relationships.

Four Levels of Visual Inquiry

Level I	**Description:** Facts, no personal feelings
A. *Identify the venue— the form of the design. Identify the media (studio tools).*	illustration, poster, package, book, photograph, Web page, advertisement, etc.
B. *State the size, dimension, and point of view (dictated by venue and media).*	painted, offset printed, collage, electronic, hand- or machine-fabricated, etc.
C. *Determine the kind of image.*	**Nonobjective**—has no referents to nameable objects in the real world. These images are generally geometric or organic lines and shapes used to create a look or pattern. **Abstract**—refers to commonly understood, nameable objects from the real world; however, the image is distorted or significantly simplified with regard to color and form. **Realistic** or **representational**—refers to commonly understood, nameable objects reflecting detailed attributes of the real world or surreal world.
D. *Identify content or subject.*	In realistic and abstract work, this is people, buildings, animals, automobiles, etc. For nonobjective, this describes line configuration, shapes, forms, and use of typographic forms.
E. *Describe the overall arrangement.*	color, patterns, textures, motif, etc. This specifies properties of the arrangement, such as vertical, horizontal, diagonal, ragged, or smooth.
F. *Research background information.*	dates, name(s), period style, "school," movement, design, or historical references
Level II	**Analysis:** Examine compositional form and its function.
A. *Discuss the use of principles of visual organization.*	Visual hierarchy to serve overall organization—unity, theme, proportion, variety, balance, movement, orientation, dominance, scale, and variations of these
B. *Discuss the use of elements of visual organization.*	line, shape, form (graphic and typographic), size, space, color, and texture
C. *Discuss the appropriate use of media.*	Includes studio or artist materials and the form that the communication assumes—venue (e.g., book, television, digital monitor, billboard, and print)
Level III	**Interpreting the Message:** Find meaning in the image. Determining the communication mode of the image provides insight as to how the image functions and how the image serves the message. Semiotics helps to decode and interpret the meaning of "signs" in media, communication, and culture. Semiotics is a field that studies how meanings are made. Consider the following modes of communication extracted from semiotics.
A. *Is the image communicating a specific viewpoint or message?*	The image is a **sign symbol**, which conveys a "one-to-one" correspondence to its referent (e.g., a stop sign and traffic light).

B. *Does the image stand for or represent something else?*	The image is a **symbol** (e.g., a cross, a national flag). Logotypes are considered symbols.
C. *Does the image physically or perceptually resemble or imitate that to which it refers?*	The image is an **icon**, which possess similar qualities to the referent (e.g., a portrait, diagram, and scale model).
D. *Does the image signify a connection to some physical or causal event?*	The image is an **index**, which shows evidence of something observed or inferred (e.g., smoke, a clock, and a footprint).
E. *Can the image be observed from a variety of viewpoints?*	The image is a **metaphor**, which is open to interpretation and can be "read" on many levels (e.g., a Georgia O'Keefe flower painting, a Brad Holland illustration, and a Brancussi "egg form" sculpture).
Level IV	**Evaluation:** Making a judgment on the effectiveness of the communication or message. An expressed opinion based on a rationale.
A. *Your judgment or opinion is more meaningful when it is based on a critical inquiry that includes description, analysis, and interpretation of the image and its message. Levels I–III initiate thought, dialogue, and necessary research of the subject, providing a rationale for your evaluation.*	
B. *You do not have to reach a conclusion in the evaluation. The evaluation can lead to further questions that require additional investigation.*	

VISUAL RELATIONSHIPS

Controlling the relationships of visual elements is the art of aesthetic judgment. Controlling graphic continuity, determining the character and quality of the elements, and deciding questions such as "how much is enough?" and "what kind should be used?" are the types of issues that make art of design. The work of arranging elements also taps one's artistic sensibilities.

Making decisions about where elements should be placed and how they should interact requires a measure of intuition and logic. The essential objective is to create visual interest while communicating the intended message. Investigative, preliminary studies allow for the exploration, development and refinement of visual relationships, and compositional arrangements that will engage the eye and mind of the viewer.

Figure and Ground

The relationship between figure and ground is perhaps the most fundamental in design composition. Shape and contrast affect the figure-ground interaction most profoundly. Keep in mind that the ground, or space around a figure, has shape as well. Shapes can exist independently, overlap one another, or have a transparent quality depending on the figure-ground arrangement.

There are three basic arrangements:

- **Simple figure-ground** arrangement is the coherent, independent presence of a shape juxtaposed in a space that serves as the ground. The space can be compressed or shallow, or it can create the illusion of depth. In simple figure-ground arrangement, the figure is positive and generally active and the ground is negative and generally passive **5.14**.
- **Figure-ground reversal** is a graphic effect in which figure can function as ground and ground as figure. Shapes form in the space between figures and create a visual inversion. The reversal can be a dynamic way to activate neutral space in a composition **5.15**.

[5.14] The playful use of typography and illustration for this self-promotion relies on a simple figure-ground relationship. All of the elements are placed against a neutral background to allow the distinctiveness of each element to read clearly with the others.
Self-promotion design by Scorsone/Drueding.

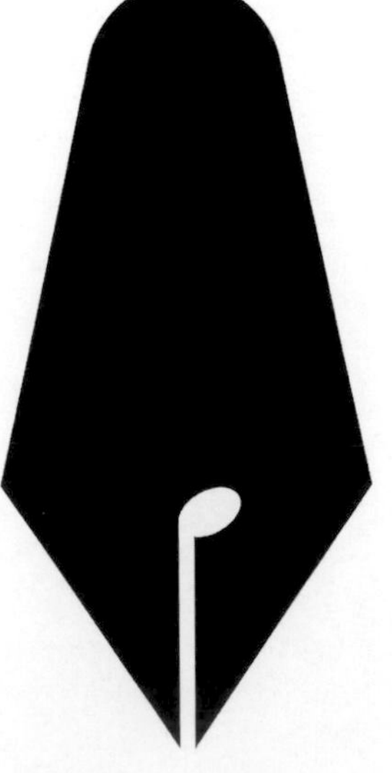

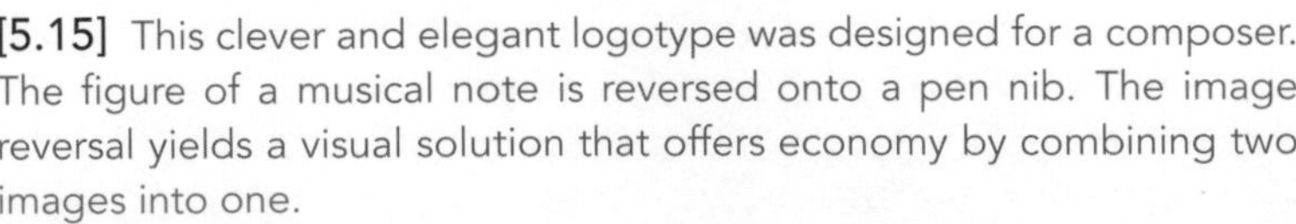

[5.15] This clever and elegant logotype was designed for a composer. The figure of a musical note is reversed onto a pen nib. The image reversal yields a visual solution that offers economy by combining two images into one.
Logo design by Dogstar.

[5.16] Figure-ground ambiguity is what designer McRay Magleby had in mind when he created the graphics for this Earth Day poster. The positive image of the mother, the profile of the head, and the resulting kiss are intertwined, engaging the viewer in a visual mystery of form and concept. *Poster design by McRay Magleby.*

- **Figure-ground ambiguity** finds the viewer uncertain about the relationship between form and space. The trick to controlling figure-ground ambiguity effectively is to create an arrangement that is disorienting yet comprehensible **5.16**.

Closure

Closure literally refers to the condition of being closed. A form that is entirely closed can be thought of as fully described or complete **5.17a** and **5.17b**. However, a form can be interrupted or incomplete and still be understood. There is a limit to how incomplete a form can be represented yet still be comprehended.

For example, **5.18a, 5.18b, 5.18c**, and **5.18d** present a sequence of illustrations of the St. Louis Arch. The question is "How much can be removed from the arch, yet still have it read as complete?" In 5.18a, 5.18b, and even 5.18c, there is enough information for the eye to complete the form. In 5.18d, however, it is difficult to complete the form in the way the viewer

[a]

[b]

[5.17a and b] Forms can be described as open or closed. In 5.17a, the open form is seen as transparent, functioning like a wire framework that you can see through. Closed forms are opaque and built from a solid mass like the one in 5.17b. Both forms are examples of complete or described closure. *(a) Naum Gabo, © Tate, London, 2011. Courtesy of Tate, London/Art Resource, NY.*
(b) Jean Arp, © 2011 Artists Rights Society (ARS), New York/VG Bild-Kunst, Bonn. Courtesy of Tate, London/Art Resource, NY.

[a]

[b]

[c]

[d]

[5.18a, b, c and d] This series of images of the St. Louis Arch provides an example of incomplete closure. *© Cengage Learning 2013.*

recognizes it. In this case, closure is about presenting form in a way that permits viewers to complete it in their mind's eye. This relationship is widely used to create visual interest for the viewer.

Closure also depends on relative position, that is, the distance from one object or shape to another. When associated shapes are physically too far apart, they have little or no relationship; but when they are positioned closer to each other, the relationship can becomes more meaningful. They can exist as complements or create a visual tension. A classic example of this type of closure from art history is in Michelangelo's painting *The Creation of Adam.* In this famous scene, God reaches his pointed finger outward toward the finger on Adam's hand. The fingers almost touch, which supports the concept of birth or creation. If the fingers were farther apart or touching, the quality of the visual relationship and subsequent meaning would change **5.19a** and **5.19b**.

Closure also depends on relative position, that is, the distance from one object or shape to another. When associated shapes are physically too far apart, they have little or no relationship; but when they are positioned closer to each other, the relationship can becomes more meaningful. They can exist as complements or create a visual tension. A classic example of this type of closure from art history is in Michelangelo's painting *The Creation of Adam.*

[a]

[5.19a] A detail of Michelangelo's timeless image, *The Creation of Adam*, presents a classic example of form completing form. *Courtesy of Erich Lessing/Art Resource, NY.*

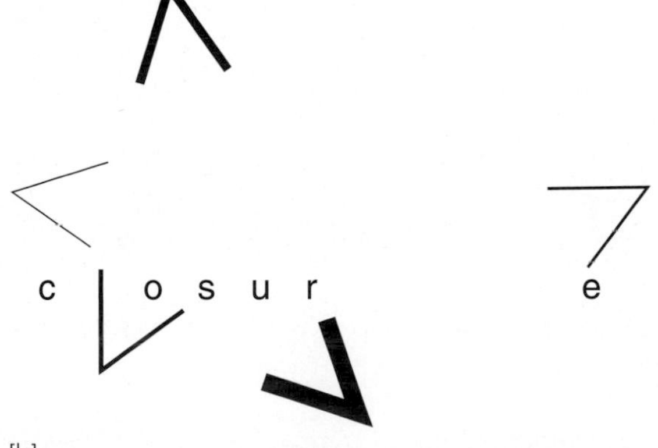

[b]

[5.19b] The *e* and adjacent angle can be associated with the other letterforms and angles by similarity. But because of the distant proximity, they do not appear as though they belong to the rest of the word. Their proximity needs to be adjusted closer to complete the word *closure* and the accompanying star shape. Presenting the five component angles of the star apart from one another allows viewers to participate more actively by completing the star shape in their mind's eye. *© Cengage Learning 2013.*

In this famous scene, God reaches his pointed finger outward toward the finger on Adam's hand. The fingers almost touch, which supports the concept of birth or creation. If the fingers were farther apart or touching, the quality of the visual relationship and subsequent meaning would change 5.19a and 5.19b.

Closure also depends on relative position, that is, the distance from one object or shape to another. When associated shapes are physically too far apart, they have little or no relationship; but when they are positioned closer to each other, the relationship can becomes more meaningful. They can exist as complements or create a visual tension. A classic example of this type of closure from art history is in Michelangelo's painting *The Creation of Adam.* In this famous scene, God reaches his pointed finger outward toward the finger on Adam's hand. The fingers almost touch, which supports the concept of birth or creation. If the fingers were farther apart or touching, the quality of the visual relationship and subsequent meaning would change 5.19a and 5.19b.

Closure also depends on relative position, that is, the distance from one object or shape to another. When associated shapes are physically too far apart, they have little or no relationship; but when they are positioned closer to each other, the relationship can becomes more meaningful. They can exist as complements or create a visual tension. A classic example of this type of closure from art history is in Michelangelo's painting *The Creation of Adam.* In this famous scene, God reaches his pointed finger outward toward the finger on Adam's hand. The fingers almost touch, which supports the concept of birth or creation. If the fingers were farther apart or touching, the quality of the visual relationship and subsequent meaning would change 5.19a and 5.19b.

Contrast

When you think of **contrast**, you think of the relationship between light and dark. That is, of course, one kind of contrast; but there are many others. A related term used often in the visual arts for contrast is *juxtaposition*, which refers to a relational, comparative placement of two or more elements.

The possibilities are endless: negative versus positive, jagged versus straight, geometric versus organic, serene versus chaotic, rough versus smooth, random versus orderly, saturated versus pastel, static versus kinetic, monumental versus diminutive, and so forth. These contrasting relationships can be visually articulated using combinations of the elements of design. Contrast serves the higher principle—variety. Achieving unity through variety is the art of arranging unlike elements and making them work concurrently. Contrast of size, order, weight, direction, configuration, value, color, texture, and form creates visual interest by presenting an opposing context that allows one to complement the other. Curved looks more curved when placed in proximity to straight. Blue looks more blue when it is surrounded by its complement, orange. Regular looks more regular when an irregular element is present **5.20a, 5.20b**, and **5.20c**.

Anomaly

Visual **anomaly** is the presence of an element or a visual relationship that is unlike others that dominate a composition. It functions as a particular type of contrast—a contrast of nonconformity.

Anomaly can create a lively, animated quality. It can be subtle or prominent. It often brings playful attention to the point where it occurs. When it is skillfully aligned with a communication message, the use of anomaly can make an otherwise ordinary design unique **5.21**.

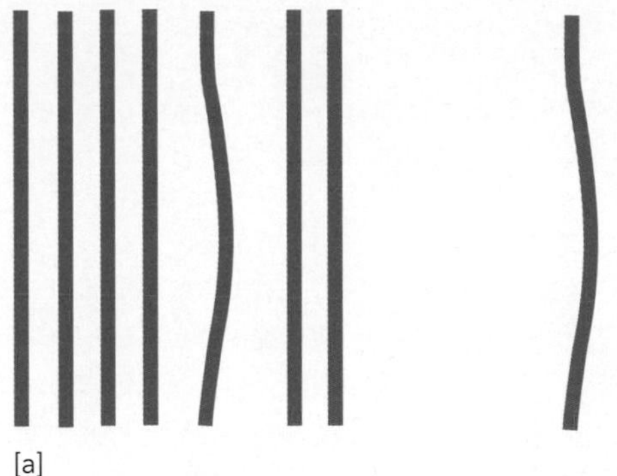

[a]

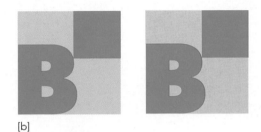

[b]

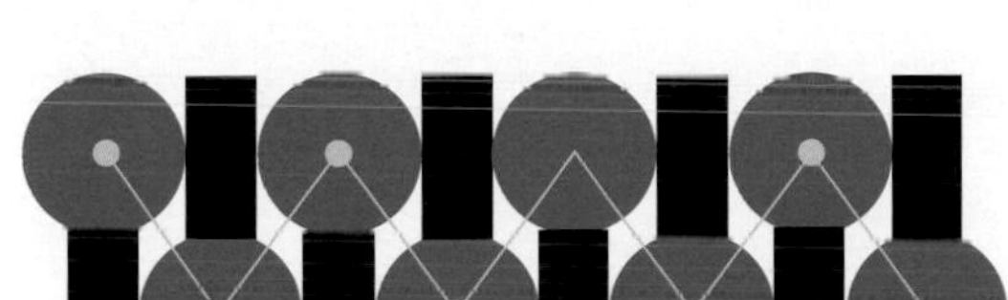

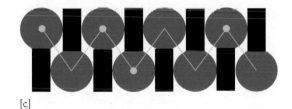

[c]

[5.20a, b and c] (a) In the context of a series of straight vertical lines, the curved line creates a tension that makes it appear more curved. (b) When placed on a complementary color field, the contrast of the blue *B* and square are heightened as compared with the neutral gray ground. (c) In a more subtle contrast, the regular rhythm of the circle and rectangle shape is countered by the intermittent rhythm of the small circle and zigzag line.
© Cengage Learning 2013.

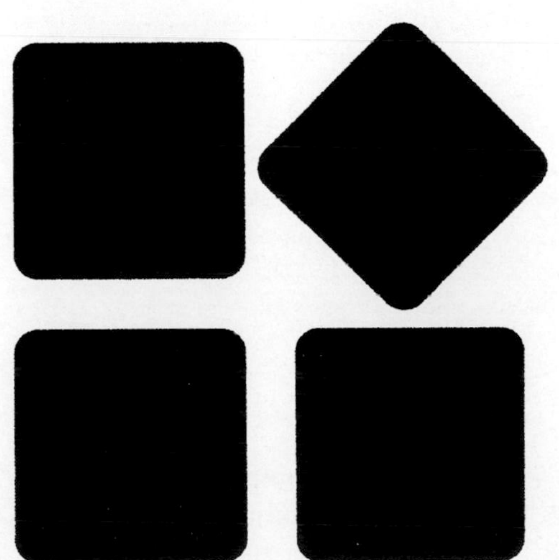

[5.21] This logo uses a four-unit grid arrangement with one different element. The diagonal unit is an example of a visual anomaly. It serves as the focal point and focus of the communication for an orthodontist whose business is straightening teeth. The designer makes a subtle but critical decision to soften the corners of the square units to represent the qualities of teeth.
Logotype design by Charlene Catt-Lyon, Catt-Lyon Design.

Emphasis and Focal Point

Look at any visual image; as your eye scans it, you may notice that your eye tends to return to one point—the **focal point**. As you attempt to find meaning in the image, the focal point usually contains the key to understanding the intent. It is where the designer wants to lead your eye. Often the element that dominates the visual hierarchy of a composition is located at the focal point. **Emphasis** refers to an area of interest, such as a place where lines converge, a light figure in an area of darkness, an area of complexity, or a detail in an otherwise uncomplicated field.

You just learned that visual anomaly creates a visual point of interest as well. Emphasis serves hierarchy. An area of emphasis is dominant and often is supported in the hierarchy of a composition by contrasting areas. Once the area of emphasis is located, the viewer tends to read all other elements in relationship to it **5.22a, 5.22b**, and **5.22c**.

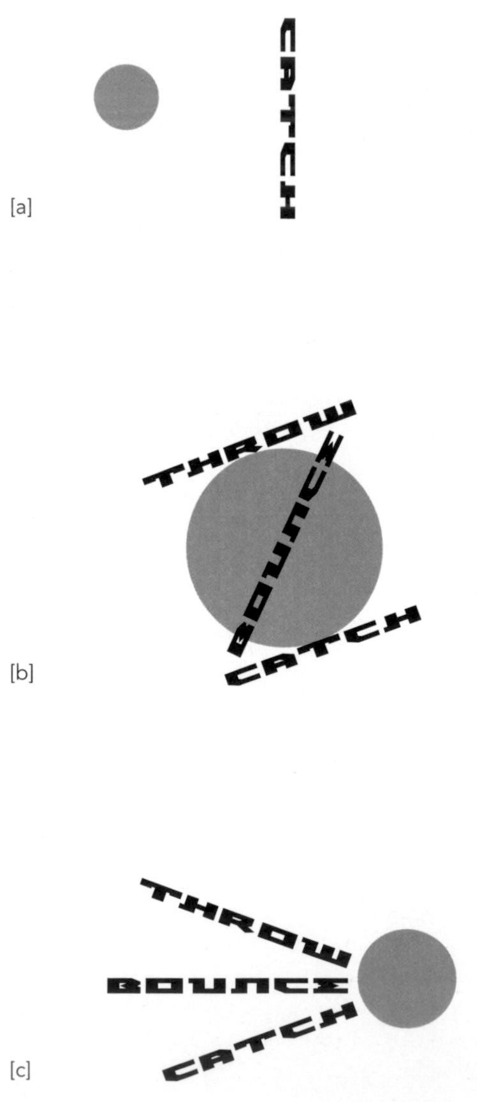

[5.22a, b and c] The arrangements in these three visuals contain the same basic elements. The dominant element in each one is the orange ball. The support elements are words that communicate an action practiced with a ball. The word elements interact with the ball, which functions as the focal point in each arrangement. In 5.22a, isolation brings attention or emphasis to the ball. It fits precisely in the center of the *T*, supporting a subliminal relationship to the word elements. In 5.22b, the size of the ball compared with the words is what calls the viewer's attention. The scale of the ball seems to be expanding as the ball presses against the words *throw* and *catch*. The diagonal orientation suggests a circular motion that reinforces the ball as a focal point. In 5.22c, an arrangement of the word elements as lines converge toward the ball. Convergence is a function of perspective that leads the eye to a point in space that, by definition, creates a focal point.

It is worth noting that all designs do not rely on emphasis and focal point. Decorative arts such as textile design rely on a regular pattern of equally distributed elements 1.8d.

Space and Illusion

This chapter and Chapter 4 has discussed the effects of color and shape interaction that can be illusory in nature. Simultaneous contrast, vibrating color, effect of color backgrounds, afterimage, subjective contour, and certain figure-ground relationships create illusory phenomena that deceives the eye. Optical illusions play a role in the design of imagery. High-contrast imagery often developed for logotypes, symbol design, and pictographs can require optical adjusting for the viewer's eye to perceive them properly. In the discussion of *gestalt*, you learned that the eye seeks order, trying to make sense of patterns, groupings, and visual relationships. Visual relationships are based on context, but they are affected by perception. Illusory phenomena have been studied to learn more about how the human eye and brain work to perceive the world. The research yields valuable insights for visual artists. Illusions based on depth cues relate to an artist's use of linear and overlapping perspective **5.23** through **5.26**.

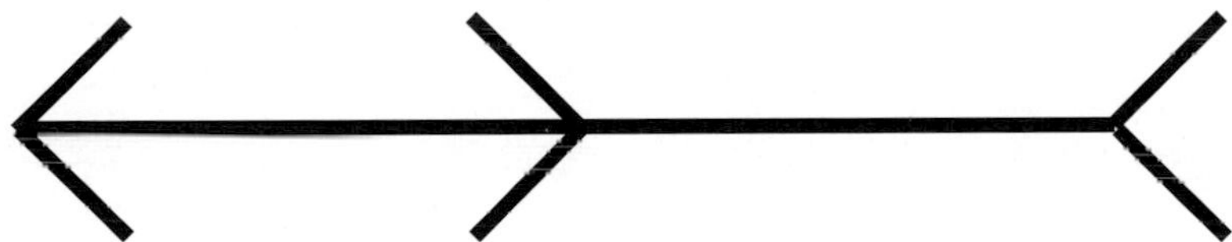

[5.23] In the Mueller-Lyer illusion, line segments between the angles "in" and the angles "out" are mathematically equal, although they appear different in length. The explanation for this is based on a person's intuitive understanding of perspective (depth and distance cues). The angles "in" are associated with closer, and the angles "out" are associated with farther away.
© Cengage Learning 2013.

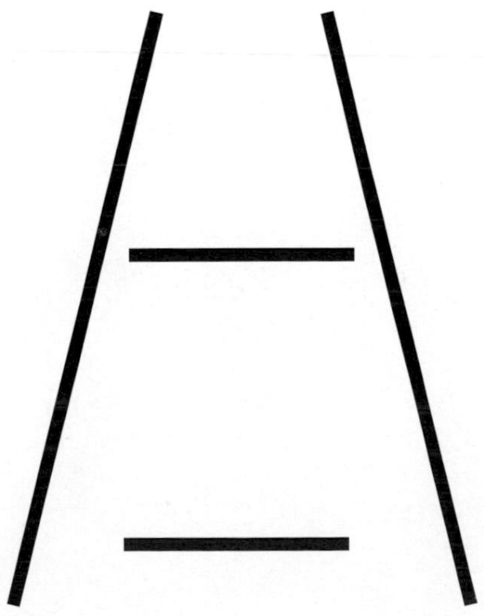

[5.24] This illusion developed by Mario Ponzo is based on a similar explanation. Both horizontal lines are equal length. The line segment that crosses the two converging lines exists in a context that you associate with farther away.
© Cengage Learning 2013.

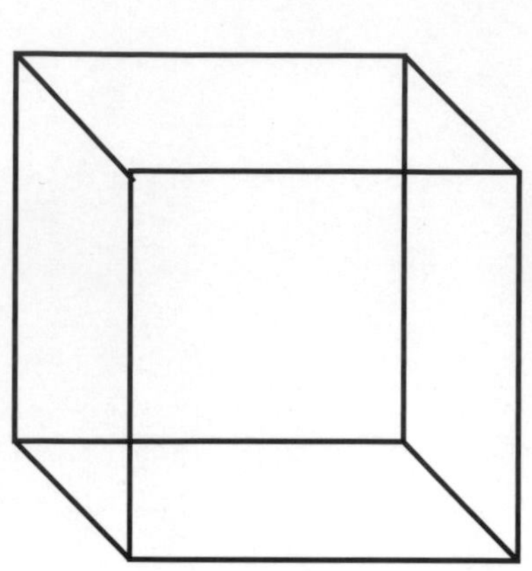

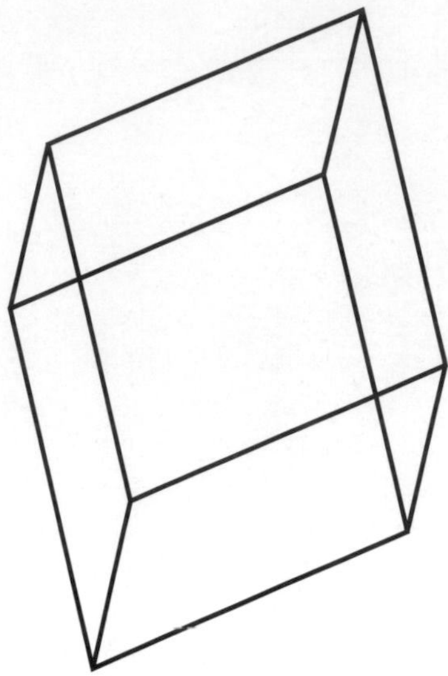

[5.25] The Necker cube (left) and rhomboid (right) are examples of depth-ambiguous figures. These figures, presented as "open forms" without a background, flip from front to back. In either case, the "fronts" are perceived as smaller.

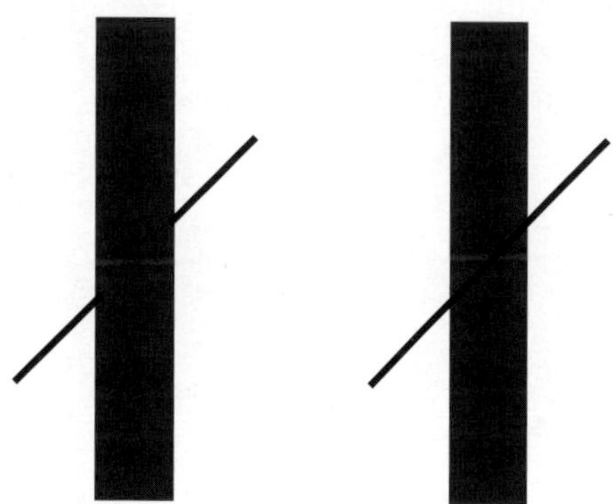

[5.26] Johann Poggendorf described an illusion based on overlapping. On the left, the diagonal line is interrupted by the rectangle—it appears disjointed. The counterpart on the right offers a different result.

Other optical illusions depend on context cues or relative size perception **5.27** and **5.28**. Graphic artists routinely make adjustments to imagery based on relative size. Making refinements to imagery that is susceptible to such effects first requires that you recognize them. While these examples are "clinical" in nature, the theory behind them applies to particular kinds of visual imagery. You will undoubtedly encounter these illusory effects. You will have to determine whether they are desired or if you need to modify the design accordingly.

[5.27] The two center circles appear different in size—the Hermann Ebbinghaus illusion.
© Cengage Learning 2013.

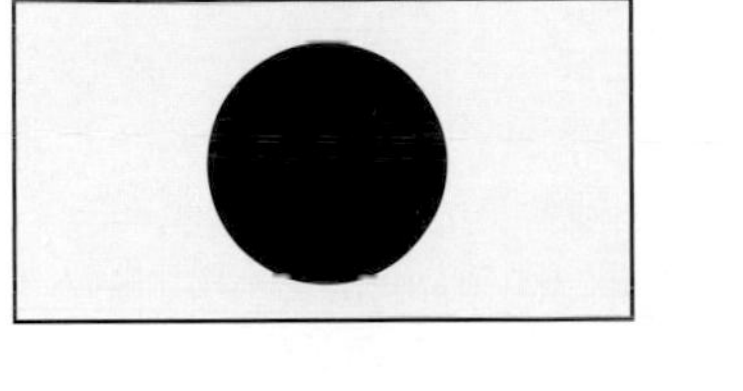

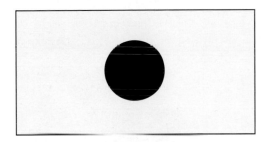

[5.28] The circle and rectangle is a variation of the Ebbinghaus illusion. They rely on a scale comparison. It has been cited as an explanation for why the moon appears larger when it is closer to the horizon.
© Cengage Learning 2013.

Origins and Inspirations

You could think of the visual world as comprised of three realms: microscopic, macroscopic, and the world in between that is experienced with the naked eye. What is curious and fascinating about the microscopic world of molecules and atoms and the macroscopic world of the cosmos is that they resemble each other. *Powers of Ten*, a film by Ray and Charles Eames, is a brilliant illustration of the scale of the universe. It zooms out from a man's hand to 10^{24}, which is to the end of the visible universe, and back in to 10^{-16}, revealing the molecular structures inside the man's hand. An important lesson here is that careful observation of natural and constructed worlds can reveal a rich source for inspiration and for design structures.

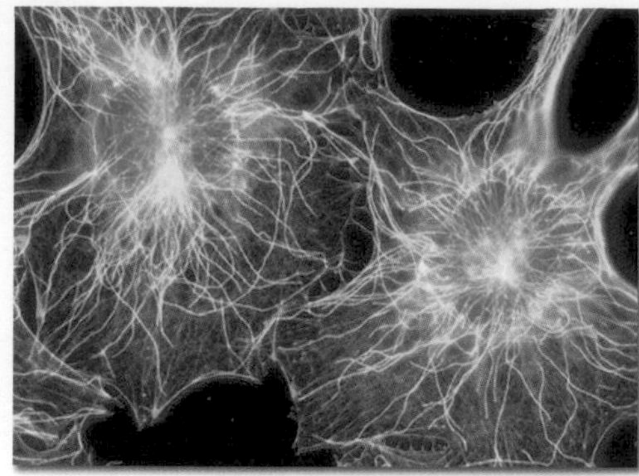

[5.29] The left NASA photo image is a view of a galaxy with enhanced color in comparison to a photomicrograph of structural protein of mouse cells. While the forms are not exactly alike, their nucleic structures resemble each other. There are countless examples of repeated and reciprocal structures and systems in nature.
Courtesy of NASA/JPL-Caltech/UCLA (left). Photomicrograph (right) by Dr. Torsten Whittman, University of California, San Francisco.

Design and Nature

Visual artists examine the world with a critical eye, often seeing what others overlook. It is important to develop an observational curiosity of the visual world, examine it, and study it. Where do the shapes, structures, and systems you use to design come from? **5.30** and **5.31**.

[5.30] M. C. Escher created imaginative spaces using illusions and precise figure-ground relationships. His inspiration and subject matter was derived from a careful examination of shapes in nature. His observations of animal forms and animal behavior yielded creative views of animals in repeated patterns with many visual surprises.
M.C. Escher's Smaller and Smaller, 1956. ©2011 The M.C. Escher Company-Holland. All rights reserved. www.mcescher.com.

[5.31] The bird and fish shapes are carefully designed to interlock as they pass one another. They share not only a figure-ground relationship but also an ecological dependency.
M.C. Escher's Sky and Water I, 1938. ©2011 The M.C. Escher Company-Holland. All rights reserved. www.mcescher.com.

You can see them in the natural world as a vocabulary of forms that are initiated by growth, built by animals, or developed from changing conditions. Shapes in nature tend to occur out of function for survival and economy of use. Some of the basic shapes in nature include the sphere, polygon, spiral, helix (or coil), and branch **5.32a, 5.32b**, and **5.32c**. From the outside, an eggshell has amazing resistance to cracking; yet from the inside, an egg is fragile enough for a weak chick to crack its way out. The hexagonal-shaped honeycomb is an efficient structure used by bees to store honey. The growth of tree branches and many forms of shells and mollusks is based on a spiral. Certain plants rely on a helix shape to coil around other structures for growth. Animals such as the squid and most stemmed plant growth are examples of branching. These basic shapes have served as content and structure for artists through the millennia. In nature as in design, they are the building blocks for more complex structures. There are many examples of how human design mimics the efficiencies and aesthetic beauty in nature's designs. Perfectly packed spherical trout eggs lying on the bottom of a mountain stream and the aforementioned mathematically efficient hexagonal honeycomb are both used in the package design for fruit and protective packing for other fragile products **5.33a** and **5.33b**.

The design of many architectural forms, such as domes, metal grids, and modular forms, owe their aesthetic beauty and structural integrity to forms in nature.

Nature often uses and reuses the same basic shapes in variation. In design, basic shapes also are used in different ways or in variation **5.34**.

Taking a close, slow look at forms in nature can offer a rich source of inspiration and a lesson in basic design. Take your sketchbook to the zoo, a botanical garden, a forest, or your own backyard. Study the growth patterns of plants and flowers. Use a magnifying glass to view details. Look at the way branches grow on trees and flowers. Make careful sketches and notes describing the things you see. You may already have a collection of shells, insects, or plant

[a]

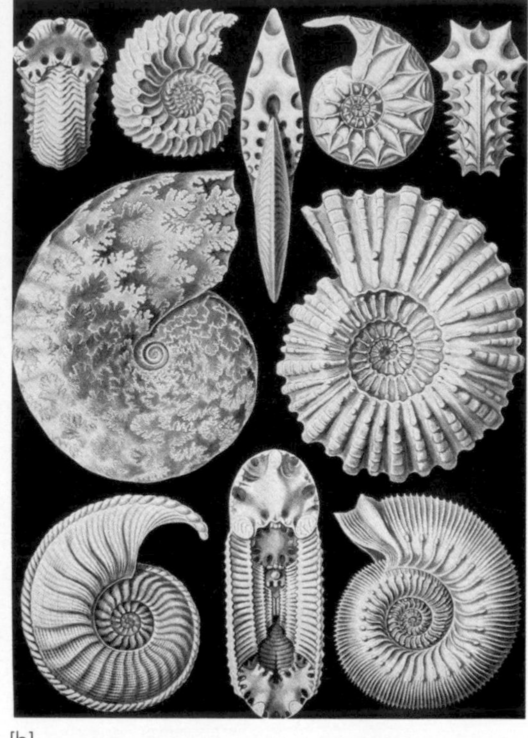

[b]

[c]

[5.32a, b and c] Ernst Haeckel (1834–1919), biologist and philosopher, made amazing drawings of organisms he studied with the naked eye and with microscopes. In 5.32a, a drawing of marine protozoa is one of a series of drawings of marine protozoa, examples of polygons, whereas 5.32b presents variations of shell forms based on the spiral and 5.32c is a page of drawings of fungi. These forms offer a combination of branching, coiling, and sphere shapes.
Public domain.

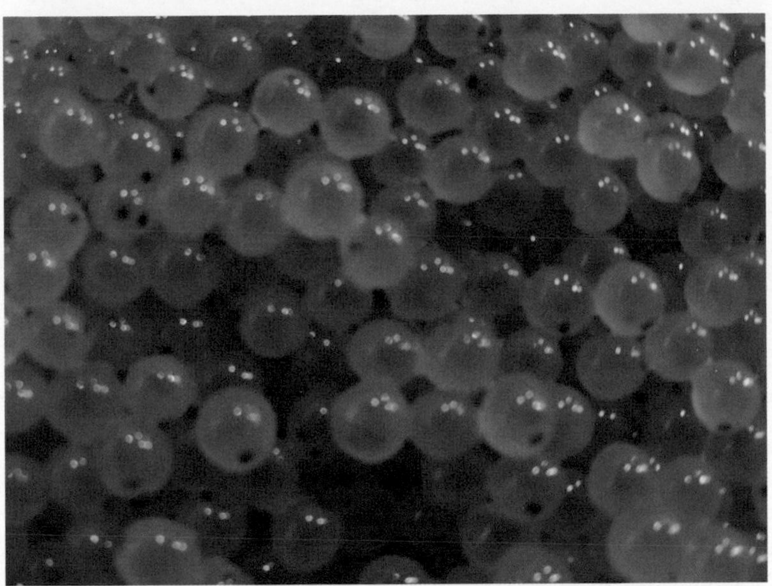

[a]

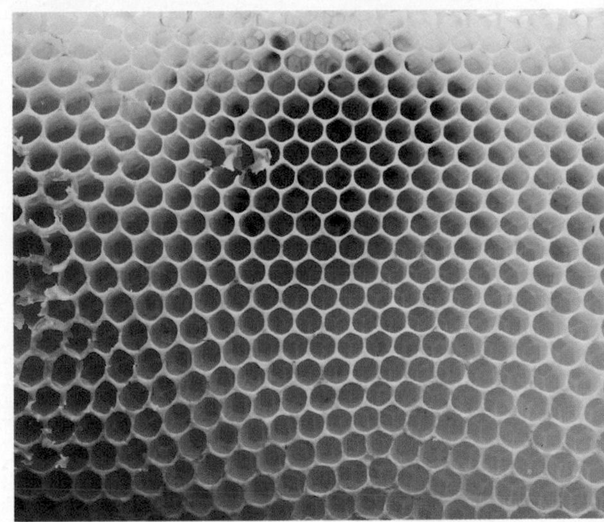

[b]

[5.33a, and b] After being laid, sphere-shaped trout eggs gather in clusters at the bottom of a stream or river waiting to hatch. It is still a mystery how honey bees arrive at a hexagon as they construct a honeycomb but it serves as the perfect modular shape for efficient storage unit.
(a) Courtesy of Nisqually Trout Farms, Inc.
(b) © Ionescu Bogdan Cristian/iStockphoto.

[5.34] This playfully enchanting three-dimensional illustration was designed to promote and enhance the DVD review column in *The New York Times*. The review column is published quarterly and often utilizes seasonal themes. The fall theme for this illustration combines an imaginative use of a leaf form as a "headdress" for the falling characters in contrast to the circular shape of the DVDs, which is incorporated into the image as a bicycle wheel.
Illustration by Chris Sickles, Red Nose Studios.

forms that you can begin to study in drawings. Collect samples of other different life-forms; you may use them as references for subjects or even design systems. Try to find examples in your nature exploration of each of the basic shapes. Many life-forms are complex structures built from more than one of the basic shapes or built from variations of the same shape. Finally, look for ways to integrate inspiration from nature into your design. Also look at how other designers rely on and use shapes, structures, and systems from nature.

SUMMARY

Organizing and arranging visual elements and information into a cohesive, engaging graphic image is the work of graphic designers. Attention must be given to the manner in which the design is organized. The key is to give careful consideration to the relationship of the elements as they come together to create a whole image. Formal control, aesthetic choices, and optical illusion affect visual relationships. Designers must work to achieve a resonance among all of the elements as they come together, like the individual sounds of a symphony. The components of overall organization, format, orientation, grid systems, eye movement, and theme function together like a transparent stage for a performance. The elements are combined to create visual relationships such as figure and ground, closure, contrast, anomaly, emphasis, and focal point, which give form to the idea. The designer is like the conductor, ensuring that the communication message and the form it takes work in coherence to serve the same compositional purpose.

projects

CONTRAST STUDIES

Objectives

- Explore a variety of forms of contrast in compositions.
- Achieve visual unity by managing variety in two contrasting compositions.
- Work with a design process that includes preliminary study of elements, composition, and application of materials.
- Work with a process that involves the refinement of hand skills to draw and paint a design image.
- Develop a visual vocabulary of lines and shapes from verbal content.
- Work to achieve economy in the relationship and arrangement of elements.
- Communicate a concept using nonobjective imagery.

Description

Design two contrasting compositions based on one of the following sets of complements: negative/positive, jagged/straight, geometric/organic, serene/chaotic, rough/smooth, random/orderly, saturated/pastel, static/kinetic, or monumental or diminutive. Use primarily basic geometric and nonobjective shapes and lines. Strive for economy in the compositions.

Choose three sets of complements to study in preliminary marker sketches. The format for the sketches is 4 inches by 4 inches.

Choose one of the sets of sketches to develop into a final compositional study. The final study is two 8-inch by 8-inch images presented together to illustrate the two contrasts. (Refer to the discussion of contrasts in this chapter.)

Limitations and Materials

Use a bristol board (two-ply or four-ply) for the final images. Work with black-and-white designer gouache to paint the final boards with flat and round paintbrushes. Mount the final studies on gray board with a 3-inch border. Present them together. This assignment also can be done as a cut-paper assignment with black-and-white cover stock.

Critique Discussion Points

How does each composition achieve unity?

Describe the overall character or quality of each composition.

Which visual relationship primarily drives the design?

How is economy achieved in each composition?

Vocabulary

contrast, unity, economy, nonobjective, negative space, positive shape, kinetic

Evaluation Criteria

Composition

Craft

Communication of Contrasting Word Concepts

Effective Use of Economy

PROPORTION STUDY WITH LINE, POINT, AND EDGE

Objectives

- Work with external and internal proportions.
- Use a grid to place design elements in a composition.
- Explore a refining process of generating elements.
- Work with repetition, scale changes, proximity, quantity, motif, and closure to produce a design composition.
- Communicate a theme in an abstract composition using basic elements.

Description

Create a composition using the golden rectangle and grid system as an underlying structure to visually convey a force of nature theme using line, point, and edge. Begin with a golden rectangle that is 11 inches on the shortest side. Subdivide the three main areas into smaller grid units using arithmetic, geometric, or triangular grids 5.5a, 5.5b, 5.5c, 5.5d, and 5.7. Ink this proportional grid system on cover stock with a fine marker and use it as a template for a design. Work to create implied alignments with elements placed in the grid system. Choose a force of nature (for example, wind, rain, snow, or flood) as a theme. Placing layers of tracing paper over the grid system and using lines, points (dots), and edges (shapes), begin generating design elements that illustrate the chosen theme. Use at least 10 layers of tracings to produce the content elements for the final composition. You can cut sections from earlier tracings and incorporate them into the final layer(s). Edit and refine the drawn elements and produce a final precisely drawn tracing of your composition. Carefully transfer the design to illustration board and paint it with black gouache. Do a color translation as an extension of the assignment.

Limitations and Materials

tracing paper, black markers, compass, straightedge, pencil, 16-inch by 20-inch illustration board, designer gouache, fine round and flat brushes, graphite paper (for transfer)

Critique Discussion Points

Discuss your process from the first tracing to the final board.

How did the grid system dictate the placement of elements?

Identify two visual relationships. How are they serving the overall design?

Identify a good design decision and one design decision you would like to change.

Vocabulary

repetition, scale changes, proximity, quantity, motif, closure, grid, golden rectangle, proportion, abstract

Evaluation Criteria

Composition

Craft

Communication of the Force of Nature Concept

Adherence to the Criteria

LETTERFORM STUDY

Objectives

- Make compositional decisions using letterforms as design elements.
- Study type as shape.
- Work with a variety of high-contrast visual relationships.
- Manage a variety of figure-ground relationships in the same composition.

Description

Produce a composition composed of nine smaller letterform compositions.

Using a variety of single letterforms, begin by generating 25 to 30 black-and-white studies that are 3 inches by 3 inches. Variety is the key—variety of typefaces, scale changes, figure-ground relationships, anomaly, closure, emphasis, orientation, and proximity in the small compositions. Cut the small studies carefully into 3-inch squares. Create a new, larger composition using nine of the small studies arranged in a nine-unit grid, three studies across by three studies down. Work to create overall continuity (unity) and rhythm from one unit to the next.

Hint: To create visual interest, partially obscure the identity of the letterforms through cropping, rotating, or reversing within the small compositions.

Limitations and Materials

Generate type from a computer or a photocopy from printed sources. For the final composition, use clean, good-quality laser prints or photocopies. Use a studio knife and metal straightedge to cut small studies. Glue the nine studies in a square grid arrangement on cover stock and mount to a piece of gray board with a 3-inch border.

Critique Discussion Points

Describe the use of variety in the design.

How is variety controlled in the overall composition?

Identify a type of figure-ground relationship at work in the design.

Describe in one word a quality that the design conveys. Point to the visual relationships that support this.

Vocabulary

variety, scale changes, figure-ground relationships, anomaly, closure, emphasis, orientation, proximity

Evaluation Criteria

Composition

Craft

Ability to Achieve Variety

Adherence to the Criteria

in review

1. What does the gestalt phrase "the whole is greater than the sum of the parts" mean?
2. Discuss two ways that format is used in graphic design.
3. What are the unique implications of horizontal, vertical, and square formats?
4. What are the advantages of using a grid in design compositions?
5. Discuss the various visual relationships that control eye movement.
6. What are the three general classifications of motif?
7. How does figure-ground reversal differ from figure-ground ambiguity?
8. Identify two visual illusions and discuss how you would compensate for their effect in a design.
9. Find in a work of professional design one of the basic shapes in nature. Describe the use of the shape and offer a reason why you think the designer chose to use it.
10. What are four of the basic shapes in nature? Give an example of how one of them relates to human design.

© Sagmeister Inc.

"Work your ass off. Try as many things as possible. Fail fast. Work your ass off more."

Stefan Sagmeister

Stefan Sagmeister is an internationally recognized and award winning graphic and motion designer. He has worked with some of the most prestigious design studios in the business including Leo Burnett and Tibor Kalman. He works regularly with icons in the music industry such as the Rolling Stones, Talking Heads, and Lou Reed. He has received Grammy awards for his CD box packaging. He works out of his Manhattan studio and is one of the most sought after speakers in the design industry. Stefan also teaches graphic design at the School of Visual Arts and the Cooper Union School of Art.

How did you get started in your career? What is your educational background?

Like many designers of my generation, I originally was attracted to the field by record albums. Then I learned about many other interesting directions within the vast world of design in art school (which I loved, I stayed as long as I possibly could . . .). I studied at the University for Applied Arts in Vienna and at Pratt Institute in New York City. Eventually I did have to start to work.

What made you decide to pursue the career path that you've chosen?

The possibility to generate work that's seen by everybody (as opposed to just a few in a gallery or museum setting) seemed incredibly enticing to me. That turned out to be true. What I did not count on that the field of design proofed to be so incredibly multifaceted that it allows for a great amount of reinvention (be it formal, conceptual, or media related) without leaving the field. I'm still excited to get out of bed in the morning.

What has been your biggest challenge in your career? Your biggest achievement?

The former: A CD cover for Aerosmith. But; I'm sadly, I'm not allowed to talk about it.

The latter: A. Possibly the *Things I've Learned in My Life So Far* series. Because we got so much great feedback. Some of that feedback came from young designers, my favorite line: After I read your book I had to go and do a lot of work.

That's exactly how I felt as a student after coming across a design project I enjoyed.

What do you believe has been the biggest factor in your success?

1. Always fresh lemon wafers everywhere in the studio.
2. Tallness.

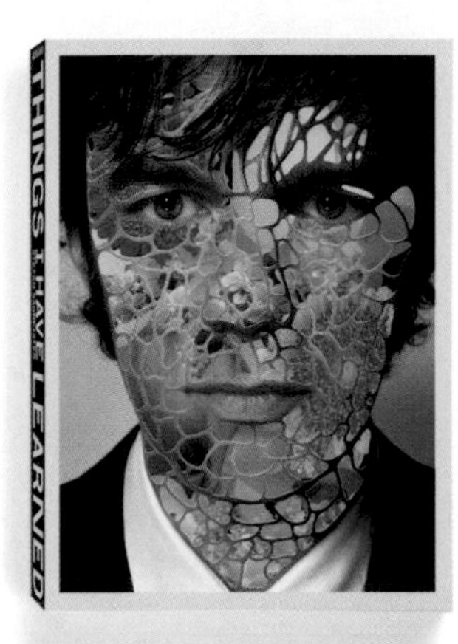

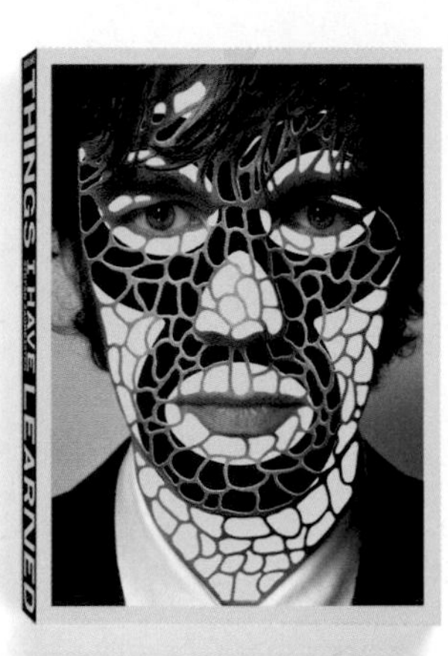

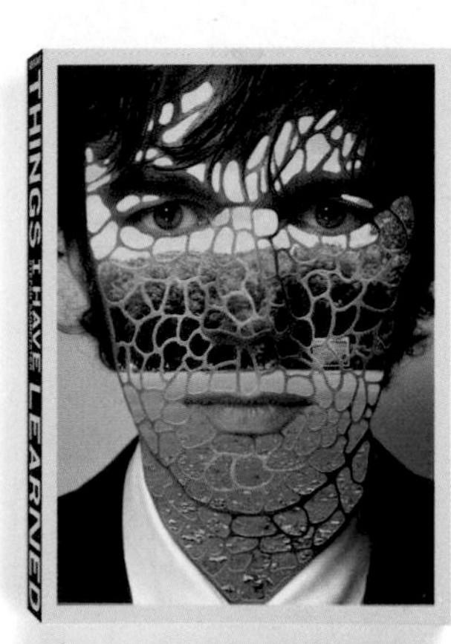

Published in 2008, *Things I Have Learned in My Life So Far* is a collection of tomes, separately bound but contained within a single slipcase. Each is a personal statement that blends design and fine art with Sagmeister's personal observations about life. The book's unique format is typical of Sagmeister's approach to design in that it takes advantage of unexpected production techniques, in this case a die-cut portrait of Sagmeister on the slip case, to give visual expression to the book's concept of change and adaptation. Sagmeister's portrait on the slipcase changes depending on which of the tomes is positioned directly beneath it.
©Sagmeister Inc.

3. We opened the studio in 1993 at the beginning of the first Internet boom when most other young studios were busy making as much money as fast as possible and few studios tried to do work they believed in. It was easy to stand out.

What advice would you give to recent graduates or others who are just getting started in a career in illustration or graphic design?

Work your ass off. Try as many things as possible. Fail fast. Work your ass off more.

Sagmeister supports the book's content with design explorations including typographic experiments like the ones shown above.
©Sagmeister Inc.

six

Research and Visual Communication

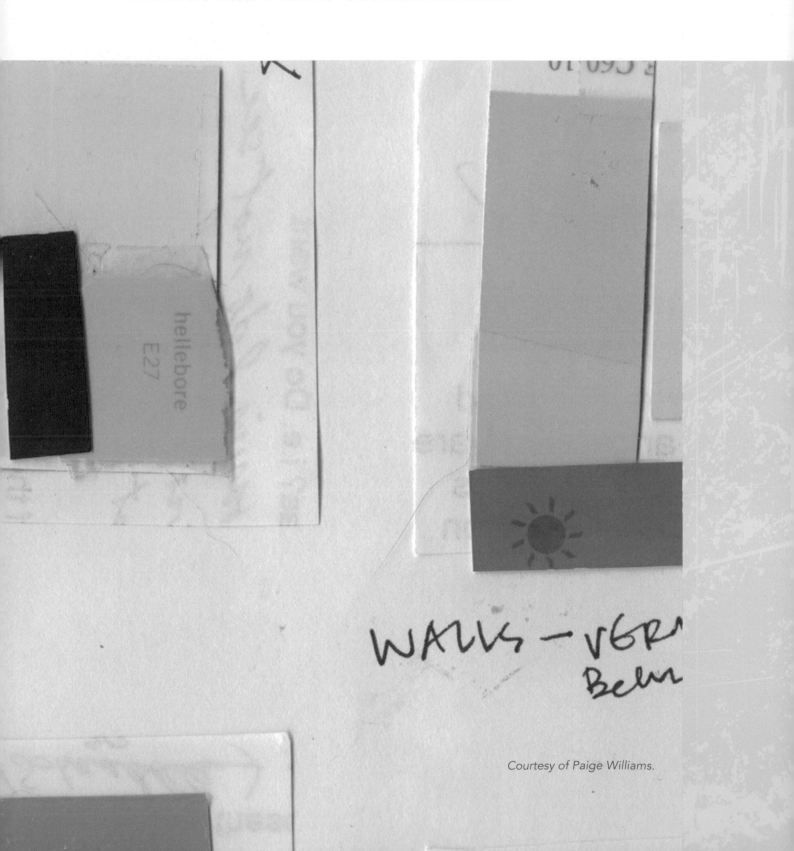

Courtesy of Paige Williams.

6

introduction

The word *research* is derived from the French term *recerchier*, which means "to thoroughly investigate." Other meanings for **research** include intellectual inquiry or examination, experiments aimed at the discovery and interpretation of facts, and the collecting of information on a specific subject. Art educator and author Dr. Laura Chapman defines *research* as "to search again." In that elegant and simple definition, Dr. Chapman captures the essence of research—an activity that, by its nature, is an ongoing process.

In the creation and production of visual art, research is often conducted. Sometimes research is deliberate and methodical; in other instances, it is intuitive and unsystematic. Intuition is a valuable form of human knowledge that relies on personal experience. The problem is that there is a limit to the depth and breadth of personal experience that each person possesses. When a problem requires a person to know something outside personal experience or knowledge, more methodical research is needed for conducting informed inquiry. But it is important to distinguish information gathering from useful inquiry and examination. An example of the former is printing pages of text and photographs about flowers from the Internet. Simply possessing the information is only the first step in conducting meaningful and useful research.

The information becomes useful only when it has been examined in the context of solving a specific problem. The problem may be to design a program for the Santa Fe Opera. If it is determined that the use of a flower as a visual metaphor is appropriate, then a particular desert flower indigenous to the high deserts of that area of New Mexico would be appropriate.

Research for communication design can be thought of as a journey that leads you to a design solution. This chapter will examine appropriate methods of research for exploring and examining the purpose of a design, the communication message, the audience, and the image itself. The chapter also will examine a variety of physical and intellectual tools used for research in visual communication.

objectives

- Explore processes and methods of research used in the field of visual communication.
- Apply methods of research to project-based design.
- Explore processes and methods for research in visual communication.
- Investigate four components of visual communication: motive, message, audience, and image.
- Present a Research Project Guide.
- Present a design criticism model for understanding design imagery.
- Explain the value of teamwork in problem solving.
- Explore the relationship between design and communication.
- Complete research projects.
- Explore a variety of research tools for the communication arts.

COMMUNICATION IN DESIGN

The incorporation of a communication objective distinguishes graphic design, applied photography, and illustration from other visual arts. Managing effective design is managing both the visual elements and accompanying communication objectives. A package or book cover must represent the contents within. A corporate logo must represent the image and nature of a company's business. An advertisement must deliver a pointed message about a product or service.

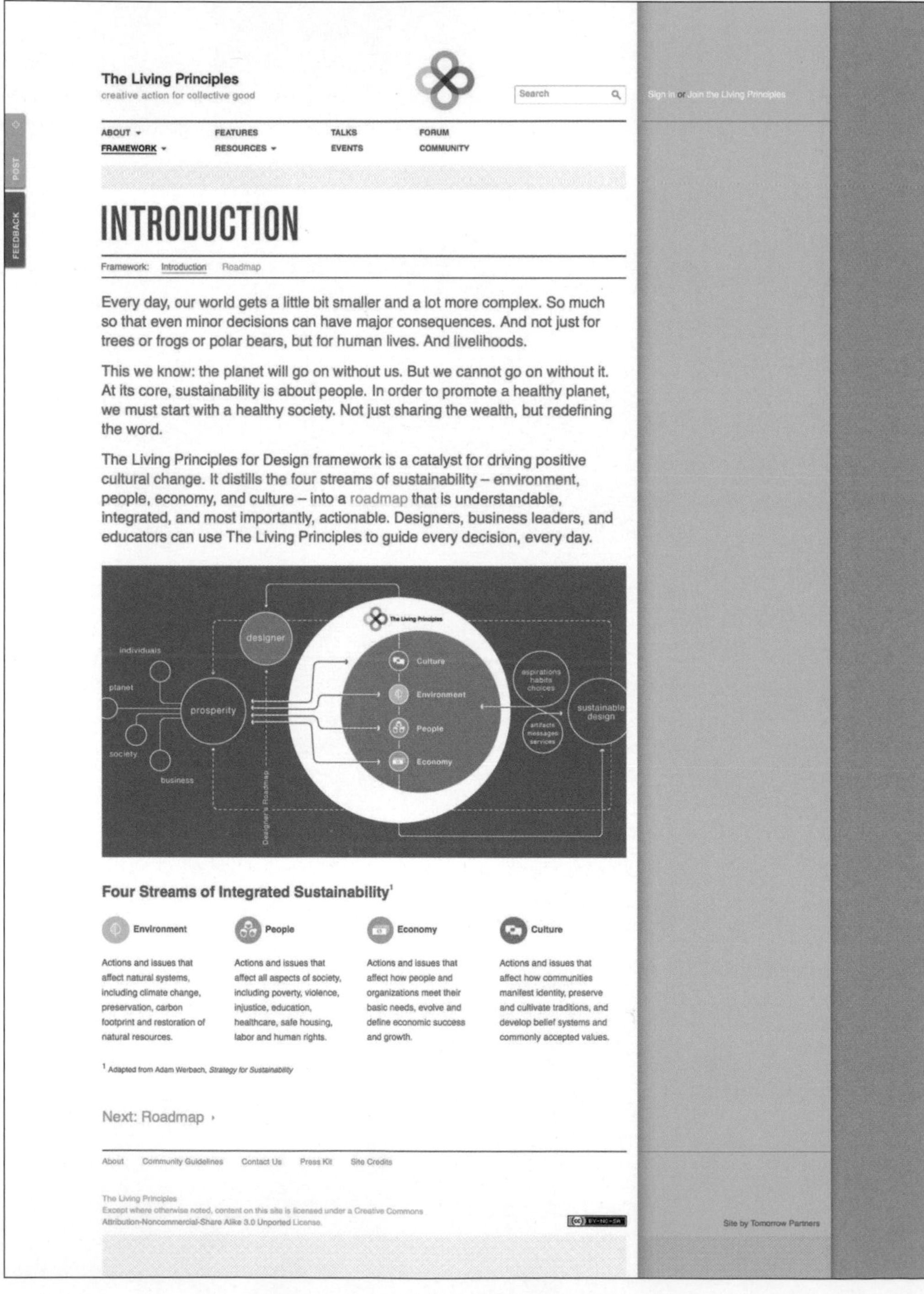

[6.1] The Living Principles are presented in this Web page as information graphics. The concept and content for this initiative is the work of a team of designers representing AIGA (the professional association for design) to promote sustainable design. The intent is that this information and its use are free for anyone to incorporate into their strategic design plan.
Courtesy of AIGA, the Professional Association for Design. Site Design: Tomorrow Partners.

Communication directs design decisions. What needs to be said by the designer and understood by the audience is the essence of communication design. It is important to understand what needs to be communicated and what to use in the design to support that need. Class assignments have many of the same components as a "real" design project. You are given a set of objectives, limitations, and a time frame to complete the work. Then you are to study the objectives to gain an understanding of what you are being challenged to do. Objectives generally contain the information you need to establish your direction. Most importantly, you must determine the communication components before you begin to explore visual solutions. In beginning design assignments, these components are more basic, but they provide the conceptual framework that serves as the communication criteria **6.1**.

It is important to understand that whether presented by an instructor or a client, the element of communication is a given that originates from the outside. It is the job of the student and the practicing designer to understand the nature of the need and develop a plan to incorporate it into an effective design solution. Once incorporated, the communication message often serves as the design objective **6.2**.

Communication design begins with verbal language. Advertising, publications, packaging, multimedia, Web design, and the images needed to support those communication venues rely on concepts that are first considered as written or spoken messages. Communication artists must learn the skills necessary to translate verbal language into visual communication.

In some ways, the verbal message is a conceptual element that must be considered in conjunction with the visual elements. Verbal messages drive the decision-making process that ultimately determines graphic content and the form it needs to take. Translating verbal concepts into visual form is a matter of testing ideas. Sometimes it is obvious that a verbal concept has limited potential as an image. For example, *coherent opinion*, as it reads, would be a challenging concept to illustrate. Having to work with such a message may require brainstorming sessions to rethink an approach so it is workable.

The concept *ancient drummer* is inherently rich with visual potential **6.3**. However, because there are many ways to interpret the concept, it is important to consider the audience, possible venues, and the communication message to guide your design decisions. That requires a clarification of the concept that can be determined by developing a series of related questions.

For example, what culture does the drummer represent? What does a drum from that culture look like? What point of view is most dramatic? Those questions define and refine the concept so it can be worked in an appropriate way.

[6.2] The objective of this advocacy design is to promote voting. The final design is a curious but effective message. It relies on the words and the image together to communicate the intended message. The essence of the illustration is saying "You have no voice." When combined with the words, the message is complete.
Poster design by Modern Dog.

Pack Your Brain

Rose Gonnella

Rose Gonnella is an educator, an artist, a designer, and a writer. Gonnella has exhibited her art nationally and internationally in collections such as the Smithsonian National Museum of American Art. She also has written numerous books and articles on creativity, art, and architecture.

Why are some professional artists and designers or students of the arts bubbling fonts of creativity that flow with a seemingly endless stream of ideas? Energetically creative people weren't born with minds filled with visual and mental information. Ideas spring from a brain (and heart) packed with experience and knowledge. Creative people are curious and passionate about learning. Curiosity is the foundation of creativity.

Creative people fuel their brains everyday by absorbing as much mental and visual stimuli as can be tolerated before passing out at the end of an evening. Even in sleep, creative people find ideas.

Upon waking, a creative person will jot down the weird and wacky juxtapositions of imagery and dialogue that comes during a dream.

1 INSPIRATION AND IDEAS ARE A PRODUCT OF PROACTIVE MIND.

Creative people are listeners, doers, hobbyists, collectors, museum goers, travelers, scavengers, revelers, searchers, adventurers—with the exploring done through far-reaching experience or simply by reading books. Creative people are hunters and gatherers who constantly look and fill their living space with interesting scraps of paper, all sorts of printed matter, oddly shaped paper clips, doodads, gadgets, and, of course, books. Creative people take notes yet understand that what they accumulate on any given day probably has no particular immediate purpose. Creative people invest in learning and searching for its own sake. The search for inspiration and ideas is an investment. Time is needed to sponge up information from a myriad of sources. Time is needed to experience.

And, in time, your brain fills up with all manner of stimulation. The stored information, images, and ideas are calmly waiting to be reordered, reconfigured, refreshed, and put to creative use. The stockpile lies dormant until a spark ignites it: you are asked to find a solution to a creative problem. And BANG, stored information explodes and ideas pop.

But you can't pull out of your head what is not in your head. Creativity does not happen in a vacuum. You have to pack your brain (fortunately there is always room for more). When you ask the question, "How do I get a great idea?" the response is, "Reach into your brain and yank it out OR get up, get out, and gather what you need." Research. Excellent ideas come from what preexists in your brain from previous research, discovery, and exploration, or from what you actively put there for the instance. If you are designing a brochure to save the whales, it is time that you (a) went on a whale watch, (b) watched a documentary about whales, (c) visit a public aquarium that has whales, or (d) read and search the Web. But don't rely on the Web alone. Experience comes best with personal field experiences.

2 WHAT DO TEETH HAVE TO DO WITH TEA BAGS?

Nothing. Isolated visual and intellectual information gathered for the pure joy and pleasure of salvaging, searching, research, observation, or accidental discovery (such as, visiting a flea market, reading a book on Northwest Coast Indian masks, poking through the Japanese bookstore near Rockefeller Center in New York City, bird watching, or coming upon a mural by Thomas Hart Benton at the city hall in Jefferson City, Missouri) will not be useful until the material is compared, related, combined, synthesized, and composed.

Meaning comes from relationships. Keeping your mind wide open to comparing and combining disparate objects, ideas, and imagery creates visual poetry and fresh ideas. A design found on the ceiling of the Uffizi Gallery in Florence might make a great composition juxtaposed with an image of clouds.

In isolation, an image of clouds is seen as itself. Seen together, an image of a floral tapestry and clouds may suggest an entirely new and evocative meaning. Some people look into the night sky and see stars. Creative people look at the stars and also see horses, crabs, lions, and warriors. Now, what do teeth have to do with tea bags?

Open your mind and let the possibilities pour in.

FOUR COMPONENTS OF *VISUAL COMMUNICATION*

1	**PURPOSE**	**Client Need**	What a client thinks they want or need	*Strategic research can determine an appropriate and effective direction*	
		Client Benefit	Improvement to current status	*The X-games are the leading action sporting events.*	
			Improved communication	*The X-games way finding program is now a gps mobile app*	
			Higher level of awareness	*All X-game events can be followed on social networking sites.*	
			Efficiency of use	*Assist fans with color coded event graphics*	
		Client Expectation	Designer/Client agreement	***Mutual trust***	*This project is important*
				Pledge	*This is what I will do*
				Deliver	*Agreed Outcomes*
2	**MESSAGE**	**Verbal Communication**	What type of message will be sent?	***Inform***	*ESPN will be broadcasting the X-games*
				Persuade	*Watch the X-games on ESPN*
			What will be received?	***Direct***	*Check out xgames.com for event schedules*
		Visual Communication	Explore the visual potential of a verbal concept	*Design pictograph symbol for each X-game event*	
			Determine which venue is appropriate	*Consistent use across all platforms: web, apps, print material*	
			Research and test response	*Test pictograph symbols for consistent response in multiple languages*	
3	**AUDIENCE**	**Demographics**	Who is the target audience?	*Gender, age, ethnicity, income, education, political affiliation, cultural preferences*	
		Psychological Foundations	How the audience responds	*Thinks, feels, behaves, interacts*	
			Audience attitudes	*Likes and dislikes*	
			Audience beliefs	*Something accepted as being true*	
4	**IMAGE**	**Visual Language**	How will the design function?	*Type driven*	
				Image driven	
			What meaning is associated with the image?	*Sign: image means what it says*	
				Symbol: something that stands for something else	
				Icon: represents what the source of the image is	
				Metaphor: open ended interpretation	
		Visual Organization	What is the visual hierarchy of the composition?		
			Which visual principles are appropriate for the composition?		
			Does the image content support the purpose, message and audience?		

[a] [b] [c]

[6.3a, b and c] Each of these instruments is a reproduction of a historic traditional drum design; from left to right, (a) a West African djembe hand drum, (b) a Northwest coastal hand drum with an eagle design, and (c) a traditional Mexican drum played with a hide-wrapped mallet. Each of these drums have a different function and purpose in their respective cultures. It is critical to specify your design direction with authentic visual references that accurately reflect your intentions and your idea. *(a) Photo by Taigi/Veer (b) © Don Klumpp/Getty Images. (c) © Danita Delimont/Getty Images.*

PSYCHOLOGICAL FOUNDATIONS AND VISUAL COMMUNICATION

Understanding relationships between verbal language and visual communication gives designers and illustrators important tools for communicating with an intended audience. An audience is a group of people with a specific profile, referred to in marketing as a *demographic*. To understand any group and the individuals in it, you need to consider the psychological foundations that influence the members of the group. Those psychological foundations include how people *behave*, how they *think*, how they *feel*, and how they *interact* with one another. You will examine each of them as they relate to visual communication.

Behavior

Behavior refers to the actions or reactions of a person, usually in response to environmental factors. Behavior can be unconscious or conscious, involuntary or intentional. A generally accepted tenet of behavioral psychologists is that it takes two weeks to begin to change a behavior. You can test this on yourself with a simple research task. Choose a kitchen appliance, a wastebasket, or another useful object that you use frequently. Move it to a different location in the room or on the countertop. In the first few days, you will notice that your behavior is to go to the original location first. As you proceed through the next few days, you will find

[6.4] This poster design is a satirical commentary promoting an anti-war message. It presents the viewer with behavioral alternatives. The pictographic images also make a comment on the obvious contrast between constructive and destructive behavior.
Poster design by Scorsone/Drueding, Joe Scorsone and Alice Drueding designers.

yourself going to the new location more often. Eventually, you will change your behavior as you train your orientation to the new location. Keep track of the number of times you involuntarily choose the new location. This example underscores how behaviors can become habits and how changing your intentions, (i.e., moving the object to a new place) can change your behavioral relationship to the use of the object.

Behavioral outcomes, or *what is determined to be a desired response*, are a key aspect in design communication that intends to persuade the viewer **6.4**. Knowing how an individual or a group behaves provides critical information when attempting to market ideas or concepts to them. It is why daytime television runs medical health advertisements geared toward senior citizens, certain sporting events advertise beer and cars, and the X Games focus on messages and products targeted to youth markets.

Thinking

Thinking is another word for cognition. The term *cognition* is derived from the Latin for *cogito*, "to think." Cognition also refers to a person's mental processes, the processing of information and intellectual understanding or comprehension. Thinking or cognitive awareness can involve the process of learning or acquiring knowledge. Communication design can involve verbal meaning and visual imagery that requires reasoning, acting, or processing information. The ability to distinguish when a design demands a cognitive response is critical to aesthetic choices and the arrangement and presentation of the overall design **6.5**. Book design, interactive information design, and educational displays and exhibits, for example, appeal to the viewer's cognitive sense and must be designed with that in mind.

Feeling

Feeling is emotional expression that produces psychological change. Expressions of emotion can include anxiety, rapture, rage, delight, animosity, or compassion. Feelings also can be thought of as sensations related to and experienced through the sense of touch, visual perception, olfactory perception (smell), auditory perception, and even taste. Graphic designers are, of course, interested primarily in visual perception when it relates to a viewer's emotional response. Images have the power to conjure feelings of loneliness, joy, contempt, and serenity. Certain shapes and colors evoke particular emotional responses **6.6**.

Communication designers can anticipate how an audience will feel or generally feels in a given situation. People at an amusement park will generally feel differently than a group at a poetry reading. An individual shopping on eBay has a different mind-set than someone walking through an airport in a foreign city. Countless scenarios affect how people feel about different situations and how different situations make people feel. Visual artists use color, shape, line, and texture in particular arrangements to communicate a mood or sense of feeling to their audience.

Interaction

The ways and motivations for how and why people interact are very complex. Sociologists and psychologists study the phenomenon of human interaction to learn the dynamics of social structures and the relationship of the individual in these structures. People experience a plethora of socially interactive situations everyday—talking to a neighbor, shopping in a marketplace, worshiping, playing team sports, attending an entertainment event, working, or going to school. When people interact, they are engaged in a symbolic social structure that provides meaning and purpose to their life. Herbert Blumer[1] is a social psychologist that studied social interaction and is known for advancing the idea of *symbolic interaction.* **Symbolic interaction** is the process of forming meaning in support of the formation of personal identity and human socialization. Blumer identifies three core principles for symbolic interaction—meaning, language, and thought. **Meaning** is central to his thesis. How people interact with one another and with objects is based on meanings the people project on to the other individuals and objects. **Language**, verbal and visual, provides a means for people to negotiate meaning using symbols. **Thought** provides a mental construct for people to interpret and reinterpret symbols. Blumer's work has an obvious underlying connection to the formal tenets of visual communication.

To communicate with a group (an audience), you need to know something about the structure and purpose of the group and a profile of the individuals in it. For example, a teacher of an introductory design class needs to know the nature of the skill levels, interest levels, ability of the group to stay attentive, familiarity with the subject, and so on, to prepare and teach the course. The designer of a sign system for a city park must consider the unique ways people interact in that environment if she is to create a successful and effective design.

[1]The Society for More Creative Speech, 1996, "Symbolic Interactionism as Defined by Herbert Blumer." http://www.thepoint.net/-usul/text/blumer.html.

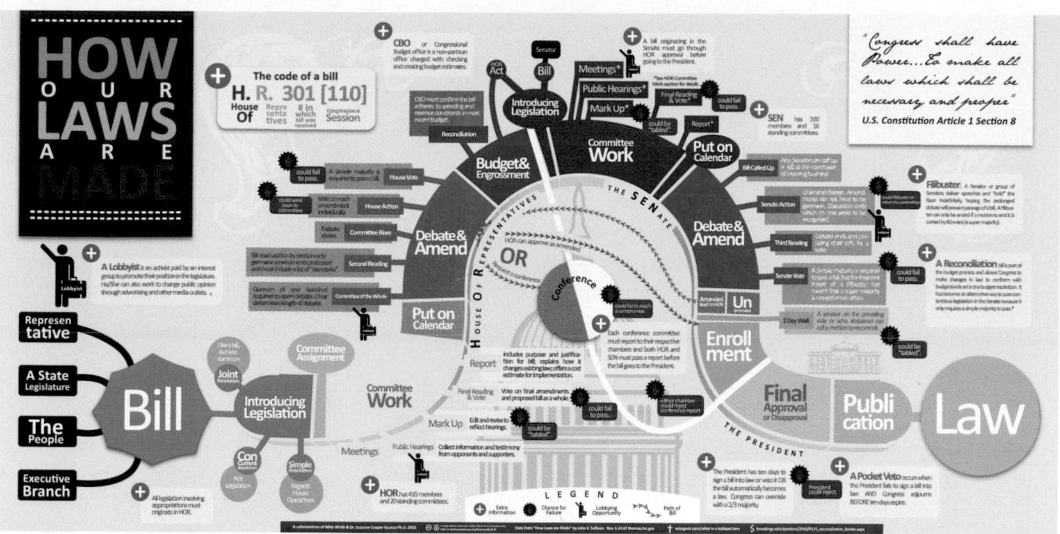

[6.5] Information graphics appeal to people's cognitive senses. Charts and graphs present information that requires analytical reasoning to process. This design, presenting the complicated process of how laws are made, provides a colorful visualization of the process with entertaining graphics that imitates the friendly look of a board game.
Courtesy of Mike Wirth Art & Dr. Suzanne Cooper-Guasco, PhD.

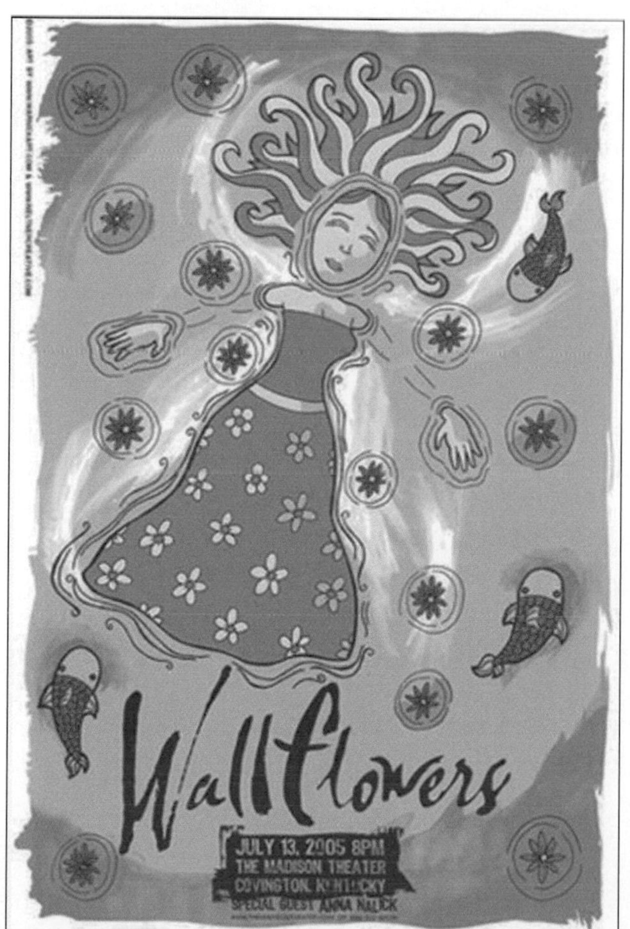

[6.6] Screen-printed poster art is a medium that often excites the senses with vivid color and imagery and with physical size. This poster design promoting the Indie rock group *The Wallflowers* depicts a female figure, fish, and water flowers floating serenely in water. The playful combination of graphic elements seems to excite the viewer's sense of sound and touch. It graphically presents the feelings of floating, weightlessness, and release. The color scheme of overall soft blue tones contrasted by muted red-orange graphic elements supports the intended feel the designers had in mind.
Poster design by Keith Neltner and Rob Warnick.

PERRY LEVELS: A GUIDE TO LEARNING

A learning environment is a complex social structure that, by its nature, is dependent on the interaction of its members. It is also a structure in which people have extended experiences. How an individual student interacts and ultimately learns within an educational structure depends on what William Perry Jr. describes as "Levels of Intellectual Maturity."[2] At this point, as a student of the visual arts, you should examine these levels in the context of this chapter's discussion of social interaction and with the goal of gaining personal insight. These levels, called *Perry levels*, are valuable to you as a student and as a future professional engaged in the ongoing process of self-education (see the sidebar *Levels of Intellectual Maturity*).

Perry's own research of his students at Harvard revealed valuable insight into the adult learner. His study offers a great example of how people generally develop as learners. The Perry levels provide meaningful insight into your own learning development and readiness to engage in the learning process. Which of these levels have you experienced? Note that although these levels are presented in hierarchical order, they are not strictly sequential in the way people experience them. Also, they are not specific to visual learners. A discussion later in this chapter will address aspects of visual intelligence and the visual learner.

Levels of Intellectual Maturity

- **Dualism** (concrete thinking) Some of the traits in this level include thinkers who believe things are right or wrong and good or bad. Knowledge is thought of as a set of truths. Every problem has a finite answer. Learners are reluctant to express a point of view. Authority figures have the ability to explain and give correct answers.
- **Multiplicity** At this level, recognition of diversity of thinking exists. Uncertainty prevails because other points of view are valid. Knowledge is a matter of educated opinion. There is no single right solution to a problem. Learners listen to experts but have a right to their own opinions. Experts explain a theory or content that is viewed as their opinion.
- **Relativism** At this level, knowledge is relative. Knowledge is not universal, but a matter of context and situation. What is true in one situation may be not be true in another. Ambiguity is part of life requiring the individual to prove reasoning for ideas. Knowledge is determined by reasoning. Based on their experiences, experts present procedures and analytic methods to help others reason and compare alternatives.
- **Commitment** The learner develops the need to take a position. Knowledge is constructed from experience, from interaction with others, and from reflective thinking. There are many potential solutions to a problem, but they are not equally valid. Knowledge is integrated. Experts are mentors that challenge a person's assumptions to support the person's learning.

Understanding these kinds of interdisciplinary theories and concepts provides an intellectual depth for your design research. They also provide you with a substantive theoretical knowledge base to formulate a rationale for design decisions. Having solid reasons for the creative choices you make gives you a distinct advantage when you present your ideas to others. If you are convincing, you will gain creative control.

[2]William G. Perry Jr., *Forms of Intellectual and Ethical Development in the College Years: A Scheme* (New York: Holt, Rinehart and Winston, 1968).

BRANCHES OF COMMUNICATION DESIGN

Communication specialists in the advertising and marketing fields understand the previously discussed psychological foundations and theories. They use them in conjunction with other profiles such as age, gender, ethnicity, geography, and income to create messages and imagery that will reach the target audience.

Designers and illustrators take the messages and craft them into visual concepts. To develop effective graphics from potential concepts, the designer must know what the communication specialist knows about the nature of the message and the audience who will receive it. A connection then needs to be made between the human psychology that drives marketing and advertising and the way communication functions in design.

The following discussion will relate the psychological foundations of human activity to the branches of communication design. It also will provide examples of each type. These branches determine the way a communication message will be delivered to an audience—that is, to persuade, inform, direct, and enhance (embellish).

Persuasive Design

Persuasive design attempts to persuade an audience to think or behave in a deliberate, sometimes different, way from what they are accustomed to thinking or doing. "Support the Arts," "Be a Subscriber," and "Buy This Brand" are messages intended to persuade. Advertising, promotional, and social advocacy designs are examples of this category 6.2.

Information Design

Information design presents ideas and concepts with the intent of educating the audience. Textbook design, Web site design, exhibit design, annual reports, charts, and diagrams all deliver information that is graphically organized and designed to assist the audience in their understanding of specific content 6.5.

Directional Design

Directional design helps people find their way through architectural, virtual, or environmental spaces. Theme parks, retail centers, public spaces, Internet navigation, and transportation systems all rely on typographic and pictographic design that can speak to broad audiences often made up of an international population **6.7**.

Enhansive Design

Enhansive design embellishes the look of a design venue. Enhansive graphics also can add a measure of entertainment value to a design application. Theme parks, retail industry, games, advertising, editorial, and electronic media all rely on enhansive graphics to present a more visually interesting and compelling product **6.8**.

It is important to realize that these functions are interrelated. Many design applications incorporate several of these categories in their concept and design. For instance, a packaging design needs to persuade consumers to choose the product from the shelf and, at the same time, give them information about the package's contents. A magazine or book needs to compel an interested consumer to pick it up for examination and offer entertainment value in the design and graphics.

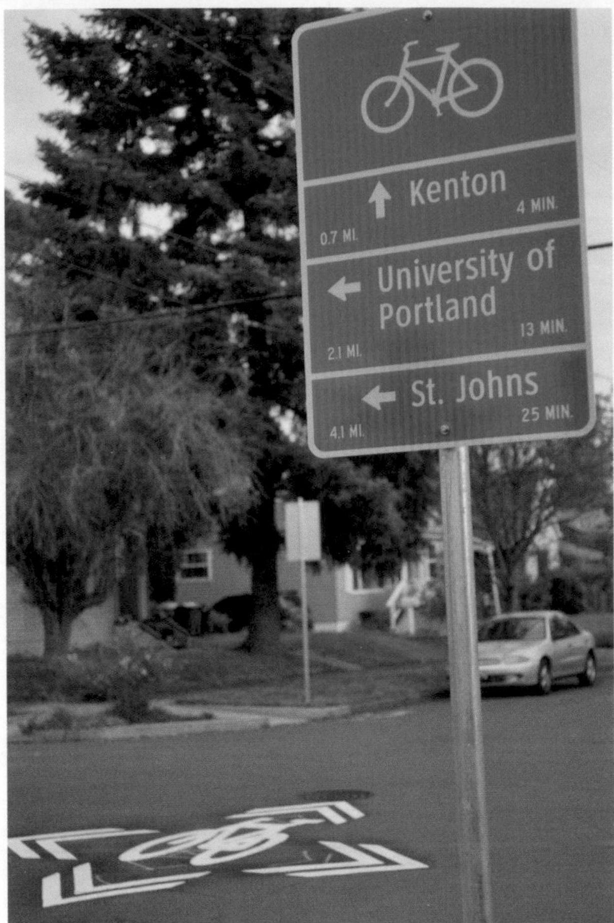

[6.7] Sign systems in urban environments aid people in navigating from one place to another. Portland, Oregon, is known as a "bike-friendly" city. Special signs like this one provide direction, distance, and time estimates for bicyclist trying to reach a destination.
Courtesy of bikeportland.org.

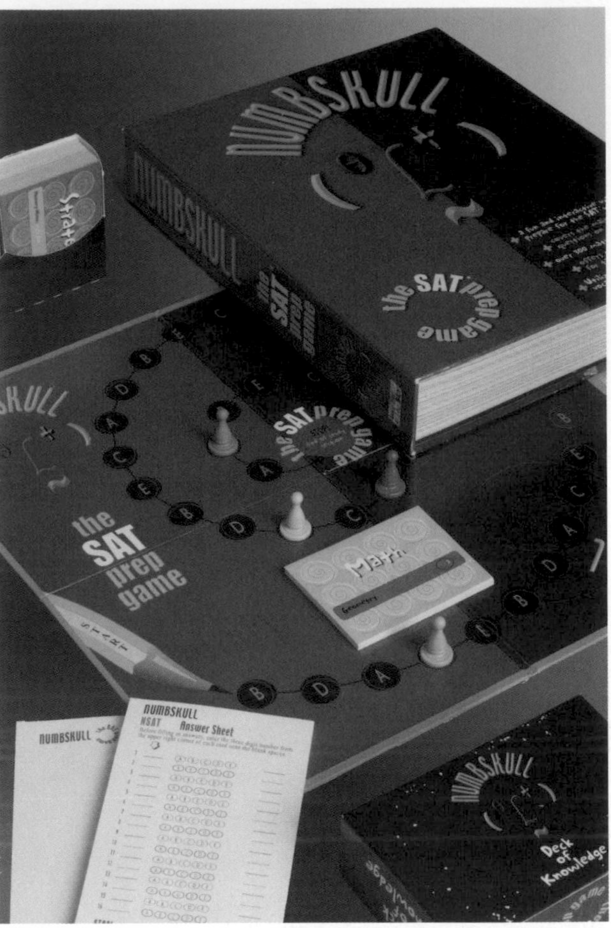

[6.8] A bright color scheme and a set of playful illustrations are used to enhance the function of this board game design.
© Cengage Learning 2013. Game design by Mark A. Thomas.

KNOWLEDGE AND DESIGN

Knowledge is the fact or condition of knowing something as acquired through experience, or you can think of it as the range of a person's information or understanding of truth or fact arrived at through reasoning. At the center of personal knowledge about any subject are experience and reasoning. The process of design requires knowledge from many sources and disciplines. It is impossible to know everything about every subject you will encounter as a designer. You will not be successful trying to solve every design problem directly from your acquired experience. Most design content will be unfamiliar. Therefore, you must develop research skills that will help you intelligently and systematically solve the problem. In effect, you are learning to teach yourself. The best way to begin is to gain a thorough understanding of the nature of the problem you are trying to solve.

Problem Solving

Solving visual problems requires a range of knowledge and skills—facility with a variety of media; the ability to present ideas, develop ideas, and identify the right idea; technical knowledge; developed hand skills; verbal language skills; research skills; a working knowledge of history and math; and a general knowledge of contemporary culture. If you run your own business, you will need to make business decisions as well. That is an imposing and probably partial list of the scope of knowledge and skills needed to be an effective designer. But the process of learning all of these skills is accumulative as you acquire and master them over time. Most of them require practice and maintenance.

Wolfgang Kohler (1887–1967), a psychologist and cofounder of Gestalt psychology, conducted an important research study by observing apes to explain the nature of problem solving. Kohler's study involved hanging a bunch of bananas just outside the reach of a caged ape. Inside the cage were two poles that fit together. After trying to reach the bananas and failing, the ape attempted to hook the bananas with one of the poles. It was too short. Motivated, the ape eventually figured out how to assemble the two short poles to make one long pole and was successful in reaching the bananas. Once the ape solved the problem, he was able to repeat his actions on subsequent tries. Kohler demonstrated creative problem solving with this simple study the first time the ape assembled the two poles to reach the bananas. Kohler referred to the subsequent learned attempts to retrieve the bananas as routine problem solving.

You can apply this lesson to your own attempts at solving problems. You tend to get creative when a problem is presented that is unfamiliar, complex, or intellectually challenging. Creative problem solving relies on invention. Invention is simply the imaginative combining of existing things resulting in something new. When you find a way to combine things creatively that are not normally associated together or that are disparate, the result can be intriguing, surprising, and sometimes brilliant **6.9** and **6.10**.

Visual Intelligence

Cognitive psychologist Jerome Bruner defined intelligence as "a person's ability to use the tools of a culture." That insightful view of intelligence recognizes that you can be intelligent in different ways—that there is no single standard for intelligence. What are the tools of a culture? Certainly, language (written, verbal, and visual) and technology (mechanical tools and

[6.9] In the Museum of Arts and Design project that we have discussed in other chapters, the designers were asked to develop product merchandise using the logo and brand. This inventive set of interchangeable wood blocks is based on a grid and two units used to construct the letterforms for the museum logo. *Product design by Pentagram.*

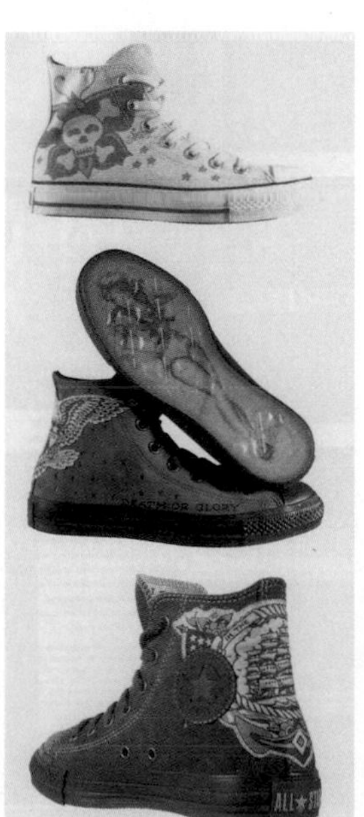

[6.10] Combining the edginess of tattoo art with an American icon such as Converse shoes may not immediately present itself as a great match. The result, however, is a beautifully elegant fashion statement and design. The ultra-hip look is the creative problem solving of a young designer who is designing for a young adult market. A clever business arrangement nets the design firm royalties on each pair sold. *GYRO Worldwide, Nick Paparone, art director.*

machines) are two of the most basic tools of any culture. Whatever a person's gift, it involves the use of language and technology to some degree. Some people have an affinity for numbers and formulas, whereas others, for working with things mechanical, organizing information, writing, managing, composing, or using languages. Those who are visually oriented tend to learn more through observation and perception than through knowledge found in books. The fact that you are studying visual art points to an intelligence that has prepared you as a visual learner. Visual learning requires an ability to think visually. Next, you will examine some aspects and strategies for visual thinking that can help you be more effective at solving visual problems.

Visual Thinking

Visual thinking is a problem-solving activity. Visual thinking is dependent on a relationship between mental and physical manipulation of an idea. A visual concept may begin as a mental idea, but there are limits to the degree to which you can develop and refine ideas mentally. To solve a visual problem or work with a visual idea, you have to manage it visually; that is, you have to give it form in the real world. A common myth about artistic process is that the artist has an idea for an image, formulates the idea in her head, and then produces the image with a mysterious direct effort or stereotypically referred to as "divine inspiration." That belief is impractical and rarely feasible. Most artists work their ideas through a rigorous process of research, practice, testing, and revision (see *Visual Thinking Is a Process* sidebar on page 229). Visual thinking is a part of the process **6.11**. Preliminary sketching, studies, and model building are ways artists externalize an idea from their mind to the real world. Brainstorming and group thinking sessions are effective in developing and testing ideas. Exploring media options and testing them to give form to an idea is visual thinking.

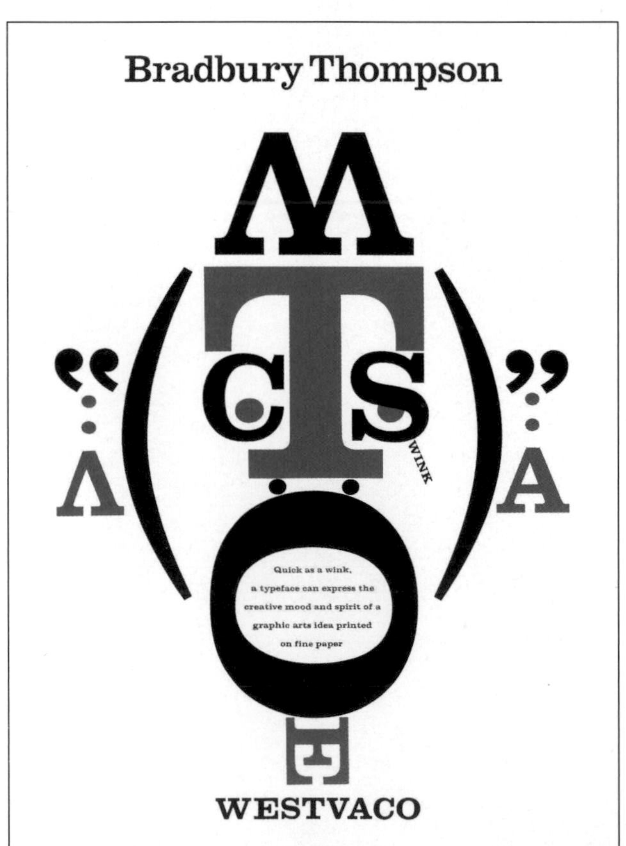

[6.11] Once the idea of creating a face from typographic forms was established, Bradbury Thompson had to consider different fonts, make associations between facial features and letterforms, study arrangements, and in this case, take a creative risk to manage this experimental idea in a successful manner. The result is one of the most memorable and innovative uses of type in twentieth-century design.

Sketchbooks: A Creative Tool

Paige Williams July 2011

Paige Williams is an artist and Professor at the Art Academy of Cincinnati where she teaches Introduction to 2D and 3D Design, Color Theory, Creativity and Criticism, and Painting. Her work has been exhibited widely in the United States and in Germany and Korea. She also conducts seminars and workshops on the subject of sketchbooks as a creative and visual thinking tool.

What kind of information do you encourage students keep in a sketchbook?

I encourage my students to include relevant and irrelevant bits and images that affect them throughout the day. It could be a color, a phrase, an image, or an idea from the profound to the mundane. I encourage them to avoid the editing process. These bits and pieces can fester and evolve, often into something more substantial and often not, but one never knows.

What kind of sketchbooks do you recommend?

I highly recommend choosing your own, choosing one you like and are attached to. Consider the size, color, binding, and look and feel of the paper. Often if you are having difficulty utilizing a sketchbook, you don't have the right sketchbook.

Do you have any tips for students with regard to keeping a sketchbook?

Always have it with you and never edit. When beginning a new sketchbook, date the front and quickly fill the first three to five pages, with anything, to overcome the pressure of its pristineness. It also helps to run over it with your car a few times to break it in; it also makes your professor believe you are using it.

Can you share any interesting stories or examples of how professional artists or designers have used sketchbooks in their work?

Picasso, who lived to be 91 years old, filled 178 sketchbooks in his lifetime.

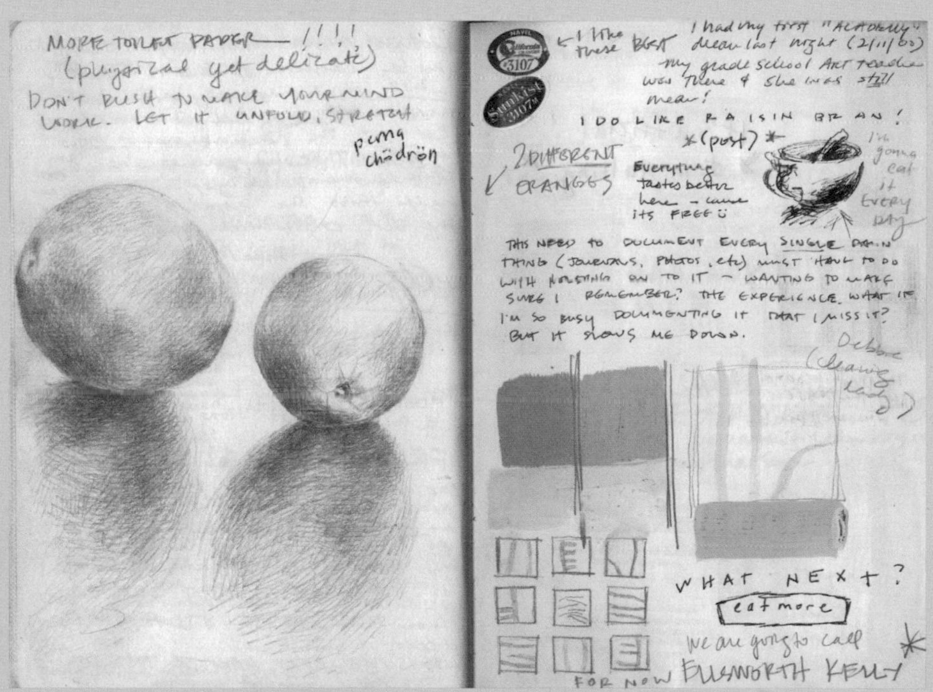

[6.12a] Observational studies, reference notes, and painted color swatches in a perfect-bound sketchbook.
Courtesy of Paige Williams.

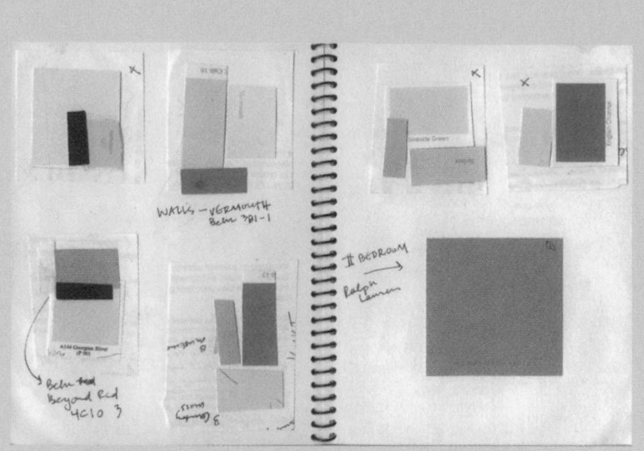

[6.12b] Cut paper and Color Aid color scheme swatches in a spiral-bound sketchbook.
Courtesy of Paige Williams.

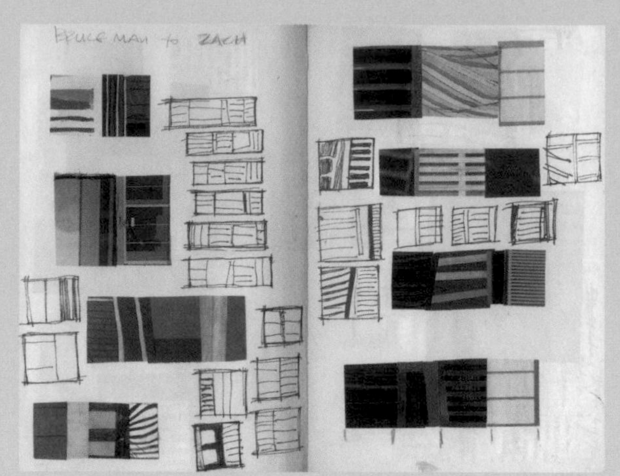

[6.12c] Collage, marker, and pencil studies using basic line, shape, and color arrangements. Notice that the spiral-bound book lays flat; the perfect-bound book is raised in the center but does not have the visual interruption of the spiral in the "gutter."
Courtesy of Paige Williams.

DESIGN AS PROCESS

Beginning a design problem can be an overwhelming task that involves many decisions. Breaking down the problem into manageable tasks and points can be helpful but does not ensure that the design will be successful. Work and skill are required to arrive at a solution that solves the problem. Some key components must be carefully researched and developed **6.13**. The Research Project Guide identifies the components and defines their role as they function in a design process.

Creative Process

Many of the projects presented in this book include visual thinking strategies that help you mange the creative process of solving a visual problem. There are many models for creative processes. You can do an Internet search or refer to books on the subject to study the models and adopt one that works for you. Most of the models have some common components or stages:

1. Identify the nature and scope of the problem.
2. Research all aspects of the problem and gather the facts.
3. Separate the big problem into smaller tasks, retaining useful information.
4. Develop and test potential ideas.
5. Allow for a gestation period, letting your ideas "live on their own."
6. Commit to one idea and execute it.
7. Evaluate the results.

[a]

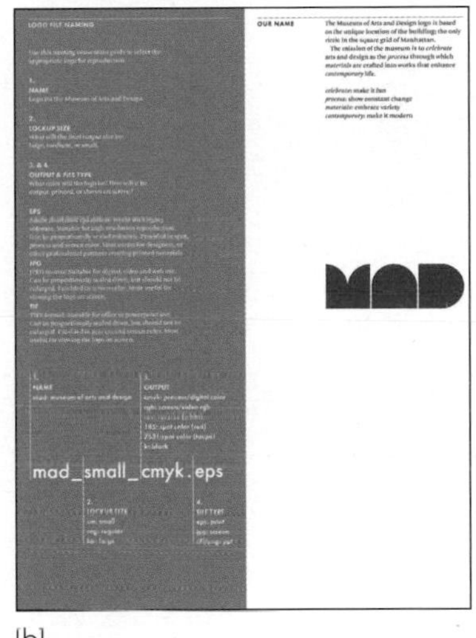

[b]

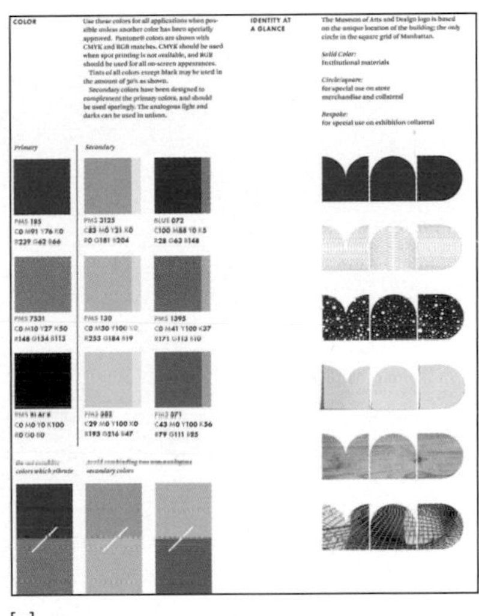

[c]

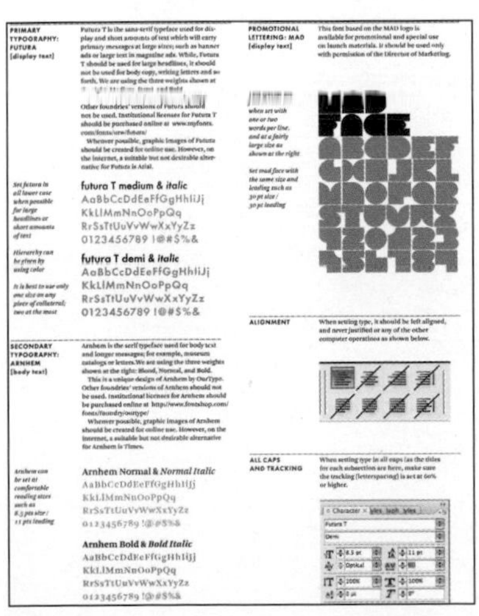

[d]

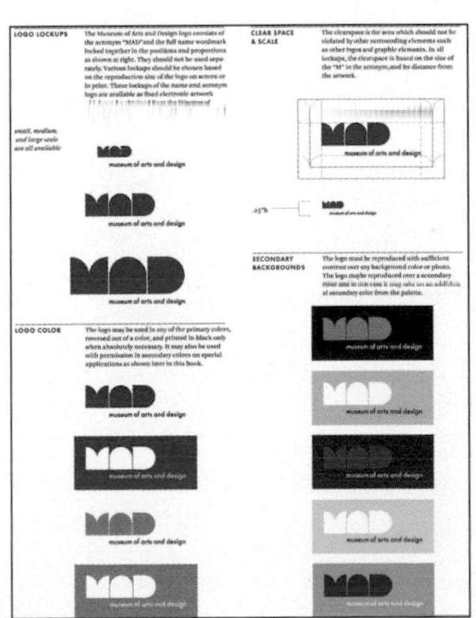

[e]

[6.13a to e] These sample pages from the Museum of Arts and Design Identity Guide constitute the result of many hours of research and design. At the point a designer provides the graphic standards for color, typography, identity use and misuse, the research is all but completed. It is not possible to provide this kind of information prior to a comprehensive concept study, visual research, and marketing inquiry.
Design by Michael Bierut/Pentagram.

Graphic Synthesis: A Comparative Case Study

This case study is a comparison of two design programs by Lance Wyman—the Minnesota Zoo and the American Museum of Natural History. Both designs use what Lance refers to as "a synthesis approach" of integrating form—in these cases, synthesizing animal forms with alphanumeric symbols. The typography of the Minnesota Zoo is designed as an extension of the animal images and became a custom typeface. The animal images of the Natural History Museum are designed as add-on shapes to an existing typeface, maintaining the original integrity of the typeface. The original reference for the zoo logotype is a moose combined with an *M*. This idea was expanded to design the numeric identifiers for various areas of the zoo.

The Natural History Museum begins with a graphic simplification of the building. Representative animals from each of the floors of the museum are combined with floor numbers. This imaginative and integrated design is an example of system design. System design is based on the development of a graphic device or structure upon which the parts of the larger design are based. Even though systems are defined and applied universally, they allow for variation to occur.

What is interesting about these two programs is that although the approaches to combining type and image are different, they accomplish the same objective.

The Minnesota Zoo

[6.14]

[6.15]

[6.17]

[6.16]

6.14, 6.15, 6.16 and 6.17 Courtesy of Lance Wyman Ltd.

The American Museum of Natural History

[6.18]

[6.20]

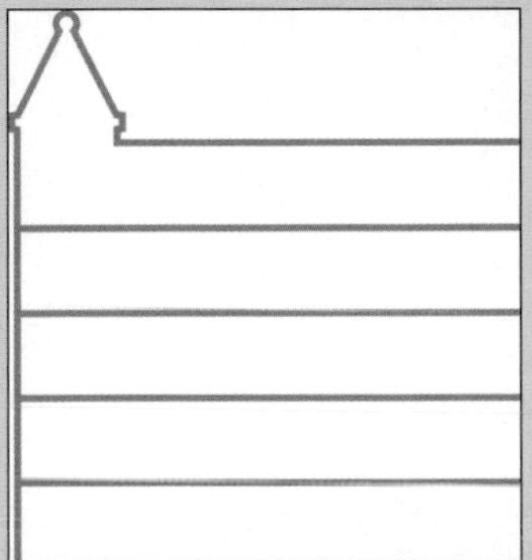

[6.19]

[6.22]

[6.21]

[6.23]

6.18, 6.19, 6.20, 6.21, 6.22, and 6.23 Courtesy of Lance Wyman Ltd.

Research Project Guide

Project Title: Give your project a name. Even though this item is first on the list, do it last.

Project Abstract: This is a brief one- or two-paragraph description of the thesis. It is a synopsis of the information presented below.

Project Goal: A goal is a big idea that is somewhat general in description. A goal serves as a conceptual umbrella. Goals are idealistic but attainable. However, goals may be achieved through a means that are different from the original plan. Sometimes goals are not achieved. This is not necessarily an indication of failure, but it can cause disappointment. Extraneous factors can change the quality and integrity of your realizing a planned goal. Resourcefulness and creative problem solving are critical skills when you must confront extraneous factors that impede your progress toward a goal.

Project Objectives: Objectives support the goal. They are linked to behavioral outcomes. They are specific to the task or project. They can be concrete and conceptual. The objectives provide a delineated outline of the project. They are the maps that the facilitator uses to navigate her way through the project. Sub-objectives contain further details of how the project will be realized.

Audience: This is the group toward whom you are directing the message or communication. The audience can be narrow or broad. The audience, referred to in marketing as the target audience, always has a profile. Even broader audiences are specially defined. Demographics are specific statistics that offer a profile about a given population. This data is critical information about human activity (i.e., individual and group behavior, attitudes, and beliefs). Attitudes and beliefs have their foundation in four distinct human activities: thinking, feeling, behaving, and interacting. To achieve the desired outcome of your objectives, you must research and know your audience.

Hard demographic research is compiled through the use of scientific surveys, focus group observation, and empirical research studies. Market-driven communications rely on this type of information.

Soft demographic research can be obtained by observing "what's out there," applying existing research data to your situation, and making inferences about social and cultural trends from information media sources such as newspapers, television, the Internet, and periodicals.

Environment: Environment is a time-space relationship that affects the use and interaction of the user with the communication. In conventional terms, the environment is where the audience engages the message over a given time frame. Sometimes the user dictates the environment; sometimes the designer dictates the environment. Often it is determined by both. The visual impact of a good design often transforms the environment. The environment can be intangible, that is, cerebral or imagined. The environment can be the design or the communication or the message itself.

Media: There are two branches of media:

1. Vehicle: The materials used to physically produce the work—paint, digital prints, dry transfer type, paper, pastels, wood, and so forth.
2. Venue: Where the communication occurs; the form of the communication—a billboard, computer monitor, book, gallery wall, building lobby, and so forth.

Strategy: Strategy determines how you will manage the project and how you will produce the imagery.

Rationale: The rationale is why you think the project is worthwhile and what the subsequent reasoning is for pursuing your idea. Use the compiled research to support your decisions.

Budget: Budget includes the number of hours, the cost per hour, and the cost of incidentals, calls, transportation, correspondence, and so forth.

Visual Thinking As a Process

It may seem odd to suggest the idea of giving structure to creative thinking, but using thinking exercises or brainstorming models to guide the creative process can be very useful for generating ideas.

Ideas generally begin in the mind, manifested by our imaginations. Attempting to re-create an idea directly from our mind into visual form often brings disappointment.

Visual thinking is the process of working and managing an idea that begins in the mind into the visual word using drawing, paper cutting and folding, sources of color, and other studio media.

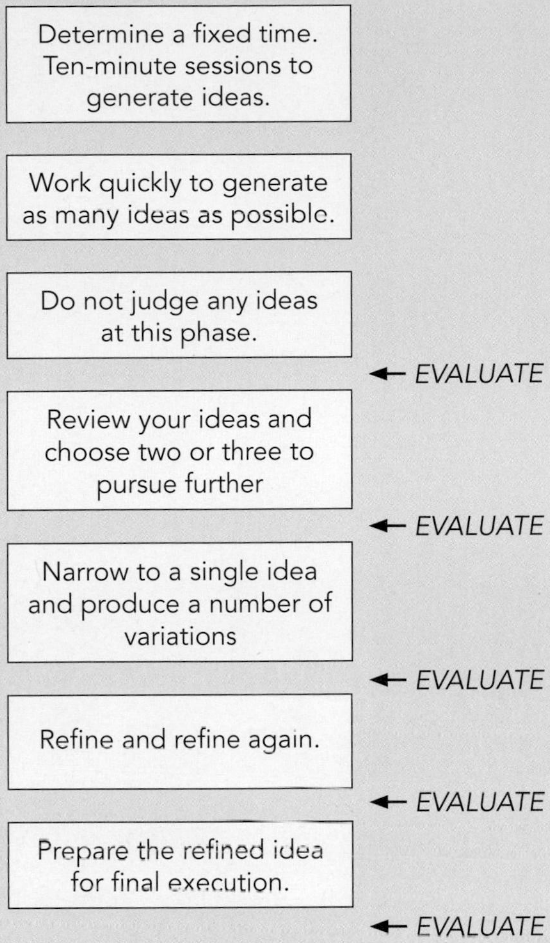

Determine a fixed time. Ten-minute sessions to generate ideas.

Work quickly to generate as many ideas as possible.

Do not judge any ideas at this phase.

← *EVALUATE*

Review your ideas and choose two or three to pursue further

← *EVALUATE*

Narrow to a single idea and produce a number of variations

← *EVALUATE*

Refine and refine again.

← *EVALUATE*

Prepare the refined idea for final execution.

← *EVALUATE*

Creative process models are not developed exclusively for artists. They can be applied to many different kinds of activities and pursuits. Try using the Creative Process Model to plan a trip, rearranging a room, or plan a party. The steps in these models are not strictly linear. You will find that skipping a step, backtracking, or repeating steps is more the rule than the exception. But now you will take the essence of the seven steps presented here in conjunction with points made throughout this chapter and consider a design process model or guide that has practical application for your projects. This process is based on a distillation of points commonly found in project models from a variety of professional sources.

What Is Risk Taking?

Risk taking in your work can yield dynamic results. Think of risk taking as exploring outside the given parameters of a project or assignment.

Introducing the unusual use of media, an unexpected point of view, or novel use of color can turn an otherwise mediocre solution into a design gem.

However, time constraints limit the number of directions you can consider, and working an idea without a plan can make it difficult to reach a resolution.

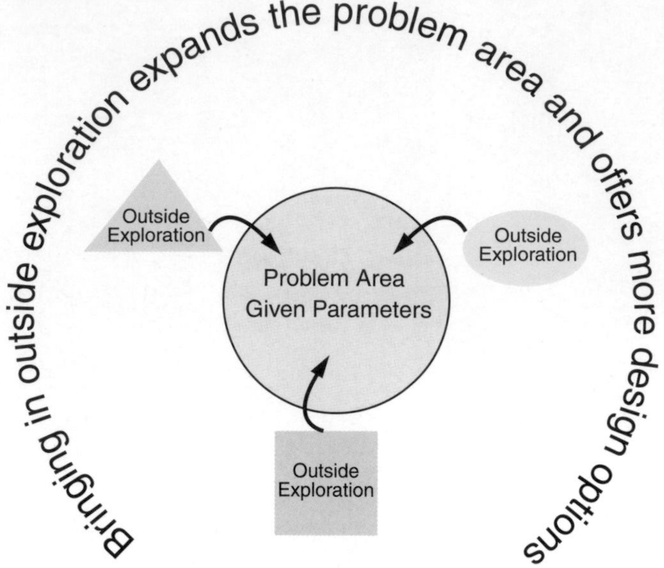

[6.24] © Cengage Learning 2013.

SUMMARY

Graphic design involves more than drawing skills, computer skills, and design acumen. A basic knowledge of academic disciplines, especially history and psychology, is significant. Most important is a thirst for lifelong learning. Proficient research skills are critical to producing informed and intelligent design solutions. Research skills also are critical to your growth and development as a professional designer. You must be able to defend your choices with meaningful and appropriate rationale to gain creative control. Evaluate your own strengths, weaknesses, learning style, and organizational skills. Strive to improve your research skills and depth of knowledge about fields of study related to graphic design. Work hard to expand your vocabulary and your presentation skills by practicing in class and with peer groups. Become intimately familiar with the field of visual communication. To generate innovative ideas, you need to know if they have already been done.

projects

CASE STUDY PROJECT

Objectives

- Discuss the creative process of a professional designer.
- Explain the inner workings of a design business.
- Conduct in-depth research on a graphic design project.
- Display oral and written communication skills.
- Prepare a formal oral, visual, and written presentation.
- Discuss the components of design process research.

Description

Select an agency, a studio, a freelance designer, or an illustrator. Choose one that is aligned with your interests. Arrange to spend an hour interviewing your contact. The objective is to gather information focused on the research, process, and development of a single project.

Limitations and Materials

This case study should follow the project from beginning to end. Use the questions on this form as a guide for acquiring the information. Complete a word-processed paper that includes the information from each question. You will present your case study to the class. Photocopy any visuals that will help explain the project.

Critique Discussion Points

Present each point in the study.

Discuss the nature of the project using the visual examples.

What flaws did you see in the firm's process?

What would you change in the firm's approach to project management?

Vocabulary

target audience, strategy, rationale, objective, venue, behavioral outcomes

References and Resources

If possible, try to locate a design firm or an individual and conduct this case study in person. Otherwise, find a design or ad agency on the Web. Do some research using the information available there and conduct the interview portion via telephone with a representative designer listed on the site.

Evaluation Criteria

Completion of the Points in the Study

Organization of Materials Presented

Depth of Research on the Chosen Case

Quality of the Oral Presentation

Case Study Inventory

Name of Contact/Individual:
Position:
Phone Number:
E-mail Address:
Business Profile:
Project Title:
Project Dates:
Client:
Project Team:
Art Director:
Designer:
Production:
Copywriter:
Artist:
Other:
Project Objective:
Target Audience Profile:
Describe the intended behavioral outcomes.
Project Strategy:
How is the project researched?
How is it executed?
Discuss the production process.
Describe the venue.
Discuss the rationale for the client's need.
What is the amount of the general budget?
How is the success of the project measured?
Other Insights:

DESTINATION THEME BOARD

Objectives

- Complete the research and production of a destination theme board.
- Provide research for the theme concept, message, audience, and imagery and elements.
- Prepare a proposal that includes information from each component in the Research Project Guide.
- Work as part of a team to brainstorm a concept.
- Produce a motif board of textures, type, color artifact, and motif that are driven by group research.

Description

Begin by working as part of a team to share background information and possible directions. Prepare a project brief that defines the motive, message, audience profile, and image profile. Refer to the *Four Components of Visual Communication* sidebar for elaboration of these points. The image profile should address questions of type style, theme motif, color scheme, and content elements. Once you have addressed those concerns, begin a visual exploration. Gather resources and references from which to work. Complete visual studies of media, composition, color, and possible arrangements. Use the research to complete a collage motif board of the assigned destination.

Assemble the written and documented research into a folder. Include the following:

1. A word-processed research brief addressing each component of the research guide and a destination profile (Use subheads, 11pt. Times Roman, double-spaced type, and a title.)
2. The visual reference materials (i.e., studies and photocopies of cultural and graphic references)

Your instructor may ask you to give a 10-minute presentation of your project to the class for the final critique.

Limitations and Materials

Each team will be assigned a travel destination and audience profile. You will work with your team to generate research on the destination. You will work as part of the team to produce the project brief and design.

The final size is 24 inches by 24 inches. Use a variety of materials, fabric, color aid, textures, graphic elements, natural material, objects, typography, and so on, to create an arrangement that encapsulates the essence of the destination. Use a sturdy foam board or comparable board as the base board. The collage or assemblage must be flat.

Critique Discussion Points

Describe the elements on your board.

How do your choices of color, texture, type treatments, and graphics reflect the destination culture?

How do your choices address the audience profile?

Why is your board effective as a visual "map" for a creative team?

Vocabulary

motif, theme, target audience, strategy, rationale, objective, venue, behavioral outcomes

References and Resources

Creative sources for materials are key to this assignment. Collect color swatches and wallpaper samples from paint stores; look to fabric stores for material and novelties and to import stores for ethnic and cultural artifacts.

Evaluation Criteria

Presentation

Research Paper

Quality of Design

Overall Rating

Destination Suggestions

Ivory Coast
Finland
Turkey
Malaysia
Nepal
Costa Rica
Brazil
New Guinea

Demographic Profiles

Gen X	1961–1981, 20 million, spending power of $20 billion
Gen Y	1979–1994, 71–80 million, 3 times larger than Gen X
Baby Boomers	1946.1964, 76 million, 29 percent of U.S. population

You can research and develop your own specific target demographic for use with this project.

in review

1. Define research in your own terms and discuss the scope of research for graphic designers.
2. What are the four psychological foundations of human activity? Describe each one.
3. What are Blumer's three core principles of symbolic interaction? Define them in your own words.
4. Give an example of how design is dependent on any aspect of symbolic interaction.
5. What are the four Perry levels of intellectual maturity?
6. Name the branches of communication design and give an example of each one.
7. Define *knowledge*. What makes up knowledge?
8. What is visual thinking? What does it involve for designers?
9. Describe the seven stages of the creative process.
10. What is the difference between a goal and an objective?
11. What are the two branches of media?

6

the designer at work

Courtesy of Debbie Millman

"Work as hard as you can. Work harder than everyone else. Shoot for the stars. Realize that only YOU can limit what you hope for. Dreams CAN come true ..."

Debbie Millman

Debbie Millman has worked over 25 years in the design industry and is President of the design division at Sterling Brands, a New York City–based design firm specializing in brand development and package design where she has worked for the past 15 years. Millman is also Chair of the master's program in Branding Arts at the School of Visual Arts and President of AIGA, the largest professional association for design. A recognized expert on design, she has hosted an Internet talk radio show, "Design Matters," since 2005. She is a contributing editor at *Print* magazine and a design writer at FastCompany.com. Millman is also the author *of Look Both Ways: Illustrated Essays on the Intersection of Life and Design, How to Think Like a Great Graphic Designer, and Essential Principles of Graphic Design.*

Why did you choose graphic design as a career?

From the time I was child, I loved making things. I made my own coloring books, paper dolls, dioramas, and even tried to make my own perfume by crushing rose petals into baby oil. I made barrette boxes out of Popsicle sticks, key chains out of lanyards, ashtrays out of clay, and Halloween costumes out of construction paper and old sheets. I even handmade an entire magazine when I was 12 with my best friend. Her name was also Debbie so we named the magazine "Debutante." We were very proud of it.

What is your educational back-ground?

I went to the State University at Albany in New York. I went there because my best friend did, and at the time, it was the best state school that I could afford. I knew I wanted to do something creative, but thought I would be a painter. I studied painting and took some design classes because I needed the credits, and majored in English literature. I also got involved with the school newspaper. The *Albany Student Press* had the largest circulation of any student newspaper in the country. As it turned out, I didn't really like the editing part of working on the school paper. What I loved was creating the paper's design.

After I graduated, I quickly realized I wasn't going to be able to pay my rent working as a fine arts painter. I also realized that the only marketable skill I had was the design I had briefly studied, supplemented by serving as the editor of the arts section of our school newspaper. I came out of college with this fantastic design portfolio of the newspaper layouts I had created for 12-page section that I did every week.

After I graduated, I saw an ad in *The New York Times* for a magazine job at a publication called *Cable View*. It specifically stated "no visitors, resumes only." I decided to deliver my resume personally figuring "What could they do, throw me out?" They hired me on the spot, and I started right away. They put me in trafficking, and I ended up working in both the editorial and design departments. I did a little bit of design and a little bit of editing. It ended up being the perfect job. I could do everything I wanted to do, and I loved it, but I couldn't live on the money.

A year later I was offered a job doing real estate advertising design, and I took it. All I did was design brochures for tasteless nondescript buildings. I found I hated doing work I didn't believe in. I quit after a year and started working at *RockBill* magazine, doing editing, writing, and design. Shortly after working there, the creative director and I decided to start our own design firm. It was 1987, and I had been working professionally for about four years. Looking back, I don't know where I got the courage to start my own company! We didn't have any money, clients or any real contacts. But we did it anyway, and in a short time it became successful and we had 20 people working for us. Ultimately, I didn't feel it was a good fit for me. When you disagree with somebody and you only have one partner, it's an argument. Currently I have five partners, so if we disagree on something it becomes a round table discussion.

At that point, I had just turned 30 and I didn't know what I wanted to do. So I took a year off and freelanced for Planned Parenthood, designing their new identity. I did a brochure for a law firm and I travelled, and I thought about what I wanted to do. I decided that I wanted to work for a firm I held in high regard at that time: Frankfurt Balkind. Through a friend I got an interview and I showed Aubrey Balkind my portfolio. He said he'd hire me, but NOT as a designer—he didn't think my work was good enough. He was responding to all of the work I had created in my entire career at that point! But I really wanted to work there, so I took the job he offered, a position in marketing. About a year later, I got a call from a headhunter and he spoke to me about a job at a branding consultancy called The Schechter Group. I had never done "formal" brand identity in my life, but it was incredibly compelling for me. When I gave Aubrey my notice, he looked me in the eye and told me that I was going to be very good in package design. He was right. For the first time in my life, I found my niche. I have been working in branding ever since and am blissfully happy all of the time. (Joking! I am actually very insecure and thus feel that I have to constantly prove myself every second of every day.)

As president of the design division at Sterling Brands, Millman oversees the firm's re-branding of familiar products and services. One of the firm's recent projects involved a redesign of the Dunkin' Donuts brand. The firm's new design incorporates many of the features of the original design, including the brand's orange and magenta color scheme. The redesign included applying the new identity design to coffee packaging, in-store coffee cups, and two new lines "Oven Toasted and "DD Smart," which contribute to the overall brand expression.
Courtesy of Sterling Brands.

You're well known and regarded for the brand development you've done at Sterling Design. How did you end up there ?

My title at Sterling is President of the design group. We do two things really well: brand strategy and brand design. In every case, we try to work diligently with our client partners to deliver fresh, inspiring, and what we hope is high-quality work. We provide a passionate point of view, what we consider to be intelligent guidance and measurable results.

In addition to my day job at Sterling, my radio show and my teaching, I spend the rest of my time as President of the AIGA, the professional association for design, and also blogging about design and culture.

What has been the biggest achievement of your career?

I became an AIGA Mentor at the high school of Art & Design in New York City. Shortly after I joined the program, I got lucky. After going to a NYC Department of Education Mentoring meeting, I met Caroline Kennedy and when I was introduced to her, she casually thanked me for donating my time to such a worthy cause. Her compliment buoyed my spirit and in a moment of courage, I asked her if she would be interested in helping the AIGA Mentorship effort. She agreed and subsequently was our keynote speaker at our upcoming launch event at the Museum of Art and Design. After that, Emily Oberman invited me to join the New York Chapter and I served on that amazing board for two years. At the end of my term, AIGA Board President Sean Adams asked me to run for a seat on the National Board, which I did. In the last five years, I have worked on every Design Legends Gala, curated 20/20 at the 2007 National Conference in Denver, chaired the 2008 GAIN Conference in New York City, and moderated the 2009 Y Conference in San Diego. The student I mentored graduated and went on to get a scholarship at the School of Visual Arts. In 2009, I became President of the AIGA.

What do you believe has been the biggest factor in your success?

I work really, really, really hard. I rarely give up. My friend Michael Surtees has said that I am "a finisher"—I have an almost obsessively compulsive need to finish things.

What advice would you give to recent graduates or others who are just getting started in a career in illustration or graphic design?

Work as hard as you can. Work harder than everyone else. Shoot for the stars. Realize that only YOU can limit what you hope for. Dreams CAN come true … you just need to work really, really hard to make them happen for yourself!

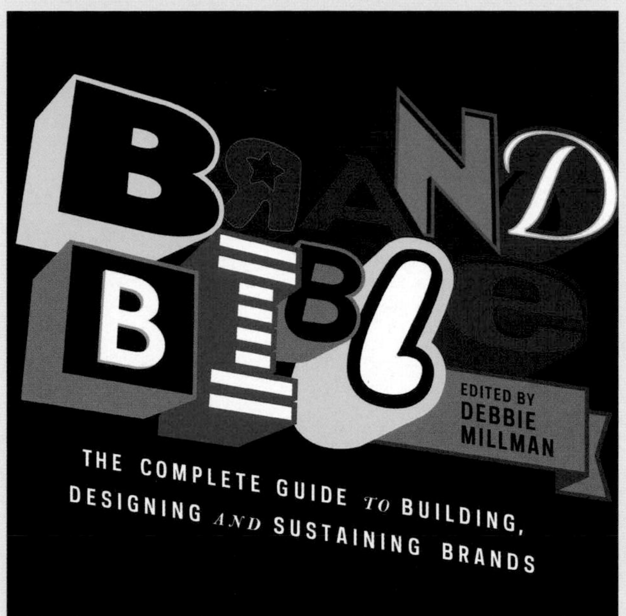

debbie millman

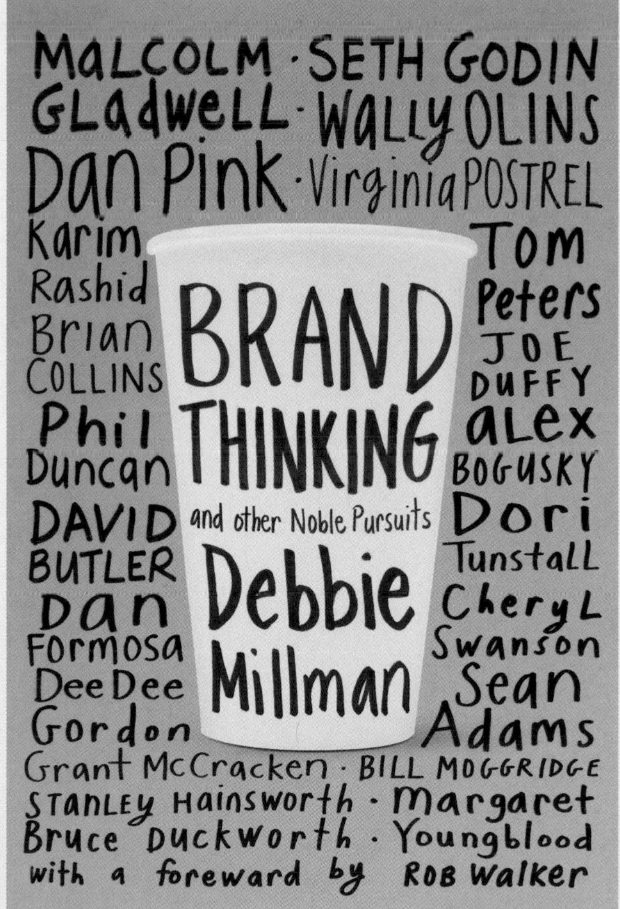

Two recent books that Millman has authored include *Brand Bible*, a guide to creating effective brand design, and *Brand Thinking*, a collection of 20 interviews with some of the world's most celebrated brand leaders.
Courtesy of Sterling Brands.

seven

Media and Technology for Communication Artists

Illustration and design by Nathan Jurevicius; animation producer Sophie Byrne, Passion Pictures of Australia.

7

introduction

You have been presented with many visual examples of how graphic design works effectively in a variety of applications including magazines, books, newspapers, and other print media. Other examples presented have included how design is used in electronic media such as television, video, and Web design. Other types of design examples have included signage, posters, billboards, and packaging.

In all instances, this book discusses how design elements and principles work to communicate verbal and pictorial content effectively. These principles and guidelines are important aspects to developing a better understanding of how to present a communication message in a way that attracts and engages an audience.

In addition to understanding how to design for different types of media, graphic designers also are involved in determining the best media for delivery of a graphic message. This chapter is devoted to the discussion and presentation of a range of media and the ways media affect graphic design and communication decision making. You will also be introduced to innovative applications that are changing how and what we design.

objectives

- Discuss the different media options available to graphic designers.
- Explain how graphic communication and media are interrelated.
- Explain how media can affect the delivery and perception of graphic content.
- Develop a historical awareness of the evolution of graphic communication, technology, and media.
- Explain how technological advancements have affected media development.
- Discuss how new and traditional media are combined in graphic communication.
- Introduce innovative technological applications.

MEDIA TECHNOLOGY THEN AND NOW

To better understand how media functions in the contemporary world, it helps to have an overview of the kinds of visual media that are used and the way they have evolved throughout the history of human culture.

The discussion will begin with what media is and does. A medium is the delivery means or channel for communicating a written, verbal, or visual message. A medium (or media if you are referring to more than one type of medium) can take any form. Examples of print media include magazines, books, billboards, newspapers, annual reports, brochures, and newsletters. Electronic media include all broadcast media such as television, radio, film, and digital print and interactivity. You experience some media, such as TV and radio, as a passive participant, meaning that you are unable to respond directly or control how you perceive or interact with the medium or its message. On the other hand, interactive media include Web sites, social media, media sharing, gaming, and mobile phone applications where the receiver of the message can respond to or interact with the media. Most digital interactive media function like conventional venues such as posters, point-of-purchase displays, signage, and other situations where the message is experienced in the receiver's environment. Throughout this chapter the discussion will focus on how these different types of visual media are most effectively used across the field of visual communication.

Media are composed of the materials and tools involved in delivering a message. In contemporary culture, people continue to use media that have been in use for centuries, such as paper and pen. However, other materials and tools used today reflect technological advances that have changed how and what we design. To better understand the various ways media function in graphic design, it is helpful to know how media and visual communication have evolved.

Early Forms of Media and Technology

As a graphic designer and communication artist, you will work with media that give visual form to verbal content, a process called *graphic communication*, or communication through words and pictures. Technology is the state of the development of tools implemented by a culture for applied purposes. We think of the concept of technology in terms of the latest scientific advances, but if you consider the definition of technology just presented, it includes the tools used at every stage of human development. People have made use of evolving forms of technology since prehistoric times. Pictorial representations of animals, human forms, and symbolic shapes were painted and carved on rock and the stone walls of caves. This early technology included the rock or stone surface itself, pigments and binders made from dirt, human saliva, vegetable juices, and charcoal and the tools to apply the pigments such as hands, feathers, bone, and horsehair brushes. In the earliest forms of media technology that have been discovered, cave paintings and rock carvings (petroglyphs), for example, all provide some insight into how these ancient people lived **7.1**.

Over time, these crude images evolved into more simplified pictorial representations, called symbols or hieroglyphics. As primitive cultures developed more sophisticated means of communication, these primitive symbols evolved into pictograms or more abstract symbols. These symbols were pressed into clay tablets, another primitive form of media technology, were then sun-dried or baked in kilns **7.2**.

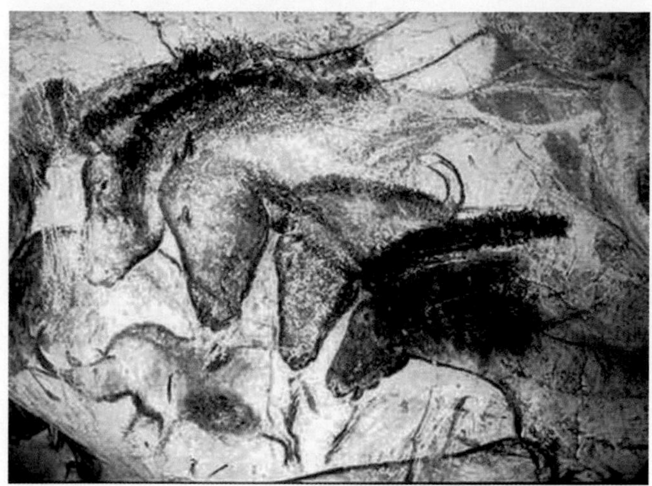

[7.1] The crude imagery painted by ancient cave dwellers gives people an awareness of the lives of their primitive ancestors.
Public Domain.

[7.2] Early pictograms, often inscribed in clay, served as the basis for today's alphabet and were used to depict objects such as an ox (left) and a house (right).
Public Domain.

Letter	Name	Meaning	Hebrew	Latin	Cyrillic
𐤀	**aleph**	**ox**	א	**Aa**	**Aa**

[7.3] The alphabet used in written communication today evolved from the ancient Phoenician alphabet.
© Cengage Learning 2013.

Ancient characters were developed and adopted first by the Greeks and later by the Romans to an alphabet very similar to the one used today **7.3**. (Also see the discussion in Chapter 2, *The Evolution of Typography*.)

During the Middle Ages, the written word was available only to the ruling class, bishops, and religious scribes. However, during this period, early forms of today's media began to take form. Bibles and psalm books were hand-assembled for wealthy merchants, the nobility, and the monasteries. Religious scribes meticulously penned these early Christian doctrines, called illuminated manuscripts, with a feather quill on vellum, a very thin sheet of calf or sheep skin **7.4**.

[7.4] Illuminated manuscripts were highly detailed religious books written by hand in gold, silver, and vivid color pigments.
Public Domain.

During the Renaissance, mass production of the printed word became possible as a result of the efforts of Johannes Gutenberg. Gutenberg developed a process of crafting single letters from brass and casting them in molten metal. Assembling these letters onto a flat printing surface that was then inked created words. Gutenberg used a makeshift press to transfer the inked text onto paper **7.5**.

Gutenberg's invention of movable type and the printing press was the first time mass communication was established through the printed word. The printing method he invented, called letterpress, was widely used for printing until the early twentieth century and is still in use today.

From the Renaissance through the Industrial Revolution, printing was the most common form of media. Newspapers, books, handbills, and posters were used to educate, entertain, and keep the public informed of current events and opportunities. During this period, visual communication as it is known today began to evolve in a way that integrated graphic and fine arts to further serve communication. Lithography, a process discussed in Chapter 2, was developed during this period of time and allowed artists such as Henri de Toulouse-Lautrec to reproduce colored imagery **7.6**.

O F

ORONTII FINEI
DELPHINATIS, REGII MATHEMA-
TICARVM PROFESSORIS, DE
ARITHMETICA PRACTICA
LIBRI QVATVOR.

LIBER PRIMVS, DE INTEGRIS: HOC EST,
ciuſdem ſpeciei, ſiue denominationis tractat numeris.

De fructu, atq; dignitate ipſius Arithmeticæ: Proœmium.

1 INTER LIBERALES MA-
thematicas, quæ ſolæ diſciplinæ vocãtur,
Arithmeticam primum locum ſibi vendi-
caſſe: nemo ſanæ mentis ignorat. Eſt enim Dignitas arithmeti
Arithmetica omnium aliarum diſciplina-
rum mater, & nutrix antiquiſſima: numerorũ qualitates, vim, & naturam, ac id ge-
nus alia demonſtrans, quæ abſolutum vi-
dentur reſpicere numerum. Cuius prin-
cipia tanta excellunt ſimplicitate, vt nul-
lius artis videatur indigere ſuffragio: ſed cunctis opituletur artibus. Ad
cuius puritatem illud etiam plurimum facit: quoniam nulla diuinitati
adeò cõnexa eſt diſciplina, quantùm Arithmetica. Nam vnitas omniũ
numerorũ radix & origo, in ſe, à ſe, ac circum ſeipſam vnica vel impar-
tibilis permanet: ex cuius tamen coaceruatione, omnis cõſurgit & ge-
neratur, omniſque tandem in eam reſoluitur numerus. Quemadmo-
dum cuncta quæ ſeu diſcreta, ſiue compoſita inſpectentur Vniuerſo, à
ſummo rerum conditore in definitum digeſta, redactáve ſunt, & demũ
2 reſoluenda numerum. Quot autem vtilitates cognita, quótve laby-
rinthos ignota præbeat Arithmetica: conſpicere facile eſt. Numerorũ Fructus arithmet
etenim ratione ſublata, tollitur & muſicarum modulationũ intelligen-
tia: geometricorum, cæleſtiúmve arcanorum ſubtilis aufertur ingreſ-
ſio: tollitur & vniuerſa Philoſophia, ſiue quæ diuina, ſeu quæ contem-
platur humana: imperfecta relinquitur legũ adminiſtratio, vtpote, quæ
A.iij.

[7.5] The classic beauty of this page from Gutenberg's 42-line Bible is timeless in its skillful handling of layout, typography, and imagery.
Public Domain.

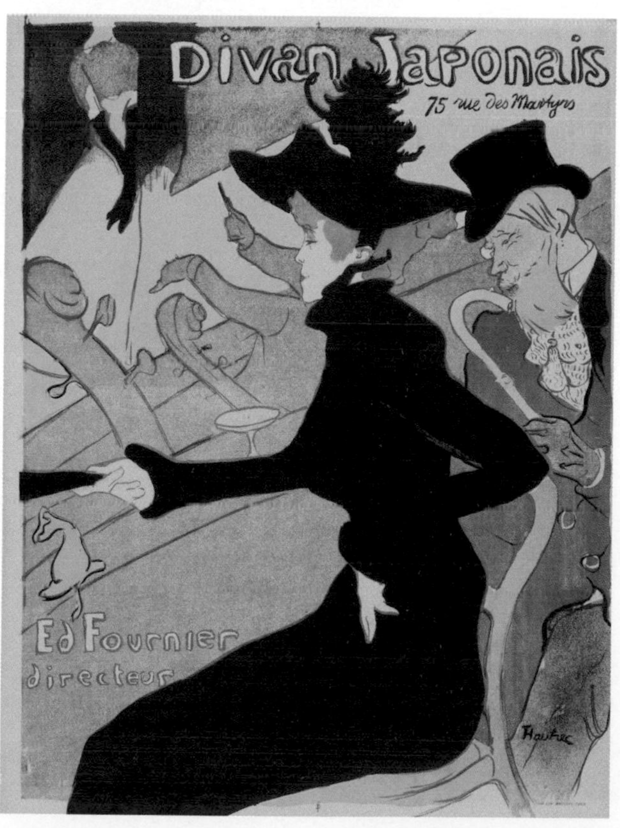

[7.6] Lithography was a printing medium that French artists such as Henri de Toulouse-Lautrec used to print color posters.
Digital Image © 2009 Museum Associates/LACMA/Art Resource, NY.

Media's Coming of Age

Mass media began to shift to electronic media with the invention of motion pictures at the end of the nineteenth century. Going to the cinema became a popular form of entertainment in the early twentieth century, initially with silent movies. The introduction of sound technology in the late 1920s ensured that motion pictures would continue to evolve as a popular form of entertainment.

Early forms of animation incorporating stop motion also began to evolve in the early 1900s. Early cartoonists such as Winsor McCay, Pat Sullivan, and Max Fleischer introduced character animation. These animated features were offered as "shorts" in theaters along with featured motion pictures **7.7**.

In the 1920s, the Disney empire began when its founder, Walt Disney, developed his own animated cartoon characters. Disney initially created a character called Oswald Rabbit who appeared in silent animated shorts. However, Disney made history when he introduced the first successful sound animated film, *Steamboat Willie*. The animated cartoon featured a new Disney-designed character, Mickey Mouse. Disney also was one of the first animators to incorporate Technicolor in animation with his *Flowers and Trees*, an award-winning animated feature released in 1932.

In addition to entertainment, broadcasting began to take hold as a news and advertising medium when the radio came into common use in the early 1900s. As its popularity and accessibility to the public increased, radio became an alternative to newspapers and other print media as a means of communicating news and entertainment.

However, one of the most important advances in media technology came into being when television was introduced in the 1930s. Television blended sound with visual impact and began to replace radio as the broadcast media of choice for news and entertainment. Although the technology for television existed in the 1930s, broadcasting was experimental in those early years. After World War II, returning GIs and their families began to spend the savings they had accumulated during the war years, purchasing homes, cars, and luxuries denied to them during the war. In the late 1940s, an explosion of television sets occurred in the U.S. marketplace, with a sales boom occurring in England a few years later. By 1950, more than 8 million televisions existed in U.S. homes and 107 television stations were broadcasting. By the mid-1950s, color television was introduced.

Graphic design for motion pictures and television began to develop during this period. The popularity of these media and the attention they drew from consumers resulted in some noteworthy design achievements. William Golden, art director for Columbia Broadcasting System (CBS)

[7.7] *Gertie the Dinosaur* was the first animated cartoon distributed for public viewing. Released in 1914 and conceived and produced by *New York Times* cartoonist Winsor McCay, the silent animation lasted seven minutes and incorporated 10,000 inked drawings similar to the one shown here. *Public Domain.*

for almost two decades, designed one of the most successful trademarks of the century for CBS. The CBS pictographic eye is such a classic icon that it still remains in use today, looking just as fresh as more contemporary logos and trademarks **7.8**.

The work of Saul Bass, another influential designer of the mid-twentieth century, also featured prominently in broadcast and entertainment media. Bass worked as a designer for the movie industry, designing posters and titles for motion pictures **7.9**.

[7.8] The iconic CBS logo was designed by William Golden in 1951. When it first appeared on television, it was featured as a translucent icon hovering in the sky.
Logo design by William Golden. Image © CBS.

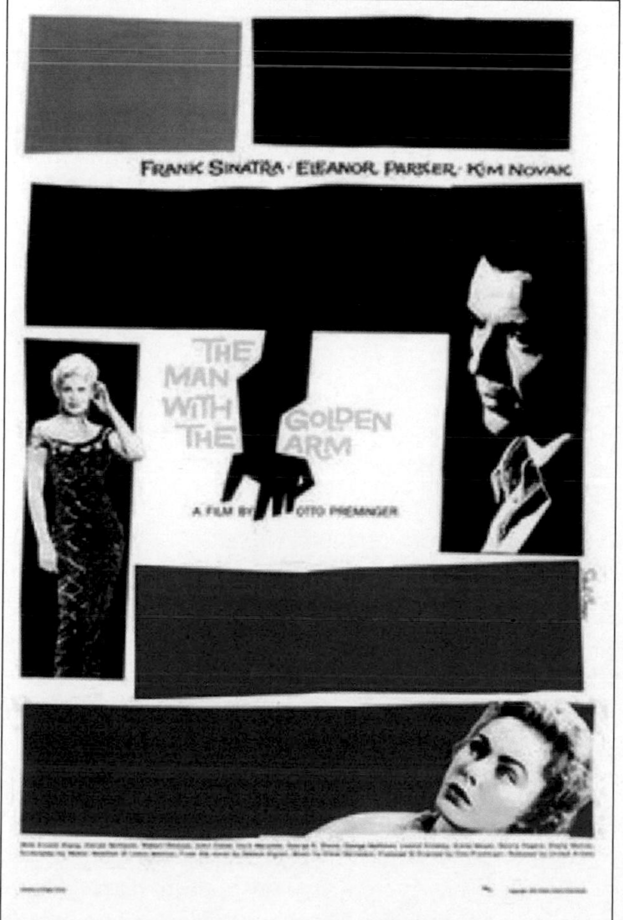

[7.9] Saul Bass designed titles and posters for more than 50 films during the course of his career. One of his most well-known designs was for *The Man with the Golden Arm*, released in 1955.
Courtesy of Otto Preminger Films, Ltd.

The Form of Media

When describing various kinds of media, it is helpful to distinguish between the media that the designer uses in the design process versus the media that is used to distribute the design product. To avoid confusion, the industry uses terminology to make this distinction:

- **Vehicle** refers to the materials used to physically produce the work. Examples include the computer, paint, pen and ink, and charcoal.
- **Venue** refers to the form the design assumes. Examples include electronic, print, environmental, and consumer product.

AN OVERVIEW OF NEW MEDIA

The end of the twentieth century heralded the digital revolution—a technological advancement that is comparable to the Industrial Revolution in terms of its impact on the way people live and work. As the Industrial Revolution moved people into the age of machines, the digital revolution pitched them into the age of computers.

The computer not only impacted the way designers work with and perceive typography, imagery, and two-dimensional design, but also profoundly affected the way designers react and interact with graphic communication. The result has been the invention of an assortment of media options the industry has dubbed "new media." Although that term is commonly used and accepted, **new media** is somewhat misleading in the sense that what is "new" now will likely be antiquated, or "old," tomorrow. But in this book, the term will be used to describe computer-generated media that goes beyond the two-dimensional realm, including interactive media, the Web, and multimedia.

New media presents different challenges for designers than conventional media. Interactivity, globalization, and blending graphic design with audio and cinematic media are among the many aspects that designers need to consider when approaching new media. Later, this chapter will discuss in greater detail how the design principles presented earlier in this book can be applied to new media. For now, it is helpful to have an awareness of what the differences are between interactive media, the Web, and multimedia and where those unique media technologies overlap and how they have evolved.

Interactive Design

Essentially, **interactive media** allows the user to respond to or control his or her media experience. Unlike books or film that require a viewer to process information in linear sequences, interactivity is nonlinear. It allows the viewer to access information on an individual basis according to his or her preference.

In its most basic form, interactivity is the ability to activate a link by placing a cursor over a keyword or an icon (also referred to as a widget) that activates an interface through touch screen or by clicking a mouse. An interface is a program designed to communicate information between computing devices or other programs **7.10**.

Before the Internet came into wide use, interactive programs were available on diskette. Some of the earliest applications were offered as educational programs and games. As technology evolved, CD-ROMs (compact disc read-only memory) allowed more digital information to be stored: animation, illustration, photography, sound, text, and video.

[7.10] Apple's iPhone interface is based entirely on "third-party" graphic elements called "widgets" or "icons." Through the use of touch-screen technology, users can literally access a global network of interactive media. Like products on a department store shelf, application icons must be designed to quickly communicate with simplified and unique graphics.
Courtesy of Computer Desktop Encyclopedia.

Since then, interactive media have become far more complex, combining audio, visual, and cinematic communications to form a body of information. In addition to Web sites, interactive technology is available on DVDs, as applications accessed on mobile phones and portable computing devices, social and educational media networking and media-sharing Web sites. Application (app) categories include entertainment and gaming, utilities, music, lifestyle, navigation, news, reference, and productivity **7.11**. Interactive media also include interactive kiosks, installations, and virtual environments **7.12**.

[7.11] DishWhere is an urban game designed as an iPhone application. The goal is to collect points by completing challenges at unique and historic restaurants and food establishments across New York City. Through the utilization of mobile technology and social communities and a single player, an ambient gaming experience is created. The game explores new gaming mechanics in the urban prototype: *screen capture.*
Interactive design by Leann Wagner.

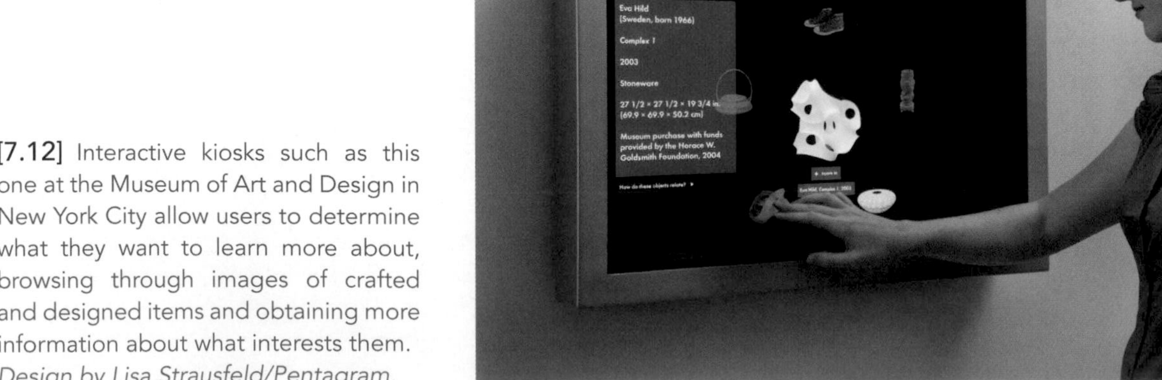

[7.12] Interactive kiosks such as this one at the Museum of Art and Design in New York City allow users to determine what they want to learn more about, browsing through images of crafted and designed items and obtaining more information about what interests them.
Design by Lisa Strausfeld/Pentagram.

[7.13] Cricket Press designs and illustrates screen-printed rock posters, custom screen prints, and illustrated prints. Their Web site features access to their inventory of posters for sale, news about events, and custom services. The graphic style of the hand-rendered type, the color scheme and "clean" design aesthetic of the site reflects the design aesthetic used in their poster design and illustrations.
Website design for Cricket Press, LLC. www.cricket-press.com.

Interactive media have changed the way we live and work. It is an integrated component of our daily lives. The design and content of interactive media largely determine which media we choose to use. Like the music we choose to listen to, the cars we choose to drive, the movies we choose to see, and the clothes we choose to wear, the media devices and interactive media we use serve as an extension of our personality, collectively defining who we are. Because this new media technology changes so rapidly and is so globally accessible, the design must be culturally responsive to the users' needs as well as their sense of style **7.13**.

The Web

The Internet was originally developed in the 1960s by the U.S. government as a covert system that would facilitate communication in the event of a nuclear attack. During the Internet's experimental stages, the government allowed access to only private users. In 1982, the National Science Foundation refined the system and made it accessible to computer research labs and institutions of higher learning. Legislation in the early 1990s made Internet technology available to public schools, colleges, and businesses. That legislation encouraged digital pioneers to develop the technology necessary to transmit words, graphics, sound, photography, and video, furthering the Internet's growth. By 1997, more than 30 million users in more than 100 countries were linked via the Internet. This figure increased to 120 million in 1999. By 2002, 580 million people were using the Internet. At the time of this writing, it is estimated that more than a billion people are connected to the Web.

Interactive Media: Present and Future

Tuesday McGowan is an accomplished, award-winning, prolific interactive designer and director based in San Francisco. She has worked for major clients including ESPN, Nokia, Target, Absolut, Oracle, and Old Navy, to name a few, and has directed dynamic music videos for Sheryl Crow, Justin Timberlake, the Greenhorns, Soundgarden, and Heartless Bastards. When asked about the state and future of interactive media, she offered the following insights:

The technology is constantly changing. Staying current on trends and tools is challenging. As a designer, clients don't know what they want and usually they are transitioning from an old model of working to a new one. With this new model comes learning and understanding industry standards and trade practices. Also designing for the lowest common denominator can prove to be frustrating. Even though we have the technology, the audience is not necessarily staying current with upgrades needed for the full Internet experience.

The field will continue to grow and interactive designers will gain more authority and responsibility. Ultimately, I see interactive designers serving as directors. This is already happening with certain production companies adding "interactive directors" to their roster. As broadband becomes more universal, we will look to Web sites to give us the full interactive entertainment experience once achieved with television. The viewer will have a greater hand in determining content, story lines, games, and interests. The blog will become a bigger presence in our experience of getting information and misinformation. This is most notably evident in politics and will serve as an issue in our democracy. Seeking out the truth will become more and more difficult.

[7.14a] Tuesday McGowan
Courtesy of Tuesday McGowan.

[7.14b] This animation was designed for Oracle's Open World conference. The story features a daredevil action adventure tale featuring a character named "O." Oracle software is featured in clever metaphors depicting specific capabilities as "O" makes it to his final destination. The strategic objective for Tuesday and her team was to signify the Oracle brand and their vast array of products.
Courtesy of Tuesday McGowan.

The popularity of the Internet has resulted in an increasingly global marketplace. As a consequence, designers who design for the Web must be aware of how they are communicating in a cross-cultural environment. In addition to developing a visual approach that will connect with a multicultural audience, Web site designers have been challenged by globalization to adapt their sites to include multiple languages **7.15**.

The Internet also has blurred the lines of media, as they are known today. Until recently, media had fallen into two camps: mass media (such as broadcasting), and personal media (such as books), where communication takes place on a more intimate level. The Internet can do both. It lets anyone broadcast content to millions of users, but also facilitates interactivity, allowing users to respond to the communication they are receiving by navigating, providing feedback, and making purchases.

This interactivity has required designers to design in a different way. Designers of mass media are accustomed to controlling the user's experience, much like traditional marketing pushes information on the consumer. Web site design is different in that a Web site can't influence a consumer's decision to go there. A Web site delivers information in a user-defined context where people experience content on their own terms. Whatever the user wants, it's the designer's responsibility to make it easy to find and accessible.

Web Technology

Web sites rely on code that allows the site to function. Since the code determines the functionality of the site, it also determines the extent of the design and how it functions. Authoring tools or software used for creating Web sites has the code built in. High-end Web design often relies on custom-built code to achieve complex interactivity by the end user. The type of code used to drive Web sites determines the parameters that dictate the design and interactivity.

Hypertext or **hypermedia** is the form that content assumes in Web design. Hypertext was one of the earliest forms of interactivity offered by Apple in the early development of computer graphics. It was bundled with a collection of programs that came with Apple's personal computers. *Hypertext Markup Language*, known commonly as **HTML**, is a language that constitutes the basic building blocks of Web pages. Web browsers read HTML documents and essentially translate them into the visual and audio information that we see and hear when interacting with a site. This technology has been adapted to the World Wide Web using **hyperlinks**, highlighted or underlined words, phrases, images, or icons that are coded to link to another part of a Web site or to a different Web site.

CSS (Cascading Style Sheets) is a style sheet format for HTML that provides layout settings that distinguish the formatting from the document presentation or the visual elements that include color, imagery, typography, and so forth. Most designers are not usually taught to write code or even understand the use of common "off-the-shelf" code programs used extensively in Web design. Learning the use of HTML, CSS, and complex "high-end" authoring tools is advantageous to any designer planning to work primarily in the world of Web and interactive design. However, there are numerous digital software programs that provide basic toolkits for Web design. These programs often limit the range of end-user interactivity. It is critical to determine the communication and functionality demands and a design strategy before choosing the software to build and design a Web site.

Multimedia

The term **multimedia** is most often used to describe the integrated interactive formats that have evolved as a consequence of sophisticated digital technology. Multimedia technology blends animation, streaming audio, and video with text, imagery, and interactivity.

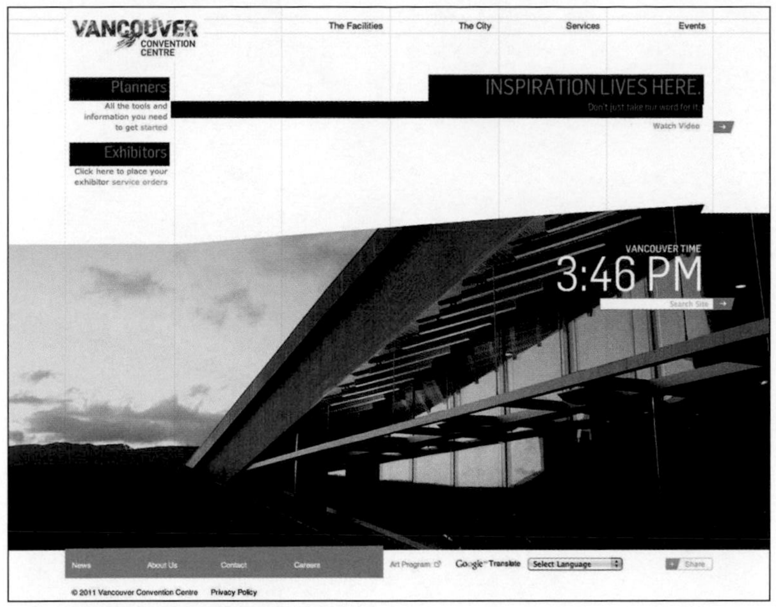

[a]

[b]

[7.15a, b] The city of Vancouver, Canada, is a vibrant cultural community. The convention center seeks to attract conferences from organizations around the world. A photograph that features the striking architecture of the center itself dominates this home page for the Vancouver Convention Center Website. The design incorporates and displays the text elements in English and numerous other languages, including Arabic, which are translated by "Google Translate."
Images courtesy of Vancouver Convention Centre.

Content vs. Presentation

Hypertext Markup Language (HTML) is the formatting or coding language used for setting up Web pages. When a Web page is viewed, the HTML code or tag tells the Web browser how to display the coded content. Although it's possible to use HTML to put together an entire Web site, today's best Web sites are created with a combination of HTML and CSS coding. While HTML works best for coding content or the information, you want the user to access such as text and imagery, CSS (stands for Cascading Style Sheets) works better for tagging presentation elements in a Web page.

If this sounds confusing, think of content as the information you want the user to access such as text and photos. The presentation is how you want them to see this information, its size, color, and so on. For example, when coding text in a paragraph for a Web page, as content it is coded as HTML. However, for presentation purposes its size, color, and font or typeface would be coded as CSS. The example below shows other Web page elements and how they would be coded for HTML versus CSS.

CSS also simplifies design changes. Rather than formatting every headline in a Web site, CSS lets you create a style for the headline tag and use that to format all of your headlines, making it much easier and much more efficient to make changes and have them applied universally. Web sites that use CSS are also more likely to comply with current standards. CSS designs are more flexible and adaptable, allowing them to be easily viewed on cell phones and other small screens, as well as larger ones.

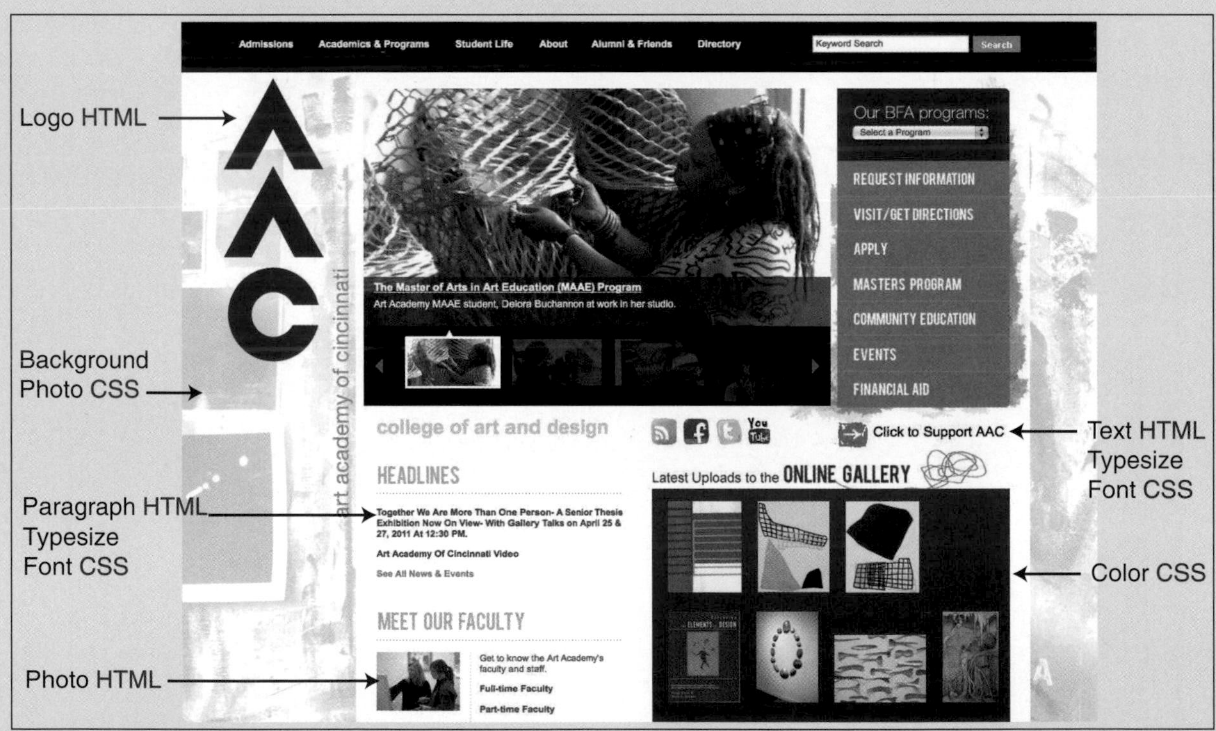

[7.16] *Courtesy of The Art Academy of Cincinnati.*

[7.17] Design studios like Mekanism, a San Francisco and New York-based production house, need a Web site that can accommodate and display motion graphics. The "screen grab" on the right represents a video animation promoting the new launch of Napster, a media-sharing venue. It can be selected to display as a low-resolution video.
Agency: Venebles, Bell and Partners. Production Company: Mekanism.

Multimedia has become an important component of today's Web and interactive technology. Today's Web sites come alive with animated graphics and audio and video technology **7.17**.

Beyond Web sites, multimedia applications include video electronic gaming, computer graphics (CG) for the movie industry, and corporate and informational presentations; and it is important to clarify that not all interactive media is multimedia. Web sites, DVDs, and other interactive technologies that are limited to text and imagery are not regarded as multimedia.

Making an audio, video, or animated sequence used to require a huge production crew with special expertise and skills. However, today's technology has made it possible for a designer to work alone in the creation of a multimedia project. Although a designer may be tempted to "do it all", designing for multimedia requires an understanding of the technology involved as well as knowledge of time-based media.

Graphic designers often collaborate with other media specialists in the production of audio, video, and animated sequences. In addition to graphic design, multimedia often requires script writing, animation, illustration, photography, live-action production, special effects, content creation, interactive developers, project development, and video and audio editing.

ELEMENTS, PRINCIPLES, AND NEW MEDIA

The design strategies discussed earlier in this book apply to the Web, interactive media, and multimedia in the same way they apply to print. Design that supports the communication goal and is directed in a way that is appropriate to the intended audience is just as important in new media as it is in any two-dimensional design application.

The guiding principles of design also apply to multimedia, the Web, and interactive media. Pages that are part of a Web site are similar to brochure pages in that they involve a balanced arrangement of graphic elements. Web pages require designers to pay attention to typography and to use an underlying organizational grid to help unify the pages and make them reader friendly. Color has the same emotive and aesthetic possibilities on a Web site and for a multimedia application as it has in print media.

Likewise, imagery that is compelling in a magazine cover, is just as likely to be arresting on a Web site **7.18**.

[7.18a to f] The JetBlue Web site uses many of the design principles mentioned in Chapter 1 of this book. A grid is used to organize information on each page. A consistent color palette, typography, and graphic approach helps to unify the pages.
Courtesy of JetBlue Airways Corporation.

Production Tip

Image File Formats for the Web

There are three image formats in constant use on the Internet: GIF, JPEG, and PNG. Each is suited to a specific purpose. Choosing the right format is important to producing high-quality, fast-loading images.

GIF—Limited to 256 colors, GIFs are smallest in size (8-bit) of all file formats. Use for graphic or noncontinuous tone imagery such as logos, graphic reductions, and line arts. GIFs can also be animated.

JPEG—This file format uses a compression algorithm to reproduced imagery in millions of colors. Used most often for continuous tone imagery such as photographs. JPEG images cannot be animated.

PNG—This format was invented specifically for the Web and is the newest of the three file formats. One version, PNG-8, is similar to the GIF format in that it can be saved with a maximum of 256 colors. Another format PNG-24 supports 24-bit color, similar to JPEG format. Howeveer, JPEG is preferred to PNG for its compression capabilities. PNG format is not recommended for animation.

However, new media design and communication differs from print in that it is time-based. Print designers often do not consider time as a factor; but on the Internet, every minute counts. Content needs to be streamlined and presented in a way that makes it easily accessible. The excessive time involved in navigating or waiting for a series of Web pages to load can alienate potential browsers or cause them to quickly lose interest in a Web site.

New media also requires knowledge of filmmaking, including the basics of working with sound and a narrative or storytelling format.

Let's look at other design considerations that are unique to new media.

Motion

Motion graphics are a major factor in new media. Motion involves composition over time and space; individual frames are not as important as the cumulative effect of these images over a period of time.

Although type on a printed page is not inherently dynamic, computer technology lets designers animate type and give it movement. Instead of composing type so that it is read in a linear format, designers have the ability to configure type so that it moves across the screen in a way that supports a verbal message **7.19**.

Motion design involves telling a story or a sequence of events and requires prior planning. Sequences that last less than a minute still need to be sketched out in storyboard format, viewed, and then revised and refined before they are actually developed. Storyboards are typically hand-drawn so they are clearly seen as being developmental. (For more information about storyboarding, refer to Chapter 3: *Imagery in Design*.)

Audio and video productions involve even more elaborate planning. Before production can begin, an outline is prepared; then a script is written. Character developers and illustrators are brought in when animation needs to be developed. Actors need to be hired and briefed when a video is developed. Sequences need to be storyboarded and revised. Music and sound effects also need to be planned and developed.

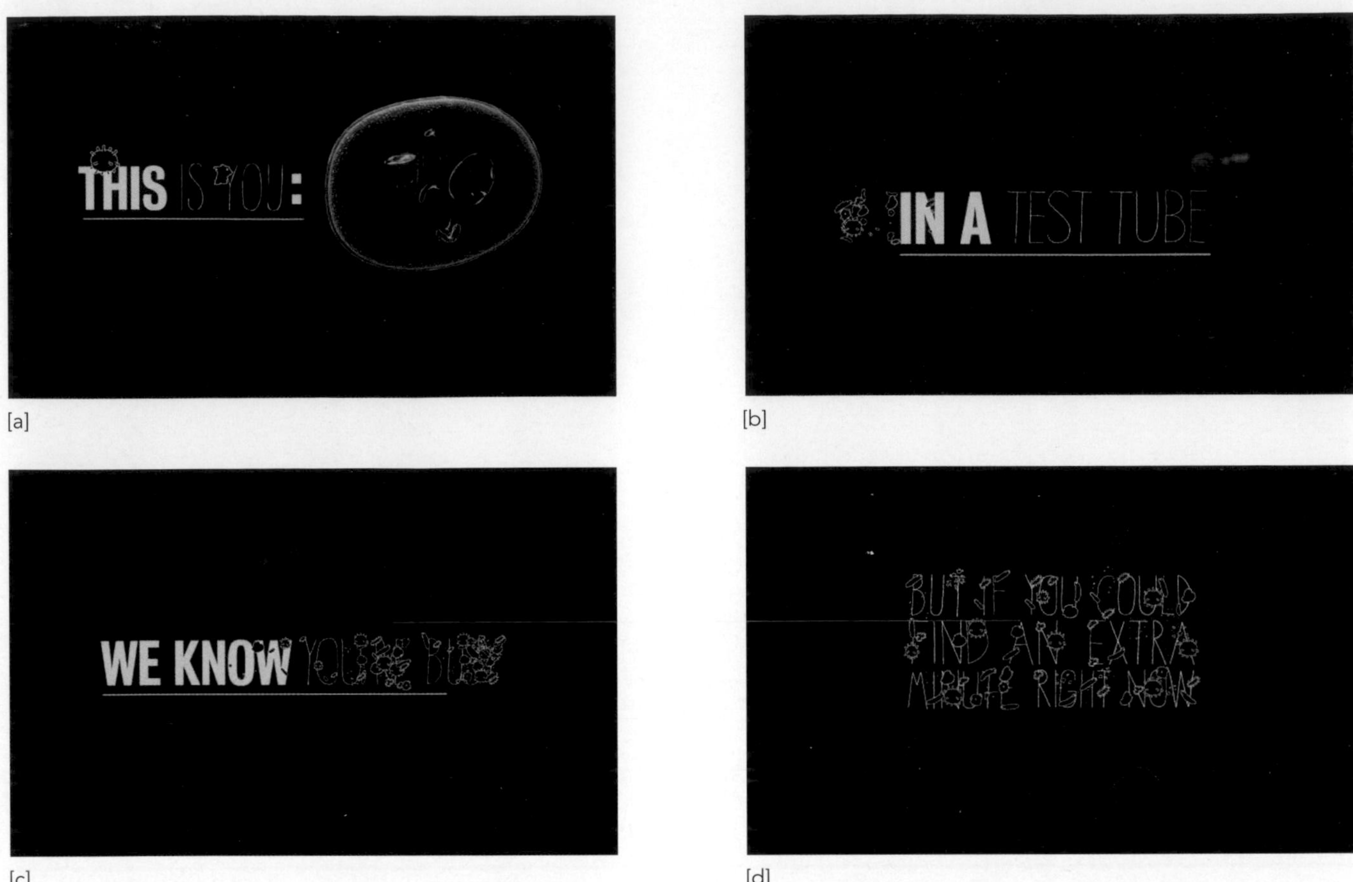

[7.19a to d] Animation literally gives "life" to this opening sequence introducing the Web site "In a Test Tube." The Web site combines user input, interactive video of Canadian environmentalist David Suzuki into an interactive parable about society's unsustainable appetites. Its lead-in "This is you, in a test tube. We know you're busy, but if you could find an extra minute right now, what would you do?" invites visitors to the site to enter in their own submissions that are posted on the site.

Web Site Design

Like any design, Web sites must meet the communication needs of the target audience and support the communication goal and purpose of the site. Often a site must be responsive to an existing brand of an organization, product, or service.

Some sites serve as sources for information, whereas others provide entertainment. Web sites also promote services, products, organizations, and events. Many Web sites allow users to make online purchases of the products they are promoting. The design of a Web site should support and facilitate these purposes.

An effective solution requires the collaboration of a team of creative individuals. A typical team includes a project manager to oversee and coordinate the work and efforts of all involved, a creative director or art director to manage the design strategy and aesthetic continuity, technical personnel to advise the creative personnel on the functional limitations and options available based on the code architecture that is being used, copy writers who generate copy and text, and, of course, the client. Individual designers can produce Web site design but as you can see, also need to be experienced and skilled in verbal, visual, and technical delivery of creative content.

Web sites employ a variety of features, which are customized and creatively delivered to engage the intended audience.

Before design options are explored, Web site designers start with a strategy for the design that includes site goals and the information to be presented, supplemented by surveys and background research to guide the strategy. The design must project a look and offer an experience that is responsive to the profile of the end user.

Web site design often challenges designers to make the most of theme and variation. Web pages must be unified and visually connected in a way that makes them work together as a cohesive whole. However, each page must be able to stand alone and work effectively by itself **7.20**.

Other considerations that are unique to Web site design are building in search engine optimization. Because search engines respond to words, words are as important as pictures on a Web site. Embedding text in graphics can prevent it from being accessed by search engines. Flash movies can also obscure content. An understanding of HTML and CSS coding is essential; knowledge of Web server administration is helpful. And, as mentioned earlier in this chapter, an understanding of narrative format, motion, and sound are essential.

As the site design and function evolves, it must be tested. Prior to the launch, Web sites can be set up to exist as a work in progress with live access by the creative team. Once a site is launched, it must be appropriately maintained and updated to keep it fresh and interesting especially to the returning visitor.

Anatomy of a Web Site

The Web site navigation and menu toolbox inventory will vary depending on the specific needs of the client. Basic menu items are usually accessed through a "Home Page," which functions much as a contents page in a publication. Home pages typically allow users to access "About," "Contact," "News," "Events," and "Profiles" navigation buttons to highlight products and services, and "Links" to a variety of other sources of information, including other Web sites and interactive social and educational media **7.21**.

Building on the general navigation and menu items mentioned above, Web site designers develop an underlying structure for a site. Users must be directed to the portions of the site that are pertinent to their needs and guided through a sequence of pages. Before they begin to design, Web site designers usually rely on a **wire frame** that serves as a blueprint for the site's logistics or a skeletal framework for how the site will function. Wire frames lack color information, typographic style, and even the imagery that will be used. Wire frames usually start as rough sketches; then they are fleshed out into more comprehensive studies that show where type and images will fall.

Site maps are another organizational tool used in Web design and represent a composite list of the pages. They are organized to help viewers navigate a Web site and are designed in a hierarchical arrangement. The hierarchy provides designers with a visual map that guides decisions about where to place design elements and information.

As you visit various Web sites, view them with the analytical eye of a design researcher and study the function, design, and contents to begin to build an understanding of this dynamic and complex venue.

Production Tip

While images may catch the eye in print, words are preeminent in Web design. The more words on your Web site, the more likely a search engine will link your Web site with a potential client. Web site designers refer to incorporating key words into your Web site's home page design as creating "search engine optimization." Not only is the choice of these keywords important, strategic content needs to be coded as html text. Embedding text in graphics or including it in programs like Flash obscures this content.

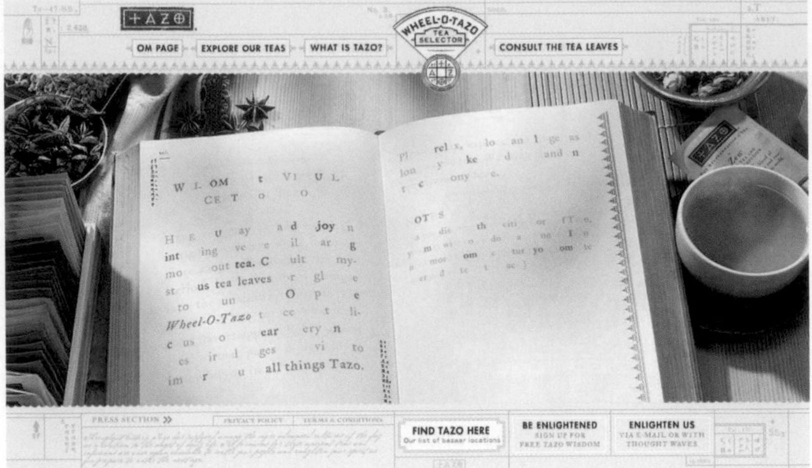
+AZ⊕
OM PAGE
EXPLORE OUR TEAS
WHAT IS TAZO?
WHEEL-O-TAZO
TEA SELECTOR
CONSULT THE TEA LEAVES
PRESS SECTION »
FIND TAZO HERE
Our list of bazaar locations
BE ENLIGHTENED
SIGN UP FOR FREE TAZO WISDOM
ENLIGHTEN US
VIA E-MAIL OR WITH THOUGHT WAVES

[a]

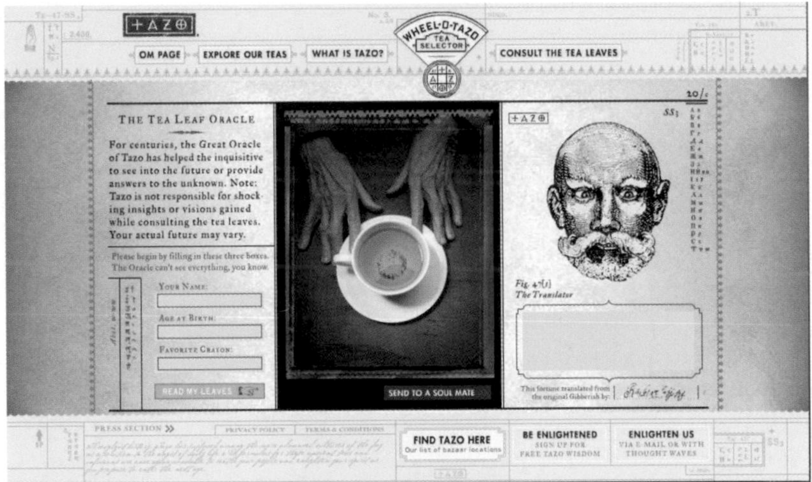
+AZ⊕
OM PAGE
EXPLORE OUR TEAS
WHAT IS TAZO?
WHEEL-O-TAZO
TEA SELECTOR
CONSULT THE TEA LEAVES
THE TEA LEAF ORACLE
For centuries, the Great Oracle of Tazo has helped the inquisitive to see into the future or provide answers to the unknown. Note: Tazo is not responsible for shocking insights or visions gained while consulting the tea leaves. Your actual future may vary.
Please begin by filling in these three boxes. The Oracle can't see everything, you know.
YOUR NAME:
AGE AT BIRTH:
FAVORITE CRAYON:
READ MY LEAVES
SEND TO A SOUL MATE
Fig. 4²(3)
The Translator
This Sermon translated from the original Gibberish by:
PRESS SECTION »
FIND TAZO HERE
Our list of bazaar locations
BE ENLIGHTENED
SIGN UP FOR FREE TAZO WISDOM
ENLIGHTEN US
VIA E-MAIL OR WITH THOUGHT WAVES

[b]

+AZ⊕
OM PAGE
EXPLORE OUR TEAS
WHAT IS TAZO?
WHEEL-O-TAZO
TEA SELECTOR
CONSULT THE TEA LEAVES
BLACK TEAS
GREEN TEAS
HERBAL INFUSIONS
To explore each intriguing flavor of Tazo in deeper detail, please select from the menu above.
Then gently roll your mouse over the image that appears
ABOUT THE DIFFERENT TYPES OF TEA »
WELCOME TO THE TASTING ROOM
This is where every delicious secret of Tazo's artful blending is kept. (Well, almost every secret.)
PRESS SECTION »
FIND TAZO HERE
Our list of bazaar locations
BE ENLIGHTENED
SIGN UP FOR FREE TAZO WISDOM
ENLIGHTEN US
VIA E-MAIL OR WITH THOUGHT WAVES

[c]

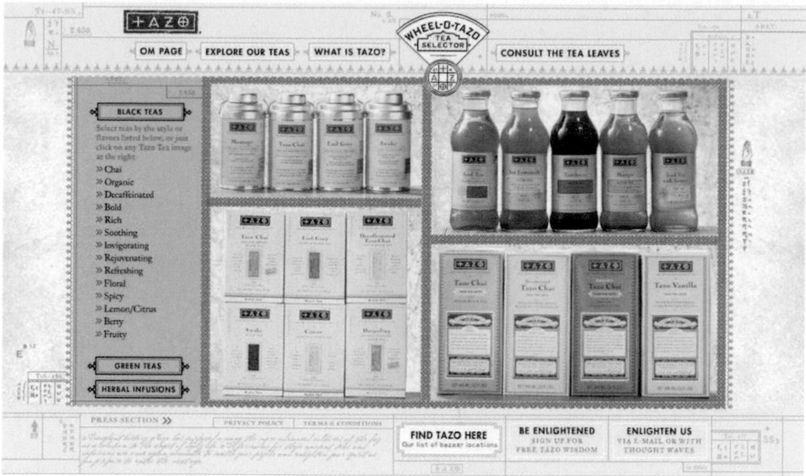

[d]

[7.20a to d] Tazo Tea creates an online brand experience for visitors to its Web site. The site's opening pages take readers through a tealeaf reading. Other portions of the site get users acquainted with a variety of tea-related products. Although the various parts of the site are different, they appear unified as a result of a consistent graphic palette. The various arrangements of these graphic elements on each page add theme and variation to the site.
Web site design by Steve Sandstrom, Jon McVey, Sandstrom Partners.

[7.21] AIGA is a not for-profit, national association for professional design with chapters in many U.S. cities. The national Web site has links to local chapters and student groups. The purpose of the site is to provide services and benefits to its over 20,000 members. The Web features reflect the non-profit status of the organization and include an RSS (Really Simple Syndication) feed that notifies users when articles, videos, and other types of content are updated.
Courtesy of AIGA, the professional association for design. www.aiga.org.

THE RIGHT MEDIA CHOICES

Not too long ago marketing and communication specialists took a shotgun approach to their use of media. Mass media such as newspapers and broadcasting were more commonly used with the assumption that sending a message to the largest number of people would be the best way to elicit a response.

However, today's communicators realize that choice of media is an important consideration in the delivery of a message. In his books, *The Gutenberg Galaxy*, *Culture Is Our Business*, and *The Mechanical Bride*, writer and sociocultural guru Marshall McLuhan asserted that the medium is the message. The various media options available today provide different experiences for their audiences. Some media are more specialized or provide a more intimate experience for the intended recipients than others. These differences need to be considered when making a decision on which medium or media to choose.

New Media vs. Traditional Media

As was mentioned earlier, some media, such as newspapers and broadcasting, reach a wide range of people. These media are also appropriate channels for disseminating large bodies of information. In a newspaper, this information would take the form of an article; on television, a program.

Magazine articles and books are similar in that they are content-heavy; however, they differ from newspapers in that they are usually directed at smaller audiences. Magazines are especially effective at targeting a specific demographic. Browsing the magazine racks at any store will yield a range of publications addressing a variety of interest areas, from kayaking to wedding planning. The industry uses the term ***narrowcasting*** to describe communicating through media that focuses on a narrow audience with a specialized interest.

Magazines and books also are intimate media in that they provide a one-on-one experience with their audience. This experience is substantially different from the shared experience of viewing a television program or a movie as part of a group of people.

Today's media planners know when to take advantage of broadcasting and narrowcasting in their media campaigns. In fact, the best media campaigns use a combination of media to deliver a message **7.22**.

Because too much information can overwhelm an audience, media campaigns often use advertising in magazines, in newspapers, or on billboards, as well as broadcast media such as TV to communicate a simple message. When an ad captures a viewer's attention, the message may include a Web site address so interested individuals can follow up and find more information by going online. In addition to corporate Web sites, online venues may include social media such as Twitter, YouTube, and Facebook **7.23**.

Communication specialists realize that advertising and promotion is occurring more frequently on the Web, particularly to target a "youth" demographic. In a real sense, new media has changed the attitudes of people as consumers. "Generation Y" or the millennial generation, for example, has grown up substantially during the period of the major technological advances we have been discussing. This generation is largely immune to the shotgun style of advertising that was effective with their "Baby Boomer" parents. They tend to "turn off" when presented with an advertising message that is aggressively persuasive. The "integrated" delivery of messages that reflect their lifestyle speak more effectively. Personal media devices and interactive deign interfaces are the ideal "new age" communication delivery system.

Online marketing is more of a grassroots approach. Online marketing is especially effective when the site becomes a venue for entertainment and information, in addition to product promotion and facilitation of online purchases. Savvy communicators realize the importance of developing a promotional strategy that ties in with online marketing.

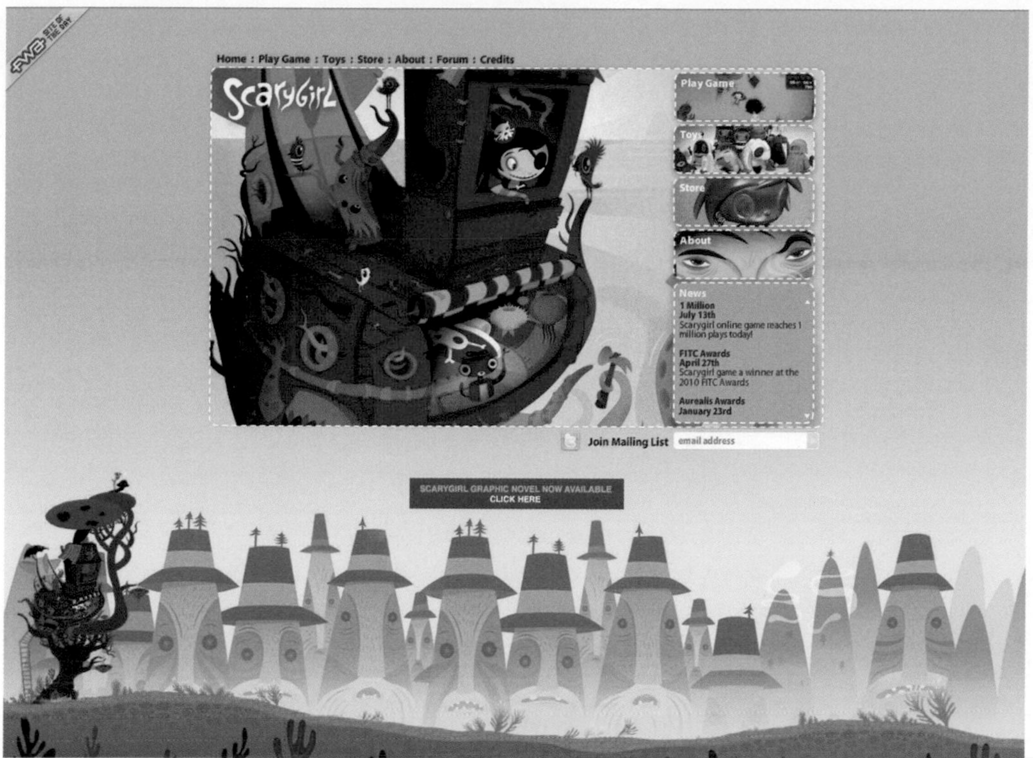

[7.22] *Scarygirl* is a wordless graphic novel that was first published in 2004. The wide range of media applications and venues for this odd character appeals to several audiences including children, teens, and a young adult demographic. The graphic novel has spawned a Web site, toy range, prints, an online game and comic and (in development) a movie. *Scarygirl* is highly imaginative and designed with a richly saturated color palette that functions effectively in both print and interactive media. The concept benefits from the crossover media applications. The online game has reached the one million plays milestone and received the Canadian-based FITC (Flash in the Can) Design and Technology award in 2011.
Illustration and design by Nathan Jurevicius; animation producer Sophie Byrne, Passion Pictures of Australia.

[7.23] Creative and educational content is often experienced on the Web through media sharing venues like Vimeo and YouTube. Jean Jullien is a French graphic designer and illustrator who lives and works in London. He directed and illustrated a short animation, *Catastrophe*, which was posted on YouTube and served as a music video for the musician Niwouinwouin. When the animation went viral, it widely promoted Niwouinwouin's music as well as promoting Jullien's creativity as a designer, illustrator, and animator.
Directed and illustrated by Jean Jullien, music by Niwouinwouin.

Expedition Titanic.com

Firstborn is a digital design agency that integrates design and technology into engaging and innovative user experiences. Based in New York City, the firm's work encompasses Web sites, online ads, viral campaigns, digital applications, three-dimensional models, HD video, interactive installations, and content management tools.

The agency was challenged to create a Web site and a social network campaign to create interest in Expedition *Titanic*, a scientific mission dedicated to the underwater exploration of the RMS *Titanic*. Ever since the ill-fated passenger liner sunk on its maiden voyage in 1912, many have speculated about what remains of the great steamship. The expedition is dedicated to answering the questions surrounding the mystery of the great steamship. Its accompanying Web site generates interest in this mission and keeps fans informed of findings and expedition-related events.

For the Web site, Firstborn wanted to capture the experience of diving 12,500 feet to the bottom of the ocean, as though visitors to the site are actually accompanying the dive team on their journey to explore the sunken steamship. The Web site simulates the experience of the underwater expedition with motion graphics that include a cinematic video and projects a visual sensibility that is scientific, as well as dark and mysterious, like the environment one would find at the bottom of the Atlantic Ocean.

When it was launched, Expedition Titanic.com created interest in the scientific exploration before it began. Since the expedition began in 2010, the Web site has provided day-by-day accounts of the expedition's journey through social media APIs.

How did you create the underwater effect with the cinematic video that simulates the expedition moving through the water and shining lights onto the three-dimensional replica of the Titanic? Can you share which programs were involved and other pertinent technical information?

"The process starts with pencil and paper. It then heads to Photoshop travels through Maya and ends in AfterEffects & Color.

We storyboard out what we want in terms of flow—how the ROV moves down to the titanic, etc. We then use Photoshop to set the look and tone—water tones, color and depth of field. Once we are happy with the look we pass it off to the 3D artist who has the tough job of recreating the trip down to *Titanic*. It's his job to make it real. He starts by creating an animatic based on our storyboards using basic shapes to represent the different objects we pass by. Once that is complete he finishes modeling and it's off to lighting and texture where the artist tries to match the boards we created in Photoshop earlier. Lastly, everything is exported in an uncompressed state so that final tweaks to color, tone and feel can be made in AfterEffects and Color. Now we're close to being done. At this point the file is exported to an .f4v and imported into Flash. Voila. It's that easy!

The process sounds much more linear that it really is; modeling is of course happening while we're storyboarding as we knew what elements we needed to create. But this should give you the idea. Long story short we created everything from scratch."

How much traffic does the site get?

"The website and social media campaign were built around RMS *Titanic*, Inc.'s expedition to the *Titanic* taking place in August of 2011; which was going to be a one of a kind mission. The program was created to educate fans, supporters, and oceanographers and increase awareness of the mission. There was no online media spend and included below are results from the approximate campaign timeline: website launch July 27, 2010 through the end of 2010.

- Site visitors that day: 5,674
- Highest traffic count on September 1, 2010 (during the expedition) at 34,541 visitors.
- Average time on the website: 8 minutes and 32 seconds
- Average page views per visit: 11
- Over 609,000 site visits and more than 6.7 million page views (pieces of content)
- 0 to 43,000 Facebook fans added during the promotion"

[a]

[7.24a] The Expedition Titanic home page offers users the chance to interact with three portions of the site. "Explore RMS Titanic" takes visitors into an exploration of the *Titanic* and information associated with the expedition.
Courtesy of Firstborn and RMS Titanic, INC.

[b]

[7.24b] When visitors to the site select "Explore RMS Titanic," an animated sequence re-creates the experience of plunging into the depths of the ocean.
Courtesy of Firstborn and RMS Titanic, INC.

[c]

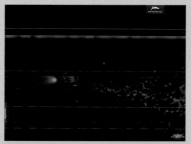

[d]

[e]

[7.24c to e] Portions of the site also lead visitors through a cinematic video tour over a three-dimensional replica of the *Titanic*'s bow. Firstborn replicated the experience of moving swiftly under water using Photoshop, AfterEffects, and Flash.
Courtesy of Firstborn and RMS Titanic, INC.

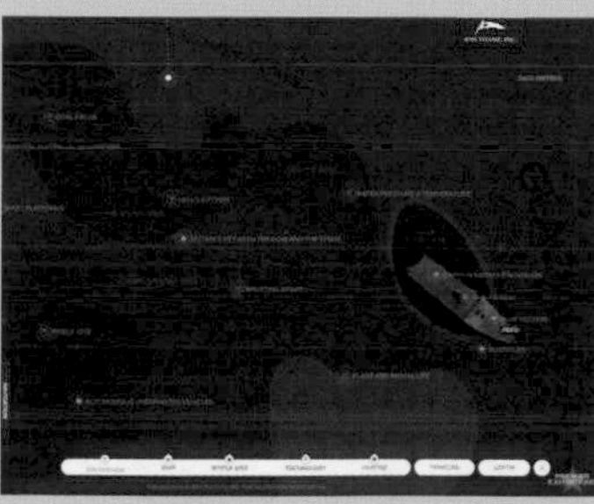

[f]

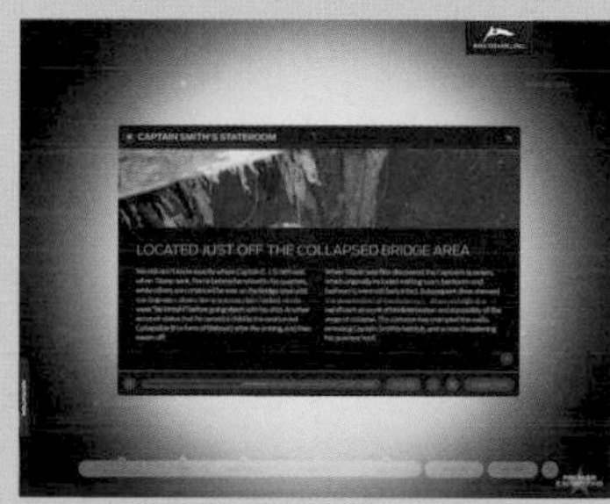

[g]

[7.24f, g] Another portion of the site features an overhead map of the wreck site where users can explore various hotspots, allowing them to learn more about the expedition and the steamship through text, photos, and videos.
Courtesy of Firstborn and RMS Titanic, INC.

SUMMARY

A medium is the delivery means or channel for communicating a written, verbal, or visual message. Electronic media can take the form of broadcast media such as TV, film, and the Web. Print media include magazines, books, newspapers, and brochures. In addition, media fall into categories where the recipients are passive participants or where the recipients can interact with the media experience.

Media involve materials and tools and, in its simplest form, consist of pen and paper. Media have evolved over time to encompass a broad range of sophisticated tools. In ancient civilizations, media took the form of clay tablets or crude pigments applied to paper-like substances. Media as it is known today began to develop with Gutenberg's invention of movable type and the printing press around the time of the Renaissance. Electronic and broadcast media evolved during the twentieth century into the realm of technologies used today. Contemporary digital media are called new media and include interactive media, the Web, and multimedia.

Throughout the history of human communication, regardless of the state of the technology, the common thread is the need for people to interact. Whether it's the "low" technology of Paleolithic people sharing the mysterious collaboration of recording the imagery of animals, figures, and handprints on cave walls or "high" technology of twenty-first century urbanites sharing music videos on mobile phones,

new media differs from print media in that new media is time-based and involves motion, or a sequence of events. However, the elements and principles of design have application in new media just as they do in more traditional types of media. Designers and communication specialists understand the advantages of the various types of media available and know how to choose and combine them to make the biggest impact on a message or campaign. Although most design requires a team approach, designers have adapted to the digital tools needed for producing print-based design. Most work in the printed realm is manageable for designers working on their own. Interactive design presents a range of technical challenges that often requires a team of creative and technical professionals working collaboratively.

projects

FORMS IN MOTION

Objectives

- Work with moving elements in a sequential series of compositions.
- Produce a short story using a consistent and limited number of elements.
- Create a storyboard or digital video pitch.

Description

Work with (1) a circular form or object, (2) a facial feature, (3) a word, and (4) a line or linear element to develop a series of five black-and-white compositions. Control the visual relationship of the elements so they work together in a harmonious manner and create a sequence. You will be managing the four compositional elements and directing their movement through the series. Essentially, this series of five compositions will function like a storyboard. To achieve movement, manipulate size, scale, direction, proximity, orientation, and value.

Limitations and Materials

Begin by exploring the potential "character" you will be creating with the four composition elements. Work with flat shapes painted with acrylic paint or gouache and magazine clips. If you are working on a computer, use digital imagery and a photo-editing or digital drawing program to generate ideas for composition elements. Once you have generated a library of compositional elements and imagery, sort and edit them and choose the four with which you will work.

Next, explore the movement and relationship of the four elements in the five compositions. You can work this stage at a scale of 4 inches by 4 inches. Use a combination of drawing, photocopying, and collage to explore solutions at this preliminary stage. Determine how much movement or change will occur through the series by studying and making incremental changes in the relationship of the elements. Use a grid of 9 or 16 units to help you make decisions about placement. Mount the five finished compositions in sequence on gray matt board.

Critique Discussion Points

How effectively does continuity of movement work in the series?

Does the series have aesthetic continuity?

Describe the narrative quality or theme of the sequence.

Does the sequence tell a story?

Vocabulary

narrative, sequential, theme, visual movement

References and Resources

South Park, Steamboat Willie

Evaluation Criteria

Source Work and Research

Achievement of Criteria

Design and Composition

Craft and Execution

HIERARCHAL PROGRESSION

Objectives

- Work with a hierarchal progression of graphic elements.
- Create a logical progression to communicate a visual theme.
- Manage theme and variation with a series of compositions.

Description

Develop a series of five compositions in three colors working with (1) a single statement and (2) a line or linear element. Start by exploring statements that communicate an idea or a theme that can be visually supported with the design principles you have learned about in the earlier chapters of this book. Your statement must consist of at least 8 and no more than 20 words. When you have developed your statement, research different typefaces to find several that support the statement's meaning. Break the statement down into five parts to develop a logical sequence of words and phrases. Each of these five parts of your original statement will be formatted and arranged in a 4-inch by 5-inch horizontal composition. Narrow your selection of typefaces to one or two fonts and explore visual possibilities by experimenting with the scale and placement of the words in each composition. Develop arrangements that support the meaning of your statement or add emphasis where needed. Apply your knowledge of balance, proximity, and proportion to develop interesting and aesthetically pleasing compositions.

You also must include a linear element in each of your compositions. Explore possibilities that support the meaning of your statement. Your linear element may be curved or straight and of any thickness. It can be repeated in each composition and throughout all five, or it can appear as a single element in any of the compositions and as multiple elements in another. When you are pleased with the compositions you have developed, select a color palette consisting of three colors that support the theme or meaning of your statement. Apply these colors to the type, background, and linear elements in your five compositions. Use your knowledge of theme and variation to create a cohesive series.

Limitations and Materials

Work on the computer to find typefaces or fonts for your statement. Work in a drawing program such as Adobe Illustrator or CorelDRAW to play with typographic arrangements in a 4-inch by 5-inch format. When you are satisfied with your arrangements, print them and use a pencil and pens and tracing paper to experiment with linear and color applications. Use the computer to add linear elements and color and to finalize your compositions as computer-generated color prints. Mount the prints in sequence on gray matt board.

Critique Discussion Points

How does the arrangement of type and the typeface support the statement's message?

How do color and the treatment of the linear element support the message?

What design principles are used to create emphasis?

What aspects of the compositions help to unify the sequence?

Vocabulary

triadic palette, figure-ground ambiguity

Resources and References

Avenue A/Razorfish, Mobium

Evaluation Criteria

Source Work and Research

Achievement of Criteria

Design and Composition

Craft and Execution

in review

1. How do television and the Web differ from each other in the ways in which they engage a viewer?
2. With what is Johannes Gutenberg credited?
3. How have media evolved during the twentieth century?
4. With regard to media, what are the differences between vehicle and venue?
5. How do interactive media, the Web, and multimedia differ from one another? What do they have in common?
6. How has the Internet affected communication?
7. What is a site map? How does it function in Web site design?
8. What is the function of HTML?
9. What is the difference between broadcasting and narrowcasting?
10. How do new media primarily differ from print media?

Courtesy of Brian Singer.

"In many professions, it's not always the most talented that make it to the top, it's those who work for it."

Brian Singer

Brian Singer is the principal and creative director of Altitude Associates, a small design studio in San Francisco collaborating with such folks as Adidas, Apple, Bent Brewing Company and Chronicle Books. Prior to starting Altitude, he had the honor of working with Morla Design, Pentagram, and Chen Design, among others. His work has garnered recognition from *Communication Arts*, *AIGA 365*, *Print*, *How*, *Graphis*, *Step*, *AR100*, and is included in the permanent collection of the San Francisco Museum of Modern Art.

He is also known as "someguy," the creator of The 1000 Journals Project, a global art experiment seeking to foster community and creativity among strangers. The project has reached over 40 countries and every U.S. state. It was recently published as a compilation book and as a full-length documentary, which was screened at film festivals and other venues throughout 2008–2009.

How did you get started in your career?

It actually started in fourth grade. Our school was putting on a play, and our class was charged with designing the program. Each student created a piece of art, and mine was chosen to go on the cover. At least, this is what I look back to, as to the reason I'm at where I am today. Just as important was, while in high school, looking through the list of majors offered by California State colleges, and thinking to myself "graphic design sounds interesting." But these events really led up to my career getting started.

While in college, I had two summer internships. These served to open my eyes to the real world, and begin to understand that design, as a profession, isn't about making art, but rather helping a company or organization communicate. When I graduated, I landed at a firm in Palo Alto, who was at the time doing a lot of multimedia work (multimedia being the buzzword at the time, as the interactive CD market crashed, and the Internet was born). I left shortly thereafter, to work for a small interactive firm, building Web sites for Netscape 2.0, 3.0, and 3.0 Gold (remember that?).

But, the limitations of the Web, and a love for the tactile, led me to a different, more traditional design firm, where I worked on corporate identities, annual reports, and other communications pieces.

What is your educational background?

I attended California Polytechnic State University, San Luis Obispo (Cal Poly, SLO). While not known as a titan amongst the design schools (as say, RISD, SVA, or Academy of Art University are), it provided me with a foundation of skills, as well as the broad experiences of a four-year college.

brian singer

What made you decide to pursue the career path that you've chosen?

I've always tried to pursue things that interest me. Other than that, I'd say opportunity plays a big role. When Apple called and asked if I wanted to do some work for them, I said yes.

What has been your biggest challenge in your career?

The biggest challenge I face in my career is figuring out what's next. It seems like creatives follow a fairly similar path in their careers. It's almost formulaic. I think I'm headed towards a different place, and have no idea how to get there.

Your biggest achievement?

To date, the work I'm most proud of is The 1000 Journals Project. I sent out 1,000 blank journals into the world. People who found them added something (writing, drawing, photographs, etc.) and then passed the journal along in an ongoing collaborative art form. The project reached 40 countries and every U.S. state. It was covered in the *New York Times*, *San Francisco Chronicle*, *Wall Street Journal*, *Entertainment Weekly*, and was the subject of a book, feature-length documentary, and exhibition at the San Francisco Museum of Modern Art.

That, however, is just the beginning. Due to the overwhelming demand (and scarcity of just 1,000 journals), I launched 1001journals.com, a site where you can launch your own project. I recently worked with UCSF Children's Hospital to launch journals within their hospital and the impact has been incredible. Meeting the kids, and seeing how the journals are helping them has changed my perception of what 1001 Journals can be. I'm currently working on rebuilding the Web site to support more organizations, and plan to launch journal programs in as many children's hospitals as possible.

What do you believe has been the biggest factor in your success?

They say, when speaking to children, that it's important to praise them not for "being smart and getting an A" but for "working hard to achieve the A." This is because work ethic plays a large part in the success of a person. Those who are raised to think they're smart often slack off, believing success will come to them.

The biggest factor to what success I've had is that I work extremely hard. There's no replacement for this. In many professions, it's not always the most talented that make it to the top, it's those who work for it. Of course, it takes a number of other factors as well (just read Malcolm Gladwell's *The Outliers*).

I'd also add that failing often has helped. While it's easy to see where I've had my successes, I've had many more failures. I've failed so many times, it's not even funny. Picking myself back up and trying again has been a learned skill, and a critical one.

What advice would you give to recent graduates or others who are just getting started in a career in illustration or graphic design?

I could write a book answering this question (and some folks already have). It sounds cliché, and honestly takes a while to figure out, but pursue what makes you happy. Of course, when beginning a career, it's hard to know what that is, so try different things, and work at different sizes/types of firms. That, and have other interests outside of the design world (science, sports, knitting, film, etc.). They'll inform your work and make you more versatile. Oh, and if you're working somewhere, and aren't learning, then it's time to move on.

Remedy Editorial is a video post-production studio based on the Final Cut Pro platform. Their identity combines the historical vernacular of the mortar and pestle, with the recent shift to digital technology. Altitude created their identity, stationery system, and Web site.
Client: Remedy Editorial. Design Firm: Altitude Associates. Designer: Brian Singer.

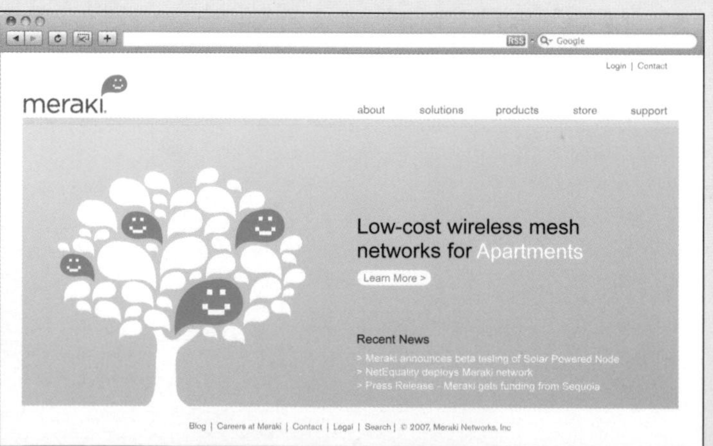

Meraki's mission is to bring affordable Internet access to the next billion people. Their wireless mesh-networking routers are in over 25 countries, from urban apartments in London, to villages in India. Altitude designed their identity, packaging, Web site, Web-based administrative tools, and campaign collateral.
Client: Meraki Networks. Design Firm: Altitude Associates. Designers: Brian Singer and Joshua Swanbeck.

brian singer

Altitude worked directly with SFMOMA to create a participatory experience for the 1000 Journals Project exhibition. In addition to a display of over 800 journal pages, viewers can become participants by contributing to the actual journals.

Client: San Francisco Museum of Modern Art. Design Firm: Altitude Associates, SFMOMA. Designers: Brian Singer from Altitude and James Williams from SFMOMA.

eight

From Student to Professional

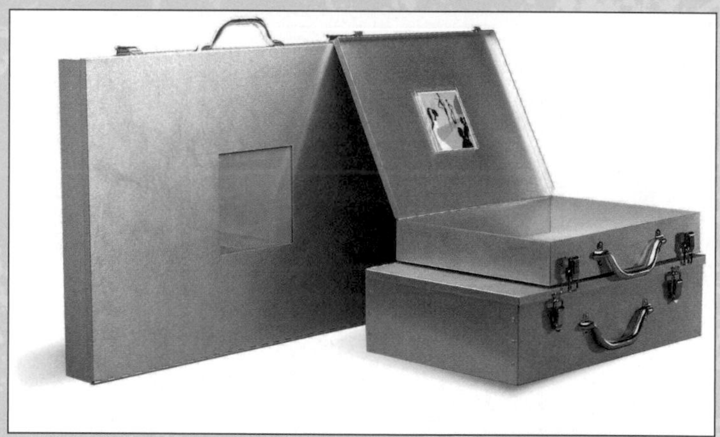

Portfolio photos furnished courtesy of Pina Zangaro

Design by Matthew Takach.

8

introduction

Students of graphic design are often in the dark about what lies ahead after their formal education.

Those of you right out of school may be tempted to take the first design job that comes your way. But because so many professional opportunities exist in the design industry, you should consider getting involved in an area of design that speaks to your personal interests and can make the best use of your capabilities. To help you determine where your best fit may be, this chapter explores specialized areas of design, the places they are practiced, and the kinds of skills these design disciplines require.

In addition to having a career direction in mind, you also will want to develop a portfolio and strategy for finding a job. The design industry is very competitive. Unlike some professions where prospective employers come to campus to recruit graduates, employers looking for designers traditionally have relied on recent or soon-to-be graduates to come to them. A portfolio plays an important role in the recruiting process by demonstrating what you have learned and how that expertise has manifested itself in prototypical design solutions. By looking at your portfolio, prospective employers can determine if and how their organization can use your design capabilities.

In this chapter, you also will discover what employers look for in a portfolio and learn how to present your work in a way that demonstrates your problem-solving and communication skills—assets for anybody seeking a salaried position, but especially important for someone who wants to be a successful designer.

objectives

- Explain how the field of graphic design developed and what it encompasses today.
- Review areas within the field of visual communication.
- Discuss career options in the graphic design industry.
- Discover what will pique the interest of a prospective employer and help land a job interview.
- Prepare a suite of promotional materials including a Web site.
- Prepare and present a portfolio of your design samples.
- Provide resources as professional tools for establishing and supporting a career.

HOW GRAPHIC DESIGN FUNCTIONS IN BUSINESS AND COMMERCE

The field of graphic design initially grew out of the need for businesses to promote their goods and services. In the early part of the twentieth century, this promotion was fairly straightforward and limited to newspaper ads, billboards, posters, handbills, packaging, and signage. Designers also were hired by publishers of books, newspapers, magazines, and sheet music.

Over the years, as marketing and communication became more sophisticated and media options expanded, design grew to encompass an ever-widening range of venues. Today graphic design touches people in so many ways that it is almost impossible to avoid. When you look at your mail, the magazines, the brochures, the flyers, and the postage stamps used to mail them all involved designers. Turn on the TV, and you will find many design applications: commercials, the opening credits for a film, or a network logo, to name just a few. The interface of your computer software, phone apps, game interfaces, search engines, and Web sites involved designers. At the supermarket, the product packaging, store signage, and tabloids at the checkout counter all required design expertise. Even the credit cards, currency, and coins you use to pay for your purchases involved the work of a graphic designer.

Design Firms

When individuals or organizations need design expertise, they usually seek the services of a design firm. Design firms provide graphic design services to all types of businesses. They are hired by other providers of creative services, such as advertising agencies, financial institutions, manufacturers, retailers, and service providers.

A design firm can consist of one person or many individuals, and the services a design firm provides can be far ranging or specialized. For instance, some design firms may limit their practice to environmental graphics or focus exclusively on brand development and package design. Design firms offering specialized services frequently serve a clientele that extends beyond the firm's regional area. Other design firms provide a broad range of services to local clients.

In addition to doing different types of design, design firms sometimes differ from one another in the aesthetic approach they take. In fact, it is not unusual for clients to select a design firm based on a look they know is a specialty of that firm. When adding to their staff, design firms sometimes seek designers whose aesthetic sense is in tune with the firms' standards.

Other design firms seek to diversify; looking to add employees who bring design sensibilities and areas of expertise the firms may not currently have on staff.

In-House Design Department

Because of the large volume of design they need to produce, publishing houses, retailers, and large corporations often hire their own designers. An in-house design department may consist of one designer or a staff of designers who work with other company personnel to develop and implement design concepts. The range of design work for in-house designers can be very diverse to very routine depending on the kind of business in which the company is involved.

In-house design departments offer designers a chance to work in an area of special interest. For instance, a designer who is drawn to fashion may want to work for a clothing retailer. Other businesses needing in-house designers include manufacturers of sports equipment, record companies, and a wide range of nonprofit organizations such as museums, charities, and

Graphic Design: An Evolving Discipline

The activity of design has evolved over many centuries. The wall paintings in the caves of Lascaux, ancient writing systems such as the Sumerian pictographic writing and cuneiforms, and the Belleville Breviary illuminated manuscript are examples of visual communication through the millennia. These and many other forms of communication throughout history have played a profound role in defining the contemporary notion of design. But the idea of graphic design as a discipline, driven by process and problem solving, was born in the twentieth century.

The Industrial Revolution spawned the need for market-driven communication, and the Bauhaus school provided a model. Since then, education, industry, society, culture, and technology have helped shape the field of design. Those forces also contributed to the nomenclature or designations that have been used to describe the areas in the field. It seems that the field is continually defining what it does by defining the various functions within it.

The field of design is a hierarchy composed of a group of disciplines that include graphic, fashion, industrial, and interior design. Each of these disciplines, in turn, is composed of specialty niches that constitute service to specific markets or industries. Graphic design encompasses work produced for print and digital communication.

Some niches are exclusively in the domain of one or the other type of communication, whereas other niches can be served by both print and digital communication.

For example, package, poster, catalog, and most publication design is exclusive to print production, whereas Web design, e-zines, and television graphics obviously function in the electronic realm. But other design categories function in both. Advertising, mail order, magazines, corporate identity, information, and promotional design rely on both print and electronic media.

Environmental, display, and exhibition design depend on a variety of fabrications, and are three-dimensional in nature. Signage systems, theme parks, trade shows, transportation systems, events, and educational exhibits are included in the three-dimensional design arena. Industrial or product design is dependent on graphic design where surface graphics and product identification are concerned.

In the advent of technological advances at the end of the twentieth century, (namely, electronic media) a move developed toward a service-dominated economy rather than an industrial-based economy and graphic design became driven more by information and communication. New professional titles such as information architect and communication designer place special an emphasis on the conceptual nature of the work.

The term *visual communication* is used interchangeably with *graphic design* but is, in a sense, more comprehensive.

Visual communication and communication arts encompass a full range of graphic arts that includes graphic design, illustration, multimedia, photography, television, film, video, and a variety of hybrid media. It is difficult to pinpoint the origin of the terminology, but it likely has evolved from the advertising industry and design education.

political groups. Many corporations support in-house design departments. Much of the work is managed and produced by salaried staff but they also rely on the assistance of freelance designers, illustrators, photographers, and verbal language experts (copywriters). Large corporations also work with design firms ranging in size from small specialty studios to multinational branding companies that take on the responsibility of managing whole sectors of their business.

Because their size allows them to put together health and profit-sharing plans that may be unavailable to smaller firms, corporations frequently can offer their in-house designers generous benefits packages and other perks.

SPECIFIC AREAS OF DESIGN

Now we will examine some specific areas of design, the kinds of expertise required, and the way a designer functions in these venues.

Advertising

Advertising agencies typically handle all aspects of marketing and promotion for their clients, developing a strategy and then implementing a plan that involves a variety of media applications. Ad agencies hire designers to work as part of a team that involves sales and marketing personnel, copywriters, production coordinators, and media specialists.

Advertising-related print design typically includes magazine and newspaper ads, point-of-purchase displays, billboards and transit ads, sales and promotional brochures, posters, fliers, direct mail, and coupons. Ad agencies also use designers to develop other media advertising, including Internet marketing, Web sites, and radio and television ads. Designers involved in television advertising often help brainstorm concepts, produce storyboards, and design graphics for television commercials. Good verbal skills and the ability to come up with creative and innovative concepts are important to designers in this field.

Although advertising agencies hire designers to work as part of their staff, they also hire other creative personnel and firms to help them in their work, often subcontracting copywriters, photographers, illustrators, design firms, and other suppliers in implementing their projects.

Brand Design and Development

Branding is designing an experience for an intended audience that includes the consistent application of a brand's logo or trademark and visual identity on all of the brand's products and services. Brand designers are contracted by a client to conceive an overall look for its product line or services and to implement the scheme on all packaging and promotional venues. Branding may include a variety of media as well as vehicle, building, and uniform applications. In addition to designing a look that will work in a range of situations, brand designers often are involved in the early stages of a brand's inception, helping to develop a name as well as a logo and visual scheme. The ability to develop a flexible design scheme that works in two- and three-dimensional applications as well as packaging is important to being successful in this field.

Design firms specializing in brand design and development are sometimes called brand consultancies and are often larger than most design firms, staffing anywhere from 20 to 200 people.

In addition to designers, writers, and administrative personnel, design firms hire production experts who understand the materials and processes unique to packaging. Clients are typically large corporations needing to promote and market their products across a broad constituency.

Interactive and Web Design

Firms specializing in interactive and Web design typically get involved in CD design as well as Web site and Web banner ad design. In addition to design personnel, firms specializing in this type of design often staff marketing and promotional personnel as well as technology experts who are responsible for doing intricate coding and staying on top of current technologies.

Firms involved in this type of high-tech work often create motion graphics and other special effects for television and film. Because interactive multimedia involves animation and sound, designers specializing in this field need to have technical aptitude and an understanding of animation, interactive design software, and Web design software as well as the ability to think beyond visual terms. Understanding how to organize information and visualize it in terms of flowcharts or navigational maps also is an asset.

Editorial Design

Editorial designers work with editors and publishers in the design of books, magazines, and newsletters. These designers range from independent freelancers or design firms contracted to do newsletter or cover designs to in-house designers employed by publishers.

Book and magazine design requires designing covers as well as working with text and imagery within a design theme that involves many pages. However, magazine and book design differs in that books represent a one-time design challenge; that is, when a book design is completed, a designer can move onto a new project. Because they are periodicals, magazines require a designer to work within an established design structure over many issues.

Knowledge of typography, an aptitude for organizing information, a love of the written word, and enthusiasm for a specialized area that a magazine addresses can be assets for designers considering this field.

Environmental Graphics

Environmental graphic designers design and develop systems of words and iconography that help guide others in identifying and finding what they need in unfamiliar surroundings. Firms offering this expertise understand how to organize information and make it user friendly and accessible, as well as how to work with signage materials and sign fabricators. Environmental graphic designers generally work as part of a team with architects, interior designers, landscapers, and other professionals involved in creating indoor and outdoor spaces. Environmental graphic designers often are brought in at the inception of a project to help in the development of an overall look and visual theme for an environment.

Applications for environmental graphics may be institutional venues (such as universities or hospitals) or recreational venues (such as museums, sports facilities, and parks).

Environmental graphics are also an important component in all kinds of transportation terminals as well as business and retail complexes such as corporate centers and shopping malls.

Pro Bono Work

Artists and designers are generally a benevolent community of creative individuals. Most donate their services to help charitable and other nonprofit organizations with visual communication needs. Donating creative services (called pro bono work) is a great way for professionals to give back. For fledging designers and illustrators it offers an opportunity to gain experience and visibility. Unlike paid projects, where a client's priorities often override or restrict the creative process, pro bono work usually allows creative professionals more freedom to develop work that showcases their talents and capabilities. In exchange for their donated time, they have a published piece with a credit line.

Young designers and illustrators often have a chance to showcase their skills by developing Web sites, posters, and other promotional vehicles for art and theater groups. Other possibilities for pro bono work include charity fund-raisers such as walkathons, dinners, and other events. Individuals involved with these causes often have a degree of prominence in the local community and may be in a good position to circulate your name or send more business your way. At the very least, you have a chance to do work with other creative professionals and organizations that has a real value for the client and real impact in your community.

Finding Work

Those involved in hiring designers say that proven capability is probably the most important factor in landing a job. You will need to develop and design a variety of personal self-promotional vehicles to manage your job search. A letterhead, résumé, business card, and PDF file of several portfolio pieces that can be attached to an e-mail, and links to social networking are key communication tools that will promote your capabilities when you contact prospective employers for an interview. Because many firms filter new hires by reviewing résumés and digital examples before scheduling a face-to-face interview, it is essential to have your work in digital format, posted on a Web site or as a PDF file.

At an interview, your portfolio serves as additional proof of your design and production capability and the way you present your portfolio shows pride in your work and the ability to package and display it professionally **8.1**.

It is critical that you ask the point person for each interview opportunity what form they prefer to view your work. Generally the preferences will be to show actual printed work mounted on boards or in book format, or presenting digital slides using Preview, PowerPoint, or Keynote. The digital presentation may be viewed on your own laptop or on a projection system or screen monitor at the company. In this case you will need to load your files on a portable "thumb drive" or hard drive.

Production Tip:

Your paper's grain direction can affect the feel of a business card. Business cards printed on cover stock can feel flimsy if the cards are printed with the longest dimension parallel to the "grain long" direction of the sheet. You can determine the grain direction by folding the paper vertically and horizontally. The fold line will be much more even when it is folded with the grain. When printing business cards, make sure that the shortest dimension of the card is printed parallel to the "grain long" direction of the sheet or that longest dimension is printed opposite to this direction.

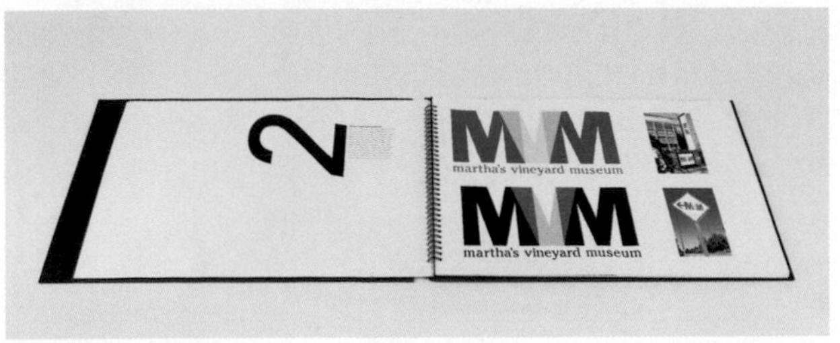

[a]

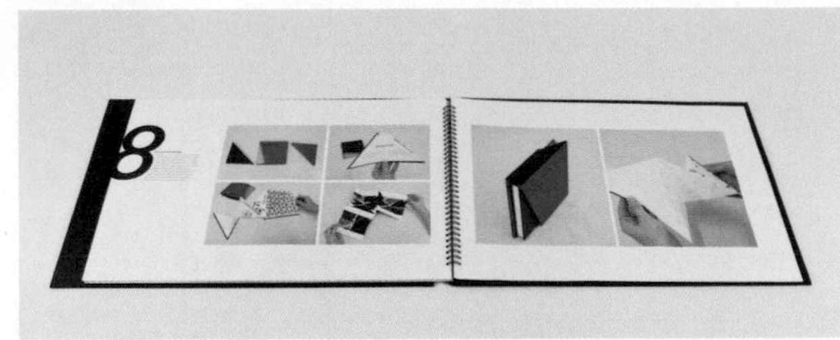

[b]

[c]

[d]

[e]

[f]

[8.1a to f] Matthew Takach's portfolio demonstrates his ability to develop a cohesive design strategy for presenting his work in publication format. His prominent numbering system (a, b) adds a unifying design element, without distracting from the presentation of the work. Measuring 20 by 12½ inches, the spiral-bound booklet allows each piece to be easily presented on a spread. In addition to showing the final piece, Takach also included thumbnail sketches (c, d) of his initial concepts to show his design process. Takach's printed résumé and die-cut business card (e) tie in with the look of his portfolio as memorable leave behinds after an interview.
Design by Matthew Takach.

Preparing a Portfolio Student portfolios should show the breadth of experience and include samples that demonstrate capability across a broad range of disciplines: logo and identity design, brochures, packaging, advertising, and one- and two-color work as well as four-color work. Including work that demonstrates capability in other areas, including Web or interactive design and illustration, also is advised.

Avoid the temptation to include in your portfolio everything you have ever done. Instead, narrow down your selection to 10 to 15 samples of your best work. Beginners tend to want to include many projects in the belief that prospective employers will be impressed with the volume of work produced. In the process, they include some mediocre work, which tends to water down the overall impression or create a sense of inconsistency. It is far better to limit your portfolio to just eight or nine high-quality samples, as opposed to including pieces that fall below the level of the rest.

Because viewers tend to remember what they saw first and last, begin and end your portfolio presentation with your strongest and most vivid samples. Bold, colorful work tends to make the most lasting impression. Balance the rest of your portfolio by mixing four-color work with one- or two-color pieces.

When you have selected the work you want to include, think about what size and type of portfolio you want. Portfolio styles can be broken down into two basic categories: (1) boxes or attaché cases that contain printouts of design samples mounted on matte board; or (2) purchased binders with acetate sleeves or bound books where the presentation of work is in publication format. Which type you choose depends on your need for flexibility, the nature of your work, and what format best serves your presentation. Alternative approaches are also acceptable if they don't impede the viewer's ability to see and understand the work **8.2**.

Many students prefer to purchase a portfolio case that is specially designed to accommodate the needs of designers and illustrators. Portfolio cases come in sizes ranging from 8 inches by 11 inches to 34 inches by 42 inches. The resource list at the end of this chapter includes several manufacturers of these portfolio cases. Although the trend in recent years has been toward smaller portfolios, you should pick a size that is large enough to accommodate your biggest piece and that is an appropriate size for carrying or shipping **8.3**.

If you want to be able to customize or rearrange your portfolio, samples mounted on illustration or matt board are easier to add to and rearrange than pages in a book or a binder. Mounted samples can be flush-mounted or displayed on neutral-colored mount board with a 2-inch to 3-inch margin. Gray is usually better than black or white because it works equally as well as a backdrop for light- or dark-colored work. It is important to keep the board size and color consistent. Nothing can detract more from your work than samples mounted on boards that are of varying color and size.

Be prepared to show concept sketches of work in progress from thumbnails and intermediate compositional studies to media and color studies. Some students supplement their presentation with a loose-leaf binder that shows some of their process sketches. Prospective employers want to understand how your design concepts develop and see what kind of alternative solutions you may have come up with. Subject and concept research demonstrates your commitment to idea development and analytical thinking skills **8.4**.

A portfolio of mounted samples contained in a portfolio case offers the flexibility of adding or removing samples, depending on the interview. However, other formats such as binders and books work if you are certain of the samples that you want to include and the order in which they are presented **8.5**.

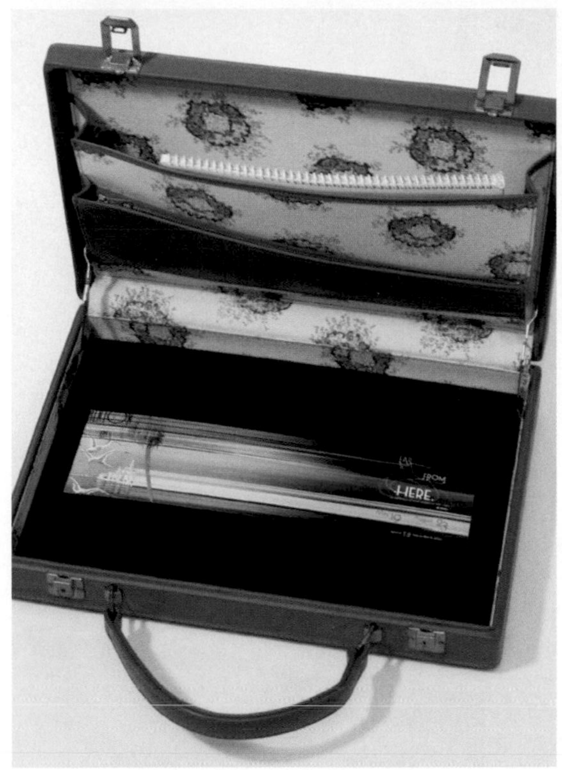

[a]

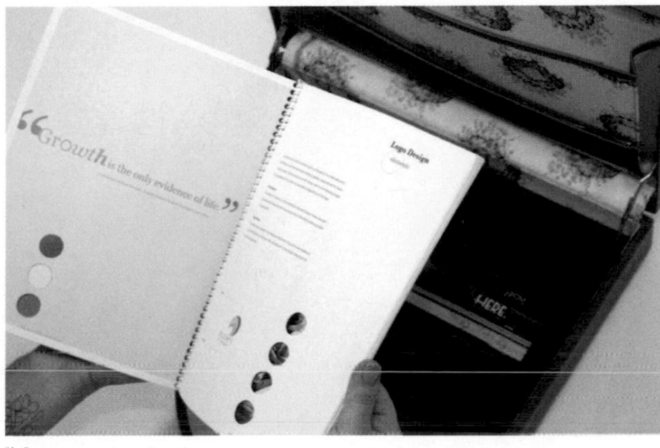

[b]

[c]

[d]

[8.2 a to d] Monica Katzenell wanted to make a memorable impression with her portfolio and also have the flexibility to rearrange and change the work she presented. Her solution was this 1970s briefcase that she found on e-Bay. Measuring 11½ by 17 inches, the briefcase was the perfect size for accommodating her work. Katzenell mounted printed samples on black matt board and cut them to fit the briefcase's interior. She uses the pocket on the underside of the lid to house loose samples.
Design by Monica Katzenell. Photo courtesy of Under Consideration, LLC.

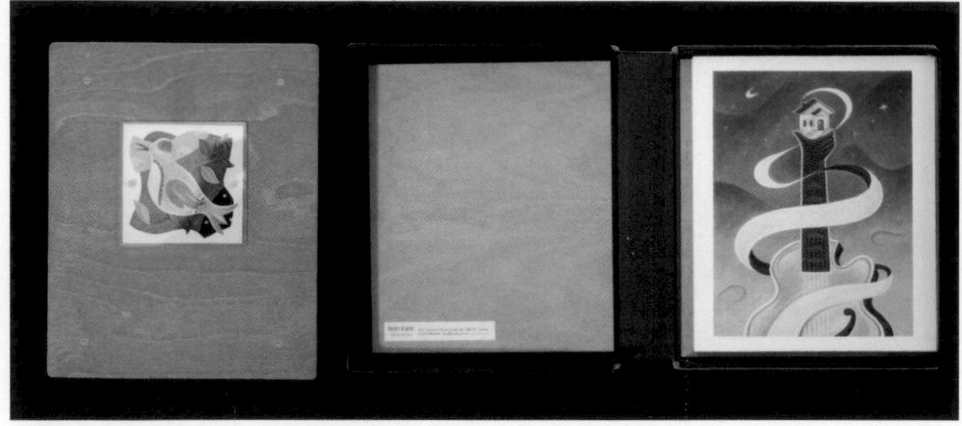

[a]

[b]

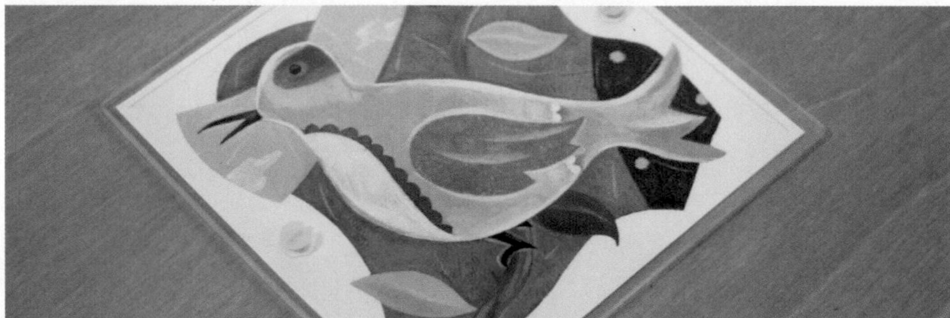

[c]

[8.3 a to c] A clamshell box purchased from a photo equipment supplier was customized by illustrator Sean Kane by attaching stained birch plywood to the front and back of the box with plastic nuts and bolts. A plastic picture frame displaying a sample of his work © was anchored to the top. The 9½-inch by 11-inch portfolio can be shipped in a FedEx box and also fits nicely into a padded laptop bag for personal interviews. Kane can substitute and rearrange the samples in his box, depending on his needs.
Design by Sean Kane Illustration. Photo courtesy of Under Consideration, LLC.

[a]

[b]

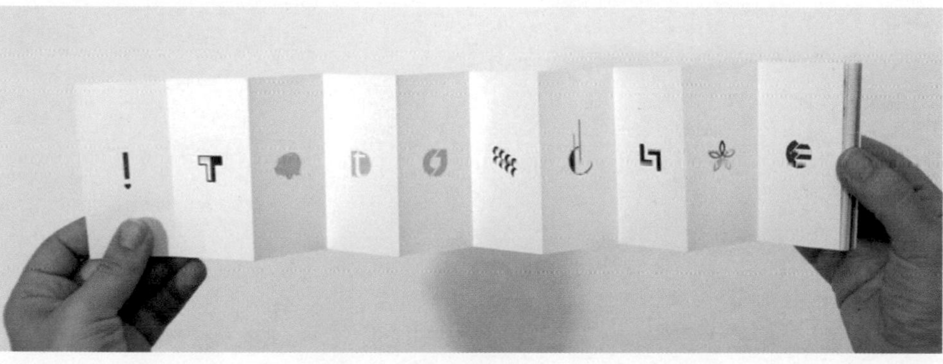

[c]

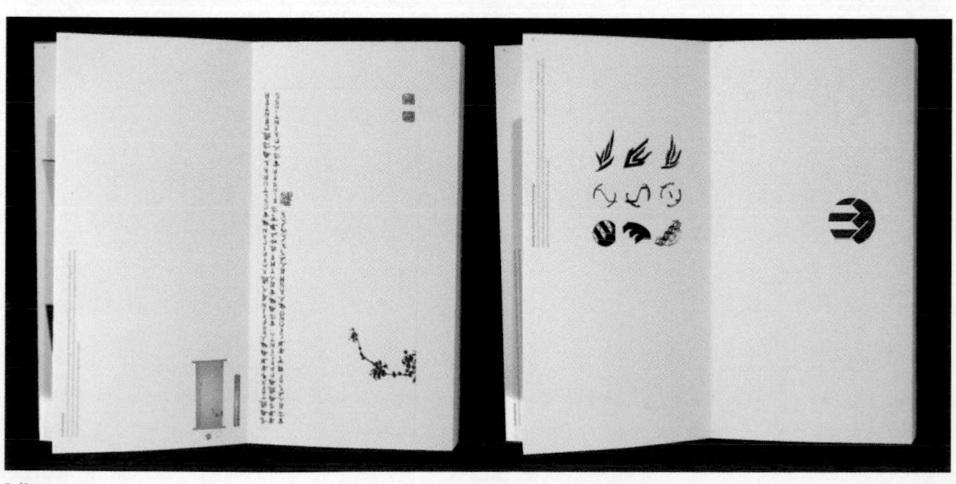

[d]

[8.4a to d] Hyun Auh chose to produce an accordion-folded portfolio that folds up neatly into a 6 inch by 11½ inch slipcase. This binding style, which originated in Asia, is in step with Auh's Korean ancestral roots and suits the minimal nature of his work. Auh's work was ink-jet printed front and back from a continuous roll of paper. In addition to finished work, his portfolio also includes concept sketches. The cover and slipcase were made from binding board covered with Touché paper.
Design by AuhDesign.
Photo courtesy of Under Consideration, LLC.

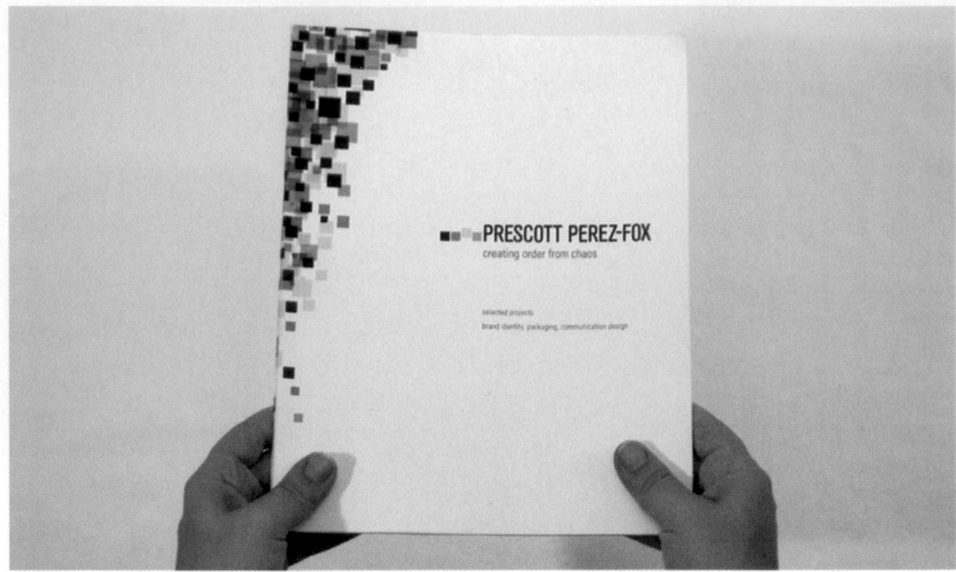
PRESCOTT PEREZ-FOX
creating order from chaos
selected projects
brand identity, packaging, communication design

[a]

We live
in a
Rainbow
of Chaos
– Paul Cezanne

[b]

[c]

[d]

[8.5 a to d] Prescott Perez-Fox chose to assemble his work in a book format that is perfect bound. A perfect bind is a book form where the pages or folios are glued together at the spine. A cover is also glued to the collected pages. This type of production would require professional printing and binding services. The result is a compact presentation that demonstrates his ability to manage the production of a multi-page publication. *Design by Prescott Perez-Fox, Art Director—Starship Design, www.strshp.com. Photo courtesy of Under Consideration, LLC.*

Presenting Your Portfolio Develop a sound strategy for organizing and sequencing the work in your portfolio and determine a set of "talking points" for your presentation. Talking points will provide cues for a discussion that will come across more conversational rather than scripted. Specific strategies will be discussed later in the chapter. Finally, rehearse your presentation. Determine the length of time it takes to present your work and yourself. Practice this on your own and in front of friends or relatives. Before you contact a firm for an interview, you should know something about the organization's work. Prospective employers want to feel as though you are interested in what they do. But more importantly, you will want to know about a prospective employer's clients and the types of projects the firm takes on so you can determine whether the situation is a good fit for your skills and career goals. Most companies have a Web site that you can find through online search engines.

When you arrive at your interview, try to position yourself at the corner of a conference table or desk so you and the viewer are looking at the portfolio together, with you sharing rather than showing your work. You want to create an environment that is conducive to establishing rapport.

Prepare a list of questions about the position and the company's policies, such as performance evaluations, areas of growth for the firm, and its expectations of employees. Remember that you, in a sense, are interviewing the firm as much as it is interviewing you. Taking that mind-set to the interview can give you a measure of confidence that will show in your presentation.

Keep in mind that you may be interviewed by a team or group as opposed to a single individual. It is appropriate to ask the initial point person about the structure for the interview, what to bring, and in what format to present it.

Seek the advice of professionals you have access to through an internship or through professional organizations or by visiting design studios and firms in your city or plan to visit them when you travel. While you are a student, professionals tend to be very open to sharing their time, expertise, and work. Once you are a peer, you are perceived as competition and have fewer doors open to you.

At the onset of your interviewing, a good strategy is to secure one or two interviews at companies in which you are not as interested. You will have had these experiences as practice for that benchmark job you really want.

Students often have difficulty thinking of their work beyond the realm of a class project. But in a portfolio interview, you need to describe your work in real-world terms. When you talk about each piece, describe the communication goal and your design strategy—how the imagery, color, or typography you chose—work in support of this goal. Mention what restrictions, if any, were imposed and what they were. It is important to let a prospective employer know how you solved a communications problem in spite of outside constraints.

Before you leave, give the person with whom you met your business card and/or résumé. These items and other venues that are used for promoting or showing your work, such as your Web site, should bear your identity and be visually linked with your portfolio. Perhaps most important of all, within 48 hours of the interview, send an e-mail thanking the interviewer for his or her time.

Career Tips

TIPS

- Subscribe to one or two industry publications to stay current with design trends and directions in the field. If you cannot afford them, make a regular trip to the library or book store periodicals section.
- Use a planner to help you manage time and projects. Establishing the practice of time management will keep you organized. Being liberated from having to remember dates and deadlines will allow you to use your brain for creative thinking.
- Join professional organizations or local groups of professionals in the graphic arts field. Some organizations have student chapters that offer events and services at a reduced cost. Some of these organizations include AIGA, Ad clubs, the Society of Illustrators, the Art Director's club, and the Society of Publication Designers. Membership is the best way to meet other young designers and professionals who can give you invaluable advice, direction about your work, and leads for jobs.
- Take advantage of internship opportunities while in school. Working alongside professionals is invaluable experience and will begin to connect you to people in the field. Consider pursuing internships after graduation with companies with which you are interested in working. Once you are "in house," there may be an opportunity to be hired as a part-time or even full-time employee.

A **Student Portfolio** Website

A Web site is a critical component of your professional toolbox. It functions as a personalized communication device that connects you to the world. The design, content, and attitude of your site present snapshots of who you are, your interests, your work, and your potential.

Zach Stubenvoll is a recently graduated visual communication design major at the Art Academy of Cincinnati. His preparation for graduation and job seeking included a personal brand and identity incorporated into a Web site. The strategy behind the site is to present his work and provide prospective employers with a sense of who he is. The contents of the site includes a home page with a scrolling banner of work samples, buttons that take the user to a portfolio page, a blog, and contact information. The attitude and presentation of the site has an appropriate sense of humor and a sophisticated sense of design that has a "clean and spacious" design aesthetic that reflects the same design aesthetic found in the work. This portfolio landed him his first job as a designer for the 2012 Obama presidential campaign in Chicago.

It is of course important that the work that represents you be of the highest quality, but you also need to present an honest portrayal of yourself. This combination will quickly identify if a potential match exists between you and a career opportunity.

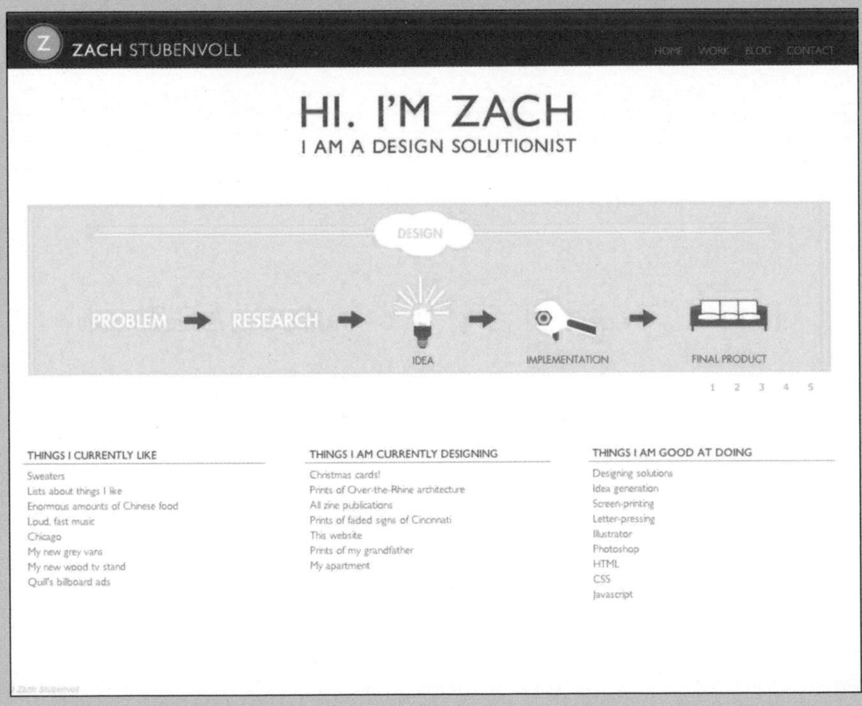

[8.6a] The home page presents Zach's interests, current work projects, and skills capabilities. The visual graphic is presented in a banner and was designed to demonstrate his understanding of the importance of design as process. This image scrolls in a five-second interval with four other works functioning as a preview to the portfolio.
Design by Zach Stubenvoll.

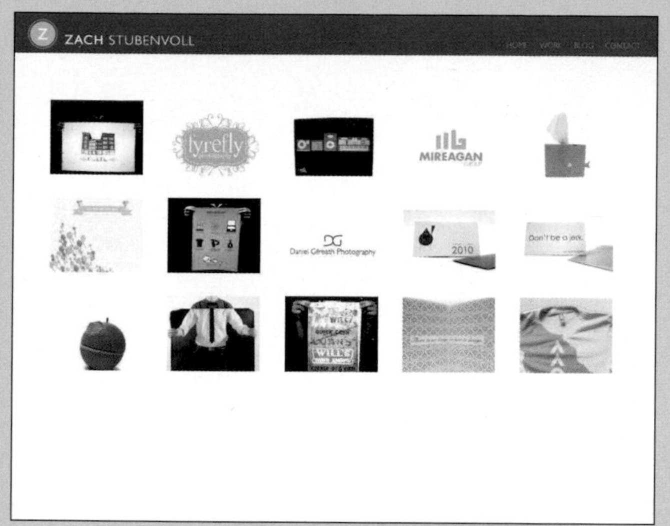

[8.6b] Zach designed a straightforward arrangement of thumbnails of work in the portfolio. Several of the works have multiple pages or views. Once inside, the navigator is able to scroll through the sequences and series.
Design by Zach Stubenvoll.

ALL THE DAY HOLIDAY
Image 1 / 2 All the Day Holiday poster series. All the Day Holiday is a Cincinnati based band. They hail from the small suburb of Fairfield. Rolling Stone has named All the Day Holiday one of the breakout bands to look for in 2009 and 2010.

[8.6c] Each work in the portfolio is described in a brief containing relevant information. This is one of two slides that present two different finished concepts for the event.
Design by Zach Stubenvoll.

[8.6d] The blog page offers interactive discussions and posts. He uses this platform as an opportunity to show works in process and his extended use of media. The page provides a link to "tumblr," a micro-blogging platform that utilizes easy use. Users can post comments, text, imagery, sound, and even video. The sign-up process is very simple and quick allowing fellow bloggers (who could be potential clients or employers) minimal time investment. *Design by Zach Stubenvoll.*

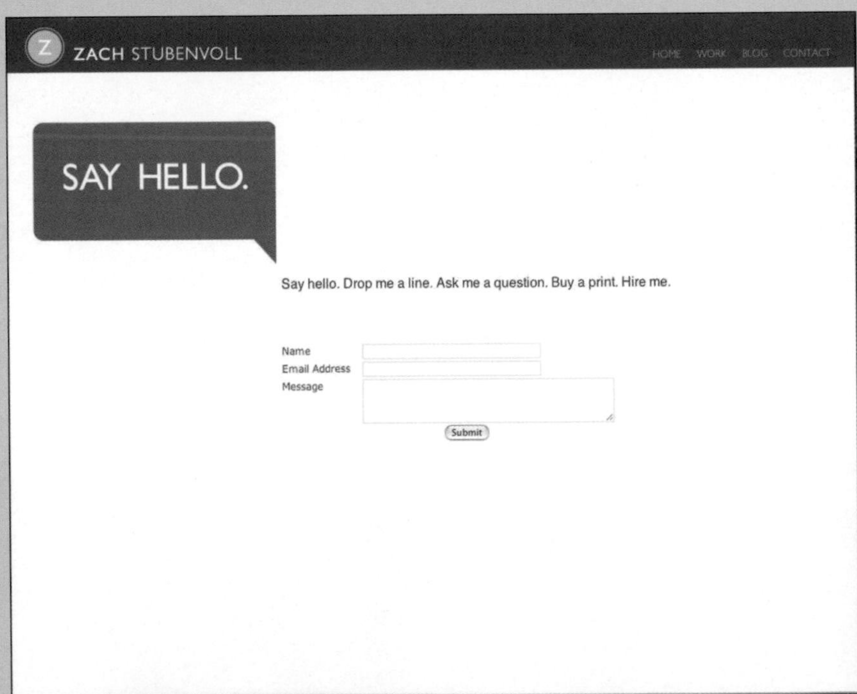

[8.6e] The contact page is direct in its design and intent. It permits interested parties to make initial contact or provide follow-up communication. *Design by Zach Stubenvoll.*

Is Freelancing for You?

Many students make money doing freelance work while they are in school and build on this income after graduating to establish a successful business of their own making. Freelancing offers many advantages to communication and visual artists, including plenty of flexibility and the chance to choose projects. It may be a viable alternative to being employed elsewhere if you have a great deal of drive and self-discipline and are willing to take on some of the business-related tasks involved in being self-employed. However, not everyone is suited to freelancing. If you think you might like to freelance, here are some important considerations to keep in mind:

- You should be a self-starter who is disciplined enough to get the job done from beginning to end. You also need to be able to work independently. If you have a tendency to procrastinate or need to have others involved to keep you on task, freelancing may not be a good option.
- Unlike a salaried job where sick days are paid for, sick days are lost time and money when you are self-employed. At times, you will be responsible for fulfilling your obligations on a project even when you are not are up to the task. Good health, emotional stability, and the fortitude to get the job done even when you are not feeling well are important attributes for working independently.
- In addition to doing the creative work, you are taking on many administrative tasks that include organizing your time and your work environment. You also need to be involved in basic bookkeeping, such as keeping track of income and expenses.
- You need to develop proposals and contracts. Other business-related tasks involved in freelancing include pricing your services and billing clients, as well as collecting on delinquent accounts.
- Marketing skills are essential to maintaining a successful freelance business. You need to be able sell your concepts and communicate your personal vision to those with whom you will be working. If you are not skilled at selling yourself or your ideas, consider partnering with someone who has these capabilities.
- In addition to marketing skills, you need to develop promotional materials. An online portfolio or a Web site, a conventional portfolio, business cards, and stationery are essential to establishing and maintaining a business.
- You have to pay for or go without some of the fringe benefits associated with working elsewhere, such as paid health insurance, pregnancy or sick leave, and vacation time.
- You are responsible for paying Social Security as well as federal, state, and local income tax on the money you make as a freelancer. In addition to filing the forms associated with these taxes, you may have other tax obligations that are specific to where your freelance business is located.
- Many designers and artists prefer the convenience and comfort of working from home as freelancers, while others go onsite to work on a temporary basis for other businesses. If you are working onsite, the government still considers you a self-employed individual operating a business. Your tax obligations and many of the bookkeeping and administrative tasks associated with running your own business remain the same as if you were working from home.

Resources

PORTFOLIOS AND RELATED SUPPLIES

Audrey Grossman Handmade

www.booksandboxes.net
Custom-made portfolio cases and books.

Brewer-Cantelmo

www.brewer-cantelmo.com
Ready-made portfolio books and cases.

Calumet

www.calumetphoto.com Archival photo boxes.

House of Portfolios

www.houseofportfolios.com
Ready-made portfolio books and cases.

Pina Zangaro

www.pinazangaro.com Ready-made portfolio books and cases.

Talas

www.talasonline.com
Bookbinding supplies, archival storage boxes.

GRAPHIC ARTS ORGANIZATIONS

ACM SIGGRAPH

www.siggraph.org
This organization is made up of a diverse group of researchers, artists, developers, filmmakers, scientists, and other professionals who share an interest in computer graphics and interactive techniques. It sponsors the annual SIGGRAPH conference, focused symposia, chapters in cities throughout the world, awards, grants, educational resources, online resources, a traveling art show, and the SIGGRAPH Video Review.

American Center for Design

www.ac4d.org
This national association for design professionals, educators, and students supports design education and promotes the value of design in the business community.

The American Institute of Graphic Arts (AIGA)

www.aiga.org
Founded in 1914, the AIGA is a nonprofit organization that promotes excellence in graphic design. With more than 60 local chapters, AIGA holds a national conference and sponsors annual competitions. The AIGA Website is a wealth of career, professional and networking opportunities.

Graphic Artists Guild

www.graphicartistsguild.org
This national advocacy organization represents designers, art directors, illustrators, photographers, and others in the industry. It publishes The GAG Handbook: Pricing and Ethical Guidelines, a valuable resource for professionals and students.

Society of Illustrators

www.societyillustrators.org
The New York headquarters houses the Museum of American Illustration, which promotes monthly exhibits and traveling exhibits of premier illustration. The group also sponsors an annual student and professional competition that recognizes the best in illustration in the United States.

The Society of Publication Designers

www.spd.org
This organization offers a monthly newsletter and an annual design competition, and it sponsors a biennial conference that alternates between new media and convention publishing.

DESIGN PUBLICATIONS

CMYK

www.cmykmag.com
This quarterly publication is a showcase of the freshest design, illustration, photography, and advertising, featuring work by students from across the United States. Students can have their work submitted by instructors.

Communication Arts

www.commarts.com
Published eight times per year, this quality journal features the best of the year's graphic communication. Student subscription discounts make it an affordable publication.

Émigré

www.emigre.com
This quarterly magazine showcases work by type designers, illustrators, and others whose work is on the cutting edge of creative graphic communication. Émigré also produces typefaces that it sells from a directory and from its Web site.

Graphis

www.graphis.com
Graphis exists as an online publication and also features annual journals of the best professional and student work from around the world. It has a reputation for featuring the finest examples of design from a variety of categories. Register for a subscription online through the Web site. Students receive discounts and access to valuable career information and direction.

HOW

www.howdesign.com
This bimonthly graphic design magazine covers ideas, techniques, and other aspects of the trade. HOW also sponsors an annual conference and competition.

Print

www.printmag.com
This magazine covers the graphic design industry and sponsors annual competitions and national seminars.

STEP Inside Design

www.dgusa.com
This bimonthly magazine focuses on how designers, illustrators, photographers, and other graphic professionals create projects from beginning to end.

Wired

www.wired.com
This monthly magazine promotes and reports on technological innovation in digital communication, computer publishing, multimedia, and graphics. Social commentary and trendy graphics reflect current pop culture.

U&lc Magazine

www.itcfonts.com/ulc
This online magazine is dedicated to typography and the graphic arts. Published by the International Typeface Corporation, U&lc's Web site offers valuable information on type, type history, and use. Fonts can be purchased from the Web site.

WEB SITES

In addition to the Web sites connected with the organizations listed previously, the following sites contain a great deal of information and links to other relevant Web sites:

www.thedesignencyclopedia.org

This online resource includes book reviews, articles, and links to other design organization Web sites.

www.designwritingresearch.org

Produced by design scholar Ellen Lupton, this Web site includes books, products, essays, and teaching materials for design educators. The links portion of this site connects with type foundries, design blogs, and sources for materials and supplies.

SUMMARY

Most of this book has been devoted to presenting design essentials, theories, and strategies. This chapter on preparation for a career in the field focuses on practical information that you may need in the future. However, the goal of your study of design is to become a professional in the field. Visualizing yourself as a working designer can be challenging at the beginning of your studies, but there are things you can do now to help you assume the role of a professional. The portfolios in the professional profiles presented throughout the book and the student portfolio and self-promotion in Chapter 8 are meant to provide a window into the profession and some real inspiration and motivation.

Continue to work on developing your design sensibilities; but also study the work of designers, photographers, illustrators, and artists. Study art and design history to gain an understanding of the world of visual communication in which you are working.

projects

SELF-PROMOTION

Objectives

- Evaluate your career interests in the field.
- Research design firms and agencies.
- Research strategies for self-promotion.
- Produce a written plan proposal for your promotion project.
- Produce the visual components to use in pursuing a job.

Description

Produce a self-promotion or communication initiative that includes the following:

A written project plan proposal that addresses the following questions:

What is the project goal for promotion?

What are the specific objectives of the project (tasks to complete, message)?

What is your design strategy?

How do you expect the recipient of the promotional design to respond?

What is your budget?

Personal identity

Logotype, symbol, image, graphic element, personal look

Apply it to all aspects of self-promotion, including letterhead, envelope, and/or shipping label and business card.

Letterhead/envelope/business card

Portfolio venu

Web site, video, CD, conventional case, cards, unique package tear sheets, and links to social networking media such as LinkedIn, facebook, Twitter, Vimeo FanBox, MySpace, and tumblr.

Optional ancillary pieces

Design the promotion as a suite of related components. Apply the design motif or look to all aspects of the promotion, including the résumé, portfolio venue, and print material. You may consider applying the identity to appropriate "leave behind" pieces that conceptually fit your promotional scheme, such as a thumb drive, mug, button or coaster for example.

Limitations and Materials

Materials to produce the self-promotion should be responsive to the strategy and objectives of your proposal.

Complete the written plan proposal before beginning the design of visual components. Word-process and double-space the proposal. Each section must include the necessary explanation and detailing to convey your intentions.

Critique Discussion Points

How does the promotion reflect your professional interest?

Discuss how the communication message works.

What was the most challenging aspect of the project?

Vocabulary

design strategy, ancillary pieces, tear sheet

Evaluation Criteria

Project Fulfills Proposed Plan

Complete Project Inventory

Quality of Concept

Technical Consistency and Craft

RÉSUMÉ

Description

Your résumé presents an opportunity for you to give prospective employers a sense of how well qualified you are for a position. In addition to stating your qualifications, the design of the résumé gives a sense of your knowledge of typography and design capabilities. Prepare a résumé that gives prospective employers an overview of your education, employment history, and professional capabilities. Design it so that it is visually in sync with your letterhead, business card, or other promotional materials. Résumé areas should be clearly differentiated from one another so they can be found easily at a glance. Use subheads to set these areas apart. Information should be listed chronologically so that the most recent experience comes first. Consult the model included with this project as a guide for structuring your résumé. The information that you feature on your résumé is standard for all types of businesses and includes the following components:

1. Your name, address, and other contact information should be prominently placed near the top of the page.
2. After your name and contact information, you typically list your postsecondary educational background, including your degree or anticipated date of graduation. State the name of the school and your degree and area of concentration, as well as the year the degree was or will be awarded.
3. Experience or employment history is where you list your job experience. This is where you show a prospective employer that you have a history as an employee. List all meaningful employment, not necessarily just the design positions you have held. State the dates you were employed, the name of the firm, the city and state where the firm is located, and the position title. Include a brief description of your duties and responsibilities.
4. List other qualifications or skills you would like to bring to the attention of a prospective employer. These items can fall under a heading such as "Qualifications" or "Achievements." You can include computer skills under this category as well as professional organizations and activities. This area also is where you want to include information that will set you apart from other prospects, such as bilingual capability, managerial experience, and military service. You also can include academic awards in this category. If you have a long list of significant achievements and awards, you may want to make a separate listing under the category of "Awards."

Limitations and Materials

Your résumé should fit on a single 8½-inch by 11-inch page and be formatted so it is easy to read. Explore format options with rough sketches. Design and produce the final version on the computer and print it on the same type of paper stock that you are using for your letterhead and business card. Produce a PDF version of your résumé if you want to submit it online or post it on a Web site.

Critique Discussion Points

Is anything missing? Does the résumé represent your experience in the best possible way?

Is the résumé easy to read and aesthetically pleasing?

Does the résumé tie in visually with letterhead, business cards, or other promotional materials?

Vocabulary

PDF, paper stock

Model

	Name Contact Information
Education	School Name City, State Degree, Major, Year of Graduation
Employment History	Firm Name, Dates of Employment City, State Job Title Job Duties
	Firm Name, Dates of Employment City, State Job Title Job Duties
	Firm Name, Dates of Employment City, State Job Title Job Duties
Achievements	Proficient in Adobe Creative Suite Deans List 2005-2012 President, AIGA student chapter Fluent in Spanish

in review

1. What is pro bono work? What advantages does it offer new designers?
2. What are some important considerations for freelancers with regard to taxes?
3. How many pieces should comprise a student portfolio?
4. Which pieces should go in the front of a portfolio?
5. Why is it important to know about a firm's work before interviewing with that firm?
6. Why is designing a self-promotion piece important to landing an interview?

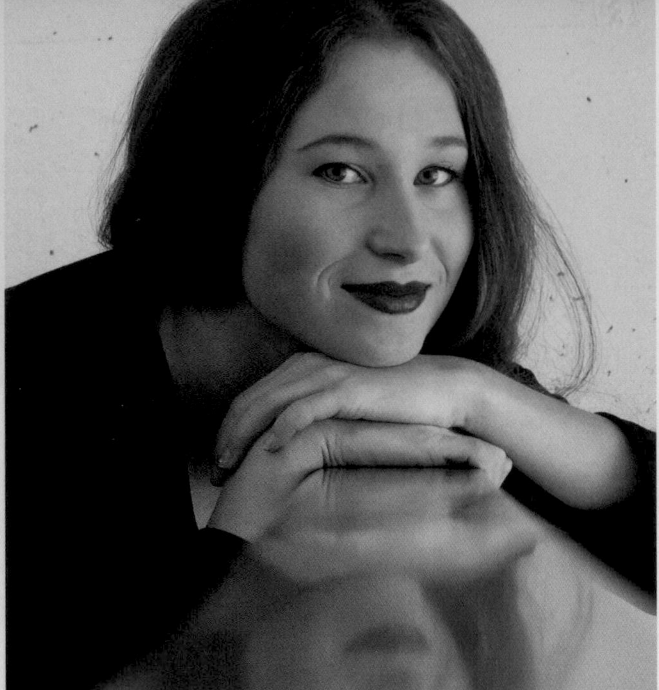

Courtesy of Janine Rewell.

> "*One aspect that has helped me in my career has been my online portfolio.*"

Janine Rewell

A native of Helsinki, Finland, Janine Rewell is a recent graduate of Rhode Island School of Design. She is the winner of many awards including a bronze Design Lion at the Cannes Lions International Advertising Festival and was one of *Print* magazine's 20 best new visual artists of 2010.

How did you end up choosing both design and illustration as a career?

I have a lot of artists and designers in my family. I was always encouraged to express myself through the visual arts. I enjoyed illustration the most. But since we don't have an illustration major in Finland, I thought it would be impossible to make a living at this. I chose to study graphic design instead since it seemed to be closest to illustration. After all, drawing logos and letters is a kind of illustration. I had been drawing my entire childhood so it was only natural to continue to explore illustration along with my design studies. During school, I started to illustrate in small magazines and after a while my style got so popular I was able to finance my studies with it. Even though illustration has always been my passion, I'm very glad that I became a graphic designer as well. Both disciplines complete and balance each other very well.

How did you end up choosing the schools you attended?

I went to the Visual Arts high school in Helsinki. It was a very good school to study art and design because it offered the chance to explore a wide range of creative disciplines and discover areas of interest and ability. When I graduated, I knew that I wanted to attend the University of Art and Design in Helsinki (UIAH). UIAH had very good exchange connections with other top universities around the world. I wanted to go somewhere where design was strong and where I could speak the language. I chose Rhode Island School of Design (RISD) because it had a great reputation and was close to New York City. It helped that I had friends who attended both schools before me who could share their experiences, both good and bad.

janine rewell

What has your career path been since you finished school?

It was good to begin freelancing while I was in school. I also did summer internships at two advertising agencies and a design firm. When I graduated, I already had a lot of connections and experience. I also learned that working in an office from 9 to 5 isn't my thing. I got a really good agent to represent me and that has helped me get visibility and credibility all over the world. Ever since I've been freelancing, I've won a lot of awards and exhibited both nationally and internationally. I've also been featured in numerous design publications, which has helped me to get more clients.

What did you find most valuable about your education?

Many years of experimentation helped me to develop my aesthetic view and style. My skills improved enormously during my time in school. I wouldn't be where I am without that guidance. I also learned as much from other students as I learned from teachers. Networking in the design student community back then has paid off now.

What do you think has been the most important factor in your success?

One aspect that has helped me in my career has been my online portfolio. After graduating I put my work online and my site was linked to numerous blogs all over the world. Design publications and magazines began to contact me for interviews and portfolio features. It really helps to be known among the design community especially if you're a freelancer. You gain trust and get bigger clients and opportunities.

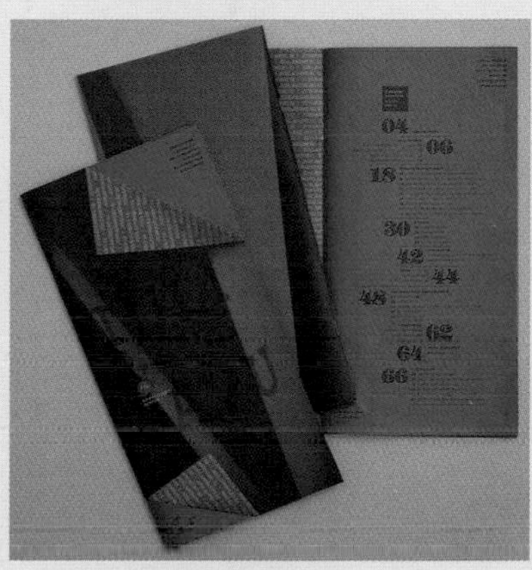

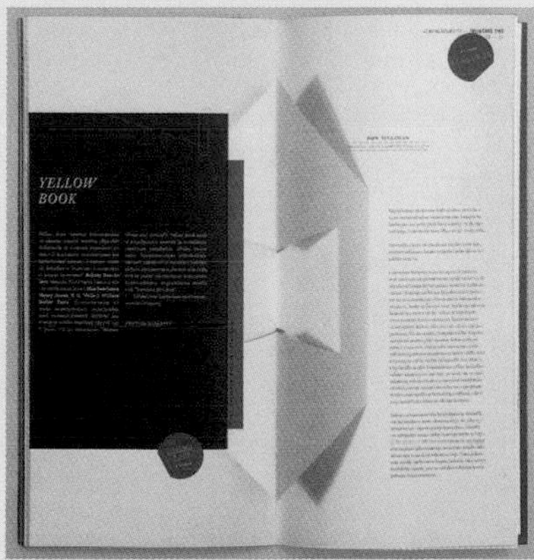

Rewell collaborated with Finnish designer Lotta Nieminen on the layout and design for the anniversary issue of *Tuli & Savu*, a Finnish poetry magazine.
Courtesy of Janine Rewell. Art direction, illustration and layout for the anniversary issue of Tuli & Savu, a Finnish poetry magazine. In collaboration with Lotta Nieminen.

The year 2009 Christmas print campaign for Nokia, commissioned by Weiden & Kennedy.
Design by Janine Rewell.

Custom-designed porcelain dishware for Otava.
Design by Janine Rewell.

janine rewell

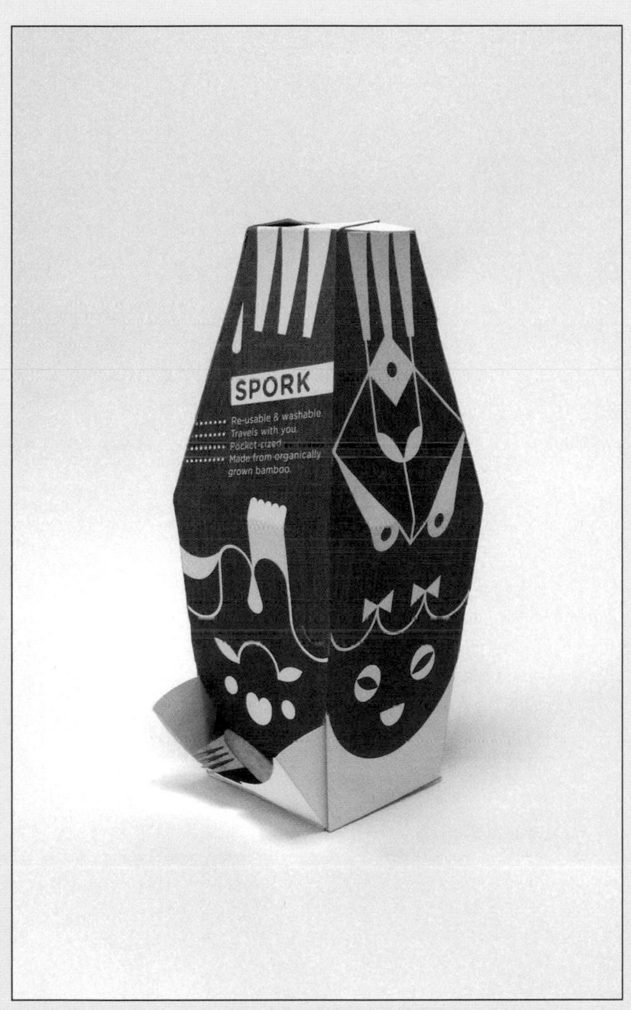

Package design for Spork bamboo utensils.
Design by Janine Rewell.

Directed and illustrated by Jean Jullien, music by Niwouinwouin.

glossary

A

abstract Images that resemble the physical world but are a simplification or distortion of the things in it.

achromatic gray A mix of black and white.

additive color system Color system of white light.

ambiguous figure/ground An arrangement that presents an uncertain relationship between shape and space.

analogous hues Color found adjacent to others on a color wheel.

analysis A level of visual inquiry involving the examination of compositional form and its function.

anomaly The presence of an element or visual relationship that is unlike others that dominate a composition.

asymmetric balance Sometimes referred to as dynamic symmetry, the art of creating balance using uneven numbers, sizes, or kinds of elements.

asymmetrical The art of creating balance using uneven numbers, sizes, or kinds of elements. In the visual arts, asymmetry or dynamic symmetry can be achieved by changing the contrast relationship of value, shape, color, texture, size, placement, or even the kind of image such as type and photograph or illustration.

audience The group toward whom you are directing the message/communication.

B

balance The visual distribution of elements in a composition.

behavior The actions or reactions of a person, usually in response to environmental factors.

broadcasting Media venue that reaches a wide range of people. These media are appropriate channels for disseminating large bodies of information.

C

CG Computer graphics.

character Individual letterforms, numerals, punctuation marks, and other units that are part of a font.

chroma The amount of colorant present in a pigment.

chromolithography Multicolored printing on stone or plate surface.

closure The condition of being closed, a dependent relationship of relative position or the relational distance from one object or shape to another.

CMYK Cyan (blue-green), magenta (redish-pink), yellow, and black.

cognition Thinking, a person's mental processes, the processing of information and intellectual understanding or comprehension.

color Inherent hues found in light and pigment.

commitment Level three of William Perry's levels of intellectual maturity; knowledge is constructed from experience, from interaction with others, and from reflective thinking. There are potentially many solutions to a problem but aren't equally valid.

complementary hues Any two hues found directly opposed on the color wheel.

continuous tone Gradations of a series of values or grays blending from one to another.

contrast A juxtaposition, a relational, comparative placement of two or more similar or unlike elements.

crystallographic The even distribution of like elements over the surface of a design usually geometric.

CSS (Cascading Style Sheets) A style sheet format for HTML that provides layout settings that distinguishes the formatting from the document presentation or the visual elements that include color, imagery, typography, and so forth.

D

description A level of visual inquiry involving the identification of facts.

design In the context of visual organization, design refers the arrangement of elements through the use of visual principles.

directional design Visual communication intended to help people find their way through architectural, virtual, or environmental spaces.

dominance The prevailing influence of one element over another, and a function of hierarchy.

drop cap A text treatment in which the first letter of a paragraph is set larger usually aligned even with the cap height to indicate the beginning of a section of text.

dualism Level one of William Perry's levels of intellectual maturity; concrete thinking, thinking in terms of right and wrong.

dynamic symmetry Managing the relationships between negative and positive space and form and counter form.

E

economy The efficient or concise use of elements.

electrophotography (1960 Photocopier) A dry printing process based on electrically charging a heated drum, which attracts toner and transfers it to paper.

elements of design Shape, space, line, size, color, texture, and typography.

emphasis Stressing the importance of one element over another.

enhansive design Visual communication intended to add a measure of entertainment value to a design application or embellish the look of a design venue.

environment A time/space relationship that affects the use and interaction of the user with the communication, and where the audience engages the message over a given time frame.

F

feeling Emotional expression that produces psychological change.

figure-ground ambiguity A graphic affect where the viewer is uncertain about the relationship between form and space.

figure/ground reversal A graphic affect where figure can function as ground and ground as figure.

focal point A single feature or mark in a composition that attracts the viewer's eye.

format The surface area that contains the design composition; the arrangement of the design components as they will be printed, cut, scored, and assembled.

G

gestalt Translated from German to mean "form" or "the way things come together."

GIF (Graphic Interchange Format) GIFs are smallest in size (8-bit) of all file formats. Used for graphic or noncontinuous tone imagery such as logos, graphic reductions, and line arts. GIFs can also be animated.

glyph A basic building block in typesetting that includes individual letters, numbers, and symbols. Groups of glyphs combined are referred to as a font.

graphic design The art of arranging pictographic and typographic elements to create a communication message.

grid A device used as a means of scaling smaller images to larger works; to break down the observed world into smaller, more manageable sections.

H

halftone Conversion of continuous tones into a dot pattern.

harmony The visual agreement between design elements. Harmony can be thought of as the desired balance or accord between unity and variety in a visual composition.

helix A 3-dimension spiral form.

hierarchy An arranged order. Hierarchy is the established order, importance, emphasis, and movement given to visual elements, from the dominant ones to those that are subordinate.

HTML, (Hypertext Markup Language) a language that constitutes the basic building blocks of Web pages.

hue The same as color, it is the inherent color referred to by a name or formula.

hyperlinks Highlighted or underlined words, phrases, images, or icons that are coded to link with another part of a website or a different website.

hypertext or **hypermedia** The form that content assumes in Web design. Hypertext was one of the earliest forms of interactivity offered by Apple in the early development of computer graphics.

I

icon An image that possesses similar traits or qualities to the referent.

index An image that shows evidence of something observed or inferred.

information design Visual communication intended to educate an audience.

inkjet printer A digital process that converts computer-generated imagery into small, sprayed drops of ink onto paper.

intelligence A person's ability to use the tools of a culture (Jerome Brunner).

interactive media Media that allows the user or viewer to respond to or control the media experience.

interline spacing/leading The amount of space between lines of type, measured in points. The term is derived from metal type where strips of lead were inserted between lines of type (alternative terms: *line spacing* and *interline spacing*).

interpretation A level of visual inquiry involving finding meaning in the image.

J

JPEG (Joint Photographic Experts Group) This file format uses a compression algorithm to reproduce imagery in millions of colors. Used most often for continuous tone imagery such as photographs. JPEG images cannot be animated.

L

language A systematic method of communicating ideas or feelings through the use of conventionalized signs, sounds, gestures or marks having understood or comprehensible meanings.

laser printer Similar to the photocopy process, which is analog, laser printing is a process where the image is scanned by a laser beam converting it into digital information that is used to produce an impression onto paper using toner.

letter spacing/kerning The distance between characters in a word or number and between words and punctuation in a line of type.

letterform The particular style and form of each individual letter in an alphabet.

letterpress Movable lead and wood type.

levels of intellectual maturity A hierarchy developed by William Perry that identifies stages of learning development and readiness to engage in the learning process.

ligature Pairs or groupings of letters that are physically joined together for the purpose of improving their aesthetic appearance.

line The moving path of a point.

line art Black and white art that has no continuous tones.

line length The horizontal length of a line of type, traditionally measured in picas, but also in inches.

linotype Machinery that produces type one line at a time from a keyboard.

lithography Also referred to as planography is printing on a flat surface and based on the chemical repellence of oil and water.

logo A symbol that represents an organization or institution.

lowercase Smaller letters, as opposed to capital letters, of a type font.

M

meaning The thing that is conveyed or one intends to convey with visual or verbal language.

media The vehicle—materials used to physically produce the work; the venue—where the communication occurs, the form of the communication.

media Any of a variety of materials and tools involved in delivering a message.

medium The singular of medium or any one material or tool involved in delivering a message.

monochromatic A single color mixed with tints, shades, or tones.

motif The appearance of the overall image in a design; there are three general kinds of overall images—non-objective, abstract, and realistic.

movement creating implied direction and rhythmic path with the placement elements as manifested through the eye of the viewer.

multimedia 1. Interactive digital format that blends animation, streaming audio and video with text, and imagery. 2. The integrated interactive formats that have evolved as a consequence of sophisticated digital technology. Multimedia technology blends animation, streaming audio, and video with text, imagery, and interactivity.

multiple master Digital fonts containing two or more original master styles, allowing the designer the ability to insert variations between the masters to create an additional range of styles without compromising integrity.

multiplicity Level two of William Perry's levels of intellectual maturity; recognition that thinking can be diverse, more than one solution can be possible.

N

narrowcasting Communicating through media that focuses on a narrow audience with a specialized interest.

new media Computer-generated media that goes beyond the two-dimensional realm, including interactive media, the Web and multimedia.

non-objective/non-representational Images having no resemblance to anything recognizable in the real world.

O

offset lithography A flat, planographic process that transfers the reverse image to a rubber cylinder from which a "right" reading or direct impression is printed.

open type Cross platform fonts that contain thousands of glyphs forming character sets that provide the designer with special characters and languages.

orientation The point of view determined by the designer; the way the viewer is meant to visually relate to a design or image.

P

pattern Elements that have an arrangement that is evenly distributed over the surface of a composition. The design creates a motif that gives equal importance to each element.

persuasive design Visual communication intended to persuade an audience to think or behave in a deliberate, sometimes different, way from what they are accustomed.

phototypesetting A photomechanical process in which type is developed onto sheets of photo paper.

pica Equal to 12 points, approximately one-sixth of an inch.

PNG (Packet Internet Groper) This format was invented specifically for the Web. One version, PNG-8, is similar to the GIF format in that it can be saved with a maximum of 256 colors. Another format PNG-24 supports 24-bit color, similar to JPEG format.

point A unit for measuring the height of type and vertical distance between lines of type.

polygon A flat sided shape comprised of three or more sides.

primary principles Affect the design as a whole and include unity, variety, hierarchy, and proportion.

problem solving The process or method of managing higher order thinking aimed at achieving a goal; it involves understanding the problem and shaping possible ways to solve it.

project goal A big idea described in a general description; a conceptual umbrella, which is idealistic but attainable.

project objectives Intentions that support the goal, linked to behavioral outcomes and are specific to the task/project.

proportion Size relationships in a composition that serve as the image area and "surface" design.

proximity The position and space given to the placement of elements in a composition.

R

radial The arrangement of elements that radiate from a center point.

rationale The reasoning for pursuing an idea.

realism/representation Imagery that replicates the real world in a descriptive manner using objects that have defined and namable referents to the real world.

relativism Level three of William Perry's levels of intellectual maturity; knowledge is relative, knowledge is not universal, but a matter of context and situation.

repetition A pattern of related or juxtaposed elements.

research Intellectual inquiry or examination, the collecting of information on a subject.

rhythm An alternating repetition of shape and space, or a planned movement of elements in a composition.

routine problem solving Applying previously established methods or sets of known procedures.

S

saturation The purity of a color.

scale Size comparisons of the internal parts of a composition—the visible elements that can be seen on the surface; scale is the relationship of size or a comparison of size from one element to another.

semiotics The study of signs and symbols.

shade The mix of black with a color.

shape A figure or mass.

sign symbol An image that conveys a one to one correspondence to its reference.

simple figure/ground The coherent, independent presence of a shape juxtaposed in a space that serves as the ground.

simultaneous contrast An illusory effect where the eye provides a complement based on a sensory response.

site maps An organizational tool used in Web design that represents a composite list of the pages. They are organized to help viewers navigate a Web site and are designed in a hierarchical arrangement. The hierarchy provides designers with a visual map that guides decisions about where to place design elements and information.

size The physical dimensions of an element or format.

strategy How a project is managed or how you plan to produce the design.

subtractive color system System based on mixing color pigments.

support principles Affect internal relationships of the design and include scale, balance, repetition, rhythm, and proximity.

symbol An image that stands for or represents something else.

symbolic interaction The process of forming meaning in support of the formation of personal identity and human socialization.

symmetric balance Elements that are arranged the same or very similar on either side of a central axis.

symmetrical Elements are arranged the same or very similarly on either side of a central axis.

T

target audience The group toward whom you are directing your message/communication.

tension The conflicting stress resulting from the strategic placement of two or more elements in a composition.

tertiary hues Colors found between primary and secondary.

texture The tactile quality and characteristic of a surface.

theme A subject or topic being represented; the quality or character of a represented idea.

thought The formation of an idea, concept, mental picture or opinion as an intellectual activity.

tint Adding white to a pure hue.

tones Grays, also referred to as mid-tones.

tracking The same as letter spacing or the average space between letters in a text block.

type alignment Arranging columns or blocks of text type in various configurations so that they conforms to a grid (ex., flush left, flush right, centered and justified).

type family A range of style variations based on a single typeface design.

type font A complete set of letterforms (uppercase and lowercase), numerals, and punctuation marks in a particular typeface that allows for typesetting by keystroke on a computer or another means of typographic composition.

type style Modifications in a typeface that create design variety while maintaining the visual character of the typeface. These include variations in weight (light, medium, or bold), width (condensed or extended), or angle (italic or slanted versus roman or upright).

typeface The design of a single set of letterforms, numerals, and punctuation marks unified by consistent visual properties. Typeface designs are identified by name, such as Helvetica and Garamond.

typography The arrangement and aesthetics of letterforms. (See the expanded list of terms for typography in Chapter 2.)

U

unity Overriding principle that is served by all others; unity is the control of variety.

uppercase Capital or larger letters of a type font (A, B, C, etc.).

V

value Lightness or darkness.

variety Visual contrast.

vehicle The materials used to physically produce the work. Examples include the computer, paint, pen and ink, and charcoal.

venue 1. The place where the communication occurs or the place where the user engages the communication. Examples include electronic, print, and environmental design. 2. The form the design assumes. Examples include electronic, print, environmental, and consumer product.

visual communication Conveying meaning through the use and management of images.

visual metaphor An image that can be observed from a variety of viewpoints.

visual thinking A visual problem solving activity dependent on a relationship between mental and physical manipulation of an idea.

W

wire frame A blueprint for a Website's logistics or a skeletal framework for how the site will function. Wire frames lack color information, typographic style, and even the imagery that will be used.

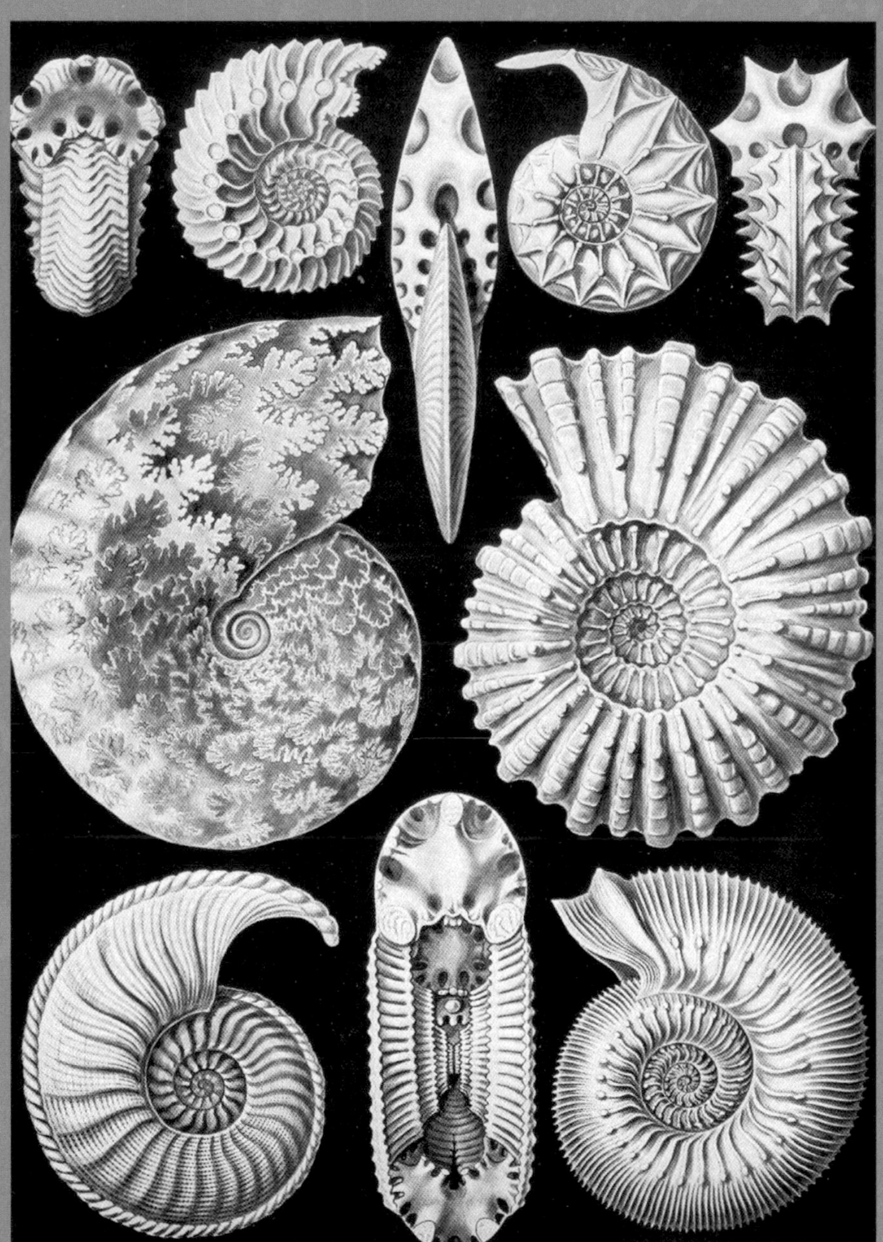
Public domain.

index

D

H

I

J

K

L

M

N

O

U

V

W

Y

Z